W9-BHK-252

QUIET MOMENTS IN A WAR

QUIET MOMENTS IN A WAR

The Letters of Jean-Paul Sartre
to Simone de Beauvoir
1940–1963

EDITED BY SIMONE DE BEAUVOIR

translated and with an introduction by
LEE FAHNESTOCK AND NORMAN MACAFEE

CHARLES SCRIBNER'S SONS   *New York*

MAXWELL MACMILLAN CANADA   *Toronto*
MAXWELL MACMILLAN INTERNATIONAL
New York   Oxford   Singapore   Sydney

First American Edition
Copyright © 1983 by Éditions Gallimard
Translation copyright © 1993 by Lee Fahnestock and Norman MacAfee

All rights reserved. No part of this book may be reproduced or transmitted in any form or by any means, electronic or mechanical, including photocopying, recording, or by any information storage and retrieval system, without permission in writing from the Publisher.

Charles Scribner's Sons   Maxwell Macmillan Canada, Inc.
Macmillan Publishing Company   1200 Eglinton Avenue East
866 Third Avenue   Suite 200
New York, NY 10022   Don Mills, Ontario M3C 3N1

Macmillan Publishing Company is part of the Maxwell Communication Group of Companies.

Library of Congress Cataloging-in-Publication Data

Sartre, Jean Paul, 1905–1980
    [Lettres au Castor et à quelques autres. English. Selections]
    Quiet moments in a war : the letters of Jean-Paul Sartre to Simone de Beauvoir, 1940–1963 / edited by Simone de Beauvoir ; translated by Lee Fahnestock and Norman MacAfee.
        p.   cm.
    Includes index.
    ISBN 0-684-19566-6
    1. Sartre, Jean Paul, 1905–1980—Correspondence.   2. Beauvoir, Simone de, 1908–1986—Correspondence.   3. Authors, French—20th century—Correspondence.   I. Beauvoir, Simone de, 1908–1986.   II. Title.
PQ2637.A82Z483   1993   93-12766
848'.91409—dc20   CIP
[B]

Macmillan books are available at special discounts for bulk purchases for sales promotions, premiums, fund-raising, or educational use. For details, contact:

Special Sales Director
Macmillan Publishing Company
866 Third Avenue
New York, NY 10022

Book design by Jennifer Dossin

10 9 8 7 6 5 4 3 2 1

Printed in the United States of America

Contents

Acknowledgments

The translators wish to thank the National Endowment for the Arts for a fellowship to support this book; the Florence Gould Foundation for its continuing help; Robert Polito and Elizabeth Dickey of the New School for Social Research; Olivier Nora of Le Bureau du Livres Français; our editor, Erika Goldman, and Charles Flowers at Scribner's. This book was also supported by grants from the French Government and the Wheatland Foundation.

Introduction

"I feel I'm on the way, as biographers say around page 150, . . . to discovering myself. Which only means that I no longer think with an eye to certain strictures (the Left, Husserl), etc., but with a total and gratuitous freedom, out of pure curiosity and disinterestedness . . ."
—January 6, 1940

WAITING FOR THE war with Germany to start, sitting in a café or Salvation Army lounge at the front, Sartre had his quiet moments to write in his journal, to sketch the meditations that would become his magnum opus, *Being and Nothingness*, to work on his novel *The Age of Reason*, and to send countless letters, usually several a day, and always one to Simone de Beauvoir, strengthening a relationship that would become almost a new social model. It was ten years since they had made their now-famous pact—to be true to the other, with allowance for contingent loves—and their cultural, intellectual, and emotional lives were now intertwined. These letters constitute a manual of attachment, permeated with the knowledge of love and endearment, of anguished betrayals within a more encompassing trust.

The letters of 1940, occupying most of this volume, give us a portrait of the growth, almost minute by minute, of the relationship, the thinker, the artist, the man. Between his writing and army duties and chess games, Sartre read everything Beauvoir could send him—*Don Quixote*, Dostoyevsky, Kafka, Faulkner, Stendhal, Heine, Jules Romains, histories, mysteries. Aware, at thirty-four, that the literary world in Paris was quite capable of forgetting him—the successful author of a novel and collection of short stories—he endeavored to direct his literary career from the small Alsatian towns near the front where he was stationed.

As he revised *The Age of Reason*, Beauvoir was working on her first novel, *She Came to Stay*, both of them realistic novels of ideas which drew heavily on their own experience and that of their circle of friends and lovers. At this stage, each called on the other as first reader and editor. Though the couple freely borrowed from life, their characters are not to be mistaken for portraits of the artists. For example, Sartre considered Mathieu, the protagonist of *The Age of Reason*, a negative model who uses his freedom irresponsibly.

Protest as he might a preference for writing to her "about nothing" because it reminded him of their rambling conversations, Sartre's letters from the front include skilled reporting—provincial character sketches at the military court martial of a deserter; the packed roomful of soldiers reacting to a tawdry representation of "Woman" as portrayed by the overpainted actresses in a fourth-rate touring company. While he was trying to reassure and advise Beauvoir about the German advances during late May and June 1940, Sartre narrated the seemingly languid approach of catastrophe, the rout of French forces and collapse of the nation such as he observed it in isolated firsthand details, as he heard it in rumors and reports of disaster denied, disaster confirmed.

Called by one biographer a "war profiteer," Sartre indeed profited from nine months in a German prison camp by writing his first play, *Bariona, or the Son of Thunder*, a subversive Christmas drama that contains some of his most lyrical writing. Captivity deepened—for the philosopher of freedom, action, and responsibility—his understanding of these terms.

With his return to Nazi-occupied Paris in March 1941, Sartre began to feel his way into an existentialist, never-orthodox, lifelong political activism. From his groundwork in drama and philosophy, he derived new ways to lay his views before an audience. His first professionally produced play, *The Flies*, a retelling of the *Oresteia*, was a protest against those who give in to tyranny, a remarkable message for an audience to hear under the censorship of German occupation.

Within the pervasive demoralization of the French collapse, Sartre had already begun in 1943 to sense the need for a new journal of cultural and political opinion. At a lecture in Brussels soon after the liberation of Paris in August 1944, he introduced his brand of existentialism to the public. The philosophy took hold within a wave of postwar euphoria, just as his journal, with Beauvoir and Maurice Merleau-Ponty on the board, was taking shape. *Les Temps Modernes*, named after Charlie Chaplin's film, quickly assumed a central position in articulating the thought of the intellectual left.

While Sartre's letters give some idea of Beauvoir's parallel course, reading her side of the correspondence completes the dialogue. Both candidly speak of their love affairs, even asking advice of the other. Beauvoir's letters, published posthumously in 1990, clarify aspects of her intimate friendships with other women, revealing that they were also sometimes sexual. After 1942, as the couple were less often apart, there are fewer letters, but some extraordinary ones—from Beauvoir living in Chicago with her lover Nelson Algren; from Sartre in New York in the late 1940s experiencing his first taste of international celebrity; and a decade later at the Irish estate of John Huston when the two men were working on a film about Freud. The two decades till 1963—when the couple stopped writing letters in favor of the telephone—saw the dual fruition of their careers and reputations, with the publication of *Being and Nothingness, Memoirs of a Dutiful Daughter, No Exit, The Second Sex, Saint Genet,* and *The Words.*

On balance, how fortunate both were in their choice of a life companion. Whatever the failings in the relationship, affection and affinity kept the two together for half a century. In the years following his death in 1980, though herself ill and far from the perceptive powers which had long been hers, Beauvoir compiled and annotated these letters. Searching for words to preface this posthumous work of Sartre's, she reached back to his youth, wryly quoting one of his schoolfriends:

"In centuries to come, my boy, literary criticism will cite 'Jean-Paul Sartre, letter writer par excellence, author of a few literary and philosophic works.' "

Lee Fahnestock and Norman MacAfee

QUIET MOMENTS IN A WAR

1940

January 1st

My darling Beaver

I'm writing to you from a warm spot by the stove, though the weather's a lot milder now. Last night we even had a thaw, and because the water pipes had burst two days ago, Paul[1] was awakened around two a.m. —while I was sleeping the sleep of the just—by a dreadful roaring. He thought it was fire, but it was water. He dressed in a hurry and dashed out into the hall, which was already flooded. There was total chaos till someone finally turned off the water. Now there's not a drop for washing, which as you know doesn't bother me much. But it's pretty annoying for the toilets, which don't flush, and where excrement of diverse provenance intimately intermingles depending upon freeze and thaw, making for a voluminous vile pudding. We "go" out of doors. I think Paul suffers and gets constipated out of shame at showing his rear end.

So today was New Year's, which resulted in nothing out of the ordinary except for some superb *choucroute* and a mob scene at the Restaurant de la Gare. And yesterday, the Eve of Saint-Sylvestre, there wasn't anything much either, except that some anonymous bastard turned the officers' radio up full blast after they'd left and accompanied the music by randomly pounding the piano keys with his fists till midnight. As for me, I scribbled away like a good boy in our digs.

---

[1] In civilian life a physics teacher, Paul was the corporal of the meteorological service in which Private Sartre spent the early months of the war; the other two privates were Pieter, a resourceful Jewish businessman, and the overweight Keller, whom Sartre referred to as an elephant seal. These names are pseudonyms, coined for the French edition. The unit regularly released weather balloons and took readings of their flight, gauging wind direction and velocity for the artillery battalion.

The countryside is unchanged—a dusting of snow, a bit of white everywhere, you'd only have to scratch it with your fingernail to get back to the usual blackness of the frozen ground and trees. I've spent the whole day revising passages of my novel, and as soon as that's done I'll get down to work on *Septembre*[2]; I'm really delighted at the prospect. I hope to have the two volumes come out at the same time, that would be best; readers could see more clearly where I'm headed. Here everyone remains the same: Paul still fretting; Mistler[3] does a thousand little things for me in exchange for my teaching. It was he who did up the packages of books I'll send to Bost[4] and to you the moment you've sent me a bit of cash and, since a private had asked me for *Quai des brumes [Port of Shadows]*[5] (mistakenly, actually, in the belief that he would find the complete story of the film) and I had asked Mistler to remind me, he came by this morning for that very reason. Since the book was in one of the packages for Bost, he undid the parcel then tied it up again. Incidentally, he's going to have someone send me Chopin's *Nocturnes* and *Preludes* so I can work on them on the piano. There are the usual family-type jealousies here between the clerks and ourselves. Needless to say, we are the targets of the jealousy. And so from the Cité Universitaire[6] to the present, it has been my lot to be envied wherever I go. But it's mostly *talk*. It's a feeble, spineless sort of jealousy which I know about only through hearsay; it doesn't even reach the level of backbiting. For instance, every morning on my way back from breakfast, as I walk past their windows, my passing arouses comment. "Ah ha! There's Sartre coming back from the café. Yes. He's seen the lovely Charlotte. The others will have done the reading without him," etc. It differs from statement of fact only in the intention of friendly criticism attached to it. But it's basically just a simple statement of fact, because they can't figure out exactly what to criticize: that I have enough money, free time, immaturity to treat myself to a café breakfast? The whole thing seems vaguely scandalous to them and every morning they bring it up as I pass by, nothing more than that. It has become a little daily scandal they wouldn't miss for the world. They're at the very bottom of the ladder. Of course it all gets back to me through the

---

[2] Tentative title of the second volume, eventually called *Le Sursis (The Reprieve)*, in his series, *The Roads to Freedom*. The first, the novel under revision, was *L'Age de Raison (The Age of Reason)*. September 1938 was the month of the Munich Pact, which delayed World War II by Allied appeasement of Hitler.

[3] A clerk several years older than Sartre, Mistler was a ready audience for his disquisitions.

[4] Jacques-Laurent Bost, youngest son in a prominent Protestant family, a former student of Sartre's who remained close to the couple throughout their lives. In early 1940 he was serving in a dangerous position at the northern front.

[5] By [Pierre] Mac Orlan. (SdB) A movie derived from the novel was made in 1938 by Marcel Carné with a script by Jacques Prévert.

[6] Enclave of university housing and other buildings at the southern fringe of Paris. In 1928–29 Sartre was living there while studying for a retake of the important *agrégation* exam, which he had failed.

good Mistler, who would prefer I take a detour to avoid their watchful eyes, but just imagine how tiresome that would be. And that's the story. I'm delighted by Stendhal's *Journal*, I'm reading the 3rd volume, his affair with Mme. Daru; it's very appealing. I'm also reading Rauschning, [7] extremely instructive, I'll even do a précis of it in my notebook[8]; and then a bit of *Provinciales*[9] and also some *Jacques le Fataliste*.[10] Tania[11] writes: "I'm reading a beautiful book that I *must* send you." I'm lost in conjecture. Could it be *Le Diable amoureux [The Devil in Love]*?[12]

No letters from you today. But since I got three yesterday, I'm not complaining too much. I have a deep longing to see you again, my dearest. We're in the slightly irritating period when my leave recedes or approaches day by day, according to changing information and the mood of the corporal in charge of drawing up the lists at HQ. But I'll fight for my rights. I'd really like to leave here within two weeks if possible. *Au revoir,* sweet little Beaver, already sleeping after such good skiing. I rise with the sun, just as you do. While you're still putting on your little skis, I've long since wrapped on my puttees and gone down to check the wind and made a sweep of the horizon, calling my findings in to the weather stations of the entire army corps. I don't sleep much, but I do feel very much alive. Till tomorrow, my dear little flower, I love you with all my might.

ᏥᎦ *to Simone de Beauvoir*

January 2

My darling Beaver
A little note, dated the 29th, from you today. My! how long ago that was, little one—for us, the troops, it's already the 2nd. But you seem so full of yourself with your skiing that it warms my heart. In the end, it's the same every year,

---

[7] *La Dictature du nihilisme* ("The Dictatorship of Nihilism") by Hermann Rauschning. A friend of Hitler's, Rauschning turned against nazism in 1935 after local Nazis set up a regime in Danzig, where he was president of the Senate.

[8] Between September 14, 1939 and March 28, 1940, Sartre filled fourteen notebooks with writings in various modes—autobiographical, literary, philosophic, political. Only five survived and were published in 1983 in France, and in 1984 in English as *The War Diaries*.

[9] Book by playwright Jean Giraudoux (1882–1944) about country life.

[10] A picaresque novel by Denis Diderot (1713–84), editor of the vast *Encyclopédie*, playwright, and critic.

[11] "Tania Zazoulich," the name used here for Wanda Kosakiewicz, a young friend and former student of Beauvoir's and at that time one of Sartre's lovers. She later acted, as "Marie Olivier," originating the role of Estelle in Sartre's *No Exit*.

[12] By Jacques Cazotte (1719–92).

handsome progress and good fun after a bit of muddling about at the start. I love hearing about all the familiar slopes. I know just what you mean when you say that fresh snow makes them easier, and ice rather trickier. I'm with you constantly. I find it hard to imagine that this letter, the one I'm writing, will catch up with you in Paris. Just think, tomorrow I'll get yet another letter—or two, I hope—from Megève, which seems odd. You're still in Megève and I'm writing to you in Paris, where you aren't and yet where you'll be arriving at the same time as this letter. And on the 4th you'll get it in Paris and I'll get more letters from Megève. It reminds me—minus the sinister part—of that story about my aunt Marie Hirsch, who lost her son, an ensign serving on a ship, killed accidentally in Shanghai; she learned of his death by telegram and then a month later received a letter from him saying how happy he was—he must have died that same evening. I'm always a bit scared that while I'm blissfully reading your letter, you might have just broken your poor little leg. But it's a very slight fear and, on the other hand, you can't imagine how nice it is to know you are so profoundly happy, it's had me beaming all day. As for the leave, we must be a bit patient, it's receding ever so slightly—not far, to about January 20th—just as we'd said, in fact. But what are twenty days? The essential thing is that I'll be in Paris in less than a month.

Tania sent me *Le Moine* [*The Monk*],[1] which of course dazzled her: it has rape, devil worship, and sex-mad monks, with surrealism in the background, and the specter of Artaud,[2] who, because she thought him crazy, has always rather dazzled her. Besides real strength of feeling in her, there's a hodgepodge of strangely demonic goods, all on the surface (why love blood if you can't stand the sight of it? Rape when you'd almost faint if some guy demonstrated his desire even slightly openly?) yet going deep. I don't know how to say it. In any case, when I leafed through it, *The Monk* disappointed me somewhat. Artaudian touches are visible but not enough to save it. Besides, to me the horrors seemed very intellectual, in the surrealist style. Yet I must admit I find it beautiful. On the other hand, *Le Diable amoureux*, which she also sent me without even cutting the pages, is a real jewel, which I read at one go this evening. The guy tells a story admirably, and he already starts out with a good grasp of the 18th century, and there's an odd character: a charming young girl, all modesty and grace, who *is* the Devil—that is, a horrible camel-headed monster. And the hero somehow manages to make love extremely well with the girl. The whole thing is set up through touches of flirtation and languorous modesty. The woman

---

[1] A Gothic potboiler by Matthew Gregory Lewis (1775–1818).
[2] Antonin Artaud (1896–1948), French playwright, poet, actor, and theoretician of surrealism.

you happy. As for me, I'd really like to have some reason in return to seem comparably poetic or romantic to you, but to tell the truth I'm neither. The war seems remote, along with my "military service" or the "field maneuvers" that are its surrogates, and similarly my sense of historicity and my well-being and whatever else. All that remains is a slightly disorderly though predictable enough administrative technique that bumbles along, and I'm caught up in it and left bone dry. I feel like a civilian meteorologist, living a civilian life that fate denied me, requiring virtues that I lack and that I try, if halfheartedly, to acquire; it's awful how many errors I make in working out the readings. Actually, they cancel each other out and scarcely show. But for instance my eyes play tricks on me when I look at the graph paper, landing where they will, and I locate the balloon accordingly. It's something of a substitute for agoraphobia: I get flustered before vast quadrilinear spaces and settle on any old square, practically demolishing it with my pencil point to stop the atrocious torture of floating about with no point of view, like a disembodied consciousness, above the checkerboard. From this I deduce, of course, that you have to be pretty petty to be a physicist. So I'm a paper-pusher by trade. For a much clearer grasp of what I'm doing than you'd get from some chronology—just imagine a warm little organic, glowing lair, filled with intimate odors and tobacco smoke, that's my day—with three little bursts of icy pale gray air for the readings. And then betweentimes lunch at the Café de la Gare, comfortable but unpoetic. And aside from my administrative duties, my technical activities—there's tinkering with the novel—and bone-dry thoughts. The day before yesterday something on bad faith, today a brief 22-page tirade on Disgust. It contains this, which I find not unappealing: "In which case, would you say that if we are disgusted by shit, it is only because we would actually like to eat it?" To which I reply, "Certainly." Note that all of this is felicitous, my little flower. But it's barren. My great joys come from the notebook and the novel, rather than being poured into the notebook and the novel. And I fear that the novel might have suffered from a certain incapacity on my part to get worked up. But what the hell, that's what novel-making is all about: a person can portray emotion without actually feeling it, can't he? To be quite honest, I must say that three or four days ago I was in the throes, not of emotion, but instead a sort of falsely prophetic aura, concerning Rauschning's book, which had really gotten to me; I was *seeing* a certain Germany, I understood its role and its threat, and I was feeling my historicity, it gave me a better understanding of the sort of people you and I have sometimes discussed, who always think in social terms. That attitude has a certain grandeur, but the other side of the coin is that one always falls short of the thoughts one has created. Because one *believes* them. Which doesn't mean that I don't believe in mine, ordinarily, but ultimately I know full well they're the product of my freedom. I believe in them without limits, that is, I believe in the system they would constitute if the little vultures didn't get me first. But they always gnaw away at you before the system is complete. There you have it. There's only one little star of moist happiness and poetry in my life, and it is you and your snow. I won't see your snow, but I will see your little self. So here it is: it's set, insofar as anything can be with the military; I'll be with you between the 25th of January and the 1st of February. There were myriad reversals and then finally they came up with the right argument, the irrefutable argument: 1. 2 meteorologists—or 50% of the force—can't be away at the same time. 2. The last leave-takers must be gone by February 15th since the first round of leaves must end by March 1st. 3. Thus with Paul being the last and leaving between the 10th and 15th of February, it stands to reason that I should leave between January 25th and February 1st (they allow 15 days because of the distance). When you get this letter I'll be at most fifteen or twenty days away from you. There's nothing to say to the Z's.[1] I wrote to Tania that I'd have five days, without adding that I would see you for two days out of the five, so our first plan still holds good.

What else, my little dear? Lévy[2] felt he had to vomit on the tables of the College Inn. Such vulgarity shocked me; I'm convinced my reaction sprang from what the College Inn means to me, at this distance: the place where I had sentimental little rendezvous with you, evenings of passion with Olga and of attentive intrigue with Tania—not to mention Bourdin[3]—and charming, friendly evenings with the Lady.[4] So after all you can see that the war makes a person sentimental, it seemed to me a bit as though Lévy had wiped his ass with my old love letters. In fact, merely explaining it to you this way, I detect a certain puritanism and delicacy of sentiment, which I can't do anything about.

That's all for now, my little flower. Send me immediately, if you haven't already done so: *money, ink cartridges, notebooks.* And rather soon too, some books. Yours are on their way. Along with *Gilles*[5] and the Romains,[6] I would like you to buy me the little volume by M. de Rougemont called

---

[1] The pseudonymous "Zazoulichs" (see letter of Jan. 1). Wanda's older sister Olga, a close friend and former student of Beauvoir's, had a tormented affair with Sartre in 1935–36. Later, she married Jacques-Laurent Bost (see note 4, letter of Jan. 2). She acted on stage as "Olga Dominique" in plays by both Sartre and Beauvoir.

[2] Raoul Lévy, historian and former student of Sartre's.

[3] "Martine Bourdin," pseudonym of a young woman Sartre somewhat reluctantly began an affair with in the summer of 1938. See *Witness to My Life,* pp. 150–64.

[4] Nickname of Mme. Morel, a rich, vivacious Argentine, part of Sartre and Beauvoir's close circle of friends from the late 1920s to the 1950s.

[5] 1939 novel by Pierre Drieu La Rochelle (1893–1945).

[6] Jules Romains, pen name of Louis Farignole (1885–1972); in letters of the previous November Sartre writes admiringly of Romains's multivolume novel, *Les Hommes de bonne volonté (Men of Good Will),* published between 1932 and 1947.

Journal d'Allemagne [*German Diary*], which I want to read after the Rausch-ning.

Till tomorrow, my love, my dearest. I love you with all my might and I'm burning to see you again.

You'll have *six* notebooks to read when I get there. But they are in larger handwriting.

⊕ *to Simone de Beauvoir*

January 4

My darling Beaver

No letter from you today. I know, it's because you're on your way home and will mail it from Paris. Very likely I won't get it tomorrow either. Time goes by very slowly without you, my little sweet. I suppose that yesterday you had your solitary Wednesday, my little sweet, which must have made you very happy. I suspect that late in the day you crept over to see Sorokine,[1] because you're very fond of her and she wants to seduce you. You are my sweet little flower and I love you very much.

I'm still going through the same old days of emotionless, uneventful comfort that rather surprise everyone around here. This morning it wasn't very cold. I didn't go out for breakfast at the kitchen of the Café de la Gare because Keller had been given a shot and so I did the morning reading with Paul, then worked on the novel, did the reading again at 11, went to get coal from a courtyard near the field kitchen. We go there in the colonel's car with an empty bag; he isn't too pleased to have it used for this purpose but says nothing; we get out the bag, I hold it, spread wide open, like a young girl with her apron under an apple tree, and the driver tosses in shovelsful of briquettes or coal dust, depending on the day, under the sad eyes of the cooks as they watch their coal disappearing. Then, after carrying the coal back to our place, I went out for lunch. Today was the changing of the guard—that is, the light infantry on the front lines came off and those here went up. They told me they were very cold and that several guys had been taken to the rear with frostbitten feet. But, with a scornful

[1] Nathalie (Natasha) Sorokine, the young daughter of strict White Russian parents, grew extremely attached to Beauvoir—see Deirdre Bair, *Simone de Beauvoir*, pp. 236, 237.

view of their present situation, they added: "We were still a whole lot better off than here." I didn't know why. Then I learned from Mistler that the 70th division had its "Red." He's a guy who fought in Spain; he came back, with just enough time to straighten things out by marrying his mistress, with whom he had a son, before taking off for this war. His kid had just died. After that, the captain of the state police called him in, grilled him, right here, and accused him of defeatist propaganda. The poor guy hardly gives it a thought, he's so completely knocked out by the death of his kid and horrified by this new war. They're undoubtedly going to dump him into a disciplinary battalion—a new unit just being formed. I read some of Stendhal's *Journal*, but oddly, at this point I find him rather annoying. In the 3rd volume I find him very self-satisfied and largely concerned with appearances. Besides, his affair with Mme. Daru is ridiculous. I think I'll find him charming again in Italy, in the 4th volume. Then I worked till four o'clock, did the reading, then the big ruckus: I had to go get the grub, because Keller is excused from service for 48 hours following his shot. Then Mistler came in—shy and discreet, he always offers something or performs some service to excuse his presence. This time he brought us some goat cheese and cognac. We drank and ate. I terrorize and rough him up a bit, describing my dictatorship of liberty and how I would force people to be free by alternating reasoning with horrible torture. He gets pretty charged up. He brought me Valois's *Le Nouvel Âge*, the magazine that naughty you should read and don't. Now he's gone off. (It's funny how we entertain at our place. Leaving aside the relative appeal of its inhabitants, the thing the weather guys' place most suggests— through its modest dimensions, its grubbiness, its comfort amidst filth, its relative independence, its strictly male occupants, and the mix of work and hospitality, as well as its collective personality—is a study-bedroom at the École Normale.) He left and Hantziger is playing his prewar waltzes on the piano, it recalls the early films, the kind you never saw, where a pianist accompanied the exploits of William Hart[2] with waltzes on the piano. And so here we are, my little sweet, I'm writing to you.

I sent off the books. But in return, do send the money. I had to borrow from Mistler and from Paul, I really do need cash. Send the ink cartridges too, this one's the next to last. If you don't, my poor good Beaver, don't be surprised if I stop writing to you for lack of primary materials.

Good-bye my little dear. Now I'm going to write to T., who's flooding me with passionate letters. I've ascended to the level of beautifully endearing legend for T. It dresses up her life, it seems virtuous and poetic to her, she has never loved so intensely. As for me, I'm still feeling unmoved.

[2] Early Hollywood cowboy star.

How I love you, my little dear, I'm sad that you've deserted your beautiful snow, where you were so intent. You seem to have made tremendous progress this year.

I send you a warm hug, my little sweet, with all my affection.

⌖ to Simone de Beauvoir

January 5

My darling Beaver

So you're home now? Today in the space of a single hour I received a letter, a telegram, and a package, all from you. As for the telegram, you're lucky the censor let it by. Can you imagine writing to any soldier in "a military zone": "Send Shakespeare immediately." It positively reeks of espionage. But it's been dispatched, the Shakespeare, my sweet. It left with *The Concept of Dread*[1] the day before yesterday, and I suppose it got there today and you're out of your bind. Thank you for the books. You know, two weeks ago, I suddenly found myself, I can't remember why, with a sudden urge to read a biography of Heine. Oh yes! it must have been on reading in Cassou's book on '48,[2] that he was a close friend of Marx's. And today's letter from you made the urge all the more intense, and I was preparing to write you to send it to me, and then at that very moment, there it was, my sweet little flower. I've already read thirty-three pages with great interest. It's well done, and I'm interested by the obviously necessary effort to relocate every event within the social context. For instance, instead of just saying, like any run-of-the-mill biographer, "As a child Heine was the favorite of his aunts," she adds, "because he was the eldest, the male heir destined to recite the blessing of the dead." You really feel the solid underpinnings of these quirky Jewish families. So, many thanks, I'm totally delighted, little charmer. Delighted too—but this time extraordinarily so—with the two thick notebooks. So much so that they're giving me ideas for rapidly finishing up the shabby little one I'm now on and going on sooner to those two thick handsome ones, so fat, so cozy, with their midnight-blue edges. I swear, nothing but beautiful thoughts must be written in them, or what's the point? Do you realize that if I get to Paris on the 20th or the 25th, you'll have all of five notebooks to read: two thin ones, two middle-sized, and one of the thick ones, besides a bit of the second thick one. The ink was much needed too; you know, with the notebook, the letters,

---

[1] By Soren Kierkegaard.
[2] Jean Cassou's *Quarante-huit* (Paris, 1939) about the revolution of 1848.

and the novel I use up a cartridge in a day and a half. In my whole life I've never written so much.

Today I went on another pilgrimage, not to reconnoiter the area, but rather for a little moisture, to get rid of a bit of my recent dryness. I was totally successful, though the two trips left me quite numb; it was cold in the truck and besides, the driver wasn't very likeable. But for me the town—so ugly, so German— had the same poetry, the same swollen face, as Berlin's. I walked around its streets doing errands, I bought everyone rubbing oil, toothpaste, large needles, soles, yarn, I don't know what-all. I had no very interesting thoughts or feelings, but it gave me back my small sense of inner poetry. I can get along well enough without it for a week, after which I miss it. Basically it doesn't take much, and the location hardly matters. Simply a bit of solitude. I am alone less than ever. There are still the three of us in the dormitory room. And the restaurant is packed these days: it's the changing of the guard, and the light-infantry men coming off the front lines treat themselves to good meals the first two or three days. After that things subside. But this morning on returning from the pilgrimage and yesterday, I had a tiny table to myself, though with one infantryman's knee against mine and another's cartridge box jabbing my rear. Still, I was able to read Stendhal, who appeals to me less and less at this stage. Toward the end there's a shabby story about marriage that's not very nice, in that he was with Angelina Bereyter at the time—and used the pretext of his engagement to announce his passion for Mme. Daru. Besides, what quantities of people he's seeing, so inept. No I don't like him much. But perhaps this is a "bad patch." As for me, I've been through tons of them in my life, and you know that last year, I wasn't much better about sincerity of feelings.

In the midst of all this, I'm happy. First of all, each day brings me closer to you so I await the morrow eagerly. My love, in much less than a month, I'll be by your side in Paris, how marvelous. But, as I wrote to T. yesterday, I really feel I'll find *you*, find *her*, but I can scarcely believe that for a short while I'll also regain my peacetime leisure, and time for which I'm accountable to no one, and a certain way of wandering the streets, without any particular reason to go this way rather than that. It boggles the mind. I love you, my little one; we won't let anyone else encroach, and it'll be a fine leave. And aside from all that, here I look forward to the morrow *for itself*, because there's always something pleasant to it. For instance, today was the day I would go on a pilgrimage for my lost sense of poetry. Tomorrow is the day I'll read the biography of Heine, when I'll explain in my notebook what I think about Stendhal's *Journal*, when I'll finish correcting the last pages of my novel. Etc., and each day I'm totally occupied and happy to wake up. I burst out of my cold room and go get dressed in the study, which is still a bit warm from the evening before, then I scan the horizon, by which I mean that I go down to piss in the snow near a pole flying a black flag, and I gauge the direction of the flag while I piss. After which I come back, eyes on the sky, I mark down the results of my observations and call them in. Then breakfast, and you know the rest.

I'm sending you a letter—is it from Tania or from me?—which will bring you up-to-date on my epistolary banter. She had gone a day without answering, and I had sent her this with a self-addressed envelope, not knowing there had been a delay in the mail. So I wrote, "Take it as a bad joke." Furious, she had chosen the worst possible options, and immediately ran to toss a letter into the mailbox saying, "It was a slightly irritated joke." So I received this letter in a handwriting that was vaguely familiar to me and distasteful, it intrigued me, and then I thought, "It's mine."

There you have it, my dear little Beaver. You've been good and written to me, I wasn't expecting any letters today, and I'm overjoyed. You cannot know how much I love you, little one completely snowbound. I hug you with all my might.

Letter returned by Tania

Kindly strike out the phrase that doesn't represent the case.

Example: I am	~~a model of virtue~~ an illumination ~~a buffoon~~
I am	~~well~~ ~~more or less well~~ not well
I am working	~~a little~~ not at all
Toward you I feel	~~a little lingering affection~~ ~~good, solid indifference~~ hatred
I am	~~virtuous~~ ~~luminous~~ capricious

AND WORSE THAN THAT

~~send you a kiss~~

I   ~~shake your hand~~

send no greeting

Signature

I'M NOT SIGNING

✤ *to Simone de Beauvoir*

January 6

My darling Beaver

Two letters from you today. I'm annoyed that you didn't get the ones I sent to Megève. I want you to know that they were very warm—and I expressed all the love I was feeling for you. I hope the books reached you. I got the mail order this morning, I reimbursed my buddies and all is well.

I'm struggling with my mother[1] about the upcoming leave, but on an insignificant point: all on her own she wrote, "Will you store your clothes here or somewhere else?" Which provoked the following response: I'll have a room at the Hotel Mistral, but I'll change at your place. She accepted the arrangement without comment and, it seems, as though it was quite natural. But now the worthy lady absolutely wants to buy me a pair of pants, and I simply won't have it; I only want my nice casual suit from Alba. We're engaged in rather animated discussion. Of course, she is offering to pay for the pants. But I want the poor woman to hold onto her pennies. And of course, too, my answers must be wrapped in mystery because of my stepfather.

An otherwise empty, studious day. There wasn't even a reading due to fog. I worked on my novel. The scene with Daniel, the one at the end, is terribly delicate. Just think, he tells Mathieu both that he is marrying Marcelle and that he's a homosexual. There's enough there to drive any guy around the bend, and besides, the situation would call for Mathieu to ask all sorts of pointless questions, which the chapter's brevity expressly forbids. I'm working it out rather well, but it's taking time. I've written some thirty pages in your handsome midnight-blue notebook. No, my most inspired little one, it isn't too thick. It fits into my pocket, and besides it's a pleasure to write in it. It was about Stendhal's *Journal*, what I think about it, which is not bloody much. I read the biography of Heine (the beginning), which inspired some curious reflections. While in fact I was praising him internally for having known how to assume his condition

---

[1] Widowed when her only child was a year old, the former Anne-Marie Schweitzer, of a prominent liberal Alsatian family, later married an engineer, Joseph Mancy.

as a Jew, and I was understanding luminously that rational Jews like Pieter or Brunschwig were inauthentic in that they thought themselves men first and not Jews, the idea came to me, as a direct result, that I had to acknowledge myself a Frenchman; it was a rather spiritless idea and above all it was devoid of meaning for me. Simply an inevitable and obvious conclusion. I wonder where it'll take me, and I'll explore it tomorrow. Since I have broken my inferiority complex vis-à-vis the far Left, I feel a freedom of thought I've never known before; vis-à-vis the phenomenologists too. I feel I'm on the way, as biographers say around page 150 of their books, to discovering myself. Which only means that I no longer think with an eye to certain strictures (the Left, Husserl), etc., but with a total and gratuitous freedom, out of pure curiosity and disinterestedness, accepting in advance that I could end up discovering I was a Fascist if that's where my reasoning led me. Don't worry, I doubt that'll happen. It interests me and I think that, beyond the war and the renewed questioning, the notebook *form* counts for a great deal in this; this free and fragmented form isn't subject to prior ideas, you write each thing according to the moment and only take stock when you want to. As a matter of fact I haven't yet reread all of my notebooks and I've forgotten any number of things I've said in them. Basically, this system enjoys the same advantages as the *Propos*, which Alain touts so lustily and profits from so little.[2]

M. wrote to me. He sounds as though he's going crazy, which suits him very well, but I'd just as soon not be there when it happens, as he has a Herculean build and I can't easily see myself playing the same role for him that you did for Ballon.[3] When I say crazy, I'm exaggerating; the symptoms are gloom, headaches, and what he calls "cerebral anemia," which obviously conceals mental problems. He writes me this mysterious sentence: "I see that Paulhan[4] is publishing you in tandem with Mauriac." What does this mean? See whether by chance the Giraudoux piece has finally appeared in the January NRF.[5] There you are, my little one. Tell me if you understand that we must acknowledge ourselves as French (with no a priori link to patriotism, of course), I'm very eager to have your opinion on that.

My little one, I so love to talk with you. See, there was nothing to say and

---

[2] Alain, nom de plume of Émile-Auguste Chartier (1868–1951), influential philosopher and teacher, whose *Propos*, short newspaper articles on the widest range of subjects, began appearing in 1903. Though a pacifist, when the First World War started, he enlisted. He wrote *Mars ou la guerre jugée*, 1921 [*Mars: Or the Truth About War*, 1930].

[3] Renée Ballon, a friend from Beauvoir's years of teaching in Rouen, whom she helped during a stormy period.

[4] Jean Paulhan (1884–1968), editor of NRF, 1925–1940.

[5] NRF, March 1940, "M. Giraudoux et la philosophie d'Aristote: A propos de *Choix des Elus*" ["M. Giraudoux and Aristotle's philosophy: on *Selection of the Chosen*"].

I'm writing four pages for the pleasure of writing to you. Oh, how I would love to see you again, my little flower.

I love you.

☞ *to Simone de Beauvoir*

My darling Beaver

The fun is gone, Pieter is back. He has been talking since two this afternoon. He's all excited, he was getting up every five minutes. "Don't you think I should go say hello to the clerks?" "Don't you think I should go say hello to the radio guys?" In each case I strongly urged him to do so; while he was there, he wasn't here. He was drunk on words and only went through one low moment—true to form—when he disappeared for five minutes to carry his knapsacks to the bedroom. "Well," he said, "it was gloomy, nobody was there, it got to me." I know very well that when I get back I'll find a sense of well-being only snug in my room, and what will make me gloomy is their mugs. Here's your ink, my little sweet. Do you recognize it? It's South Seas blue. But so delectable that no doubt the paper is taking sips of it. But that's a detail. You know, with this ink and despite Pieter, since yesterday morning I've written 81 pages in the first midnight-blue notebook. South Seas blue on Midnight blue. You can just imagine how beautiful it is. Today's 39 pages are on my relations with France. Just a recital of the facts, the kind of thing you like. I've only gotten to the recital but tomorrow I'll do the theory. Only I'm somewhat scared that Pieter's return will make me lose time. For instance at the present moment there are four of them in this little room, Mistler, Pieter, Keller, Paul. Paul and Keller aren't saying anything, as usual, but Pieter is talking to Mistler, and already it takes concentration to write to you without hearing them. I've only written in my notebook, I haven't worked on my novel, and I haven't done any reading. By tomorrow I'll rectify that, at the risk of seeming rude. For today it's all right: he just got back.

Otherwise, the day has been quiet but lacked the virtue of being studious. I don't like that, right now I'm a bit annoyed. I got a letter from you, my little angel . . . (I just stopped talking to you to bawl out Pieter, who hasn't once stopped talking for the past half hour. Mistler had gone, Keller and Paul were reading, I was writing, and that beast was finding ways to ask questions like,

"About that report from the N.M. Office on the 95 francs, did Captain Munier answer?" etc. I said, "Pieter, would you like a book?" And, unstrung by his return from leave: "I'm not speaking to you, Sartre, I'm speaking to Paul." "But, Pieter, you're boring the shit out of Paul; can't you see that he's reading?" "He's old enough to tell me if I'm boring him, Sartre. Kindly don't butt in unless it's something that directly concerns you and me." "But I'm speaking on behalf of everyone, Pieter. If you only knew how peaceful we were when you weren't here." "I do as I please, Sartre," he repeated ten times, looking furious as a sheep, "I do as I like. You certainly like leaving filthy handkerchiefs lying around the bedside table." "Then good, let's make a deal, Pieter: I'll chuck the hand-kerchiefs but you'll keep your trap shut." "I'm not making any deals." "Because you fucking well don't keep to them." The argument stopped dead right there, I don't know why: dead stops like that just happen. As if it had run out of steam. Nary a peep from the others. Keller, who hates him, must have been secretly happy to see him get bawled out. In any case, since then—for ten minutes now—complete silence has reigned, which is a step forward. He must find it bitter to have gotten himself bawled out on his first day back, but the contrast was too great between my absolute tranquillity yesterday and this chatterbox today. Tough.) End of parenthesis. Which I close on a pessimistic note, actually, because now he'll keep quiet this evening till bedtime, but tomorrow he'll be chattering again, he's like a bird. Received an amusing letter from Tania about the Moon Woman,[1] who "wants to be a lioness after this war the way Youki[2] was in '19" and who's going at it already, as you can see. She wants to dump Blondinet[3] for the Argentine painter and begs Tania to see him from time to time and tell him good things about her when he's alone with her. I find that very naïve. It seems that the painter had the phonograph with two legs coming out of it that we saw at the surrealist exhibition. There you have it for today, my little one. I'm sorry not to have been able to read more in the Heine biography. It's well done.

My little one, my dear little one. I wasn't unmoved, after all, by Pieter's return. It made me see Paris so close, through him at first, and then also because I'll soon be leaving too. Since he's come back, there's no longer any *compelling* reason, it seems, for me to stay here (actually there is—the sequence of leaves—except that I have the illusory feeling I'm leaving after Pieter) so now there's only a formless void separating me from you, which is simultaneously enervating

---

[1] Marie Ville, nicknamed thus because of her dreaminess. Sartre had an affair with her in Berlin in 1934.

[2] Nickname for Fernande Barrey, formerly married to the painter Tsuguharu Fujita (1886–1968) and then to Robert Desnos (1900–45), the Belgian surrealist poet.

[3] Nickname for Jean-André Ville, philologist husband of Marie.

and exciting, and in the end that's why I bawled Pieter out, I think. I love you so much, my little dearest, I would so love to have your little arm in mine and stroll about with you. I hug you with all my might.

☜ to *Simone de Beauvoir*

January 8

My darling Beaver

Things are going much better than yesterday, we've absorbed Pieter, who's totally dazed and not talking anymore. But earlier he thought he had to snore all night, he's a real noise machine, that guy. I whistled, but in vain, so I grabbed a table by the leg and banged it on the floor, very hard. He sobbed like a young fawn, and then a second later his snoring poked around some and, when he had collected it, resumed full blast. I beat on the floor again and the little performance started up again. Finally, I romped the table so hard that he jerked up with a start, grabbed his flashlight, turned it on, trained it at me, berserk, while I closed my eyes and artfully played the sleeping angel. He went back to sleep right away but didn't let out anything except little yaps, very soft and lulling. At four in the morning I finally fell asleep and got up at six-thirty, all this to explain why I'm hurrying to write to you, though it's not past eight, for fear of falling asleep. You must have had a good laugh the other day at the solemn praise I was according Heine for his fidelity to his Jewishness, you who already knew that one year later he'd gotten himself baptized to qualify for the civil service. It really doesn't matter, this repudiation *for nothing* is rather interesting, because it was basically a bit of gratuitous dirty work. The book is really engaging, you're right, though perhaps Heine himself gets somewhat sacrificed to his *situation*. You can still see him well though, in rough terms you can clearly sense what he was. Only the details are missing. I feel he seems very Jewish and that he (somewhat) resembles Rosenthal in *La Conspiration* [*The Conspiracy*],[1] because of which Nizan has grown in my estimation. Also a desire to read Heine's *Complete Works* in German, but that's for peacetime. On the subject of peace, here's some good news: it is definite that within 2 or 3 months they're going to recall to the rear all those over 30. The paperwork on that began right here today. We in particular are a case apart, and it is the National Meteorological Office that will handle it but at least you can see that it's underway. So no more Postal Sector and of course everything that goes with it. Naturally

---

[1] The first novel by Paul Nizan, Sartre's friend from École Normale Supérieure days.

you can see the advantages, my little sweet. I think you can begin to rejoice with, of course, all the prudence appropriate in the face of military decisions.

Today no letter from you, nor any from T. I suppose there's been yet another log jam; only one little letter from my mother. Did I tell you, the restaurants are closed now till 5 in the evening, so I can't have lunch out anymore. I ate some white beans here, not unhappily. Though I did go out on the sly for a coffee at the Café de la Poste, since the post office has been set up in a little mauve hotel located between the town and our hotel. The room to the right, on the ground floor, is occupied by the postal clerks, the one on the left remains a café. So you drop in on the postal clerks, you casually inquire if there's any mail, you go to the back door and slip into the café, which is locked up with closed blinds but filled with the regulars, who are playing cards and getting gently soused in the semidark. They left bit by bit and I stayed on alone, writing in my notebook with four other delinquents, guys who'd been on guard duty the day before. The night before, as guards, they had come into the same café to chase out the delinquents, but the next day, liberated from their obligations, it was their turn to be delinquents. So I was writing about France. I've done the theory and done it well, but don't worry. I'm not turning fascist, far from it. I saw the whole thing clearly, and I believe you will agree with me. Anyway, it's always the same: historicity, being-in-the-world, *my* war, etc. I've already filled half a midnight-blue notebook, but I have more work cut out for me since I still have an entire large one, and besides, the other day I bought four little ones. I'll surely bring you six of them and perhaps seven or eight, you'll have plenty to read. Perhaps you know that I also have a theory of consciousness-nothingness; it's actually not entirely ready. In a word, I was writing about the motherland when there was a loud knock on the café door and someone tried several times to open it. The four delinquents got up, whispering, "The cops! The cops!" They were right, it was the police doing their rounds. They had to go around by the back door, and so we had time to make it up to the second floor of the hotel, carrying our beers, schnapps, coffees, and went into the office of the health service, where the guy watched dumfounded as we entered. The gendarmes took forever, I finally went back down quite calmly and exited through the post office, but I lost a glove to the affair, since I was looking for it at the moment the cops arrived, and the woman who owns the place shoved me onto the staircase by the shoulders without leaving me time to find it. I also finished the last chapter of *The Age of Reason*, I'm going to revise the previous one a bit then I'll write a little monologue for Boris, which will go much earlier, and it will be time to go off on leave. To see you again, my charming little one, my dearest. Do your planning well so that we'll see everything we should and be happy.

I love you.

⟡ *to Simone de Beauvoir*

My darling Beaver

I got a letter from you today. But only one. Only one from T. Yesterday's are missing, so it seems. Perhaps I'll get them tomorrow. Well anyway, I know what you're doing. You've seen Merleau-Ponty,[1] and what you wrote amused me because it tells me that in France the very same methods are employed that the newspapers deplore so vehemently when the Germans use them. You seem bright-eyed and bushy-tailed, and your gaiety makes me happy. Yes, my little dearest, we'll soon see one another again; I yearn for it.

Somehow today I'm going through a little crisis of self-confidence—an occurrence rare enough to merit the telling. There are a multitude of small causes. Today I've just finished *The Age of Reason*. There are only ten lines still to correct, which will take one hour tomorrow, and the prospect leaves me almost speechless. I'm saying to myself, "This is all there is," and I find it paltry, too paltry. Perhaps after all the book suffered somewhat, not directly from the war, but from my changed point of view about everything. I've been a bit numb about it all this time and in particular, curiously, since you read the 150 pages done in November. Yet you told me it was good. I'm not really sure what went on in my head. Was it the need to change Marcelle?[2] At any rate there it is, I'm not pleased with it, I'd have liked it to be good and *sincere*. Mind you, I well know that you have to lie all the time in a novel. But at least you lie to be true. And it seems to me that the whole novel is something of a gratuitous lie. And here I've been working on it a year and a half! I have a perfect right to feel a bit disgusted. Besides, I've reread my five notebooks, and they didn't make quite the good impression I'd been rather counting on. It seemed to me there was vagueness and superficiality, that the clearest ideas were rehashes of Heidegger, that basically since September and the stuff about "my" war, etc, I'd done nothing but laboriously develop what he takes only ten pages to say about historicity. In addition, I'm reading the biography of Heine, which grabs me, as it did you. But, now that I'm "grown up," biographies don't give me the same easy joyful charge they did ten years ago. Instead this one rather defeated me. My life seemed pretty futile next to his; he'd done lots of underhanded things and had a very weak character, but he had lived so superbly within his situation, as you put it. As for myself, I realize that I waited till the war to decipher my

---

[1] Maurice Merleau-Ponty (1908–61), a leading phenomenologist; during their senior year he and Beauvoir had been the two top students at the Sorbonne. He was a teacher through the 1930s and an officer during the war. Coeditor (1945–52) with Sartre of the journal *Les Temps Modernes*.

[2] The mistress of the novel's protagonist Mathieu.

situation somewhat, and I also see that I have no great talent for that: I don't lack goodwill, but I should also have the sense of history he had. Well, there it is, I'm a very humble sort of fellow tonight, my love. Doubtless I won't be so tomorrow and your letters in which you'll strain to gently show that I'm a very good little person, not so despicable as all that, will find me on the crest of a wave, and instead I'll be irked by the faint demurrals you'll have come up with. I wonder what I'll write now. It would be wise to go on, in a way. But, in another sense, if it disgusts me that doesn't make too much sense. And what can I write? I'm feeling myself out. Don't worry too much about this fit of modesty: it's hardly more than daily ups-and-downs.

Aside from that, nothing new, I'm still playing the monk. Today it was icy underfoot and I only went out to get grub. You would have laughed, to see me on the road with my mess kit, canteen, and flashlight, tottering along with tiny steps like a little old lady. The day's true little pleasure was your letter. Greater than usual, because there'd been nothing from you yesterday. I love you much, my little one.

I send you big hugs and kisses, my love.

⟨⟩ to Simone de Beauvoir

January 10

My darling Beaver

So I wrote you a self-deprecating little letter. Today, it's all gone. To be sure I'm not delirious with pride, but I'm back in a proper frame of mind, I mean I'm doing what has to be done without thinking about myself at all. Today there was a terrific wind (60 km an hour), and what's more, it was − 12°. Just imagine the readings that take place, as they must, in open countryside, and those blasts of icy air hurtling over us, filtered inside our clothes. It was so strange, beneath a perfectly pure sky with traces of pink, all that forbidding open ground around the building which bit, clawed and pinched the moment we went out. Right now it's still meowing at our windows, and there's a little trickle of cold filtering between the sashes of one window. This morning at eight, on my way back from the reading, one of my arms was frozen up to the elbow. Afterward, when I started moving it, I had those fireworks sensations you get when you've banged your funny bone against the arm of a chair. But please understand that all this is *fun*, it gives me a sense of struggle, and particularly of nature laid on with a trowel. In addition to which, the icy ground makes a person dance like eggs in a pot. Nonetheless I stubbornly refuse to wear my overcoat—it's a matter of honor. But then, people say, you who are so fond of the cold outside, why can't you bear it inside, why must it always be 18° or 20° in the room where you spend your time? I know the reason, I wrote it down in my notebook. You'll read it.

There's the shape of the day. And my only sorties, since the restaurant remains off-limits. As army rations have decided to be foul these days, my lunch and dinner consist of a piece of bread. This, together with my diet, will make me slim as a reed when I get to Paris. It's drawing nigh, my love, the pace of the leaves is accelerating; still just one poor little fortnight to go and that'll be it. I hardly think of anything else anymore. This morning I finished the novel. I mean totally finished, we won't say any more about it till Paris. And this afternoon I mused at length upon a play. I wanted a city under siege, pogroms, who knows what else. The subject, properly speaking, wouldn't come. Then all of a sudden what do you suppose I began? Stories for Uncle Jules. At first with a sort of guilt, because it's futile. But then it occurred to me to put in loads of things in the form of banter, and in the end it's amusing me a lot and exciting me a bit. Here's how it begins, to convey the tone.

"That morning my Uncle Jules came into my room and said, 'Nephew, so you've been stealing money.' " I figured I'd do some writing between the two home leaves (if you like the genre, which you can tell me in two weeks), it will make for an odd little gratuitous book, along the lines of *Er l'Arménien*[1] and *Légende de la Vérité*,[2] but now, since I no longer have any of the faults that made the style intolerable (symbolism, mannerism, etc.) I wonder how it will turn out. That's the event of the day. Aside from that, there's some reading: Stendhal's *Journal* (IV) which is turning completely charming again; and an inept January issue of *NRF*, without my article, which they sent me along with a long insipid poem by Mauriac, a Cocteau that doesn't know when to stop, and an Aragon, which I only leafed through and found very bad. That's all. A long letter from my darling Beaver, nothing from T., who however wrote yesterday, "I love you generously (don't laugh)."

That's all, my very dear little one, my tender little Beaver, I love you so much and so well you are my dear little heart. In fifteen or twenty days I'm seeing you.

When you send the books, would you kindly add two pads of paper like this?

---

[1] An unfinished text written about 1928 and published in *Écrits de jeunesse* (Gallimard, 1990). Inspired by Plato and Hesiod as well as French writers and thinkers, Sartre mythologized such philosophical topics as Contingency, Evil, and Art.

[2] An early work that was never published in its entirety; a portion appeared in *Bifur*, June 1931; and in Sartre, *Selected Prose*, 1974.

❧ to Simone de Beauvoir

January 11

My darling Beaver

I've just given a little lecture on American literature to Mistler, simply to hear myself talk a bit. Now he's here beside me, reading Stendhal's *Journal*, smiling with that almost besotted inner bliss of his. It's nice and warm here in our place, but it's the last day for that. There's not a single briquette of coal left in the whole region. I have no idea what we'll do, since it's −12° or −13° out. In fact, that's rather exciting to a graduate of the school of hard knocks. But there's only one problem, that I won't be writing anymore. To begin with, a refrigerated body is not terribly conducive to thought, and anyway, my frozen hand won't be able to hold on to a pen. Well, we'll see how it all turns out. Yet I'm in the mood to write, though I'm very wary of what I'm doing. When I was talking about Faulkner to Mistler, I felt like a fallen Walkyrie, what with the little satiric volume I'm writing: all his stories of murder and blood suddenly seem to me the only serious literature. But after all there's no harm in trying for twenty days. After which you'll be the judge. Here's the idea. It will be a small volume of literary criticism in which I'll talk about the laws of genres. Of course there would be a discussion in dialogue on genres and later the story as illustration: 1st, a fairy tale (to distinguish the allegorical fairy tale—Maeterlinck—from the true popular fairy tale); 2nd, the narrative; 3rd, the short story; 4th, the chapter of the novel. An explication of the genre followed by the story. I begin by justifying myself for writing obscene material and by explaining the literary work in general, the whole thing in the form of playful paradoxes which obviously run the risk of annoying. You'll see, you'll be the judge. In any case, by writing the dialogue I'm proving I can do excellent stage dialogue. I have the feel for this dialogue. I lack only a subject. That's put off till after the *Tales of Uncle Jules*. All the same, from what you know now, do tell me if you're wary or if you'd encourage me. It's in simple, lovely style. But it's marvelous how *easy* it is to write a simple, lovely style. Ten times easier than writing in the rough and muddled style of *The Age of Reason*. Now I understand why I'm such a drudge and others aren't. It's because I've adopted a style for my novels that may be neither better nor worse than others but is quite simply more difficult. So much for intelligence. Of course I'm no longer working on my notebook, I don't have the time anymore. And yet I must still add one or two little things, which I'll do tomorrow. However long the war, I'll return with fifty volumes and be able to just sit back and relax for the rest of my days.

As for life here, it's mostly one long bath of warmth, interrupted by brief bursts of anger, which make Pieter say "living together is difficult," and pierced by shafts of glacial—though not disagreeable—cold (readings, or when we go to get the grub). On Pieter's say-so, we took off at noon to go to the Café de la Gare, but it was closed and we had to turn back in cold that bit our ears. To show you the old-woman type of idleness that afflicts all these people, you should know that this failed attempt furnished the material for the entire day's news. Everyone had seen us going off and wanted to know where we were headed, or else, if he knew, to make little comments. Anyway, I lunched on bread and chocolate and dined on the same, because the army rations were too foul. This makes three days that I've been living off bread and chocolate, if I don't come back slim as a reed, there's no God left in heaven. Don't worry: the restaurant is open in the evening, and if I were hungry I could drop by. But those are my best hours for work, and all things considered, I prefer to stay here.

There, my little sweet, that's all there is. If you only knew how I long to see you. This whole period seems like a rather long-winded epilogue before my trip to Paris. Actually, I tend to vaguely confuse Leave and Peace, out of failure to see beyond those ten days. It's not so much that I imagine they're going to last indefinitely, it's rather that I can't imagine my life going on after them. They are terminated by a definitive and slightly tragic limit that could as well be my death as my return to my sector. But how beautiful and pleasant they seem from afar! My mother seems as sensible as anything, the lovely woman; she seems definitely decided on letting me wear my light-colored clothes. So everything is going very well in that quarter. And you, my little one, I'm going to see you and talk continually with you and squeeze your little arm. We'll go to bed early, since we'll be chased out of everywhere at eleven, but we'll get up, military style, at seven in the morning, and go running all over the place. I love you so.

I love you, my sweet, I love you with all my heart.

Bost is taking it all with a stiff upper lip.

✣ to Simone de Beauvoir

January 12

My darling Beaver

That's enough; a moment ago I tore up the first six pages of *Stories for Uncle Jules*, I was ashamed to be writing it. There was a smugness about it, and flourishes (frankly dictated by the genre), and little set pieces, all of which gave me the shudders. And besides, as I told you, I felt like a fallen Walkyrie. So I returned to my plan of writing a large-scale play with blood, rape, and massacres, and you would have seen me all afternoon looking sad, gnawing on my fist— which is my way of looking for a subject, as you know—to such a degree that Paul, who keeps a sharp eye on my failures, asked me with an ironic and indulgent superiority whether I felt low or had received some bad news from home. I snapped at him to mind his own business, and was actually very cheerful; I was fully and enthusiastically launched on fashioning a *Prometheus*, a dictator of liberty who ended up in those celebrated tortures. It gave me my little moment of enthusiasm, because my aims are lofty in literature, and I sang "The Man I Love" while I did the reading, which made the theodolite wobble on its legs. And then after reflection, the symbolic quality of *Prometheus* disgusted me. It's not that symbols *per se* can't be used, if at least it is done discreetly, but I've so abused them in my mad youth that they give me indigestion. A jumble of metaphors from *The Legend of Truth* came to mind and in the end that's where I am now. I fear I'll be mired down a day or two longer in search of a subject, and will finish by returning honestly to *September*. Honestly, but with mild regrets. It seems to me that I have drama running through my head, and I would like to use some of it finally. And what better time could there be than now, since I have the leisure?

Wait a minute! you'll say, so you weren't freezing after all, you who had no coal left? That's because this morning, after two or three rather difficult hours (reading at $-15°$ with a wind that could knock the horns off a bull), weary of vegetating in a room where we were burning our newspapers to keep the temperature at 4 above, we learned through Mistler, our spy, that the clerks were about to steal some coke from the public baths. We went over and came back with three bags full. As a matter of fact it wasn't robbery, and what we took was duly noted by the guard. But lo and behold, coke is a weird kind of obstinate coal, which, once it lights, broils us, then dies out and stubbornly refuses to rekindle. But generally speaking, we are warm. Nothing else to say. We went over for a drink at the Café de la Poste at one, and for the first time in three days I ate something more than dry bread: the field kitchen had pea soup, which I really like.

I haven't received your little daily letter, my dearest, which left me feeling that something was missing. I got one from T., which tells me nothing about you during the evening at the Théâtre Français (but the play delighted her),[1] but she returned the very next morning to the "Bar des Champs-Elysées, which the Beaver discovered," which indicates, I think, very good feelings.

Really, my dearest, my little flower, except for you, who might well kill yourself, by now I don't mean anything to the rest of the world (aside from my mother). And that's funny in my case, because I had everything I could wish for. But *presence* is essential. I say so without any sort of bitterness, amused to be a corpse, a fossil for that whole crowd, because I actually feel very much alive. It counts as experience and besides, I promise myself to slough off my old skin, if I so choose, at the end of the war, since basically not one of those good ladies will have acquired the rights of fidelity. What do you think of that, do you find me too easily and too conveniently skeptical? In any case, that would only be because you shower me with blessings through your tender little letters, with your whole way of being, and that when one has that, one becomes demanding with others.

I love you so much, you, little paragon. It's so easy to live and be happy when you exist.

❧ *to Simone de Beauvoir*

January 13

My darling Beaver

I'm copying out for you the beginning of a letter that opened with these words: "I'm writing to you in a quiet moment: It's nine o'clock and we're thirsty, so I've just sent Mistler and Pieter off to buy some wine, it's my treat. When they return, we'll doubtless drink and get a little raucous." There was more to the letter, and I'll copy it all out—but, sad to say, Pieter came in with the full bottle when I'd finished two long pages, snatched my glass to fill it in a fit of generosity, and spilled all the wine on your poor little letter. Alas, my little sweet, I'll therefore have to begin it all over again. He stood there sheepishly, because they're all scared of me. ("We can't nail you on the big things when you bawl us out," Pieter said to me, "so we make up for it on the petty ones.

[1] *Right Your Are! (If You Think You Are)* by Luigi Pirandello (1867–1936). (See *Lettres à Sartre*, vol. 2, p. 32.)

But that doesn't matter: you're so hard on us when we bother you. What a load of guff you say to the poor jerks. You're hard on all of us!") But after having good-naturedly called him a dimwit, I rapidly came to a decision: I wouldn't write to T. who hasn't written to me, or to my parents who can get by for once without a letter from me.

This evening we convened a little salon. Mistler came, and Pieter spoke in an interesting way about the life and death of the Jewish colony of the Rue des Rosiers, since it appears to be just now ended. Meanwhile Keller, these days a poker-faced practical joker, had secretly slipped a long rubber tube behind Paul's books with the opening right beside Paul's nose. After which Keller lit a pipe and blew clouds of smoke through the tube. Paul, getting it right in the face (he despises tobacco), grew upset and said, "The room is saturated with smoke, and we're getting convection drafts." The rest of us, meanwhile, nearly died laughing about it—even I, my good Beaver, I was red in the face and had to tell some story about rats to justify my hoots of laughter. I have to say the smoke had its charms as it swirled around at table level, like a cat chasing its tail, beneath the dumfounded scientific gaze of our corporal. We plan to repeat it every evening.

Aside from that, of course, a day of absolute calm. Everyone's going off on leave and surely it will be my turn in ten days or two weeks. Actually Paul is going to bring it up with the captain, since it's as much in his interest as mine. Two nights ago I'd been so cold ($-7°$) in my room that I slept last night in the readings office on a mattress we found in the hall. It was voluptuous. Today, we were on KP, Pieter and I, which consists of doing not one fucking thing: we sort of sweep the premises (Pieter), we fetch the coffee (me) at 7 o'clock, we pick up the rations at noon (Pieter) and supper in the evening (the two of us, since we have to carry flashlights) so, as you can see, from 7 in the morning to 6 in the evening I have it pretty hard. Keller and Paul do the readings. Tomorrow it's our turn. You're probably thinking that I've begun *Prometheus* or some other vast enterprise. But far from it, I haven't even thought about it. I've written long ruminations on Destiny. Once again it's historicity. It impresses and amuses me to see how, "under pressure" of events, an historic thought has been released within me and now won't stop, me who up to last year was an absentminded little fellow with his head in the clouds, an Ariel. Ultimately I'm now haunted not by the social but by the human milieu. And that's pretty funny, since I'm a regular here, in perfect solitude (the Assistants[1] don't count) and feeling not the slightest social constraint. You remember our impression of a Kafkaesque war when we were in the Gare de l'Est and you felt I was departing for the East

---

[1] Sartre sometimes called his colleagues the Assistants, picked up from Kafka's *The Castle*.

out of some heroic, guilt-ridden stubbornness without any real urging from anyone. (Oh, my sweet, I do love you so, I remember that night walk in a deserted Paris, how close I felt to you, that's something very powerful between us.) Well, I swear, it's the same thing here. We're doing our service but with a strange and constant sense of being volunteers, we have no leaders, I don't have to put on a public face, I neglect washing and grooming. (Paul reported that they had said to him in the kitchen, "Your buddy's a celebrity in the division." And I don't believe that "celebrity" is intended as a compliment. And this evening, d'Arbon, a huge semi-idiot, an ironmonger in civilian life, said while I was washing the mess kits, "Sometimes the guys talk such crap." "Oh?" "Yeah." A silence and then d'Arbon chortled: "They say things like you're a teacher!" "Oh? So what?" "And so you're not a teacher." "Yes I am." He was eating something, and he had to spit it out lest he choke.) And yet in this state of liberty and solitude I feel all around me a terrific human pressure, that's what keeps me constantly alert.

Here ends the copied-out letter (with flourishes, of course). I got two long letters from you, little flower. How come you're talking to me about Mme. Medvédeff?[2] You must have noted with great amusement that I hadn't forgotten her name. She was a fine slip of a girl, who certainly seems to have fallen out of favor, according to her note. But I'd like you to correct one or two of her essays, my good little one. The better to preserve a few little distractions for the future-demobilized.

This evening, you know, I was musing that I'd soon be with you, in civilian clothes, in a Paris restaurant just as in the past (we'll go to the Louis XIV and to Le Relais de la Belle Aurore) and we'll be making slurping sounds as we wolf down a good meal, and it left me flabbergasted, I could hardly imagine that it all exists. Oh my love, how I long for this leave. And the omelettes! Today I remembered about the existence of omelettes! it's been three months since I've had one. As for sausages, on the other hand, I've had all I want.

That's all for tonight, my little sweet, my love. Do you truly feel how much I love you, how you are my little flower? We are as one, my little sweet, together we make for one. Or just a half. I love you.

[2] See *Lettres à Sartre*, vol. 2, p. 35. She was teaching in Sables-d'Olonne and had asked Beauvoir to correct her dissertation.

✢ to Simone de Beauvoir

January 14

My darling Beaver

All day long I've been daydreaming about a topic for a play. In the end I sank into total despair. Everything was contemplated but nothing stuck, from *Prometheus* to that famous ship loaded with Jews whose story had tempted me for a while. And then nothing. Nothing at all. I wrote a scene for *Prometheus* and tore it up; you know what a burden I am to myself and others during such periods of gestation. To top it all off, wanting to reread a passage from my novel, to at least confront something I'd finished that had a little solidity, I found it atrocious. So I screwed up all my courage and redid it, but I still don't think I've got it right. With that I wrote almost nothing in the notebook. Such was my day, with its empty dreams. I must say that here we have the right temperature for dreams. 25° to 30°—enough to put you to sleep for life, it's rather awful, you can feel your whole body in your head. It's the wretched coke: either it doesn't burn or it burns too hot. It's obvious that anthracite is better.

There's going to be a brief postponement in the leaves, my sweet. Nothing much, perhaps five or six days, but I think it would be wise not to expect me before February 1st. My sweet, have patience, that virtue born of war. But don't worry. This is not some way of gently letting you know that I won't get any leave at all. It is simply what I am telling you, only that and nothing more.

I got a letter from you with a most unfair postscript. You accuse me of not sending the books to Bost, and you call me "bad little fellow." But it is now almost a week since I sent him *twelve*. He will surely have received them. On that score I, for one, have almost nothing left. Quickly send me the Romains and that *Gilles* that's boring you so. I think that if I'm not writing I'll read. I don't quite know what to do with myself.

T. dutifully wrote me a long epistle but she's annoying, I don't know why. I think I must have gratuitously got the idea that six months' absence was much too much for one so young, and consequently I'm rather cross at her for forgetting me. But without passion, what the hell. You're absolutely right, my sweet, when you say that I'm as sensitive as you to incongruities. I don't think I let any get by. Yet I must say that at first I am ever full of indulgence for the incongruities of young ladies.

That's all for today, my little dear, my darling Beaver. I love you with all my might, you are my little flower.

◈ to Simone de Beauvoir

January 15

My darling Beaver

Yet another studious day. Pieter and Keller went off to get hydrogen, it was their turn and I didn't get my poetic little morning. But it was unimportant, and I worked well. Philosophy, alas, neither play nor novel. That doesn't matter, it needed to be done. This morning I reread Heidegger's lecture *What Is Metaphysics?*, and I spent the day "staking out a position" vis-à-vis his on the question of Nothingness. It wasn't very well constructed, but now it is. You'll see it when I come home on leave. You may well find that my notebooks are turning too philosophical, my little judge. But I really have to do some of that too, and besides I was just writing in my notebook today that the philosophy I'm writing must be rather moving for others because it is personal. It plays a role in my life, protecting me against the melancholy, gloom, and sadness of the war, though by now I'm trying neither to protect my life after the fact with my philosophy, which would be sleazy, nor make my life conform to my philosophy, which would be pedantic, instead now philosophy and life have really become one. On that subject, I read a beautiful sentence of Heidegger's that could apply to me: "The metaphysics of human-reality is not simply a metaphysics *on* human-reality; it is metaphysics coming . . . into being *in the form of human-reality*." All the same, for the "cultivated public" there will be boring passages. On the other hand, a few turn out to be racy: one on holes in general, and another quite specifically on the anus and love, Italian-style. This will compensate for the other.

Aside from that, I treated myself to a little entertainment during the afternoon, by reading *The Sinking of the Titanic*.[1] Quite diverting. But after fifty pages I couldn't resist peeking at the ending, and once I knew the guilty party I couldn't go on. Speaking of which, my little sweet, the moment you get this letter you'll have to send me some books, as I have none left. And if you haven't read the Romains, send it anyway, please. I'll send them back scrupulously.

So, my poor little one, you had heard that they canceled the leaves. They didn't say why, but it isn't hard to figure out: there are new threats to Belgium and Holland. I learned that last night a bit before writing to you, and it was rather a blow. I, who had been talking to you the night before about the walks we would take together and the omelettes I'd eat. But above all I'm longing so to see you, my little dear. But you know it's only a very short delay. Once again, these threats won't come to anything, in four or five days the leaves will start

[1] By John Dickson Carr.

up again. And since they have to complete all of them they'll accelerate the pace. So you'll see me almost at the appointed time. Actually they're saying on the radio this evening that German-Dutch tensions are decreasing. Except that last night no one knew anything at all. But I "took it on" and digested the blow in a way that did me honor. This morning I was in a great mood. Not so the three or four poor guys, quite devastated, who were supposed to leave yesterday and didn't. In fact it was the colonel's turn to go, and on account of that he's still here. *But above all don't worry.* I'm *sure* to come within the next two weeks, or thereabouts; this is merely a tiny inconsequential hitch. Yesterday it hit pretty hard because we knew absolutely nothing.

No mail at all today. From anybody. So I'll have six letters tomorrow, which will make for a good day. And there you have it. I've begun my ninth notebook. It's the second large midnight-blue one that you sent me. When I get there I'll be bringing you *seven*, for sure, you'll never have read so many at one time. And we'll record a small one in confidence between the two of us about the leave, which we'll show to nobody, particularly not to our intimates, on *the stay* in Paris.

I love you so, my little one. Yesterday I felt how much I need to see you. You write that you feel me "at hand," and I so love that; yes my love, I'm almost there within your little paw, which I kiss fervently.

❧ *to Simone de Beauvoir*

January 16

My darling Beaver

I'm writing to you earlier today because I haven't had a thing to do all day (overcast skies, no reading) and was therefore able to work away quietly. First, at constructing that little theory on Nothingness, which you'll surely admire, since 1st it eliminates Husserl's recourse to *hylē*[1]—2nd it explains the oneness of the world for plural consciousnesses—3rd it allows a *true* transcendence of realism and idealism. That's all well and good. But I'm not explaining it to you because I want you to be present at the creation, as it develops in my notebooks; you'll enjoy it. After that, weary from chasing after a grandiose topic that required

---

[1] Greek for "matter." Hylomorphism, the central doctrine of Aristotle's philosophy of nature, viewed every natural body as consisting of two intrinsic principles—one potential, the primary matter (*hylē*) and one actual, the substantial form (*morphē*).

considerable persuasion, I modestly and sensibly went back to the novel. There was a chapter to be done on Boris, which I began. Basically, why shouldn't I take it up again now and recast my novel? I'm still warm and yet far enough from the first chapters for their faults to stick out. So here is what I suggest to you: what would you think of writing to the Lady for her to send the manuscript by registered mail? (Or perhaps someone at La Pouèze might be coming to Paris and could bring it in, it's no more than a week away.) And then you could send it out to be typed in duplicate, and I'd bring one copy back on my return from leave. Or else, if you think it's too expensive to have it typed, I'll bring it back in manuscript form: given our sedentary life, there doesn't seem much risk. What do you think? If you agree, you could write as soon as you like to the Lady. If not, state your objections.

So, I'm writing on Boris, and it's going well, I think it will be appealing. And then I read Heidegger and began *As I Lay Dying*.[2] (Do send the books, my love, the Romains, *Gilles*, and then if you're not too poor you could add one or two little surprises not on the list. Thank you, so very thoughtful sweet little one, for your offer of food. I just got a whole package full from my mother, and besides, if I wanted some, I could get it here.) I got *one* letter from you; I was expecting two because I didn't get any yesterday. It was Saturday's.

My little darling, I certainly understand how you could feel so numb while still being happy, and how that can be a way of missing me. I feel very much the same. In the long run we're hardened, and besides, there are all the little annoyances (suspended leave, etc.) which we must face with a stiff upper lip, so we feel an aridness within, but it's a vaguely depressed aridness. Me too, my love, I'd like to have your little arms around my neck, to kiss you and talk to you. Fortunately there are these letters, or I would have no way to tell anyone about the things that interest me. Note that I say this cheerfully: there are the letters, and there is the notebook—and fortunately for me I've half forgotten what it's like to have at my side anyone at all, let alone you, who's interested in what I think and feel and who can understand it. I've forgotten that, just as I've forgotten omelettes, and I have no conscious need for it, I enjoy writing down my little ideas in my notebook, and I think about you reading them. Except there's this, the other side of the coin is I come up dry. But not when it comes to you, my love, I want you to understand that. Oh no, I remember lots of your little facial expressions, and they do move me. But when it comes to facing things, and people, and landscapes, and when it comes to my writing . . . there used to be a sort of emotion that somehow flowed along with the ink in my pen when I listened to Johnny Palmer at the Café des Trois Mousquetaires while

---

[2] *By William Faulkner. (SdB)*

writing my novel—and I can't say that it directly inspired this word or that phrase (though even that might be possible) but it gave me sympathy for my characters. Instead, now it's more conceptual. I see what they have to think and do, but coldly. I'm curious to know whether that changes the novel (soon you'll tell me), whether it takes away a sort of density or not; it is a sort of crucial experiment on the lying that exists in books.

You know, on what we were saying about Jews, you haven't convinced me in the least. You write: in that case (if to acknowledge oneself as Jewish was demanding rights for Jews as Jews) then to acknowledge oneself as French would be to turn chauvinistic. But that's not so. The expression *rights*, which I must have used incorrectly and hurriedly, set you off on the wrong track. The problem is as follows: does acknowledging oneself as Jewish entail a subsequent suppression of the race and the collective representation "Jewish"? (in that case the acknowledging would be done keeping in mind the immediate historicity of the individual, as for instance to acknowledge oneself as bourgeois in order to eliminate the bourgeois class, knowing very well that, even if one *helps* to suppress it, it would be as a bourgeois, and one would remain a former bourgeois after its suppression, except that afterward there would be no more bourgeois) or else, isn't it possible too that in acknowledging oneself as Jewish one recognizes a cultural and human value in Judaism, in which case the principle one would use for inspiring oneself to struggle against anti-Semitism would be not that the Jew is a man but that the Jew is a Jew. And naturally one should not *stop* at his Jewishness. All such acknowledging moves beyond, toward the man, which I'll explain to you. I am not deciding and it isn't up to me to decide, but the two attitudes still seem possible to me.

Au revoir, my little sweet, my little dear. This is a very long letter, and I haven't even told you my doings. But that's because there's nothing to tell. You live for me.

Till tomorrow, my little flower. I send you a great big hug.

⚛ *to Simone de Beauvoir*

January 17

My darling Beaver

I've just written to the Lady, imagine that! I'd been wanting to for a long time. And then to Martine Bourdin, who had sent me a long and typically hazy letter, except for one solid element in the cloudbank: her address. She was complaining bitterly that I hadn't written to her. But where could I have sent it? I'm not sending you her letter, which is of no interest. I replied in the "great lover" style with which you're familiar. I got two dear little letters from you, so charming, one from the 13th and one from the 15th. Look here, my sweet, you don't have to talk to me about our memories. Of course not, I'm not insensitive to them or to anything that comes to mind about our lovely excursions. It's true that those you mention left me cold, I don't know why, perhaps from contrariness, but here's one they revived, which moves me to tears for love of you: when we were coming back from the center of Naples (say, from the Museum) by trolley, the trolley stopped at a piazza beside a church, the end of the line. Children were playing around the piazza and we went back to our Hotel Umberto, arm in arm, your little fist in my hand. Do you see it? It was a charming little piazza. Will we find *that* again, my love? I don't know. Not right after the war, in any case; I suppose we'll be very poor. But it was luxurious, and I only ask for my two annual months of complete solitude with you. We'll continue our trip through the Pyrenees, we'll return to the Causses, we have plenty to do, you'll see, and a slew of little adventures will come our way again.

So there you are, a bit in love with your little Sorokine, my love? But, at the very least, you shouldn't drop her? What's going on? Such a lot of affairs and loves you're enjoying, little one!

As for me, I labored diligently. Wrote on the war and the new concept of *alliances*. Worked too on my novel. I really enjoy what I'm doing (young Boris). I had a lot of fun describing the Avenue d'Orléans: it seems so poetic, and I've regained the kind of emotion for my characters I used to feel last year, simply through imagining the corner of the Rue d'Alésia and the Avenue d'Orléans[1] on a beautiful evening in June. Aside from that, last night Paul protested to Captain Munier because there wasn't enough to eat. As for me, I don't give a shit, I eat a little toast (we make it on our coal stove) and from tomorrow on the restaurant is opening at noon, so I'll go. Nonetheless, Captain Munier sent a lieutenant to protest to Captain Lemort. And this morning, who was it that got bawled out at the field kitchen—me. "You never come to do the peeling, that's why there aren't enough potatoes," said Captain Lemort. "Captain, Sir, we have a dispensation from the colonel, in addition to which, permit me to note that we've been complaining that there weren't enough *noodles*." "Ah ha!" he said. "That's because they don't give us more than that." And he turned on his heels. The Acolytes told me later that they'd foreseen that sort of dressing-down and were satisfied that it was my turn to get picked on. "Because you're the most incisive," said Paul.

Something else: home leaves are starting up again tomorrow or the next day.

---

[1] In the 14th arrondissement, where he nearly always lived. L'Avenue d'Orléans is now L'Avenue du Géneral Leclerc.

As you know, all troop movements were indeed stopped. But now this morning they have begun again. 4 radio guys from here were to leave for the Maginot Line. For two days they were all stopped. And then today they left, and the fifth, the one who was supposed to go on leave the day before yesterday, was sent to the center for troops going on leave, where he'll await the start-up, to set off. So we're losing only a day or two.

So that's the story, my little charmer. I love you with all my might, and I'm bursting with longing to see you. But I'm being good. I don't want to let myself get carried away before being sure about leaving. My love, how I love you.

ᕉᕙ *to Simone de Beauvoir*

January 18

My darling Beaver

What a charming little letter you sent me—it wrung my heart because you seemed so eager to see me and you had even shed a little tear and then what news would you be getting the very next day? That all leaves had been suspended. But listen, my sweet, suddenly they've been reinstated this very day and even with an accrued percentage. Tomorrow Paul will speak to Captain Munier for me, and I'll know my exact departure date: it will certainly be *at the very latest* February 1st. My love, when you get this letter I'll be ten days away from you. But it's too late to change a thing about the sad day you must have spent when I wrote that all leaves had been suspended. That's what made me hesitate to tell you about it; you see, I thought that it was probably unimportant (though it was extremely unpleasant the other day) but that the words made it seem important. The first day I merely said, "There's a slight delay," without specifying. And then the next day, I felt constrained as I wrote because I hadn't told you the truth, I found it unbearable and I said so, actually pretending a degree of assurance that I didn't entirely feel. But the next day everything was fixed up and then I regretted the slight commotion I'd doubtless caused you. It's annoying to tell the truth *by letter* because the truth corrects itself with time while a letter is a brief moment fixed in time that flies off to the correspondent and can easily land like a ton of bricks on her head: in the long run, if I had told you *nothing*, you wouldn't have noticed a thing. Yes, but then our relationship would have been on false ground for a few days. It's the same old question of false security: yours would have been complete but *false*. Besides, what if it had actually turned out to be serious? If the leaves had been suspended for a month? My love, don't worry, I will always tell you the truth (with at most 48 hours' delay, as in this case, enough time to examine a question of conscience) except that it's irritating to think that *today* you've received my Tuesday letter and will only get this one on Saturday. Well anyway, yesterday's was already completely reassuring and besides, the newspapers must have filled you in.

Except for that, my sweet, I don't know what happens to the passing days: at night I find I've accomplished almost nothing at all. Today I had three readings to do and then, this morning, the fire wouldn't catch and it was −23° outside— so you see what I mean. Our teeth were chattering till around 10:30, it was 3° or 4° in our place and then all of a sudden the fire took and in no time at all turned the place into a furnace. Of course I didn't work, my hands were frozen from the reading: they were two holes at the end of my arms. It's surprising, you know, the real cold, it's pretty terrible but also semivoluptuous. I always go out without an overcoat to enjoy those treacherous baths, I know of nothing that penetrates so profoundly. The heat stays on the outside. But you remember those condemned men in Kafka's prison who read their sentence with their bodies, through their flesh. Well, one gets that feeling, it seems as though there's something exterior that you learn to know with your intestines, your liver, your spleen, etc. And then when we come in from the reading to a room that's not too warm, it's also surprising how you get the feeling that you're a little dynamo manufacturing your own cold, it seems to emanate from you in waves to the middle of the room, and each shiver has a metaphysical aspect. When all is said and done, I love it. Right now it's nine at night, it is −20° out, tomorrow morning it'll be −25°. But all of this is to tell you that up to 10:30 I didn't do a thing. At that point I began to jot down a few things about innocence in my notebook. And then it was readings time again, and then we went to lunch with Pieter at the Restaurant de la Gare, which is permitted again. During the afternoon I read a bit in Glaeser's *Classe 22* in German. (Yesterday a guy came in without knocking and said rather dryly as he held out a book, "Here, I'm returning this." Then he went off again.) And it was *Classe 22* in German, which, needless to say, I had never lent him, then I worked on "Innocence" and my novel. Then reading then work again then dinner and Mistler appeared with a bottle of white wine (it's the new ritual, we take turns treating, a liter of white every evening) and then here we are, I'm writing to you. Tomorrow I don't have a bloody thing to do and will work even more. I've got to hurry a bit if I want the chapter to be finished when I bring it to you.

That's the way my life's been going, my sweet. Still happy, of course, but I'm bursting to see you. This time, we're on, I can reassure myself and begin to count the days. In not much more than a week I'll be with you. Let's see, where do things stand? Is my mother bringing you my civilian clothes? That's extremely prudent of her. If by chance she didn't, we'd have to ask her for them since I don't want to walk around Paris looking like a stuffed parrot, not even the first night.

I love you, my sweet. These days, something is in the process of ending, our first long separation. I'll be seeing you again, and completely at leisure I'll cover your dear little face with kisses.

❧ to Simone de Beauvoir

January 19

My darling Beaver

A half hour ago, we got a cat. He's as fat as Toulouse's[1] fat, neutered cat, and rather noble. Keller gives him enormous portions of meat and tells him, "Mull that one over." As for Paul, he says, "A cat's reaction is very funny when he sees himself in a mirror," and he chases it into corners holding out his pocket mirror. We also have some coffee, canteens full of good coffee that the cooks make for us (the officers' cooks, you understand—not the ones in the field kitchen). In short, we're settling in. Just the moment, of course, when they're beginning to talk about leaving. In any case *I'm* leaving, my good Beaver: on February 1st, *at the latest*, I'll be at your side. Paul went to see Captain Munier, who telephoned HQ. It's definite. Just think that when you get this letter I'll be *eight days* away from you, nine at most, my little flower. How happy I am, my love.

Today what did I do? I wrote about the first sergeant and then about solitude. I enjoyed it. You know, we always used to wonder what it meant to "be alone" (alone in a crowd, etc.). That's what I was trying to clear up. I never once touched the novel, but tomorrow I'll work on it, because I find it entertaining. I don't know why, but devoting the same number of hours to work, I'm working more slowly. Is it fatigue? A fatigue that seems neither intellectual nor physical, but rather something closer to disgust? I wouldn't know how to explain it, but that's the way it is: 150 pages from September 1st to November 1st (of the novel) and 70 pages from November 1st to January 15th. But I must say that I was writing a great deal in the notebook. Which means you will have six and the start of a seventh. Oh my dearest, when I think how delighted I am that I'll be

---

[1] Nickname for the couple's friend Simone Jollivet.

seeing you again, and that right now you're still somewhat wary and anxious and don't even know that the leaves have been restored!

This evening I gave a lecture on sexuality to Mistler, in front of the Acolytes. I had him drooling. Aside from that I had lunch at Charlotte's and didn't do a bloody thing all day from a strictly military point of view. I didn't read anything either, I don't know what happens to the time. There was no letter from you.

There you are, my little one, I'm a regular little bundle of joy. My dearest, whom I'll be seeing again, I love you with all my might.

Listen carefully: 1st—the moment you know the exact day of my arrival, you'll have to reserve a room at the Hôtel Mistral.

2nd—if by chance my mother telephones you to find out the exact date, give her the *day after* the actual day I'll be arriving.

3rd—don't wait for me at the station, after all, because Pieter's Rosette missed Pieter there, it's a frightful mob. To save half an hour, you run the risk of losing an hour. I'm arriving at five in the evening. Wait for me instead at a café near the Gare de l'Est. You'll have to write me the name of the café and its exact location in your next letter.

✑ to Simone de Beauvoir

January 20

My darling Beaver

I didn't get one of your letters, yesterday's. I really enjoyed reading the one I got today. Your little Sorokine seems quite charming. I love how she turns hateful when she has to leave, and then how she brings you a bite of pastry in the afternoon as a peace offering.

As for me, I launched into a metaphysical study. It is agonizing and difficult but it's paying off. It goes with the ethics, of course, in such a way that the notebooks become a brief treatise on philosophy. I worked all afternoon, not unsuccessfully, on the *Mitsein*.[1] This morning on the novel, with relish. And then I began Glaeser's *Classe 22* in German. Along with three readings, that's all for the day. But the day is pleasant because it has a charming future nearly

---

[1] Sartre feels that Heidegger's very general account of *Mitsein* ("being-together") has to be supplemented by an analysis of how one can apprehend oneself in the same way that one is perceived by another consciousness—as an object and devoid of the transcendence central to one's personal sense of one's being.

at hand. In ten days I'll be seeing you, we'll stroll about so serenely. There are still a few little bridges to cross and then we'll be there. Why do I want to go to the Relais de la Belle Aurore? I don't know, my love. You know, I sometimes run through my head the places we've been together, and now this one tempts me, now another. So, if I'm writing to you I mention the one that's just going through my head. It was the neighborhood that appealed to me, and the hors-d'oeuvres. But the little Louis XIV, well, that's a must, that's another story altogether. And the Ducottet, of course. And perhaps, who knows, why not the Pierre? How about that? And the Lipp, because after all we'd want to be at Saint-Germain. I love you, my little one; how lovely it will be to get up very early and go for a walk. You know what I've been thinking? That by getting up at six in the morning we could go have a drink at the Dôme without too much risk of being seen. I would so like to go there with you.

A moment ago I didn't do a good job of explaining what there is that's strange about this attempt to put together a metaphysics. Basically what we've been doing up to now, good little phenomenologists that we are, was an ontology. We were looking for the essences of consciousness à la Husserl, or the being of existents à la Heidegger. But metaphysics is "ontic." You get your hands onto the material itself, it is no longer essences that you consider (what provides an eidetic—the sciences of possibles—or an ontology) but rather out-and-out concrete and given existences, and you wonder why it's that way. In general, this is the way the Greek philosophers proceeded—there is a sun, why is there a sun? Instead of asking "What is the essence of all possible suns, the solar essence?" or else "What is the sun-being?" It's more barbarous but more fun. Aron could only approve of what I'm doing, because he always encouraged me to do some metaphysics.

That's all for today, my little sweet. T. sends me letters delirious (for her) with love. Through fear of some slight suffering, that odd little creature barricades herself in and forgets you so long as she doesn't expect to be seeing you and, when that becomes possible, she abruptly remembers that she's fond of you. I sympathize with her, right now, I think I'll be very nice, and effortlessly so, when I see her again. She's a good girl, with a tendency toward fibbing, she's a bit of a slut though with some class. After her fashion. She feels in a sharper, fuller way than her sister, but ultimately she senses her situation in the world very strongly, though hazily.

My dearest, how I love you and how I long to see you. We two are one, my little jewel.

☙ *to Simone de Beauvoir*

January 21

My darling Beaver

Now for a tale of disaster: I've broken my glasses. Fortunately it's only the frames. It happened just a while ago, when I went to pick up the grub. We have to go through a low passage that's hot and steamy, where the meat cooks in a huge black cauldron. Before going in, I put my glasses in my pocket—otherwise, going from $-10°$ to $+20°$, from dry cold to hot, dense dampness, they steam up and I can't see a thing. But today the cook accidentally tipped over the mess kit, I bent down to pick it up, my hip and thigh met, and, caught in that vise, my glasses snapped in two. This evening, kindly Pieter wrapped the break in the frame with rubber taken from a readings balloon then made a splint, and I'm wearing all that on my nose. It chafes the skin and hurts my eyes, but I'll hold out well enough like this till Thursday. On Thursday I'll go to town to get the hydrogen tanks, and I'll make a detour to a still bigger town, where I'll get the frames replaced.

That's the major event of the day. Another is that not one letter came today. The train was ten hours late, and so we'll have two mail deliveries tomorrow, one in the morning at nine o'clock and one in the evening.

For the past few days I've been sleeping in our study on a mattress, because it was warm, and also for the pleasure of leaving Pieter enclosed in his cocoon, and I can sleep alone. It's somewhat offensive to Keller, who has such a proprietary sense that he stays here, wilting with sleep till about midnight, with a lover's jealousy, so as not to leave a soul behind him within these walls. As I said, I slept there last night, very well, so well in fact that in the morning I heard Paul bellowing for me in the hall: it was seven-thirty and I had completely forgotten to get up. I was on KP duty, which in this case means taking mail to the post office and bringing coffee from the field kitchen. I got the letters in under the wire. But I couldn't get any coffee, I had to run to the bakery to buy some chocolate. It was charming, I followed a path in the snow, just as at our winter resorts. And then in the end the colonel's cook made us some superb coffee. Following which I worked on the metaphysics till noon. I think it's really interesting and new, what I'm doing, it's not at all like Husserlian philosophy, or like Heidegger, or anything else. It seems more like all my old ideas on the perception of existence, ideas stillborn because I lacked technique but which I can now develop with all that phenomenological and existential technique. I'm extremely eager to show this to you. It's very odd in spite of everything, how the war and the sense of being slightly "lost," have given me a certain hardiness; I mean it's allowed me to go forward without ever being preoccupied with finding out whether or not I was in agreement with my earlier ideas—nor even whether from one day to the next I was in agreement with myself. This way of thinking pays off well and, eventually, you find youself agreeing with yourself, and it has the merit of not being forced. Lunch at Charlotte's with Paul and Pieter. Then we came back up here. There are a few little snags with HQ about my leave, but Captain Munier promised me, in tones that left no room for doubt, that I'd leave on February 1st, and I think we can trust him completely. The difficulties are actually ones of pure inertia: generally speaking, HQ's idiotic plans would amount to having me leave on the 10th at the same time as Paul. But that's what the captain couldn't allow, since that would make two out of four in our unit gone at once, which, at the slightest hitch (the illness of one or anything else of that sort), would run the risk of eliminating the readings altogether. So there's no solution but to send me off earlier so I can be back on the 15th and Paul can leave then. There's no other solution *because* the leaves must *all* be taken by March 1st, meaning that the last to go must be off on the 15th. The captain is within his rights incidentally, because the instructions relating to leaves state very clearly that the sequence of leaves can always be modified according to service needs—and it has actually been done here a hundred times. Except HQ would be obliged to make slight alterations on its lists, and you can't imagine the power of inertia of a military administration. But authority will win its case, particularly because Captain Munier is Staff Captain and consequently can do as he pleases. I am filling you in on all of this to be meticulous, my sweet, while assuring you that on the 1st of February at 5 o'clock—or at the latest the 2nd, which is a Friday, if I leave on the 1st, you'll see me arriving at the Gare de l'Est in uniform. How happy we'll both be, my sweet.

I'm feeling some sense of loss without a letter from you. I should get 3 tomorrow. The one of the 17th, which is still missing, of the 19th which I should have received today, and the 20th, which should get here tomorrow. I have no idea what you're up to.

This afternoon I worked on the novel and this evening Mistler came and I talked to him about the war in Spain. It's become a ritual: in the evening someone brings in a liter of white wine, they settle in, I speechify, they listen. After which I tack up on the wall a little poster Pieter made for me: "Those assembled are hereby requested not to bore me shitless." I terrorize them mercilessly, the way I used to terrorize people in Berlin. It's odd how my relationships (École Normale—Berlin—here) are identical across variations of age and communities; Mistler fills Brunschvicg's role and Paul, Klee's. Right now, with these I have the kind of domination I wished for, which isn't imperialism but allows me a regal peace, and that means a lot. I'm absolutely and truly my own master, just as in civilian life. I've been lucky.

Till tomorrow, my sweet. You'll get this letter the 23rd, and there'll only be eight days separating us. Incidentally, it's likely we won't be staying here much longer.

I love you with all my might, my little flower.

✣ *to Simone de Beauvoir*

January 23

My darling Beaver

No letter from you today. That's because of a railway accident that cost the lives of 7 men on leave and wounded 40 others. After this, we look upon our departures with cautious glee. As the sergeant said, "Were they going off on leave or coming back?" "Coming back." "Oh well, in that case!" For the record, I would just as soon have it happen to me on my return, if it had to happen at all. In any case the mail delivery hours are off schedule, we get letters in the morning (with forty-eight hours delay from their posting) and it's surprising, after that the day stretches out before us, blank and dumb. For instance, it is four-thirty and I'm writing to you to have a bit of contact with you, because I won't be reading your dear little flyspecks at all today. It used to break up the day so well. I received a pleasant letter from Tania and then this note, surprising to say the least, from *Marianne* (signed André Roubaud).

M. Sartre—Meteorological Post—Sector 108 (that's the address), and on the sheet below the heading:

"Dear Sir,

"We would like to consider a possible contribution from you. Would you be kind enough to contact me in the near future so that we might set up a meeting.

"Yours truly, etc."

This letter confirms my view that in this phony war nobody takes servicemen seriously. Serves them right, actually. But people at home certainly do have a weird idea of what being at the front means.

What have I done today? First, last night I went to bed very late (around one) and the cold suddenly took me by surprise (last night it was $-25°$, which means $-6°$ or $-7°$ in our bedrooms). I must have stayed awake for two hours, and then this morning I had a little cold sore on my lip, I was really scared of appearing before you with a blister like the one I had on my return from Greece.

But by this afternoon it had dried up. I was in a bit of a daze as I went for coffee this morning, but now I'm fine and I wrote all morning on that idea of totality and of worthless morality that we discussed.

Paul and I went off for lunch at the Café de la Gare, and a soldier near us came out with the (baseless) idea that we would soon leave, at which Charlotte said, looking at me, "Then I won't see my handsome little fliers anymore." Now wasn't that ironic, she's not insensitive: you can't imagine how disgusting I can be with my beard, my sideburns, and the string holding my glasses on my nose. Today the captain was saying to Paul, "Will he shave off his beard when he goes on leave?" "It is still undecided," Paul said. And the captain and lieutenant raised their arms to the heavens, "That would be a real pity. It goes so well with his getup and those glasses." Never fear, I'll shave it off anyway; my mother writes me that on that score you both have agreed to put pressure on me. I don't in the least want to stroll about Paris a whole evening in my uniform, you know. So do give my mother a phone call, to have her leave the clothes with the concierge, and you could pick them up by taxi. Or any way you like. Do get them a few days ahead of time so it doesn't look too obvious. You'll receive a telegram, because the whole thing will be official by the 30th or 31st. For your part, send me the address of the café near the station where you'll be waiting for me. Send it *the moment* you receive this letter, because it will get to you on the 25th or 26th, and I'll receive your reply the 29th or 30th. If I put in my telegram, "Arriving such-and-such date agreed café X," wait for me there, but if there's no café name in my telegram, that means I won't have gotten the letter. And in that case wait for me at the Trois Mousquetaires (or, if it is closed, at the Rallye). Finally, one other thing, you can't always trust telegrams. So I'll keep on writing up to the last day. If you don't get a telegram, trust to what you see in my last letter.

My love, these are very businesslike letters with the scent about them of arrival, wouldn't you say? I'm so happy to be going to Paris. How happy we'll be, we two, my dear, dear charming Beaver. I love you.

ᴓ *to Simone de Beauvoir*

January 24

My darling Beaver

What's all this, you little scoundrel? You're not overjoyed about my leave? Unfeeling little wretch! You can believe that I too, seeing a guy who'd returned from Paris overcome, felt a sort of disenchantment that hasn't gone away. But that's all part of the game, you know. If they were to cancel it, just to see, the two of us would start braying like donkeys. But actually there's no question at all of their canceling it, and when you get this letter, no doubt on Friday, I'll be *six* days away from you. As for me, taking it as of today, I'm thinking that in a week, at this very hour, I'll be on the train ready to leave. I'll be traveling for twenty-six hours and the first evening I'll probably be a bit groggy, but so happy. I wrote to my mother to do up a bundle of my clothes and leave them with the concierge, whence "I'll have them picked up."

Today was largely taken up by a long argument with Pieter, whom I'd called a lazy bastard because he was using his hernia as a pretext for not taking part in coal duty and who, with righteous indignation, listed the services he had rendered the community since September 1st, 1939. Paul got mixed up in it, and they reproached me for being hard-nosed and pretentious. I reproached them for being weak and stupid, we said some of those irrevocable things that can only be said within the bosom of a family and which we say every ten days, and then we went out and did the reading. I'm sparing you the details of the argument, I haven't even entered it in my notebook, it's so much like all the others. Aside from that, I worked on my novel, the chapter on Boris is coming along rather well, and then I wrote a bit on metaphysics, I really think it's rather good, what I'm doing. I'm coming back to dogmatism by way of phenomenology, I'm keeping all of Husserl, the being-in-the-world, and yet I'm reaching an absolute neorealism (in which I integrate the Gestalt theory). Well! you'll say, what a hodgepodge. Well, in fact, not at all: it is very sensibly organized around the idea of Nothingness or pure event at the core of being. I got a strange letter from a moderately interesting student named Chauffard,[1] who didn't want to play the disciple and "resisted" with all his might last year. He writes to say that in June he was hesitating about undertaking an *agrégation* in Letters, but that I had advised him to focus on philosophy and that it had been a decisive day for him, because then he grimly decided on Letters just to screw me. "So this year I began that agrég. in Letters. For three months I more or less took the courses in French and Latin. And then, 10 days ago, I most courageously chucked the whole thing because I was too bored, and now I'm trying to do some Philo. At that point, ten days ago, I was very pleased with myself, and considered myself a clever guy. And then the other day, as I was telling this story to some guy, I added, 'Yet Sartre had clearly told me I couldn't do French' and that took the wind out of my sails. I truly believe that this was the real reason for my giving it up. I truly believe that from October on, I had decided I wouldn't be going on, which pretty much disgusted me. I'm telling you this so that you'll be on your guard. You must already know it, actually, but you are powerful. I mean

[1] *Who later became an excellent actor. (SdB)*

that next to you, the compass doesn't point north. I don't mean to charge you with a responsibility that isn't yours, incidentally. I was free, at least I hope so, but I'm telling you this because I simply had to tell someone." He enclosed with his letter, mysteriously, a long epistle that a Normalien in philosophy who's been drafted wrote to his wife and in which, bracketed by two terms of endearment, he complacently lays out Antoine Roquentin's theory of Existence.[2]

I received your package this evening, thank you, my sweet. I immediately began *Gilles*, which is dry and irritating—it seems altogether vile. I'll finish it but only dragging my feet all the way. I've scarcely glanced at the Romains volumes, which look as though they had really fallen back into the mediocrity of the first in the series. So we'll chalk up *Verdun*[3] to luck.

So that's that, my sweet. At this moment I love you so very much. As you know, my disenchantment involves the air of Paris, the pleasure one can get from the restaurants, I don't know what else. But not you, little Beaver. Oh, as for you, I'm longing to be with you and kiss you and then, as I used to say, "to take you and explain my theory to you." I'll certainly read your novel right by your side while you're reading the notebooks—all of which delights me.

I love you.

I received an invitation to a Chagall exhibition (Galerie Mai—12 Rue Bonaparte) sent by Gérassi[4] (?) and I'm counting on both of us going to it.

ᏬᎧ *to Simone de Beauvoir*

January 25

My darling Beaver

Today it's definite, you won't have to long to wait. I already told you so the day before yesterday, I think, and besides, you eventually got your four well-packed pages, you must have laughed. But this evening my hand and eyes are tired. I've filled *eighty* pages of notebook, I don't know if you can believe that. Because this morning as I woke up, I got an idea of the way I construct a novel and the way I imagine it; it struck me (what Lévy said was irking me—that I didn't have a novelist's imagination, and I knew that you had discussed this with

---

[2] In Sartre's first novel, *Nausea*. Antoine Roquentin is the narrator/protagonist.
[3] One volume of Jules Romains' series of novels, *Les Hommes de bonne volonté*. Sartre particularly admired *Verdun*, with its panorama of World War I.
[4] Fernando Gérassi, a Spanish painter friend of Sartre and Beauvoir.

B.[1] and that you said to him that in Faulkner you can easily tell what is invented). And I wanted to put that in my notebook. I began this morning, I haven't done anything but that except for KP and I've just finished it.

It's rather odd to see how a novel works itself out. But I guess it's true, I don't have a novelistic imagination. That doesn't mean I'll write worse novels than others, but only that I'm not "made" for the novel. Very soon you'll be reading the eighty pages; when you get this letter I'll be five days away from you. I can't believe that I'll be leaving yet I'm fully living my departure, things are leaving me, I feel a sort of instability in these quarters where I used to feel snug as can be. A sort of joy pervades the place and at the same time a faint regret at the thought that I won't be returning here, I'll be finding my unit elsewhere on my return from leave. It feels like an epic journey. Aside from that, nothing new. I'm reading *Gilles* with disgust, *Classe 22* with enjoyment (because it's in German). I've made up with Pieter. But as they keep an eye on me and always try to screw me, Pieter, who had started *La Douceur de vivre*,[2] which begins with a savage attack on some intimate journals, poked the book under my eyes opened to the proper page, with a snicker. I'll copy the passage into my notebooks because it's right on the mark, but I want to defend myself. I'd like you to know that a Japanese magazine has written to ask for 8 typed pages, for which they'll pay appropriately, because "my works are very much appreciated in Japan." I won't write the 8 pages but, as you're certainly thinking, my nose is twitching as I read this. In other matters, Koyré has written that he'll accept anything at all from me for *Recherches philosophiques*.[3] I'm groping around for something I might write for him on Nothingness. To tell the truth, that depends on you. It's that I have greedy little proprietary thoughts about everything concerning my notebook, I wouldn't want to deflower it by speaking elsewhere with style and form on what it addresses casually. If, as you read it, you believe that on publication one could, or rather that one *would have to*, delete passages that are too technically philosophical, then Koyré will have Nothingness. If on the other hand you think that *the history* of my thoughts on Nothingness, as it is written day by day, is as interesting as the ideas themselves, then he'll have something else, anything at all. You be the judge. You know, you'll have *eight* notebooks to read.

My love, I would indeed like you to write to the Lady to have her send the novel to Poupette. Do it immediately. And you'll also have to send what you have at your place, but wait for me, since I have another 75 pages to include.

---

[1] Probably their friend Jacques-Laurent Bost.

[2] The exact title of Jules Romains' novel is *La Douceur de la vie* [*The Joy of Life*].

[3] The philosopher Alexandre Koyré edited *Recherches philosophiques* (*Philosophic Research*), which in 1936 had published Sartre's essay "The Transcendence of the Ego."

Poupette will send you, collect, two of the typed copies, you'll keep one and send me the other.

Well then, my little flower, you see you're getting three pages after all. It's impossible to do less when writing to you. I love you, little Beaver, you are my dear love.

No letter from you today. But 3 yesterday.

❧ to Simone de Beauvoir

January 26

My love, my darling Beaver

I received, a day late, a charming little letter from you in which you seem not at all indifferent to my coming. The idea puts you on edge, my little sweet, and you complain out of some vague fear that it'll keep you from working. But look at how happy we'll be! To tell the truth, I've gotten neither confirmation nor cancellation, nothing has changed, the captain jokes about my beard, which I'll be shaving off before February 1st, and what a dreadful pity that'll be. But nary a detail. Don't worry, with the military that's a good sign. Their minds are slow and reflective, and the ideas take a long time to ripen before manifesting themselves.

Today I've really been a bit lazy, I read *Gilles*, which annoys me as it entertains me. I find it very unfair toward Breton (Andre); I'll go so far as to agree that shabby and vaguely crime-novel scandals exist in Breton's life, like the story of Paul Morel,[1] nonetheless it's too easy to consider him purely in light of this shabby taste for scandal. Surrealism was something other than that and Drieu is only writing bullshit about what—not Breton or Aragon—but surrealism has been. And besides, I'm always disgusted by any guy who complains about his own times. He breaks me up when he writes about his contemporaries: "I allowed them to steal my soul." In his place I'd be ashamed, because ultimately he didn't have to do that at all. I'd be so ashamed in fact that I'd never again think of accusing my contemporaries, I'd accuse myself. He's really such a little ass. And since he condemns communism, so much for him. But it's hilarious after all, that he goes looking for them in the literary salons of the IVth Republic; he seems to forget entirely that there were *also* some workers who were communists.

[1] A character in Drieu la Rochelle's roman à clef *Gilles*.

The whole thing reeks of official morality. From the point of view of the novel, it isn't always so badly done (when Paul Morel has his breakdown and Galland goes to his house) but it's a botch, badly put together. There are essential scenes he doesn't deal with (the relationship between Galland and the policeman), essential characters he skimps (the policeman, for instance) and needless repetitions and incoherent stuff. But some situations are noteworthy: for instance that little Jewish social climber who arrives in Paris quite unhinged and chases after her mad lover.

I worked some on the novel, some in the notebook too, and that's it; as for the rest: three readings. These are good monkish days. Tomorrow I'm going for a hydrogen tank. I'll take a detour to a large town where I'll get a haircut and replace my glasses frame. Incidentally, *L'Imaginaire*[2] will come out in the first two weeks of February, and they have asked me, if I should be in Paris, to stop by the publicity office. I'll do it at those times when you're at the lycée; it will be really fun to autograph all those books, me the private. There's a Japanese magazine that wants me to submit something, but I courteously replied in the negative, because the Japanese are bad characters. No letters from Paris today, yours was the one I should have gotten yesterday. And that's all, my love. This is yet another humdrum letter. But you know, I'm swept up in the joy of leaving and of seeing you again.

Till tomorrow, my little sweet, my sweet little flower. When you get this letter, you'll be 4 days away from seeing me. I send you a big kiss, sweet little face of the old well-trod path.[3]

⳹ *to Simone de Beauvoir*

January 26

My darling Beaver

I'm dead tired, I tried to write a few lines of the novel and found myself daydreaming over the page, scribbling "store window," and I was back in Arcachon with little you. So I gave up. I *am* writing to you but if that doesn't wake me up, I'll go to bed without writing to the others. Actually, it's fairly voluptuous to feel that sleepy when nothing's holding you to terra firma.

---

[2] Published by Gallimard. The translation appeared in 1948 as *The Psychology of Imagination*.
[3] A woman whom Sartre had rejected reproached him for preferring Beauvoir, an "old well-trod path," to herself.

This morning I went to get a tank of hydrogen, with Keller, in a camouflaged truck. The driver was pleasant, a photographer in civilian life, which is doubtless why they made him a truck driver. He was wearing a gorgeous lambskin coat, and his face was lively and dark. Next, we went to the big city, and we had unimaginable difficulties getting there. Snow was coming down and frosted over the windshield. No windshield wipers, naturally. The driver said, "We'll have to take serious measures," and he peed on a rag then wiped the windshield with it. The results were most satisfactory. In the big city I bought some glasses and had myself shorn, but not excessively. I couldn't resist the pleasure of having my beard and sideburns trimmed, to see what sort of a pugface I'd have, but rest assured, those appendages will be eliminated in good time. The weather was threatening, really magnificent, gray sky, avalanches of snow, flocks of crows in the fields and even on the road, and crowds of little sleds. We got back at noon, and I had *choucroute* at Charlotte's. And this afternoon I waited for the mail. There was a pile of letters, one from T., one from my mother, and two from you. That's nice. Paul just came in and told me that Captain Munier had gone in person to HQ about my leave, and that they promised him I'd leave on February 1st, which puts me in Paris the evening of the 2nd. He prudently enjoins me, by the way, to count on something between the 1st and the 3rd, so as not to be disappointed. In any case, next week for sure. So I'll get there Friday or Saturday. You'll have confirmation in good time, my little flower. I do know the Café-restaurant de Vieillards. There's a room just below street level, you go down two steps. That's of course where (in that room) you'll wait for me. But it would be pointless to get there at 4:30 if you have something else to do. Theoretically the train gets in a bit after five, but it's not unlikely that it'll be an hour or two late. Get there at 5:15 or 5:30, that'll be soon enough. My dear little one, my love, in less than a week I'll be seeing you.

I'm pleased that you like *The Castle* and that you think it's better than *The Trial*,[1] that's my view completely. But what an odd idea you have, that nobody should write unless they produce something disturbing, as Kafka does. That's not absolutely necessary. It depends on each person's nature. There's nothing like that in Dos Passos—nor, basically, in Faulkner. I'm terribly eager to read your novel, I dearly hope that the first part will constitute a masterpiece. Yes, my love, we'll have lots of chattering to do, and even at that, we won't entirely make up for lost time.

Au revoir, my sweet, till tomorrow, I love you. How happy we're going to be.

---

[1] The Castle *and* The Trial, *by Kafka. (SdB)*

❧ *to Simone de Beauvoir*

January 29

My darling Beaver

I love you with all my might this evening, but I'm going to write you only a wretched little note because Mistler came in at nine-thirty with chocolate and cognac. These days I am so mean to him that he brings presents whenever he comes. I reversed myself, accused myself of being capricious and decided to be nice, talking to him for two hours nonstop, on theater and film. And here it is midnight.

What else have I done? I'm having a good time; I noticed that right at the beginning of this war two books were published which, for different reasons, both attack surrealism: the Romains and the Drieu, and I attempted to say what I owed to surrealism. I'm not through yet, but it's most entertaining.

When it comes to my leave, I'm rather disgusted, I don't yet know anything precise. They'd promised, now they're complaining that it's very difficult, they want to recoup two or three days. Of course it's still within the very first days of February, perhaps even the 1st, but I don't know anything more precise. It annoys me for your sake, my little flower, because I know that you don't like to just sit on your hands waiting. I'm doing so, but if you only knew, my little one, how much I long to be with you, with your arm in mine. I love you so much.

You know, I've gone two days without a letter from you. If I weren't to see you within a week that would make me very sad, but I know I'm going to see your dear little Beaver face, and I can put up with a small delay in getting the letters.

Till tomorrow, I love you with all my might.

❧ *to Simone de Beauvoir*

January 29

My darling Beaver

This was a pleasant but uneventful day. The kind that's easily forgotten. I did some readings, finished *Classe 22*, halfheartedly wrote about *Gilles* in my notebook, and did a bit of work on my novel. Betweentimes I lunched at Charlotte's, and this evening talked a while with Mistler. My influence over him is so great—because of his own failings—that since the day before yesterday he won't even dare pee into his chamber pot at night. I'd told him it's disgusting, and he'd solemnly pleaded that he was an old man, but I refused to accept his excuses. Day before yesterday he took up peeing out the window and proudly told me about it. Since then there have been yellow blossoms in the snow beneath his window every morning; every day the sight of them turns Paul's stomach. And yet because of this docility I don't like him anymore or find him entertaining. I can't look him in the face anymore as we talk. Come to think of it, I'll jot that down in my notebook. I'm not underhanded, I do look people in the eye. Though in fact that's wasted effort since with my walleye, they think I'm looking at their ear. But when I react to some guy with a certain nauseating unease, I sheepishly consent to everything he says, trying to avoid his glance. This evening I literally couldn't look at him. At times I was able to force myself to, but then I would involuntarily avert my eyes. For the moment he's gone, and all is quiet. Keller is asleep over a book and Pieter is doing his wash in a pan with some "Persil," which foams up and hisses a bit, and he's scrubbing his handkerchiefs in it. Paul's in bed; he goes to bed at the stroke of nine, his need for sleep is as great as his need for food. That cat's here too, "The clerk," as Keller calls him. All is quiet and pleasant though the same things happen every day. I'm putting myself in the shoes of the man I'll be in a year or two rereading these letters with you, trying through each letter to recapture some nuance of the day when it was written, but today I can't help that man, can't find anything that makes the day special, that makes it something particular, it's only good for adding to a slew of others, to constitute an indistinct mass that I'll call my wartime. It's probably because I'm about to go on leave, I'm more inattentive about everything involving this place. Indeed, my love, when you get this letter, it might well be the eve of my departure and two days to my arrival. How happy we'll be, we two . . . We'll choose a meat day and go to La Villette for a meal at Dagorneaux's, where they say the food's so good. And another time we'll go to Ménilmontant and Belleville. I realize I gain a small benefit in coming so late: the cafés will stay open till midnight, which means we'll have evenings out just as late as in peacetime. I love you, my dear little flower.

Till tomorrow, I have two letters yet to write you, and then I'll be there.

✤ *to Simone de Beauvoir*

January 30

My darling Beaver

I got your little letter of the 28th, which you tell me is the last. But in fact I could very well have gotten two more if you'd written them, for even allowing that I do leave on the 1st, departure is at 19:00 and the mail gets in at 14:00. I'll get those two little letters anyway, I hope, because yesterday's and the one from the day before haven't yet reached me but I do expect them tomorrow. Right now, am I leaving on the 1st or the 2nd or the 3rd? I haven't the foggiest. Certainly no later than the 3rd. But the military administration is pretty good at spoiling in advance even the smallest pleasures it dispenses, allowing a lingering doubt up the the very last minute. So, my little flower, stay flexible and nebulous like me, not overprecise. The important thing is that within five or six days I'll be at your side, I'll wrap your dear slim little self in my arms and we'll be marvelously happy, we two. I love you so. You wrote me a very sweet little letter, my love, and I'm awfully moved to think that with my arrival you'll again have "those things that matter." It's delightful to be able to enjoy one another as we both do without the slightest fear of disappointment between us. O my little paragon.

What to tell you about life here? It snowed, so we benefited by not doing a reading of darkened skies, I did as I ought and worked away in my notebook this morning, on my novel this afternoon. I finished a chapter on Boris and his meeting with Daniel, I'll probably touch it up for a while tomorrow. And the following days—if there are any—I'll touch up some obvious weaknesses in the entire seventy-five pages. Meantime, lunch at Charlotte's where I finished *Vorge contre Quinette [Vorge Versus Quinette]*.[1] It's relatively entertaining, and besides when it comes to talk about the surrealists, I'd much prefer Romains to Drieu. All things considered it's more intelligent. You've probably noticed with annoyance that in these past few letters I've been saying Drieu the way Mme. Verdurin would say Rimsky.[2] It's not an affectation of familiarity on my part— though everyone at the NRF says Drieu—but the name is really so interminable that I feel an overwhelming lassitude when I have to write it out. This evening, benefiting from your advice, I also poured over the beginning of Aragon's novel[3]

---

[1] By Jules Romains, part of the multivolume series published in English as *Men of Good Will*.

[2] A character of bourgeois vulgarity in Proust's *Remembrance of Things Past*, referring familiarly to the Russian composer Rimsky-Korsakov (1844–1908).

[3] *Les Voyageurs de l'Impériale* [The Upper-deck Passengers, published 1942], episodes from the early life of Louis Aragon (1897–1982).

in the NRF, which I'd only glanced at. I agree with you that it's well written and, though he didn't live through it, you get the impression that he has pretty well caught a certain "1889" flavor, but its psychology is quite feeble. So much for that. All this is terribly literary news, my poor little one, but what else would you have me say? It seems that some days yield such small details when you look at them, some aspect of the cold or of the house or the relationships between the people here. Yesterday was rather like that. Then there are others, for instance the day before yesterday and today, that go by without so much as a glance. It's not that they're any emptier. But you know every day here holds treasures so discreet that you have to dedicate yourself entirely to discovering them. We're going to be leaving here, for sure. I won't be coming back to this little haunted hotel on my return from leave. Our successors are already coming here on reconnaissance, and they "visit" the place with an eye both timid and critical, exactly like someone visiting an apartment up for rent. "Right! And just what is this? And what do you do with it? And how do you go about . . . ," etc.

There you are, my little one. I'm getting less enjoyment than usual out of writing to you, actually, since I know that I'll be seeing you. The little letters I write to you or get from you seem meager nourishment. It's *you* I want to see, my little one, you and your little smiles, it's with my lips that I want to tell you my stories and from your lips I want to hear yours. I love you, I have a great *need* to see you. How about this: the first evening we'll go to Ducottet for dinner, it's an excellent place to meet again.

I send you a tender kiss, my little flower.

As for me, I'll continue writing right up to the day I leave—or rather till the eve of my departure, and you'll get a telegram.

⭗ *to Simone de Beauvoir*

January 31

Hey there, my poor good little Beaver!

I'm about to hand you a big disappointment. I'll tell you right off that it's only a matter of a week's delay, at most ten days. But, well there it is, you were waiting for me, you were waiting for the telegram, you were all ready to go off to wait for me in the little café below street level, and now you'll have to go back to counting the days. My little one, my dear little one, how I hope this doesn't hurt too much. Actually I know very well that it won't be real pain since you *know* I'm going to come, only it means a sort of violent nervous disappointment, with tears I imagine, and then it causes a sort of unjustified mistrust of the future; after this I'm afraid you won't dare cheer up again and all your joy at waiting will be spoiled. My little one, my dear little one, do tell yourself that, awful as it is it's only a *delay*, it's no more than ten days of waiting, it doesn't in the least mean that they're taking away our leave in an absolute sense. It's just that they're awfully good at spoiling the small pleasures they dispense, because we would have found these ten days delicious and full if they'd simply been given to us, just like that, generously and without our having to beg for them, instead of which, after false starts, you wind up telling yourself that those ten days aren't anything much, after so many hopes and so many bitter disappointments. But don't say that to yourself either, my love. Remind yourself that you'd have gladly gone to New York for forty-eight hours, simply to see the skyscrapers, to bring them into your life. My love, it's the same here. Ten days are nothing when it comes to time, but they're enormous because we are going to touch one another and exist for one another, we'll intertwine our lives; later we'll have the patience to wait, and to share all we've experienced since you left me. I love you so much.

As far as telling you what's happening: well, nothing. We were simply beginning to find being in the dark pretty dubious. So Paul went to find Captain Munier, who had sent a big malicious imbecile to settle the question the day before. And Captain Munier, who had firmly *promised* it for February 1st (or I would not have allowed myself to give you that hope) but was very busy today replied, "Well, what d'you expect? It can't be done. I have no idea when he'll be leaving." "But then our leaves will overlap and that's just what you didn't want." He shrugged: "Well, what d'you expect? So they'll overlap. In any case we'll be off duty." So that's that. When will I be leaving? At the latest on the 15th: all leaves *must* be over by March 1st. I don't dare tell you to count too much on anything earlier because I'm already guilty of having given you false hopes, but in the end I don't really think I'll be leaving *last*. Consequently, stay loose and expect me on the 8th or the 10th. And don't be too nervous, my sweet.

Which leaves the question of Zazoulich. What shall we tell her? Frankly, I think the best course is to take the bull by the horns and tell her you have no idea anymore when I'm coming (I'll write something along those lines to Tania tomorrow) and that you can't make the decision when to leave before knowing exactly.

As for me, it depressed me somewhat at first, and then since I want to be tough, I recovered in twenty minutes or so. You're the only thing I'm anguished about. And besides, this way I'll be left hanging two or three days without a letter from you, without books and without money, it's really annoying. Do begin writing me letters again every day, my little flower. And *the moment you get this letter* send me five hundred francs, and choose three books on the list to send me immediately. If I don't have time to read them before I leave, at least I'll need them to read a little on the way.

My dearest, my little flower, I love you so much, I so want to see you. Be very patient, after all we're nearer to seeing one another than we've ever been. I send you a great big kiss.

You will have eight notebooks to read instead of 7.

❧ *to Simone de Beauvoir*

February 1st

My darling Beaver

Just a quick note. Now everything is changed and I'm leaving the 3rd or the 4th. But this time it's real. I went to HQ and tomorrow morning I'll have my physical. So you must *count on me* without fail for the evening of the 4th or the evening of the 5th. The rendezvous is fine where you told me, I remember the little café very well. My love, how glad I am to be seeing you again. You'll get this letter the eve of my arrival, perhaps that very day. You'll also get a telegram to give you the exact time. But if you don't get one on the 4th, it would be best to go to the rendezvous anyway, because sometimes they take a long while.

I'm so glad, my love. This is my last letter, and in three days I'll be kissing your little face. I love you.

❧ *to Simone de Beauvoir*

February 15

My dear little Beaver, my love

I still can't tell you very clearly just what I'm feeling in my head, but I can say your little face, eyes brimming with tears, which I saw across the shoulders of the soldiers in my compartment, completely overwhelmed me with love. How beautiful it was, my darling Beaver, I know of nothing more beautiful in the world than that face, and it made me feel so strong and filled me with such humility to think that it was *for me* that it was so beautiful. My love, I'm not at all sad but in a strange, loving state, and right now I still can't think of your face without bringing tears to my eyes. I wouldn't want you to have been sad, my love. I imagine that the lycée had to have dried you up slightly. But there must have been that empty interval. (I saw you slowly turn on your heels and leave), that was painful and made me heavyhearted, thinking that you were sad and that I couldn't take you in my arms and give you a comforting kiss. Now it is past, and it is irretrievable. And yet we are truly one, my little flower, truly one, I love you even more, if that's possible, since this leave than before. I won't tell you that you're perfect, because that irritates you, and in fact it is just the sort of guff that Xavière and Pierre[1] would say to one another with a sly complicity. But you are what I know best in every way, all that I love you have and you have it best. I love you with all my might. These aren't just "tokens of affection," what I'm writing here.

The guys on the train were a bit exhausted and glum. But toward the end, one played the banjo and they sang. It wasn't bad at all. I read the detective novel (middling), slept, ate, began the *Bismarck*, all of it in a state of tender upheaval that occasionally bordered on remorse. I was afraid I hadn't been nice enough during my leave. My love, I eventually found a reason for remorse: I gave your little knife to Tania. You know, my little love, as long as I was here, I was terribly fond of that little knife. Only it didn't cut at all anymore, and above all it didn't matter anymore because I wasn't off at war, I was in Paris. But I was wrong, and I'm beginning to miss it, to miss its little leg and its little gilt foot. My charming little one, it's getting very awkward writing to you. I have one more little topic of remorse, but I'll talk to you about it tomorrow. I'm in a garrison similar to the ones I described to you, and I'm writing on my canteen amid infernal comings and goings. I got here at four o'clock, it's now five (you're probably with Bien[2]) and I'm leaving again at 9 this evening. I'll get to the "embarking station" at 4 in the morning, and I guess I'll get in around 8 o'clock.

My love, I love you with all the strength of my heart, I wish you were here. I send you a kiss for your little cheeks.

You've written a beautiful novel.

---

[1] *Main characters in* [Beauvoir's] *L'Invitée [She Came to Stay.]* (*SdB*)

[2] Bianca Bienenfeld, a friend of Beauvoir and Sartre. In *Mémoires d'une jeune fille dérangée* (Paris, 1993), Bianca (Bienenfeld) Lamblis spoke of the sense of betrayal she had felt reading the published letters of both Sartre (in which she is known as Louise Védrine) and Beauvoir.

❧ to Simone de Beauvoir

February 16

My darling Beaver

Here I am, back. It seems odd to be writing to you. And particularly to commence again the deluge of daily letters. On my horizon there is you, dear little one, and that's all. How I love you, my sweet, what a jewel of a leave I spent with you.

It's possible that we might go to rest camp on March 2 for 3 to 6 months. That should please you, my little dear. I want you to know it's a *strong* possibility. I'll spare you the evidence, but no one talks about anything else around here, and that was all they talked about on the train. It seems to be well-founded, and actually it is true that after six months at the front the divisions leave for a long rest period at the rear. You can be happy for many reasons, among others that I'll get 48- and 24-hour leaves. I must tell you that receiving this news on arrival contributed no little to consolidating a self-enforced undaunted mood.

As for the story of my trip, here goes: from 9:40 to about 16:00, train. I wasn't sad (there were some who were grim and everyone was quiet. Toward the end one guy played the banjo. It made a rather strong impression) but I was feeling overwhelmed. There was above all a feeling of tenderness for you; for Tania in quick flashes—and also a vast feeling of disorientation and little habits acquired during leave—including habits of *seeing*, perceptual patterns that suggest your little smile, for example, now shattered in this new reality. But once again it wasn't sadness, I was even almost happy, I think that if ever a state of emotion merits the name, this one could be called pathos. I read. After that I got off the train and found myself in some profoundly gloomy and dreary barracks, where we were packed in like cattle. Nothing but dog tired or complaining guys. But I strongly felt that gloom and sadness are a matter of will, for I felt it all around me but was not in it, and I didn't want to be in it. Dear God, my sweet, when I think that during my earlier military service I allowed myself to be overwhelmed because I was going to Saint-Cyr for five days. How shameful! There were cans of beer there and I drank some, a continuous movie and I was tempted to go, but it seemed like cowardice, a way of escaping the black atmosphere of the barracks, and I went back to mine, which smelled of damp wood and wound up being marvelously poetic. I settled down to writing my letters then moved in close to the stove and set about warming up, butt to butt with the other soldiers, smoking my pipe and happily thinking of you. And now and then I'd remember Tania hugging me and saying, "My best beloved, my best beloved" and that shook me up too. But it's odd: today, memories of Tania have dried up, and there's no one left but you. My love, if you only knew how I've loved you these past two days, you wouldn't ever ask me what a feeling in my head is and you'd nevermore call me a whited sepulcher. But I have to say that I'm still guarded about my feelings, they could very well rear up again. Particularly yesterday, because then I'd have been in a pretty shabby state. Upon which, at 21:20 they had us leave the barracks, and we went to pile into a dark, frigid train (because the heating pipes were frozen). The train pulled out, in total darkness, my neighbors began to flail about, cursing because their feet were frozen, upon which I advised them to get off at the first stop and go to the front car where there was a better chance the pipes weren't frozen. I for one took the initiative of getting off and running the whole length of the train in the snow. And indeed the first car was warm as toast and I slept there blissfully till seven in the morning. After which I had a good conversation with my neighbor, who told me his captain is a diviner who verified the location of his sections by means of a pendulum. When the pendulum told him that a section was not at the appointed place, the captain would pick up the phone and bawl out that section. The guy said this objectively, without making any judgments. But when he was through he added, "*Incidentally*, he's a jerk." Around seven-thirty, off the train, new barracks where I drank a glass of coffee and chatted with some guys who were still very grim and then a bus brought me here. I got off all alone, the others had gotten off earlier or were to get off later. It's a small town[1] with twists and streets sloping downhill with lots of steep pitches, it creates a pleasant little motion. I went at random down one street and, at the bottom, I went flying head over heels with all my gear. A passing soldier recognized me and took me to HQ. From there I went to the Artillery Division, where I was greeted with the smiling indifference I expected. Except for Pieter, who latched onto me and took me right off to a bistro to gossip about one and all. Paul's on leave, Mistler's gone off to the Army Corps HQ. As for the site, I'll tell you more in detail tomorrow, but in short: good restaurants, appealing little town, *absolutely* not a bloody thing to do. But we in the weather unit have no place to ourselves. We're living, 14 strong, in a room the size of yours, and it's pretty rough going. So I'll go in search of a place of our own. I have some ideas. Today I got back to my notebook. I'm not sad, just empty: the important thing is to acquire new habits or, as Mistler says, "make a niche for myself."

So there you have it, my little one, those ten passionate days are now laid to rest. But there'll be others, and perhaps very soon. My dearest, I think that by now you mustn't be too unhappy. I would like to have you feel how I love you,

---

[1] Bouxwiller.

my little one, and how at one with you I am. Like you in the past, I have the feeling that I didn't tell you enough how much I love you.

With all my heart I would love to be kissing your little cheeks.

Don't forget

Selbona[2]
2 boxes of halva
ink

And if possible, send a little money. (But of course no need to send five hundred francs.) But do note that next month you'll have to make it up, because I'll borrow from Pieter.

✺ to Simone de Beauvoir

February 17

My darling Beaver

No letters today. I'd wisely warned myself there wouldn't be any, that letters sent the 15th could only get here on the 17th if they were mailed before 14:30, which was impossible for you. So I wasn't terribly disappointed, though I won't have the feeling of having linked up with life here again until I get some letters. For the moment I'm a bit disoriented, I haven't made a niche for myself. Everything seems hollow, but it's an odd feeling, as though all the hollow things are slowly filling up right before my eyes. For instance, this afternoon I felt that Staff Sergeant Naudin's profile as he leaned over his notepaper was once again taking on some sort of value in my life, reachieving it in this new light and in this new room. It's my life here that's beginning to shape up again. Little impressions are surfacing, some distances that seem familiar (for instance to the Hôtel du Soleil, which Pieter calls our CP [Command Post] of the AD). But as a whole it isn't too appealing, there's no querencia[1]; how appealing was our cramped little querencia in Morsbronn, where the four of us lived, which reeked rather profoundly, according to the clerks. Here the village is not unappealing, and they fucking well leave us in peace, we're treated like kings. Only where to

[2] Photographic paper.
[1] Sartre and Beauvoir appropriated this Spanish word from bullfight terminology—the place in the ring where the bull feels safest; thus, a haven, good for work and thinking.

go? There are ten of us in one tiny little room, Courcy promenades sententiously up and down, his heels creaking pensively, sometimes hollering, "*Que vouliez-vous qu'il fit?*" (a corruption of: "*Que vouliez-vous que la bonne y fasse?*" I'd left him at the Boniface[2] stage in Morsbronn, this corruption and contraction provides some measure of the passing time). The staff sergeant repeats his stories here for the tenth time; at the moment he wants to "shave off Papa Stalin's mustache" and dreams we'll be sent as an expeditionary force to Finland. Incidentally, he'd go to pieces there, since he's as susceptible as an old woman to the cold. To reassure you, I permit myself to tell you, as I softly retorted to him, they'll send an expeditionary force to Finland *only if* they've previously fulfilled the slight and insignificant formality of declaring war on Russia. The others aren't saying much but they live, which makes for some noise. During the morning I sit in a large sad café where they tolerate me though it's off-limits. At noon I go to have lunch in the adjoining restaurant. So far so good. For eleven francs. They kick me out at 1:30. Then I resign myself to going to the clerk's place. They're installed on the ground floor of an affluent little house, comfortable but minus any mystery, with none of the ruined charm of our Hôtel Bellevue. The house, smack on the main street, is in a row of eight similar houses, painted gray-blue and very Germanic. They all used to belong to a prince. But now the houses have been bourgeoisified and one bourgeois family gave up the ground floor. We can hear them moving around overhead. So, from 2 to 5 I stay there, I read a bit—today I worked on my notebook, I spoke about your "unrealizable situations"—you know, what Elisabeth[3] feels all around her. And I stashed my leave among those situations. I also recounted my return (what I had written you yesterday). At five o'clock I return to the café, which is filled with the military, but military that babble along amongst themselves without dedicating their noise to me (the terrible part about the Division HQ is that each person expressly addresses his noises to everyone else, they are penetrating noises. Those in the café are frothy noises) and I can write my letters there. Well anyway—just as in November—I volunteer to take the watch at the AD in the evening because I'm all alone there. And that's it. Just to add that this morning I had my physical, as everyone must on return from leave, and this afternoon I toted some wood to the carpenter for sawing. Consequently I wasn't able to get much accomplished. Tomorrow perhaps I'll get back to my factum,[4]

---

[2] The last three words of the nonsensical puns are obviously based on this name.

[3] A *character in* She Came to Stay. *(SdB)* In *The War Diaries* (pp. 197–99) Sartre describes Beauvoir's view of "unrealizables" as things that are all around us, which we can think from afar but never truly *see*, happenings like a mark of success which we clearly imagine in anticipation through our hopes, but which vanish when sought through the present of success.

[4] Sartre originally used "factum" to refer to his first novel, *Nausea*; here he is talking about his second, *The Age of Reason*.

I'll work on the Jacques-Mathieu chapter so as not to lose time. I'm not sad, my little one, but I'd really like some letters. I would really like you to enclose your little self in your letters again, like a genie in a bottle; for the moment it is wandering free, and more than once my heart has sunk because it is so far off. I love you so much, my little one, so much, so much, and since I have absolutely nothing to do here, not the least little reading, I find it absurd to be so far from you.

I love you with all my might.

It seems that Emma,[5] though she has no clear idea of what will happen to her, is nonetheless and on the off chance going about preparing for your visit. She wrote me so just this morning.

My love, don't forget to ask the Lady to put in a good word to Tournay for Tania.

The Japanese embassy (publicity office) tells me that my "volume of short stories *The Wall*" has been translated into Japanese. But there must be some mistake: it's only the one short story by that name.

Jacques Chardonne has sent me his most recent book, *Chronique Privée [Personal Chronicle]* in which he writes: "I will make bold enough to state that Marcel Arland's *Les plus beaux de nos jours [Our Most Beautiful Days]*, Henri Fauconnier's *Noël Malais [Malay Christmas]*, Paul Morand's *Milady*,[6] J-P. Sartre's 'La Chambre' ['The Room'] have in common that mysterious and in-alterable quality of by-gone novels that we still read." My head's a little swelled. I'm a bit pleased that it all still bubbles on gently despite the war.

✑ to Simone de Beauvoir

February 18

My darling Beaver

I finally got your long letter a short while ago. How pleased I was, my little sweet, to see that you've not been too shaken by my departure. I saw you move away so quietly, with such an odd mechanical suppleness, that I greatly feared

---

[5] A fictional name for Sartre, used by the couple to evade censorship when planning for Beauvoir to make a forbidden visit to him at the front.

[6] Chardonne (1884–1968), novelist and essayist; Arland (b. 1899), writer and editor at *NRF*; Morand (1888–1976), diplomat and fiction writer.

a bit too much emotion. My love, I'm so pleased to be a source of happiness for you and never, even now, a source of sadness. My little one, yes, I would so love to kiss your "old beaten-path" cheeks, which please me more than anything in the world. I love you. You know, these days, try as I will to hoist myself up to authenticity, there are times when my courage fails shamefully from being away from you. Nonetheless I have remained as true as before the leave. The others, Hang and the staff sergeant, for instance, are laid up. It has turned Hang into a defeatist. And generally, on the train and in the barracks I saw that the man on leave is nastily shaken, which somewhat justifies my mother's thoughtless comment, "They say that leaves shouldn't be given because they go back with worse morale." So I can certainly allow myself a few little instances of annoyance. And yet it's done, you know, I've found a niche for myself. It's above all an intellectual niche, actually. I've got plenty to do, which makes me happy: I'm beginning to see glimmers of a theory of time. This evening I began to write it. It's thanks to you, do you realize that? Thanks to Françoise's[1] obsession: that when Pierre is in Xavière's room, there's an object living all by itself without a consciousness to see it. I'm not sure if I'll have the patience to wait for you to see it when someone takes you my notebooks. On that subject, my love, you haven't had the time to tell me what you thought of my theory on *contact* and *absence*. Do tell me.

As for my day, here it is: first off it was Sunday. Here a person begins to feel it again. Every morning I have worked and read at the Hôtel du Soleil; it was rather cold because the maid couldn't manage to light the stove. I'm engrossed by the war of '70. You gave me a book by Duveau on that subject (I know him through Maheu,[2] he's sad, he keeps a private journal but his book is intelligent), I found a book by Chuquet here on the war, and besides that I have Ludwig's *Bismarck*, it makes a whole and it's interesting. At noon the light-infantry friends of Pieter's came by and we lunched together. This time by some miracle they were interesting, but I think it wise to save what they said for my notebook. Some light-infantry men I don't know got mixed up in the conversation and were interesting too. Then I went to get the mail: a long letter from you, one from Tania. Yours really excited me, my love, but T.'s irritated me. I don't know why, it seemed less pleasant than the two others, and more importantly I suspect her of having written it the following day and dating it earlier. In the long run that's not so important, but in one fell swoop it punctured the type of trust I'd granted her out of pure stupidity.

[1] Again, referring to Beauvoir's *She Came to Stay*.
[2] René Maheu, friend of both Sartre and Beauvoir when they were studying for the *agrégation* exam. It was he who nicknamed her "le castor" ("the Beaver") for her industriousness and the similarity of her last name to the English word.

I went out for a walk to calm down and saw a charming spectacle: some soldiers, girls, and kids coasting down a steep street on a sled between two rows of spectator-soldiers who pelted them with snowballs. Upon which I came back, calmed down and restored, and worked on Time till the dinner hour in the café which, for lack of anything better serves me as querencia. While I think of it, I have not a penny left. If it is possible without putting you out too much, send me a hundred francs, my little one. And don't forget the package.

That's all for today. Right now I'm alone and in fine spirits. I'm writing to you. I love you so much, so much. Yes, my love, it was a very wonderful evening, the one at the little O.K., and we'll go back there, I had a splendid leave. (But not "precious," I'm discreetly complaining about that in my notebooks.)

Here's a little anecdote for your edification: the wife of Private C., whom I know, came to see him, with papers in good order. She has some *genuine* cousins in the region. When she reached a large city near here she asked some man to find her a taxi. He was from the military police, he had her arrested. They grilled her for three hours. Following which she confessed and they were kind enough to authorize her to see her husband for *24 hours* (she had taken off for a week, bringing along her cat because nobody could take care of it). In other cases they have been less kind and have punished the soldier that was being visited. But that's because we're still very close to the front lines. If we were in the rear, the women could come as they pleased.

My dearest, my little Beaver, I love you with all my heart.

❧ *to Simone de Beauvoir*

February 19

My darling Beaver

No letter from you today. Just a word from Tania. For now the mail clerk has gotten it into his head to distribute them himself, it's annoying, they get here later. Still, I'd have liked to know how you're doing, my little sweet. But perhaps you haven't had time to write, above all don't feel badly about that. But on the other hand, *do not fail* to write to the Boxer.[1] Did you answer the insurance

---

[1] Alfonse Bonnafé, who taught with Sartre at Le Havre 1931–33 and 1934–36. Sartre had eagerly participated in some of Bonnafé's boxing classes—hence the latter's nickname.

company? I got two letters and I'll answer them tonight. Do the same, remember that poor Russian driver who was so appealing and refused my tip.[2]

I'm spending all day today in the restaurant of the Hôtel du Soleil, and I find that time is dragging, not to put too nice a face on it. These home leaves are a bit upsetting to their beneficiaries. Three guys here have already gone nuts. Not I, but from time to time I feel that I won't be seeing you again for a long time, and try as I may, I find that hard to take. You know, I even miss doing the readings somewhat, they gave a meaning to the day, and the little bits of reading and writing were sandwiched in between them, compact and dense. For now everything seems wide and slack. We have too much time.

Nonetheless I've begun a theory of time that's quite good, I think; it is giving me some trouble but is paying off. Anyway, it isn't finished. I'm only working on my little notebooks, but I think that by tomorrow morning I'll get back to the novel. There are two things I can still write: Jacques-Mathieu and also Daniel's furious walk when he has just left Boris on his way to Marcelle. It would be sweet of you if you could prod Poupette[3] a bit, though obviously the typing has to take a good long while. But I'd so like to have precise, attractive work, it would change my mood considerably. As for books, no point sending any now, but on the 28th when you get paid you must mail me off a whole slew. I'll send you a list tomorrow. We still don't know a thing about our possible departure. If you have no money right now don't send anything, poor little one, don't deprive yourself. I can easily make some arrangements with Pieter. Only you'll have to send 1,000 francs on March 1st. Is that too difficult?

I'd like you to know that T. tells me (nicely) that there are passages in my notebook that "profoundly shocked" her and that she's completely undone because I have an "intimate life" and she thought I didn't.

There you are, my little dear, a very empty letter but what else can I tell you? To tell the truth it is I that am empty, I can well imagine that at other times it would have occurred to me quite naturally to tell you about the café where I'm ensconced, about Hantziger's return, about whatever. But it isn't even that I don't feel like it, it's that I'm not even thinking about it. And you know, you shouldn't be jealous of the notebook; as of today there's nothing in it but the theory of time. Above all don't think I'm depressed, my love: its just a little melancholy that will quickly pass, one must find one's niche, and that's that.

I love you with all my might, my little one. I wish you were here; then, everything would be fine.

---

[2] During Sartre's leave, a taxi in which he and Beauvoir were riding was struck by another. The Russian driver had asked for a letter of supporting testimony from them.

[3] Beauvoir's sister, Hélène, who was typing *The Age of Reason*.

๑๖ *to Simone de Beauvoir*

February 20

My darling Beaver

I've just received your moving, strong letter. It really shook me up to think how much I was present for both of you and how you spoke about me. I find young Bost very appealing, and I feel that you are right to think that after the war one will have to live *for* him and try with whatever means at hand to keep guys of his age from becoming Brice Parains.[1]

O my little one, I'm still very moved by that brief time I spent with you; never, even in Brumath, have I felt so forcefully how much I loved you, little paragon, my sweet little Beaver. You know, I haven't mentioned it before, out of coquettish modesty, but I'm not at all insensitive to the praise you heaped on my Sumatra.[2] It encouages me, as my old grandfather used to say, and I'll get back to work this very day. I certainly thought that chapter had turned out well. I'm going to go back over the whole thing to bring it up to that level, I promise. My little one who knows so well how to revive my joie de vivre whenever I've somewhat lost it. Thank you too for the beautiful pipe, I'm smoking it as I write, it's very fine and sweet. I gave the halva to Pieter, who carried on about it so, that I bawled him out. At this very moment he's eating a big chunk with great satisfaction. As for the ink and envelopes, everything's fine, but would you believe that the package arrived in tatters, though intact.

I'm definitely never leaving the Hôtel du Soleil again. It's off-limits, but they put up with us all day long. From time to time I pop over to the Artillery Division to see if everything's going well and then I come back here. I worked on the notebook this morning and cashed in on a few little ideas we had in Paris, you and I, notably that the desire for authenticity was either entirely inauthentic or else was authenticity itself (on that subject, did the notebook you sent me get lost or else did you forget to send me one? But in any case there are some here and I have two in reserve, there's no rush). This afternoon I wrote my letters to the insurance people about the accident on the Pont Alexandre III. You do the same, naughty one, if you haven't already. And then I wrote to Brice Parain "about the generations." Right now I'm going to read a bit and then set to work

---

[1] Brice Parain, a philosopher friend of Paul Nizan, worked as a reader at the leading publishing house Gallimard. In his April 30, 1937, letter to Beauvoir describing Gallimard's acceptance of *Nausea*, Sartre describes Parain as "intelligent, nothing more . . . a guy who thinks about language . . . " Whereas Bost, on his first leave, spent partly with Beauvoir, was reading *The Age of Reason* in manuscript and other of Sartre's new writings with great admiration and planning to support Sartre's political activities after the war. (*Lettres à Sartre*, vol. 2, pp. 86–7.)

[2] A night club frequented by the main characters in *The Age of Reason*.

again on the novel. T. didn't write to me today. It's a bit strange, two days after having been so likable, there's something going on beneath it all; perhaps she finds something fishy about the story that you didn't move out of your place. It annoyed me a bit yesterday and the day before, but today it makes no difference and I'm working well. Tell young Bost—or, if you don't see him, write to tell him—that I feel very warmly toward him and will write him.

Till tomorrow, my sweet little Beaver, my dearest, I love you with all my might. I long to kiss your "old beaten-path" cheeks with a "religious" tenderness, my little one.

✤ *to Brice Parain*

[February 20]

My dear Parain

I'm terribly sorry that our conversation the other night degenerated: we have more interesting things than that to say to one another. Sorry particularly that you could even think of me as a representative of the generation of 1930 putting that of 1914 on trial. Nothing could be further from the truth, and a strange thing develops out of each of our conversations, namely that you grasp the slightest pretext to put your generation acrimoniously on trial *instead of my doing so*. I grant you absolutely *all* that you say in your letter, and I certainly swear to you that I'm not proud of my generation, nor ashamed either. I scarcely think about it. I simply spoke to you about it to show you how much levity there was on the part of Drieu in speaking of a France in decay and disarray, whereas the young people like those I knew when I was twenty, who are now men, were indeed marked by the cold-fish type of gravity for which you reproached them the other day. But what I require is the possibility of judging a man, it hardly matters whether it's Drieu or any other, simply as an individual without someone throwing his generation in my face. I'm not talking about metaphysics (while I do find it brash to claim that the only nonhistoric judgment must be that of true or false). Nor am I trying to deny that Drieu happens to have a mind molded differently from mine under circumstances I never experienced. That would be worse than puerile. But it's not fair to deny me Drieu when I want to judge him, and then abruptly shove his "generation" at me instead, telling me it's the same thing. That's like asking me to believe the moon is made of green cheese. Drieu the individual is *of* his generation, agreed, and he has experienced the problems of his generation. But that is not to say that he *is* his generation. To use a phenomenological expression, one is-in-one's-generation as one "is-in-the-world" ("*In-der-Welt-sein*"). Which always assumes that one transcends one's generation in the direction of self. And that is the level where I want to judge Drieu, not some other. To put it another way, the generation is a *situation*, like a class or a nation, and not a *state of mind*. So I repeat that though you had to transcend an identical situation, I would never think of subjecting you to the same reproaches that I level at Drieu insofar as he "transcends" his generation. No more than I would think of judging you as I would Blaise Cendrars or Giraudoux or Aragon who, after all, are closer to your generation than to mine.

What I find profoundly engaging and appealing in you is the generational sensitivity which is raised to a *Weltanschauung*; I find that very difficult from Drieu's poor acerbities. In my opinion, you are precisely the image of an "unhappy consciousness" and quite the contrary, in my universe you represent a moral value. I tell you this so that in the future I can call one of your contemporaries a jerk without risking the surprising discovery that I have unwittingly attacked you.

As far as politics, don't worry. I'll go it alone, I'll follow no one, and those who wish to follow me will. But the prime necessity is to prevent the young people who went into this war at the age you went into the last from coming out of it with "unhappy consciousnesses." That is possible, I believe, only for those older men among them who go through this war with them.

You have my current address; if you have a moment from time to time and if it's not too much trouble, do write to me.

With warm and friendly greetings.

⚛ *to Simone de Beauvoir*

February 21

My darling Beaver

An honest stranger very kindly sent me your little lost letter. It didn't tell me anything new but I was pleased to have it, since you had written it—and I also got another long one, which deeply moved me, my little sweet. Have no fear, it's with the dear little expression of a few mornings ago that I see you now, my little Beaver. It is not vanishing quickly, and I love it so much.

My little one, I feel freed of a great weight to learn that you serenely plan to get back to work. I'm in fine spirits, but I miss working. I'll do that Jacques-Mathieu dialogue conscientiously, but it's forced labor. I had planned to delete it, but cannot, I'm somewhat sorry I didn't bring back the manuscript. At least tell Poupette to type it as quickly as possible. I read a gripping book that admirably complements my views: *Plutarque a menti* ["Plutarch Lied"].[1] You read it, I think, at La Pouèze. That Pierrefeu was extremely intelligent, it's like a Critique of Military Reason and there are lots of things in it that I'd had an inkling of in my notebooks. I've just finished it, and I'm also reading [Georges] Duveau's *Le Siège de Paris*, which I got from you and which is most entertaining. Tell me whether you've read it, and I'll send it to you. It teaches, among other things, that for utopians like Drieu and even Guille, who put the golden age in the past, that in '70 at least things were just as they are now. You'll have a better understanding of what I'm trying to say once you've read it.

So, I'm a captive in this large café-restaurant. In the morning I keep watch from the windows of my room for the instant the shutters open. Then I cross the street and enter. It's still very cold and deserted, there's a large cast-iron stove that's just been lit. I stand in front of the stove while a maid sweeps the long rectangular room. It's a hotel café, incidentally, and that's the impression you pick up from minute details—from the multicolored tablecloths for instance, from something sinister and drafty. To get into a working mood I read Goethe or Schiller, in German, standing up, and I feel in my bones that I'm in some 18th-century Jesuit refectory, whereas in Morsbronn or Brumath it was the Middle Ages. A rational sun upon the thaw outside contributes to that impression. The proprietor comes in—her husband is in the army, she runs the hotel with her parents-in-law—then her son, who is six and converses with me. Breakfast: a glass of coffee, three rolls like those in Brumath and butter. Then I read and work. Yesterday evening and this morning I got back to work on my novel. A few scattered soldiers. Then Pieter comes and talks while he lunches. He has told me some delightful stories about the days when he was, as he calls it, "chasing skirts." I'll tell them tomorrow, because I foresee that having exhausted the description of my typical day I'll have nothing left to tell you. So then, reading. If you'd like to know, I'm at a large table at the back near a window and two steps away from the stove. Every day I come to this spot. I have piles of books and papers around me, it looks like an office. Around noon we go to the restaurant. It's a "mixed" restaurant, civilian and military. A very odd effect, since the civilian side is generally pensionnaires. They're here at every meal, husbands and wives of a certain age, dressed in black, proper. There is also the mysterious couple composed of an atrociously ugly young woman and a hunch-backed young man, with a limp, elegantly dressed, not ugly, with a sad face; they don't exchange a word, come in and go out by different doors and yet have

[1] By Jean de Pierrefeu.

lunch, regularly every day at the same little table, with a look of ancient hatred. And then transient families, noisy and happy as in peacetime. And then mixed in with that some soldiers, not very many, looking quite stern, like those you saw in November. There's not as much discord as you might think, instead they cancel each other out. At 1:30 they shoo away the military, the civilians go about their work, and I stay here by one of those odd favors I've obtained wherever I've been since I've been in the army. It continues to surprise me, because God knows I'm not at all the sort to obtain favors. Nonetheless it's a fact. All afternoon I'm steeped in this droll atmosphere, familiar to you from occasional glimpses through a window of a family boardinghouse dining room in Rouen, after lunch and already set for dinner. Through a large bay window I can see soldiers going by in the street. That's where I generally write letters or read. Around five o'clock darkness falls, and with that the military gain rights to the café. So I go back to the café, which is full of soldiers, I have a cup of coffee while reading some Goethe, then I write in my notebook amid the hubbub, interrupting myself to watch the billiard players, sometimes civilians, sometimes military. At seven I eat two rolls (I don't know what strange modesty made me write "two." Actually it's three). And I read Le Siège de Paris. Then I write for a while, and finally around 9 o'clock I return to the clerk's office, where I write in solitude, then go to bed. It isn't monastic, the way it was in Morsbronn, it's less memorable and less poetic—it's nothing at all or, if you like, it reminds me of a civil servant's life. But since yesterday it feels set, the whole thing has taken on a sort of intimate quality that makes me feel it is "mine."

Very good news: the second series of leaves begins today. I'm firmly counting on being there around the 1st of May and perhaps a bit earlier, the end of April. This time around it isn't pie in the sky; the list hasn't been changed, and we had begun on November 20th. I left February 3rd. So, since we're starting up on February 22nd, I should leave May 5th. But actually it goes by service branches, and Mistler and Keller who were before me aren't part of the Artillery Division anymore. So that puts me in the neighborhood of April 25th. Which really won't seem too long, this time around. Particularly since they're still talking about going on a long rest period.

I got a most passionate letter from T. "I love you like a presence, enthusiastically . . . I am totally penetrated by you." On the other hand she admits she hadn't written in the preceding days: "I didn't love you enough for that." I find their mode of existence strange but basically comprehensible (which doesn't mean acceptable). With you and me, the moment of separation raises our emotional level to fever pitch. But as for them, they put themselves to sleep and go numb for three or four days to avoid the brief period when it might seem painful. Well anyway she's fond of me, as she should be.

Well, how's this for a letter? Hey, my little sweet, how I do love you, how I'd love to hold you in my arms. I love you with all my might.

✑ *to Simone de Beauvoir*

February 22

My darling Beaver

Here's a good bit of news: Pieter's going off on leave tomorrow evening. I didn't dare hope for as much. Since last time I left one month after his return, to the day, that would have me leaving about April 10th, which means in roughly a month and a half. They are hurrying with the leaves for a whole slew of reasons. (If ever you should speak about this to Z., don't forget to take it as quite *natural*—and expected—that I should arrive around April 10th. Didn't I say, come to think of it, that I'd be back 2 months after leaving? We'll use the same story of 5 days. Only this time, since the weather will be good, and to spare you the fib about the trip to see Poupette, I'll see my parents *in the evening*—or at least on certain evenings; we'll see each other all day, you'll go out with Z. till 11, as usual, and then you'll join me at the little Hôtel Mistral.) Doesn't that work out well? Actually *you must* call Pieter (Magasin "Chez Gaston" 255 Rue des Pyrénées—MEN. 63–59) for any enlightening details, or else go to see him. *But* if you get his wife on the telephone or if you see her at his place, he asks you to pretend you don't recognize him, because he kept mum with his wife about your November escapade. As a matter of fact, he has nothing truly urgent to tell you, simply some details.

My sweet, what gems your letters are, and what pleasure they give me. If you are indulging yourself with slight feelings of bereavement, as you say, then that's just as it should be. You're a wise little one, you too. O my little sage, the idea that in one brief month and a half I'll see you again has completely reinvigorated me. Besides, it will be good weather, you'll put your little arm in mine and we'll go for a walk, like the twin octopi. My love, since then I have attached myself to you more and more.

Don't put yourself out for the 100 francs, my little one. Pieter will lend them to me before leaving. *Do not send them.* You can wire 1,000 as soon as you have cashed our paychecks.

What have I done today? I've read Heine's poems in German, which entertained me. A bit of Goethe's *Faust*, the end of *Le Siège de Paris* which I'm having Pieter take back to you, and some witticisms by Chamfort. I painfully but correctly wrote on the Future. From that, I begin to get a total understanding of Heidegger's theory on the existence of the future, at the same time I'm constructing another that has the advantage of giving *reality* to the future, while still preserving the consciousness's translucence.[1] Ultimately the theory of Nothingness is more productive, I believe it to be true. For instance (lots of things are based on it, but I'll give you the basic idea): is it possible to conceive of *desire* other than as based on a *lack*. But for something to be lacking from human-reality, it must be constituted in such a way that something can, theoretically, be lacking from it. Now, neither the psychology of states, nor Husserl, nor even Heidegger have taken that obvious truth into account. If it must be possible for consciousness in general to lack something, then the existential nature of consciousness must be that of a lack. Think it over carefully, it is *impossible* to conceive of desire other than stemming from that. Tell me what you think about that.

I also jotted down Pieter's confidences on his "skirt chasing" and I wanted to share it with you but, all things considered, there are 14 pages of it in the notebook, you might as well read it there.[2] For the moment the soldiers are quietly playing cards all around the café, Pieter, suffering from a typhoid shot but healed by the prospect of leaving, is gazing at them indulgently, and I'm writing to you. It's 8:12, I still have to write to T., to my mother. Have you answered Cavaillès? I'm doing the same.

My little sweet, I love you, you are my little everything, my everything little. I send you kisses for your little cheeks and little eyes.

⚬⚬ *to Simone de Beauvoir*

February 23

My darling Beaver

Just as you predicted, I'm completely undone by this Bourdin affair. It hit me like a ton of bricks, and Lord knows I hadn't seen it coming. I read four pages, which were foaming with rage, from Tania. The thing that makes answering difficult is the existence of letters written by me to Bourdin, which she showed to Mouloudji[1] and in which I'm having fun playing the Lothario, you

---

[1] *War Diaries*, pages 229–234.
[2] *War Diaries*, pages 234–9.
[1] An Algerian actor-singer friend of Olga and the couple.

remember. Another aspect, as you clearly pointed out, is that Tania learned nothing she didn't already know. Luckily, to begin with there were two *false* facts that I was able to refute: she suspects me, according to what Mouloudji said, of still maintaining a relationship with Bourdin even now, and she thinks I was still sleeping with Bourdin when I was sleeping with her, which is false. 2nd. She believes I told Bourdin that she (Tania) was in love with me and that I was sleeping with her, which is also false, given that when I mentioned Tania to Bourdin, I didn't think that she was in love with me, and we had no physical relationship. My good faith is intact on those two points. As for my physical relationship with Bourdin, I resolutely deny that it was emotional and that I was playing the satyr. That much is easy, there's no proof. Then, I'm playing a cheap trick, but one that Bourdin quite deserves, I'm sending an open letter to Bourdin that Tania is charged with mailing, and in that letter I tell the Bourdin story to Bourdin just as it was. I'm sending you the draft copy. The letter is better, but this will give you the tone. Now, is it a "mistake" in the sense of when you said "you'll commit other mistakes" or is it a disaster? I don't know. If I were in Paris I'd fix things up, but I'm not there and Mouloudji will pursue his advantage— on the other hand there are the notebooks. If they're taken in the wrong way, they'll get mired in loathing; Tania's letter is certainly intent on avoiding the worst, since she ends it thus:

"Forgive me, I am doing my best not to let this obscenity fill me with childish loathing. But I just can't help feeling a terrible physical anguish, as though someone had put some meat in front of me, and besides, I think of the melange of bodies in which I must have participated without knowing a thing about it. Till tomorrow, I love you anyway, but I'm uncomfortable and it has to wear off.

"Tania"

and she adds a PS: "Note that I've said all and that it would have been easier to keep it all to myself. But I think that no duplicity of mine would have sufficed."

Those last lines leave much hope, for she's already defending herself against a possible bawling out by claiming the rewards of candor (because I'd told her that last year, instead of going into a panic, she should have told me everything). What do you think?

For you, my sweet, there are some modes of conduct to adhere to. Vis-à-vis Z. you must say: 1st That I never said anything of consequence to Bourdin and that I didn't speak to her about Tania except evasively, as just somebody. That's true, incidentally. That one evening I told Z.'s story in general terms and without naming her.—2nd That my relationship with Bourdin ceased on the 1st of October and was extended by five or six meetings in October without my sleeping with her. Incidentally that's true. That I saw her again only once in June and that she seemed crazy. Again, it's true. That since then she's been pursuing me, but that I've dropped her completely. Again, that's true.—3rd As for the notebooks, be sure to remember that for the most part you have *not yet read them*. In fact, it wouldn't be a bad idea if you reclaimed them at the earliest possible moment to read them, and thus prevent her from giving way to gloomily mulling them over.—4th Try to keep me up to date, get Z. to talk about it the day after you get this letter, or the day after that, to see more or less whether my explanations have calmed things down. And the moment you receive this one, let me know how serious you think the whole affair is. It seems to me that nothing is ever serious with the Z's and that nothing is ever forgiven either.

As for my personal state, well, here it is: of course it has shaken me up, because I feel warmly toward T. and besides I've been enough of a bastard for it all to seem wrong to me. And in actual fact the Bourdin affair is over. Besides, at the time I was wracked by violent anger, which gave me the brilliant idea of writing a letter to Bourdin that I'd have T. read. It's a mean trick on Bourdin, but it's funny how hard I'm becoming with people. I'm sick of phony situations and I want to be left in peace, for too long I've been constrained and disgusted by a false sensibility. At the same time, and thank heavens, it hardened me against T., this was no longer the pleasant little character I'd been seeing during my leave. The fact remains that I'm still on edge, and I'm wearing you down with this whole business.

The thing is that aside from that, my sweet, there's nothing else to say. I worked as I should on my novel this morning, and it moved along, I also wrote a few little things in my notebook, and then I really went to great lengths to help Pieter leave. Hey, little one, seeing him go really does something to me, I'd love to be in his shoes, meeting you again in our little café at the Gare de l'Est. You, little charmer, how I love you, how it moves me to think of you, what a pleasant leave we had. My little one, what I once told you remains true, you are the optimism of my life. Nothing can be bad if you exist. But I would so like to see your little face of flesh and blood, to kiss it.

৯৵ *to Simone de Beauvoir*

My Beaver

Here's the draft of the letter to Bourdin:

If you wish to retain some slight devotion to my memory, no point trying to share it with others, my dear Martine. Above all, there's no point spreading it to the four winds, revised and tarted up. Your indiscretion, which was reported to me, forces me to tell you exactly what I think of our affair, so that if you're unable to contain yourself you can at least tell it properly.

I never loved you, I found you physically pleasant though vulgar, but I have a certain sadism which was attracted to your vulgarity nonetheless. I never—from the very first day—intended to have anything but a very brief affair with you. In your own romantic head you spun an entire pretty fiction of mutual love, which was alas forbidden by a prior vow, and I let you have your own way because I thought it would make the breakup less painful for you. But the reality was much simpler. During September I was already a bit bored with you, and you remember how often you complained during the day that I was going to see my parents or some friends. That's because I wasn't having a very good time with you. At the time my letters, which were exercises in passionate literature and gave the Beaver and me many a good laugh, did not entirely deceive you. Deep down you really believed that I did not love you. And when I got to a rendezvous late, you thought I wasn't coming at all, that I'd abandoned you. The affair was to end on October 1st. Since the threat of war had brought the Beaver home, I stopped seeing you a week earlier and through some stupid idea of compensation, I admit, I offered to see you four or five times in October, which I did. It was awkward, you were there near me, you seemed to want to start up a physical relationship with me again, you'd throw yourself at me and then abruptly push me away, and you would claim I broke my word and wanted to take up again what we had agreed to break off. I was too polite to contradict you, but it wore me out. I showed up less and less, I would forget to write, you sent me a bitter letter breaking it off, I leaped at the occasion. There's an affair, I thought, not always proper perhaps, but properly ended. I'd confess that the liking that you'd inspired in me for a few days had long since faded, one tires of sadism and vulgarity. Besides, on top of all that I had to endure your noble chatter, your philosophical claptrap, it gave me a headache. Particularly, I must admit, when you talked to me about the theater. Finally we went for several months without seeing one another and I had quite forgotten you, when you wrote me a letter in June, you seemed unhappy and the Beaver advised me to see you. I saw you for two hours, and you seemed altogether mad, we set up a second rendezvous and I didn't show up. Since then you took it upon yourself to write me numerous letters which I didn't answer except *once*, prodded by curiosity, because you seemed to have gone through some rather amusing things. So I replied, but in such a way as to have you understand that it was all over. In your letter you said to me, "Sartre, Sartre, don't you want me to kiss you anymore?" I replied, "Well, why not, kissing you isn't that disagreeable." You called that resolutely boorish letter "playful," and from that moment you understood, though you did write me twice again. So, if you tell the story again, don't say that we still have a relationship. Instead, say that I have profoundly forgotten you. And if, for lack of anything better, you find some pleasure in bringing up among friends our physical relationship in September, that's your business, though I find it profoundly repugnant. In any case, do me the great kindness not to invent three-quarters of what you tell.

So that's how you should tell the story. Incidentally, the last time, you wrote, "Why do you find me cheap?" Well! now you know: because you tell obscene, base, concocted tales that you mix in with the sentimentality of romance novels.

✿ to Simone de Beauvoir

February 24

My darling Beaver

How happy I am to be writing to you, it's rather like seeing you. I'd so very much like for you to be here, your little hand in mine, me entertaining you with the weird times I'm going through. Because I am going through a weird time. It's not so much the outward situation, though that's strange enough, because things are on a pretty shaky footing with T. But it isn't so much what it's about, though I'm wretched at the idea of losing T. The main thing in all of this is that I'm very profoundly disgusted with myself. You know that happens to me rather rarely, and even then, there's my tendency to distance myself emotionally from my actions, which makes things still bearable; but, well, I'd really like to know how you see it, my little judge. I'll lay out what I think for you, and above all I'm not asking for absolution but for you to give it some serious thought. And then you'll tell me what you think, upon reflection, little golden mouth. I'll take it as a verdict. Here we go:

I agree with you, and it is very irritating of Tania to withdraw in disgust because someone *tells* her what she already knew. And she herself, it seems to me, has passed through far too many hands to be so shocked. To be sure, her affairs aren't obscene, but still there are a few that aren't much better than this. So as a person she isn't implicated, it's rather that she, like her sister, has a sort of ability to judge and to isolate ugly things for consideration irrespective of herself. Well, in the first place, if I look at myself in that light I judge my relationship with Martine Bourdin as disgraceful. To begin with it's only too true that the affair did not have to take place. I had no illusions about its value, and, if I had had, a few hours of conversation would have sufficed to open my eyes in plenty of time. I blinded myself somewhat voluntarily. What need did

I have for that girl? Wasn't it simply to play the neighborhood Don Juan? And if you excuse me because of sensuality, let's just say, first of all, that I have none, and that minor skin-deep desire is not an acceptable excuse, and secondly that my sexual relationship with her was disgraceful. Here what I admit is less what I was with her than my sexual personality in general; it seems to me that up to now I've behaved like a spoiled brat in my physical relationships with people. There are few women I haven't upset on that score (except, as it happens, T., which is funny). As for you, my little Beaver, for whom I've never had anything but respect, I've often embarrassed you, particularly in the beginning, when you found me rather obscene. Not a satyr, certainly. That I'm quite sure I'm not. But simply obscene. It seems to me that there's something terribly rotten in me and, you know, I've been vaguely feeling that for some time because, in our physical relationship in Paris, during my leave, you were able to see that I'd changed. Perhaps the power of our physical relationship is fading slightly, but I find that it's becoming tidier. In any case, with M. Bourdin, whom I did not respect as I do you, whom I did not treat with consideration as with T., I was indeed disgraceful. Don't start imagining bacchanalia, nothing happened beyond what I've told you. But it's the atmosphere of sadistic dirty-dealing that comes back to me now and disgusts me. So that what I've been feeling rather forcefully since yesterday is that whatever T.'s faults in this affair—I'm the one who pays. And not only for M. Bourdin, but for all of my past sexual life. I'll have to change that. Do you agree, what do you think about this? I feel rather thoroughly sullied by the whole affair, and I feel there's absolutely nothing to be said for it. It actually ends sordidly (a year and a half after its real end) just as it began, with Bourdin's complacently disgraceful accounts and by my letter to her, no less disgraceful.

Thus, first accusation. Added to which, there's another that irks me: what sort of a person do I appear to be through my notebooks that could have so powerfully shocked the sisters Z.? Oh to be sure, I don't delude myself about their opinions. But all the same. When she began, T. was clearly predisposed toward me, and yet she was instantly revolted. What do you think of it yourself? Actually this is secondary.

And finally, my darling Beaver, yesterday T. wrote me a letter beside herself with rage in which the thing that particularly infuriated her is that Bourdin speaks of my "mysticism" for you. Today I wrote: "You well know that I'd walk all over everyone (even the Beaver) despite my 'mysticism' to have a good relationship with you." The end justifies the means, but I was not proud to have written that. Because of you as well as because of her.

Conclusion: I've never known how to lead either my sexual or my emotional life properly; I most deeply and sincerely feel like a grubby bastard. A really small-time bastard at that, a sort of sadistic university type and civil-service Don Juan—disgusting. That has got to change. I've got to swear off (1) vulgar little affairs: Lucile, Bourdin, etc.—(2) big affairs undertaken lightly. I'll keep T. if it clears up because I'm fond of her. But if it doesn't clear up, it's all over, my career as an old rake will be over, period. Tell me what you think of all this.

Which didn't keep me from writing a few pages in my novel this morning, my sweet, and scads of pages in my notebook this evening on a subject I find entertaining: my lacking the sense of propriety. Only, I'm writing about myself at arm's length, if I may put it that way. You reproached me somewhat for complacency, on reading my last notebooks. Well, I swear that I feel no such thing.

Nothing else, little one. To outward appearances, it looked like me in a room of the café rewriting and reading, then me in a room of the restaurant reading and writing, but a lot was going on in my head. You must admit that it's unheard-of to learn modesty at thirty-four.

My little one, my little dearest, it's only with you that I'm all right, and that doesn't come from me, that comes from you, little paragon. I love you so much, my little sweet, I would so like to squeeze your little arm and cover your little old cheeks with kisses.

Above all, don't think that I'm *despondent*. I'm rather calm. Though grim.

Tomorrow I'll send you a list of books to buy for me when you have cash.

Underlying all this is the fact that I thought nothing could ever tarnish me, and I now realize it isn't true.

No letter from T. today; I was expecting that. But no letter from you either, and that leaves me all alone in the shit.

ᴼᵗᴼ *to Simone de Beauvoir*

February 25

My darling Beaver

Here's a list of books. If you're really sweet, you'll buy them for me *the moment* you have your monthly cash. Or some, at least.

*

The Commune Lissagaray

The Commune. I don't know by whom in *Anatomy of Revolutions,* the same series as Cassou's book on 48. You'll look into it?

The Life of Goethe—Ludwig

William II—Ludwig

Journal—Renard[1]

The volume of the Goncourts' *Journal* that deals with the siege of Paris and the war of '70 (a rather inexpensive edition of it came out two or three years ago)

Don Quixote

The Life of Baudelaire by Porché. See if another biography of him hasn't appeared in the series called Lives of Illustrious Men (Gallimard), in which case you'll have to buy that one too.

Thank you, my little one. I love you so much.

* (*In the margin*). These are the ones that interest me most at the moment.

৵৹ *to Simone de Beauvoir*

February 25

My darling Beaver

I'm so pleased: I've received two little letters from you. I feel a lot better. Things are always better when you write to me. I feel I'm with you today, and I think that since you are so sweet with me I mustn't be all that bad.

Of all things, today I received a slim volume of poems called *Cicatrices de songes [Scars of Dreams]* from an epistolary admirer by the name of Alain Borne. I read them, irritated that I couldn't understand the poetry, and without a pause set to work writing one "just to see." Here it is, I give it to you for whatever it is worth, I also entered it in my notebook, as a sort of penance.

Melted, the screech of light beneath dead trees.
Into water, the thousand lights of water that hide their name
Melted the pure salt of winter, my hands chap.
Between the houses I drain the sweet, rich caulking of the air
And the sky is a botanical garden that smells of growth renewed.
At the windows of great vacant halls
Powdered phantoms watch slow black glue run down the streets

[1] Jules Renard (1846–1910), whose seventeen-volume *Journal* was published 1925–27 (in English, 1964).

Melted the needles of white joy in my heart
My heart smells of fish.

Venomous springtime just beginning
Do not harm me
My heart was so inured to pain
And now unsettled by spring

Springtime commencing in my heart
May you burn like a torch
May the torrid stone of summer
Touch and dry the supple grass

With scorched breath I slid over the rock
And the seeds burned, torched by the wind
With icy breath on the snow
I slid hard and transparent
And the world was made of marble and I was the wind
But now the exile of spring has returned.

You can offend me all you like in your critique. I don't feel very proud of it myself, I look upon this offspring with surprise, quite surprised to have dared speak of my heart and say *tu* to the spring, but the genre demands it. It is precious, incidentally, because it gives you a glimpse from inside of what the poetic state is all about.

Aside from that, a policeman evicted me from the café this morning with a good dressing-down, and I went up to the second floor to the place that will henceforth be my sole refuge so long as I stay here: the Soldier's Center set up by the Salvation Army. It's one large room formerly used for showing movies, and the end wall is covered with a screen. It is set up with pious affectation, there are long tables, checkered cloths on the tables and bouquets of flowers—just imagine!—on the tables. Fifty silent soldiers sit there, reading, writing, playing cards. It suggests a mix of an English club, the old folks' home, and the local library. An alert little old lady, who looks mean and hard, wanders through it, wasting her energy checking up on things. Don't feel sorry for me, I'm certainly much better off here than in the Division HQ and basically just as well off as at the café. The old woman trots around unobtrusively, the soldiers don't make much noise, they exhibit that indescribable drabness of males who regularly attend church. There's a radio that plays a few tunes discreetly, this morning I was almost overjoyed to be here. On Tuesday they're giving me a shot for the first time against typhoid. It knocks some people out a bit but not others. If you get no letter that day, that will mean it knocked me out. I'm rather pleased to have it finally out of the way. I'll take a room here, as Pieter did, and stay over if I feel tired.

My love, you're anxious about my leave: how to *hide* five days. But here's your answer: you'll see Z., for instance three evenings out of five, and I'll see my parents during that time. To begin with we'll have the whole day up to seven-thirty in the evening to see each other (you'll eat at the lycée), and then when you leave Z. around eleven-thirty (don't go to live in her hotel again, precisely so that you can sleep elsewhere with no problem), we'll still have the whole night to ourselves. That way we'll see each other more and more pleasantly than in February, and we'll be able to take long walks. In addition, we'll have two evenings to ourselves after all, which will vary the schedule and allow us a bit of night life. But I don't actually find that life too pleasant in Paris. Is that workable? It seems to me it will do very well, if we stick to our guns. Incidentally, I might be *altogether* free at that time; things seem to be going very badly with T.: she wrote me a letter beside herself with rage in which she dragged me through the mud, and since then two days have passed and she hasn't written again. She must have a deep-seated resentment of me. As for me, I've written pages and pages of justification, I even sent a letter of Bourdin's clearly demonstrating that I no longer have any relationship with her, but I don't know how she took it. I know very well that T. *cannot* take it upon herself to break off. But she is capable of pulling some lowdown dirty trick with her Creole or V. Brochard's guy or someone entirely different, and that I will not tolerate.

That's all I've been up to, my sweet. I am as one with you as possible, and your letters have completely bucked me up. I love you with all my might. Take good care of yourself, little one who burns the candle at both ends, get some good rest and work dutifully.

I send kisses for your little eyes, my darling Beaver.

⟅ฺ *to Simone de Beauvoir*

February 26

My darling Beaver

So now someone else has stolen your subject? Cocteau, in *Les Monstres sacrés*. There's a trio in the third act. But it looks flimsy. I suppose you'll go nonetheless. It's not a mortal blow. There seems to be a rather pleasant first act.

On another subject, you'll admire this envelope, typed by my very own hands.

It happened yesterday evening, there were some annoying people at the Division HQ who prevented me from going to bed or doing anything worthwhile, so I took the typewriter and typed out six envelopes for you, six for T., two for my parents. I got letters from nobody today. No mail from Paris, which means my dealings with T. are at a standstill. In spite of the typed envelopes, I won't write to T. again till I get an answer to my explanation. I think that's good politically: the first and second days I sent letters bitterly and violently defending myself, offering proof (because her 2 major complaints are false: I never spoke about her to Bourdin, in any case I didn't say that she was in love with me and that I was sleeping with her—I have not maintained a relationship with Bourdin since last October 15th)—then a third and calmer letter in which I put myself in *her* shoes: I understand that you feel soiled, I'm horrified that you might be soiled, etc.—a fourth, tender at the start but slightly threatening near the end: I do not understand how you could accept those stories without the slightest favorable reaction toward me, without reminding yourself what, as recently as yesterday, I meant to you. And now, supposing that this cloud of letters can have won the day, I'm holding my peace till she answers. I ultimately think it's not too serious, it simply erases with one stroke of the pen all the benefits acquired during those three days, which puts us six months behind. It will definitely be worked out on my next leave. What do you make of it? I think the only way to make her forget those ideas completely is to make her anxious and ashamed to have had them. That's why I'll pretend I'm in a bad mood for a while. Meanwhile, she may do something stupid, but basically that's the best route. If she's good and disgusted with herself after one of her drunken binges or halfhearted secret screwing-around, she might not be disgusted with me anymore.

You see that from every point of view I'm a lot calmer though without any news of that little world. Today I particularly regret being out of contact with you, I seemed so stupid when I came out of the Division HQ emptyhanded without any letters (I did get your 200 francs, little one, many thanks, I'm afraid it shaved things pretty close for you?). I'm still working at the Salvation Army Center, but on Sunday it gets noisy as hell, like the café Rouge, because they put a loudspeaker above the screen, and the radio, which used to be discreet, now bellows from morning till night. Fortunately ten years of café life have trained and immunized me. As though it happened yesterday, I still remember my annoyance at the radio—discreet and intermittent though it was—when I was writing *Nausea* in the Café Thiers in Le Havre, and my Elderly Gentleman brand of reflections on the progress of mechanical arts. Incidentally, those were happy times, my little one. You were in Rouen, I in Le Havre, I hadn't yet been to Berlin, that year remains the sweetest in my life. It will come back, my little sweet, we'll have our peacetime idyll, ourselves, old "sacred monsters." (Excuse me, in my naiveté I hadn't realized that when the radio bellows like this it's because they're showing a film on the screen. A film glorifying Finland. I think that lots of them hadn't been aware of it any more than I. It's because the room is flooded with daylight and electric light, and you can see a few gray shadows on a white background. The white background is, of course, snow. I understand now why the music was sporadic and interrupted by horrid detonations, which I'd assumed were atmospheric discharges: they were cannon fire. I also understand why from time to time a man was speaking; I'd thought he was giving commentary on a soccer match.)

Tomorrow I get my shot, but it mustn't amount to much. I alerted you yesterday on the off chance I might not write, but I'll try to write a short note anyway. I took a room at the hotel to be quiet and have a bed in case I get a fever, because otherwise I wouldn't know where to go. I find it rather amusing, because I think a bit of fever would supply some material for the notebook.

Aside from that, little one? Well, nothing more. (The movie's almost over, but another is starting, it's rather awful. So much so that I wonder whether, when I'm through writing to you I won't just *watch*, perhaps that's the best way to endure the thing.) As I said, nothing: last night I read Michel Durand's *Barbara* out of curiosity, to finally know what Durand could do, he who criticizes others so much. Well, it's simply abject, boulevard trash with no verisimilitude or interest, and vaguely copied from lightweight American films like *New York–Miami* and *The Extravagant Mr. Deeds* (he stole the tuba gag from that), and also old hackneyed French stuff like *Mlle. Josette ma femme*. Then I went to sleep, rolled up in my covers. This morning the driver Klein woke me up, and I went out for breakfast at the café, then the Center. Then lunch at the restaurant—Center again, and here I am. Yesterday I read *the Life of Alexandre Dumas père*, lifted from our landlord's library, and that prompted me to lift *The Three Musketeers*, which I read with delight and admiration just a while ago. I also have *The Charterhouse of Parma*. And I still have *Marat* and the end of *Bismarck*. The novel is inching along. It's easy but not a whole lot of fun. It won't be gripping either, and it shouldn't be so. It's simply a necessary chapter, that's all. In a couple of weeks it'll be finished. On that score, tell Poupette to send me *the manuscript* with a typed copy, when she's through typing it, because the corrections are easier to do on the written page than on the typed, at the point I've now reached. The handwritten looks perfectible, whereas the printed is confined to a mediocre and obdurate imperfectibility. Basically it's the notebook that's not going anywhere. Yet there are lots of things to say, but for the moment I've hardly anything beyond my emotional life and I've forbidden myself to allude to it.

And that's it, my sweet. That's all, except that I love you so much and that I feel in complete communion with you. I yearn to see you.

I love you.

Already *ten days* since I left you.

৵ *to Simone de Beauvoir*

February 27

My darling Beaver

It's one-fifteen, I got my shot at 10 o'clock, and as you can see, I'm none the worst for it. All the same, I'm writing to you in a hurry for fear of turning wooly before the end of the day. But I wanted to wait for your letters to answer them. But now the problem is I don't have Saturday's.

T. still isn't writing, nor I. About that whole business, I'd really like to know more and to get your opinion. But you probably know no more about it than I. She must have gotten my explanations on Monday, and if she answers, the letter will get here tomorrow or Thursday. But as for you, you could tell me the *importance* of the whole affair. In your lost letter you probably also talked about the Bost-Zazoulich relationship such as you were able to grasp it from Z. But I know absolutely nothing about your little world, it's a bit annoying because things are in full swing there: things are happening in people's heads and conversations, and I'm getting no information at all.

You ask, my sweet, if I've stopped being sad. No. Not really. After two days of restiveness, Friday and Saturday, I definitely calmed down on Sunday and Monday; the present—with the Center, the taste of my pipe, the reading, etc.— has built up a thick crust around me again; I wrote in my notebook that I was tasting the "dreary sweetness of living." Only time drags along because it is completely centered on the mail hour, and that's the point, the mail is disappointing: nothing from you yesterday, today a letter "from afterward," you know, it seems to me, the ones we write after a long long letter in which we exhaust the subjects and exhaust ourselves, that's what is driving me wild, that they've mislaid the one that must have been voluminous. No letter from T. So right after the mail, I have to get back to waiting. Very patiently, but even so it's a wait that provides a sort of very slow glide along the present. Do tell me about everything.

Paul returned this morning, and, contrary to my expectations, was so chipper

I thought he was drunk. I took him out for a cup of coffee, then around nine-thirty, I went down to the hospital, where some twenty guys were waiting, the last to get their shots. It took longer than I'd thought precisely because we were the last group, into which they'd stuck all the remnants; we waited in a dark corridor, illuminated by the blue light from the painted windowpanes; I talked politics with a photographer-driver, the one who'd urinated on rags to clean the windows of his car. And then around ten-thirty they pushed me into a small room where the medical officer was giving shots. It was over so quickly I didn't even notice it, I felt a slight prick and said to myself: he's looking for a good place with the tip of his needle. But not at all, it was all over. That's the advantage of being fat: the skinny ones suffered. Upon which, wrapped for once in my overcoat, I came back to the Center. I was able to forge ahead on the novel till half past twelve, the hour at which I went to get the mail (as you know, we have to eat lightly the first day) and then, after that, I came back to write to you. It is two o'clock, and I don't feel a thing, except perhaps a small node under the armpit and a slight pain in the back. They gave me the shot in the left shoulder blade, and my left hand is cold—whereas the right is hot, but it's not un-pleasant—in fact, it feels like *hot fudge*.[1] And that's it, my little sweet. Did I tell you that I reread *The Charterhouse of Parma* with boundless admiration? It's terrific. You have to be biased, like young Bost, to compare the Sumatra scene to Stendhal. There is a wealth of invention and detail in that novel that literally dumfounds me.

My sweet, you are right to say that never has our love been so necessary and so strong. I feel it every day. You are a little sage, a marvel of a little creature. Yes, my darling, we'll have a beautiful leave. And, you know, at the moment they are talking about *one month*, which would bring me to you around April 1st.

I love you so much, so much, my charming, my sweet little Beaver.

৵ৡ *to Simone de Beauvoir*

February 28

My darling Beaver

At the same time I got your Saturday letter, which had gone astray (always put *Postal Sector* spelled out, that's why it got lost, you make an S that resembles

---

[1] In English in the original.

nothing on earth) and your Monday letter. Good Lord, my little one, how you interested and instructed me. I'm going to answer you fully and on everything, because I too would like to chat with you for a long, long time. First I want you to know that I got a repentant, passionate letter from Tania, who isn't even trying to maintain an obstinate superiority, as you put it. She begs pardon as though from delirium and right off the notebooks are enthusiastically accepted: "During this irritating trimester, which has slipped through my fingers without giving me anything, without enriching me, your notebooks are the only abundant thing, which has given me more and enriched me more in a few days than everything else in the past three months." So that's settled, I'm really pleased. Which reminds me, if Z. should mention it to you again, tell her without insisting that I gave you all pertinent explanations and that you are convinced of my innocence (*if she seems to believe that you are up-to-date on it*—but I've not said a single thing that would give that impression).

But what can I tell you about your whole letter? It moved me. I'm in the process of changing. I want nothing but the *pure* now and you understand what I mean by that: my feelings for T. include nothing very elevated, but they *exist*, I rage when she bawls me out, I worry about her, I'm moved when she is tender, etc. And to be sure, it is profoundly regrettable that I put things on such a footing that to express a moment of strong affection I'm obliged to say, "I love you passionately." And it's too bad I have to lie to her about you, etc. But all full of sneaky little ways and little fibs as it may be, this affair is right, because I am fond of T. The war has made me intimate with hierarchy. Don't complain about it, it is not what showed me the infinite distance separating my affection for you from all the others—that I already knew—but rather it taught me that I must not be negligent or casual toward you, since our love is so strong and noblesse oblige. But next it showed me, slight though this may be, that I have deep feelings for T., and it is so seldom I have deep feelings that they have become precious to me. And besides, it persuaded me to put an end to my life of little conquests. If I expected to be around after the war, it was not to chase skirts but for completely different things. But then, precisely because my amorous life was *over*, I mean as a sharp break, I had to keep no more than what I could really assume *for myself*. Well—since there was no question about you—it had to be T. I want to break off completely with that shifty sort of generosity that has me spending hours and hours with people who aren't worth a damn to me, under the pretext that "it would be just too rotten to hurt them." I feel I'll be rather hardheaded about that, from now on. I want to *care* about things, I've had enough of being a cold fish or stony. So I don't want to spread myself thin and spoil my possibilities of loving people and things while dispensing claptrap to people I don't care about. I agree with you completely: we should only do things we would acknowledge. And up to now I haven't. I know: there are ignoble aspects to my relationship with T. It's ignoble of me to have to write, "I'd crawl all over everyone (even the Beaver, despite my mysticism)." But I'd like to explain to you—here we're getting around to Bourdin—in all this grubby business there's something totally new for me. I'm not just paying it lip service, the way I used to do "the right thing": I'm in it up to my neck. I find that repugnant, but I want it, it's fulfilling. I say to myself: The end justifies the means. And that's precisely it, I want the end.

The letter to Bourdin was abysmal. Totally agreed. But you can't imagine what perverse joy I found in being so far gone I'd do something that rotten. All things considered, it's the first time in my life I've done anything like that. I've often been a bastard out of frivolity or lack of consideration, but never, strictly speaking, have I done something so rotten as represented by the mailing of that letter. But up to now I've always been too cold to do it. I think I told you what a feeling of plenitude I got from that moment of anger in a café in Rouen where I'd seen red to the point of agreeing to do battle with a customer even in public. That was just about what came over me the other day. You see, the thing that disheartens me is the world of half-measures and half-lies into which we (you too, my little one—and perhaps I'm at fault for that) allowed our lives to sink into a quagmire. When suddenly, there was something I cared about above all. I don't mean T., you must understand, I feel no passion for T., you know exactly what my feelings are. Instead it was to preserve unspoiled those three days which had, after all, hit me rather hard (what spoiled them was my lies), not to let them fade into memory, instead to recover the note of tenderness I had taken three years to have her know: so as not to fail in her eyes. Do you understand that for a few hours one can want that more than anything else in the world, yet without feeling passionate about the woman? My state of mind on Friday was a very odd one. I didn't think all this just then, but a while ago when I was out walking with Paul. What I was feeling on Friday was that if it were possible to do devious but fruitful things to get back T., I would do them. And besides that, of course, I was crazy with rage against Bourdin—who, you will admit, was rather indecent to go and recount the details of our affair to a little boy of 18 in order to arouse him. Besides, she very well knows that Mouloudji is an intimate friend of T.'s, so I'm not sure there wasn't some calculating thought in her head—and if there wasn't, there was unpardonable flightiness. I'm not telling you this by way of an excuse, I well know that you're right and that she deserved to be bawled out *about the present*, but that it gave me no right to rake over the past. I'm simply explaining how she seemed dirty and sneaky, that dame who goes around airing her affairs in front of anyone at all, it's like urinary incontinence. Actually, yes, I did hold her in high regard, but that ended a year ago.

In June I could barely stomach her—I saw her once, you remember; the way you described her after seeing her at the Dôme, you terrible little destroyer, had furthered the undermining, and finally her last madwoman letters. For a long time I've been thinking that I was mistaken about her and that she was just no good; I didn't entirely admit it to myself, and that was one release in my fury on Friday, being able to say to myself with dawning understanding that she's the lowest of the low. A relief against myself, not against her. Again, all this is not to justify, but to describe. Then the idea of that letter came to me and right from the start I knew it was a rotten business, and I wanted that rotten business, even to the point of copying the letter over twice to polish it. Note that the primary goal was in no way to hurt Bourdin, but for T. to read it and become convinced of the truth in what I was saying. And in other respects—we're none of us simple people—while convinced that I was condemning myself to be up to my neck in garbage and sacrificing Bourdin's distress to T., I was *convinced* that T. wouldn't send her the letter, because she's too lazy, because she'd be afraid that Bourdin would guess where it was coming from, which would give her the upper hand on T., and also because the Z's are satisfied with symbolic victories. And in fact I was avidly hoping she wouldn't send it—not for reasons of morality or to spare B.—but because after all the other would have been able to amend certain details in the letter to Mouloudji with supporting proof. It's even yet a bit more complicated than that: I couldn't remember B.'s address, so I sent an envelope simply reading "Martine Bourdin," and I told T. either to have Mouloudji deliver it or to send me the address and then I'd send back a fully addressed envelope. Well, when I realized she might charge Mouloudji with the task, I feared he might not deliver it, because he could pretend to have delivered it and bring back an untrue report of B.'s reception of it. And when I imagined that T. would give me the address and that eventually the letter would go off by mail, I hoped that on the contrary T. wouldn't send it, because that would avoid all dangerous reactions from Bourdin. And then the next day I had some unsettling thoughts about Bourdin's possible collapse, but not too seriously, because I sense things poorly at such a distance. But the important part was the way I allowed myself to be carried away as I applied myself to doing something I took to be a rotten trick as though I were only too happy to do something bad, of being carried away to the point of doing something bad. And besides, I think something lingered on from my affair with Olga: a sort of inner hardening which results in my *not wanting* to begin that sort of thing again and lose what I have for reasons of morality. It's not that I totally approve of myself in the Z. affair in which I was decent—and if it were to be repeated I'd do it again—but it's because *you* were involved. In other words, I understood that I had made up my mind to sacrifice T. at a first sign from you—2nd to sacrifice all the others to T. In one sense it's a sort of moral test; I already felt that slightly in Paris, during my leave. I'd really like you to tell me what you think about that, my little one.

Conclusion: my relationship with T. is back to normal, I severed all ties (of course) with the person I was on Friday. It seems to me that the crisis ends on the best possible note for me. Never again will I have such libertine and coarse affairs (or at least not for a long time). We'll try to draw conclusions from all this on my next leave.

My very dear little one, here you have a very long letter and I haven't found time to tell you how much I love you. You know, I fear that in writing to you about all this, it might bewilder you, you might find me sneaky, vile and base. Little one, I need your good judgment more than anything else in the world; give me a good tongue-lashing if I deserve it, please. I love you, my dearest little Beaver.

Count on me between April 1st and 15th.

ৰ্তচ *to Simone de Beauvoir*

February 29

My darling Beaver

No letter from you or from T. today, there must be a delay in the mails. I do need to talk to you and, as though by design, never have your letters been so infrequent. Not through your fault, my little sweet, but through the mail's (do be sure to write Postal Sector 108). You know, a very unpleasant fear sometimes overtakes me, one that I fend off by pretending to find it absurd, but it's not really so, and that shakes me up. I'm afraid that in the (justified) severe attitude toward me which you now have, it might have been very unpleasant for you to read in my last letter that I'd written to T.: "I'd crawl all over everyone . . . , etc." not so much because of yourself as because of the sort of universal lie it smacks of. My love, it would be the hardest blow of all if I displeased you so much that one day you could not write to me at all. You know, right now I'm in an odd state, I've never been this uneasy with myself since I went crazy.[1] Get this straight: I'm not at all crazy, but there's a certain

---

[1] In 1935, Sartre had a doctor friend give him mescaline to see its effects. For several months after he had frightening hallucinations and thought he was going mad.

way of being outflanked, taken from behind, somehow screwed by ideas, a sort of emotional and moral unbalance, that I hadn't experienced since my days of madness. I don't want to play on your pity, and I know that there's no such thing as an excuse. But picture for yourself the weird return from my leave, still in the throes of civilian memories, that letter from T. breaking in on a sort of tender revery for her.

Since yesterday, I've had no idea what I want or rather what I feel. If T. had written to me pleasantly as she had begun to, and without this Bourdin business, I would have continued to have the same tender, full affection for her I'd had in Paris, one with *value*. But after the furious letter she sent to me, followed by five days of silence, I've had one idea alone, after the first day's passion: to harden myself, but it turned to restiveness and passion. I read, I wrote, I didn't want to think about it. So I found myself *outside* of the affair again, and when I got her letter, instead of feeling the joy I'd expected, I was mostly *reassured*. Everlastingly the same boorish reaction that I really hoped not to have and from which I wasn't spared. Particularly since your letter, arriving at the same time and saying, "She thought only of the way she would appear to Mouloudji," thereby reducing T.'s moods to their true proportions, made me still more boorish and cynical regarding reconciliation. At the same instant your severe letter put me through the ringer somewhat. The whole thing set up a strange atmosphere. It lasted all through yesterday and this morning, but all the same I didn't feel the restiveness of the previous days. This morning I was strangely "sensitized." I read the account of the loves of Fabrice and Clélia[2] (for the twentieth time) with real tears in my eyes, and at the same time I was annoyed at playing the sensitive soul in the realm of imagination. Thereupon the mail, no letter from you or T., my restiveness started up again; as I write, I'm very restive, particularly because of you, because I don't much suppose that T. has fallen back into a rage. Particularly since your letters seem too short to me at the moment (though they are good and long, my love). I'd like to ask you questions and discuss everything thoroughly, my love. Well, that will come soon. My sweet, how I need you, now much charm your presence brings for me and your sense of balance. I love you. I'm afraid I must seem slightly underhanded to you with all the lies I'm entangled in, I fear that my true image and what I am with you might be slightly soiled—just as the Bourdin affair soiled me in T.'s eyes, but with more reason. I'm afraid you might suddenly ask yourself, in the midst of so much politicking, of total lies and particularly of half-truths: isn't he perhaps lying to me, isn't he telling me half-truths? My little one, my darling Beaver, I swear to you that with you I'm totally pure. If I were not, there would be nothing

---

[2] In Stendhal's *Charterhouse of Parma*.

in the world before which I would not be a liar, I would lose my very self. My love, you are not only my life but also the only honesty of my life. That's because you are what you are. I love you.

I began to think about writing on my relationship with people, but there again I have to lie, because T. would want to see the notebooks. I struggle to rearrange as little as possible, but it winds up weighing me down.

My yesterday's letter was stupid, but, beyond all I told you above, I had a slight fever during the night, it scarcely woke me up but dazed me for the whole day. I was a bit under the weather. In your letter you'd told me so many interesting things I wanted to answer, and then I don't know how I missed the point and my letter turned into a plea. What particularly struck me was your saying that I grant myself an advantage over people and that I find that what is lying for me is actually a good enough truth for them. That *is absolutely true.* But how I would like to talk to you about it.

My love, don't infer too much from this letter. Tomorrow I'll get your letters, and I'll be fine. I love you with all my might, I wish you were here.

༖ *to Simone de Beauvoir*

March 1st

My love, my darling Beaver

I have your Tuesday's letter and I'm awfully relieved. But you mustn't be too afraid that your letters have a pretty good whiff of reprimand; you've got to rub my nose in what I've done. Or else aren't you my little moral conscience any more? I've been going through strange days, I swear, and I'll have strange, powerful memories of this town where nothing happens from dawn to dusk, where I exist in the Salvation Army Center without budging for one second and where, without leaving my chair, I experienced passion, crimes of passion, remorse, and I voluptuously indulged in the first great lousy act of my life (I mean the letter to Bourdin). In the larger picture, I suppose it will seem on the poetic side; besides, I'm only half here, because April 1st is already looming and between the 1st and the 5th I'll be with you, my sweet. I feel that this whole period will be set to rights, stamped, buried, only when we two have been able to talk about it together. It's as though you have a little seal and have to stamp everything I see. You're certainly my little absolute as well, believe me. Not metaphysically, because I do metaphysics all by myself like a grown-up, but morally. To conclude, I believe what you think is: 1st that I played a gratuitous rotten trick on Bourdin (the letter won't be sent, I suppose; T. isn't saying any more about it)—2nd that henceforth I must act in such a way that nonsense like this never again happens in our lives. Is that it? I agree with all of it. I promise there won't be any such affair in a good long while (long after the end of the war, of course, because otherwise it would be too easy). Anyway I'm really disgusted. Besides, it would take up much too much time. Besides, I think I've changed: I no longer want to "seduce." Everything was always a story of seduction, I see it all clearly now as I write about it and, once the woman was seduced, I was flabbergasted to have her on my hands. I hadn't *anticipated* that. Now it's all over because I like to have full relationships, and they, on the other hand, can begin only once the ceremonies of seduction have been completed. More and more, not only you but also my *relationship* with you is precious. And for seduction that's somehow "conjugal," I mean within an officially established relationship, T. is more than enough.

Speaking of which, I received a letter from her too. A rather mendacious one, given that it is dated Tuesday and was obviously (from clues that I'll spare you) written on Wednesday. No doubt she wanted to hide an evening with the Creole or some other nonsense (but I'm not anxious, it's all quite innocent). Essentially, the thing is that she's riddled with guilt regarding me, "introspective and anxious," as she puts it, and that everything is going swimmingly. The way it seems to be transpiring, as she explained at length, is that she was aware of going into transports while she was doing so, and she was taking a sadistic pleasure in it and did not have an easy conscience about it. All is well.

I find that game of truth or consequences very entertaining. If I really understand it, in order to play well, a person has to give proof more of presence of mind than of sincerity.

Till tomorrow, my sweet, I send tender kisses for your little old cheeks, I love you with all I have.

◦⃝◦ *to Simone de Beauvoir*

March 2

My darling Beaver

How can it be that you haven't received my Tuesday letter? I think you must have gotten two the next day, because I'd written faithfully. And all was going very well for me. There are surprising delays and surprising bursts of speed in the mail service these days, you'd think it was an accordion.

My sweet, how sweet of you to advise me to take a little querencia-room. But just consider: 1st That it amounts to 250 francs additional a month, minimum. 2nd That I'm very comfortable at the Center, where I like to work, because there's noise. 3rd That the bedrooms *aren't heated* which, up to the 1st of April, at least, is a deciding impediment.

Because of which I remain here. Reliable information has it that in a while we'll be going to the rear, perhaps for the whole summer. We'll be a winter division. Last night I saw someone rather well-informed who told me that. It was an Alsatian, and I carried on a rather strange conversation with him (on an entirely different subject) but one that cannot be discussed here. Incidentally I haven't yet put it in my notebook because I was absorbed with writing about my relationship with others. Since the day before yesterday I've written *a hundred* pages on that, just think of it, and without exhausting the subject. It's too bad, actually, but I'll have to write about Olga, about Bost, you, and Tania, and so I'll have to shamefully falsify it. So I stopped *before* the Olga affair with a few enigmatic phrases, such as T. might use, announcing a total transformation, which occurred soon after. It was quite entertaining. I clearly saw the sources of my imperialism and of all the rest, but now I'm slightly disgusted, as happens each time one speaks about oneself too much. What else was I doing, incidentally, in all those letters of justification I've been sending you? But now I'm not going to think about myself for some time, those affairs are all buried, we won't drag them out in the open again till we're together once more.

As for me, my little dear, I've worked all morning and read, guess what? Émile Ollivier's *L'Expédition du Mexique* (Second Empire). It's extremely entertaining, it goes very well with Bismarck and the war of '70; I'm beginning to get a feel for the odd atmosphere of the period. And then I lunched, got your letter and a letter from Hermann, who tells me that my factum on Emotions[1] has come out. You should know that the article on Giraudoux will appear in the March NRF. It's been announced in *Les Nouvelles littéraires*. If *L'Imaginaire*[2] comes out too, that makes a good literary month. You'll be getting copies of the *Émotions:* would you please, 1st, drop one in Tania's pigeonhole—2nd, give one to Pipette if she's still there, for herself and entrust one to her for la Dérouille—3rd send one to Bist[3] if he likes the idea—4th drop one off at my parents' when convenient.

---

[1] *Esquisse d'une théorie des émotions (Sketch for a Theory of the Emotions)*, Paris: Hermann, 1939.

[2] Paris, Gallimard, 1940. *The Psychology of Imagination*, New York: Philosophical Library, 1948.

[3] Sartre is playing with the names of Lionel de Roulet (a former student of his who a few years later married Beauvoir's sister Poupette—given as Pipette here), and of Bost.

Something else: you'll have to send me a thousand francs, my little one. If we sent the Z's to Laigle, can we perhaps get by?

Finally one last little touch: there are going to be cards after all. I don't in the least think it will be a nuisance for you. But would you see to it that T. doesn't do anything stupid; help her with it (at the same time that you'll certainly have to help Olga, who's scarcely less incapable. Find out whether she'll have to have an ID so that they can issue her cards to her). I find mine just right and fortuitous. It's funny that here it is the rich army personnel like Hang who are protesting against meal regulations, in the name of individual liberty, whereas the establishment of Censorship seemed an excellent decision to them. Political censorship has been abolished, incidentally, did you know? The newspapers bear some rereading now that they're less empty.

So that's all, little one. It's a letter of ideas, but what can I do? Nothing's going on, I'm here, I read and write. But I'd really like you to feel how much I love you and how close to you I am all this time.

With all my might I send you kisses, my dear dear little one.

ⳙ to Simone de Beauvoir

March 3

My darling Beaver

This whole day slipped right through my fingers. Outside it was a real Sunday, with just the right kind of pale sunny weather and people strolling up and down the streets, a heartbreaking Sunday. But I scarcely noticed it. At the Center it was Sunday too, because of the vast number of "peasants" who came to town. Given the tasks demanded of them, the 160 HQ guys ordinarily here represent an aristocracy. And on Sunday the nonentities from the batteries or the infantrymen who are in the surrounding villages descend on the place. The Center is filled with the heavy, impassive faces of ill-formed, hefty guys with fat gnarled hands, sitting there dreaming away in the state of military waiting, looking like the seedy regular army soldiers that you see hanging around army post towns, simply a bit aged and leaving you with the distinct impression—and it's something not generally visible hereabouts—that the French soldier is a peasant. Last Sunday, I forgot to tell you, there were three of them wandering around on the lookout. All of a sudden they catch sight of me: "Hey, Bud, movies, got any around here?" "No, there aren't any." Then, sotto voce, "And the whorehouse, where's it at?" It seemed very *8:47 Train*.[1] They were profoundly shocked when I told them there weren't any. So this all makes for very special Sundays here. Except that the day is totally discombobulated, because these last few days the mail has always arrived at noon, today the mail clerk who was on leave came back, a strapping customer you don't want to mess with, and he brought us the mail at 4 o'clock. So up to four o'clock it was a long morning for me. And the afternoon was all squeezed in between four o'clock and nightfall, I spent it playing chess. Incidentally, there was no mail. Yes there was, one letter from *Le Figaro littéraire* which I'll send you because it's worth its weight in gold, and two copies of my *Théorie des émotions*, which I read with some disappointment. The theory is shown but not demonstrated. The preface is the best part. But nothing at all from you. It's Sunday that's the problem. It seems a blank day, with a "letterless moment," not too long to get through, soon it will be tomorrow. But the thing about all these mishaps, these disputes and deluges of blame poured down on me, is that I'm virtually killing time here. I'm not at all miserable, there's even a particular charm to each day, but I haven't regained my pre-leave serenity.

That's all for today, little one. I've gone back to my novel and neglected my notebook somewhat. The novel is entertaining me—on the unemotional side. Just a while ago I heard some tunes on the radio, I went up and listened—it was that cheap music that moves me, the *Johnny Parker* sort of thing and, worse yet, sung, I could swear, by Jean Tranchant. No matter, it moved me tremendously, and with a sort of emotion I've long forgotten because ordinarily I'm most unemotional and spill my guts into my notebook with a sort of hostility. You know, the kind of emotion that swept us up—or rather that swept me up—and you caught it, too, my little sweet—one night when we'd had a bit to drink in Montmartre. It was about myself—something like: I too used to write things that could move people (why "used to," one wonders), and this brought on self-pity. For two weeks now, I have to add, conscientiously abiding by your say-so and T.'s, I've been guiltily thinking of myself as a scoundrel. But, rest assured, I'm not losing sight of the fact *too* that I am a scoundrel. And then the Salvation Army lady, no doubt considering the songs profane, turned the knob, and I came back to write to you. Alas, little one, how I wish you were here beside me, how I wish we could shed our little tears about our fate, as we used to do. How I would love to hold your frail little body in my arms. You, my little Beaver, you who are me. I love you so much.

There are no more typed envelopes, but I'll do some more this evening since you like them.

---

[1] *Le Train de 8 heures 47*, play by Courteline, pen name of Georges Moineaux (1858–1929), author of satiric comedies.

⟨⟩ to Simone de Beauvoir

March 4

My darling Beaver

Today I get your letter of the 2nd (written the 1st), which delights me because it tells me that you're convinced by what I've written to you. My sweet, you'd be truly flattered if you could see how poorly I bear up under your disapprobation. I writhe beneath it like the Devil beneath the foot of the Archangel Saint Michael. Only I have to tell you that I *can't at all* remember what I wrote to you that convinced you. It's not that it was invented on the spot, but in the end I've written so much on the subject that I don't remember the exact choice of arguments that found their way into the first letter.

You see, that's rather what I was trying to tell you two months ago when I said that without half trying you can feel buried here. Think of the number of people who aren't loved *any other way* now. They know very well that their old lady is faithful, they know she'll be happy to see them again, and that after the war they'll resume their life together. But if they're the least bit clever, they feel too that while they're bored as hell here, there's nothing left for them in the old lady's heart but a bit of dusty bone. Fortunately *you*, little one, you can't love that way—bonily; I'd grow sick on that, I need to feel your love, and I feel it so powerfully, in its smallest detail, deeply. I love you. I have to say too that with T.'s odd feelings, one often feels betrayed but never entirely done for, I don't know why. Speaking of that, everything's going beautifully. She writes, "I have only you, you are what I know best in the world: that's how I love you." T.—spineless, not always proud of herself, and completely lost in the world— needs me, and even if I'm far off she needs to think from time to time that I exist.

You ask what I think about things that Bienenfeld said to you about American novels.[1] But there's nothing to say: yes, American novels are like that and ours are different. When we were contemplating writing a novel and were preoccupied with technique, the question was knowing to what degree we could assimilate the American *technique*, which is excellent, to *serve our purposes*. By that I mean—but it has been settled once and for all—precisely to what degree is the concern for putting ideas in the novel compatible with the technique of novels without ideas. But then, we know the answer: it involves accommodation, etc. But it would be absurd to say: Hemingway's novels, which have no ideas, have good technique, so you have to write novels without ideas. On another point,

---

[1] Beinenfeld had admired the gratuitousness and lack of thought in American novels (*Lettres à Sartre*, v. 2, p. 97).

to return to that matter of gratuitousness, one must be cautious: in reality *nothing* can be gratuitous in art because art is first of all unity. Whether it's a painting of Picasso or a novel by Stendhal or Kafka, you'll never find anything that doesn't *serve some purpose*. And I had noticed, reading A *Farewell to Arms*, how far Hemingway's art is from granting gratuitousness its place, for instance how the place he accords the uninteresting episode about the purchase of a revolver in Florence is then justified by the role that revolver plays. And you yourself wouldn't accept putting just anything at all in your novel. The thing is that the necessary must sometimes—not always—be able to take on the aspect of the gratuitous. It will have that look only *at first*, when it is initially encountered: for example we speak of a character who had not yet been mentioned, we describe a stroll without any direct connection with the subject. But a hundred pages further on, it will become necessary because it will be linked to the rest by a hundred bonds. Which leaves the only remaining problem: have you managed to give the appearance of the gratuitous to episodes which are *in fact* necessary? I for one calmly answer *yes*. But I assure you that when I congratulated you for the fact that *everything* has import, "under the appearance of the contingent and the gratuitous" was understood. Otherwise we would have a mathematical demonstration, which would be a bore. Besides, if after a hundred pages and through a thousand changing episodes the reader is gripped by a stifling impression of necessity (with the "life" of the characters—which is gratuitous—being preserved), what would be the harm in that, I ask you. At any rate, you well know it's not a question of style.

Bist wants to become an officer candidate? I fear he might find a life that's less arduous but a hundred times more disagreeable. I'm not sure it's not better to scorn superiors without being party to it than it is to rail against one's equals, within a sort of complicity. He alone will decide. But I think he won't find an Anselem there—or anything as nice as the guy from Belleville who sends him to see his wife and his buddies. Incidentally the guys doing officer training are given a pretty rough time. No frills. No time off, without those great periods of vague degradation when the soldier is left on his own. Besides, they're often at greater risk. Anyway, what he should obviously be told is that there is *absolutely no moral reason* preventing him from doing what he considers the least unpleasant. For military service, the choice is clear. For war and particularly for *this* war, you'd have to reconsider the question in so many different ways that it becomes impossible.

My love, here I am sending you whole volumes. Fortunately *nothing* happened yesterday, or it would take me six pages more to tell you what I've been doing. Just bear in mind that I'm getting my shot tomorrow and that I'm in fine fettle today.

Another thought: from all indications, it seems I'll be on leave around the 24th or 25th of March at the latest.

There's confirmation that we will be going to rest camp. Perhaps for the whole summer.

My love, my darling Beaver, it would seem marvelous if I could see you in three weeks, and then very easily after that.

I love you with all my might.

ᵔᵔ to Simone de Beauvoir

March 5

My darling Beaver

Two letters from you today, one of them so sweet, Saturday's in which you told me so carefully that you don't consider me too much of a bad boy. My love, I'm so happy that we're so close and that you feel so strongly how much I care for you. You're so right, this year is "paramount" and we should not have missed out on it. It seems like a "trial" and I believe that it's good this way that in the midst of a life that is of necessity undertaken somewhat blindly, and that's put together without perspectives or with false perspectives, there's a time of trial that allows us to verify everything and get it back in focus. And it's so great, my dear love, my little one, to think that the one thing that has the least chance in the world of changing, so true and satisfying, is our shared love.

I got my second shot this morning, but that was five hours ago and I'm not feeling it at all. Perhaps my head is a bit woozy, if one were to really look hard. I even ate a sausage sandwich. I'm at the Center, and I'm working on my novel (you know, in the evening I type, encouraged by my success with addresses, so it will simply need to be inserted in Poupette's manuscript when it arrives). Tonight I'll sleep at the hotel. My supply of books is exhausted, and I really need to have you send more. Within a few days I'll send back those you tell me to, I've got to finish the *Bismarck*, the only one still not finished. On my leave, I'll choose some novels, because I'll have read only history and austere stuff these last few months. But while I think of it: If I'm getting there around the 25th of March we'll need money for the first days. At least 1000 francs (if you're getting paid the 30th). How will we go about it? If it comes down to that, I could actually borrow 500 francs from my mother for a few days.

My sweet, I have a tremendous desire to see you, I'll squeeze you like a lemon. I love you so, sweet little Beaver.

⚭ *to Simone de Beauvoir*

March 5

My darling Beaver

Just a brief note to complete the book list. I'd like *Solitude en commun [Solitude in Common]*—by Margaret Kennedy.

And a little book by Ludwig that might be called *Août 1914* or *La Drame d'août* on the declaration of the War of 1914.

I've just received *Guillaume II* and *La Commune. Guillaume II* looks enthralling. I hope to find something concrete in it about that troubling business: the role of *one* man in a social event. I know Aron will say it's one layer of meaning among others. But even granting that, the meaning isn't simple.

I love you.

⚭ *to Simone de Beauvoir*

March 6

My darling Beaver

Only a short letter today since I don't have much to tell you though it's not for lack of caring. I don't quite know how to characterize the life I'm living here, stuck in this Center where I almost never have a table to myself and where one can hear the most varied of sounds, including the bounce of the celluloid Ping-Pong balls. It's no longer the life of a monk, unless it's a cenobite. And to me the Center itself has an instability about it; sometimes hospitable (during the morning when there aren't too many people), sometimes a little bit heartbreaking, when my querencia's completely denied me by intrusive mutterings. It's an odd sort of a place whose outstanding characteristic is its structural link to an old Alsatian hotel where I have my meals, so that for lunch I go down one flight and when I have to pee I go up one flight and find myself in a corridor between two rows of hotel rooms. It's one of those objects that you don't see except in the course of a war and, I'm telling you, because of all that, it's profoundly unstable, I don't know what to think of it. In addition there are relatively few windows for such a large room and they look out onto a courtyard, so that, from morning to evening, there's electric lighting, which has its own sort of charm. Also there are strange variations of temperature. For example today it was freezing here, while at other times it's stifling. Today it's infested with the men who've been inoculated. And that'll go on for several days because shots are being handed out every which way, which on the whole makes things less appealing. Incidentally, I got a shot yesterday too, as you know, and I spent the night in the hotel in a room on the third floor, quite rustic, with—of all things—a huge French flag in one corner, fully unfurled, doubtless the one they hang out on parade days. It seemed a little eerie going to bed with that fetish in my room, but I slept like a log from 10 o'clock to 7, and today I'm fit as a fiddle and had a positive feast at lunch. So that's that for shots.

For the rest of the day, I read a great deal and worked not much—except on my notebook, where I arrogantly wrote: "I am the monstrous product of capitalism, parliamentarianism, centralization and officialdom." Sad to say, it's true. I'm intrigued by Ludwig's *Guillaume II*, which is well-done and terrifically interesting. I'll send it to you with the *Bismarck* if you haven't read it. *La Commune*, which I've begun, is somewhat disappointing, but perhaps you'll like it, as you liked Cassou's *48*. In any case, all these books give me a glimpse of what history ought to be. For instance in *La Commune* there's a felicitous attempt to show the influence of the myth of Paris the great city (Caillois is quoted) on the Communards. I also worked a while on the novel, but I'm not rushing it because in any case I'll have done all I can do on it well before getting the typed manuscript. And that's that. Time here is a bit like an accordion, sometimes it bubbles along, sometimes it hangs heavy. What with the home leave that's just over and the one just three weeks off, I haven't been able to regain my wartime sea legs; and in this old folks' home, which feels so little like war, one can feel it even less. Crazy life. I've made one friend, the little newsboy, who's fourteen and keeps coming to bum cigarettes off me. He prowls around me and converses with me totally unintelligibly; I suspect him, incidentally, of procuring women for the soldiers.

And that's it for today, my dearest little Beaver, my love. It's true that your letters are never long enough, but you must realize that it is not your fault, it's just that my best time comes when I read them. If you wrote fifteen pages, I'd still want more, and I always reread them three or four times. I love you so much.

My very dear little Beaver, I love you tenderly.

⊶ *to Simone de Beauvoir*

March 7

My darling Beaver

No letter from you today, but that was as expected. Still, it depressed me some, my sweet. I love your little scrawls. You're still stubbornly using that "South Sea blue" ink, which was a failure, and I can tell in advance when there's a letter from you the moment I see the tip of a letter sticking out of the bundle of mail with FM [Military Franking] written in that pompous, contemptible color. Today I thought it was you again, but instead it was a letter from T., T. butting in with the same ink. I didn't like that at all, because my passion for her has cooled; these moral and emotional "tornadoes," as you call them, have exhausted it for the time being.

Aside from that, I had a lovely day. Not so much in the morning, because the officers requisitioned the Center for a conference. Which is typical of them: they all have their own little spots to harbor them, if they want them, plenty of restaurants where they have their own food. But no, they have to prove to the men that nothing belongs to them, that an officer can always take everything away from them. It's all the more intelligent in that this morning there were twenty or so of the vaccinated who had no idea where to settle. So I went back to the Division Headquarters and spent an hour with the clerks, who have distinctly fallen to abject depths. It isn't even funny anymore. Then around eleven I went back up to the Center, and at that point things picked up as ideas on history came to me and I wrote them down in my notebook. I went to lunch, got the mail, then went back up to the Center and got back to writing and reading *Guillaume II*, which is truly astonishing, less because of Ludwig than because of the protagonist and his entourage. Then again I did some writing. A young man with glasses struck up a conversation, and I was going to get back to work when an old redheaded lady who acts as entertainment director here said, "You're always writing, you'd be better off playing some Ping-Pong with me." That morning she'd been circling around me—I annoy her by reading so much—and spotted Ollivier's *Commune*. "Oh! oh! A Communist?" "Why no, Madam." "Well I for one think we should send all Communists to Russia. I spent four years there and I know what it's like. We should do what they do in America: if you don't like it here, why don't you go there? And without even giving them the travel money: they can just march their tails right out of here!" Such an extremely military expression surprised me coming from such a mouth. But the fact is that the dame isn't from the Salvation Army, she's some sort of a volunteer and my bet is she's worn out more pairs of balls than the French army has pairs of boots. Not absolutely insufferable, however. So I agreed to a game of Ping-Pong. She beat me in the first game, I beat her in the second, and we were beginning the third when the ball spun off and got stuck under the stage. We had to move plank after plank, we were down on all fours, sweating blood. Upon which she was called off elsewhere and the game stopped, but we'll give it a go again tomorrow. Well there, my little one, do you remember in Rouen when the two of us used to go up over the Brasserie l'Univers (I think it was called) for our little game? But, you know, I don't miss those days, I miss *you* yourself, little one. After the Ping-Pong I worked on the novel—and it went well. And now I'm writing to you. I'll still send this letter to the Rue Vavin, but now that I think of it, T. will be moving out in three or four days, Olga isn't there anymore, one week from now nothing will prevent me from writing to you regularly at the Hotel. If, at any rate, they leave for Laigle.[1]

Au revoir, my sweet, my love. I love you so much. I would so like to see your little face again. You know, it still upsets me when I remember how it looked the morning I left.

ᦕ *to Simone de Beauvoir*

March 8

My darling Beaver

How deeply I was moved today by your little letter in which you tell me how guilty you feel about giving me such a bawling out. But, my little one, I'm no longer sad at all, I want you to know. Besides, you *must* scold me when I deserve it, just as you must be harsh about my novel if it isn't any good. I love you so much, my little flower. Oh yes, I certainly feel how you love me, and I so love the way that you love me. I so long to see you. And voilà, we have a little problem, perhaps it's nothing: we haven't heard a word from Pieter, who left on leave two weeks ago and should have returned yesterday morning. He's probably sick. As soon as we know, Hang will leave, and this won't delay him more than two days. But if he's still sick when my turn comes up, will they let me leave? That would leave Paul all alone for two weeks. And what if there were readings to do? Well, there it is. If you want to know more, telephone Mme. Pieter for me, to ask her for news of her husband. Perhaps she will give you more news than I'll have at that moment.

---

[1] Sartre, pretending a more distant relationship with Beauvoir when confronted by the jealousy of the Kosakiewicz sisters, usually addressed letters to Beauvoir at one of the lycées where she taught, fearing the sisters might spot his letters to her at the hotel desk.

Aside from that, nothing, my little one. T.'s moving out, and from then on I'll address my letters to the Hôtel du Danemark (after confirmation from her, however). Here I diligently wrote about Guillaume II. But that's not a subject for you, little devil! No, of course not, but one must write about everything. And I've almost completed the chapter on Jacques.[1] But perhaps I'll redo the whole thing. Besides that I sawed and chopped some wood, because I'm the one who lights the fire tomorrow. The last time it was disastrous, the clerks had to rekindle it after I was done. I'll make sure I do it right this time.

This is a poor little letter, my love, but that's because I have nothing to say. And I've written so many and such long ones that you can well forgive me this one.

My love, it's so good to be with you, I'd so love to squeeze your little arm. I love you as much as I possibly can.

๛ *to Simone de Beauvoir*

March 9

My lovely Beaver

Herewith a very newsy letter, though I feel so tenderly toward you, but today has been very eventful, and we must discuss it.

First, *I've been recalled to the rear*. Not today or tomorrow, but within a month or two at most. Here's the story: Captain Munier had written to the colonel in charge of Meteorology asking if he couldn't recall our arms, given that we weren't using them and were auxiliaries. The colonel's reply arrived today: "Impossible to recall arms but am recalling men." The readings posts, as the meteorological positions closest to the front, must be occupied by soldiers on active service, not auxiliaries, and he's going to take the measures necessary for us to be recalled as soon as possible. Captain Munier was wringing his hands and wanted to make us sign a protest, but Paul, who values his hide, was unshakable. So we are to leave the division. For the moment there's a possibility they'll withdraw us just fifty kilometers from here. But first, that would already be much better. And then, there's almost no chance of it. It's likely that I'll do a six-week hitch at Saint-Cyr, something like one 24-hour leave per week and two overnight leaves. You can imagine our delight. My sweet, we'll never again be separated for such a long time.

[1] In *The Age of Reason*, brother of Mathieu, the protagonist.

That brings me to the leave. At the earliest (thanks to Pieter's providential delay—he arrived this morning fresh as a daisy) I'll be in Paris on March 26th. But I think it's best to hurry up and take the leave because, with this change of assignment, it'll be that much under the belt. If I return to Saint-Cyr right after, so much the better. So you'll have to negotiate a loan of a thousand francs *right away*, from Gégé,[1] say (or the Lady).

I received a letter from the chairman of the jury for the Prix du Roman Populiste (members: Duhamel, Romains, Durtain, Thérive, etc.)[2] informing me that I'm a candidate for the aforesaid prize and asking me to write a letter stating my candidacy. The prize is 2,000 francs, which is not to be sneezed at. *However*, if I write a letter of candidacy, I'll be labeled a populist. Or will I? Please advise immediately. My first impulse was to refuse, but perhaps you'll feel that this business of labels is a complete sham and that, ultimately, 2,000 francs is most palpable. We have others to think of. You decide, my little conscience.

Paulhan writes that Wahl and Brunschvicg[3] decided to take *L'imaginaire* as a doctoral *thesis*. They'll publish the thesis, deleting the first part (which already appeared in *La Revue du Méta*). I'm agreeing, provided there's no secondary thesis to write. Does that seem right?

Also received a letter from Monnier,[4] who says that my signature has changed, that it's become "aerial." A letter from T., asking me for cash. You were to send me 200 francs. *Would you give it to her when you have it (as soon as possible)*, I'll work out something with Pieter.

Whew! When I add that I also received the *NRF* with my article on Giraudoux[5] (and that Pieter, whom we'd thought dead, got in this morning) you can see how emotionally fertile this day really was.

And in other respects empty. That's certainly the paradoxical side of it. For outside of that, *nothing*, as Heidegger says. Yes there was something: the actors of the Théâtre aux Armées were rehearsing behind the screen and snatches of music reached me. It was poetic and moving.

My love, how happy I am this evening. In two weeks I'll be seeing you again, and perhaps after that we will hardly be apart again—at least for a long while.

I love you so much, my sweet, so much.

---

[1] Geraldine Pardo, an old friend of Sartre and Beauvoir.

[2] Georges Duhamel (1884–1966), novelist; André Thérive had given a bad review to *The Wall*.

[3] Jean Wahl, a Sorbonne professor very impressed by Sartre's upcoming publication *L'Imaginaire*, had suggested he submit it as a thesis, which would qualify him for teaching there. Léon Brunschvicg (1869–1944), dominant figure in French philosophy between the wars.

[4] *Adrienne Monnier, who directed the bookshop called L'Ami des livres, used by many writers at that time. (SdB)*

[5] *Reproduced in* Situations I. *(SdB)*

*   *   *

1) If you write to the Lady for the money, do it immediately and tell her we'll reimburse her on the 1st.

2) I'm writing to T. that she can count on 200. But if there are difficulties, write to me about it and I'll tell her it's not possible.

3) You haven't said whether Bonafé has been called up.

✑ *to Simone de Beauvoir*

March 10

My darling Beaver

I got all of two letters from you today and the most recent was dated yesterday— which means that you must have mailed it yesterday morning at 7 o'clock on your way to the lycée. It's very good to have such fresh news. They were two extremely brief little notes, but the two together made for one big one. I whole-heartedly approve your idea of putting the touch on Toulouse[1] (1,200 francs). It will be for only ten days, after all, which shouldn't be impossible. Otherwise, the Lady. Paulhan is an odd bird. According to your letter of the 8th, *L'Imaginaire* is already out. Splendid, but his letter was mailed *in Paris* on the 7th and consequently he had to know that the book was on sale at the very moment he was proposing a delay in publication. I don't give a damn, but I must admit he's an odd sort. And why didn't he tell me about it a month and half ago when Wahl was sounding you out on the subject? If Wahl didn't do it himself, that must mean Paulhan had taken it in hand himself. I suppose this Machiavelli, for whatever unknown reasons, didn't want anything to do with that scheme. I tell you this to sketch in the character because, so far as I'm concerned, it leaves me cold particularly since I could still offer something on Nothingness or any-thing else if the spirit moved me. About the Populist Prize, I'm still hesitant. I saw that Troyat[2] had won it, and there's nothing particularly populist about Troyat. I await your decision. However, I've got to get it—the prize—if I put myself forward for it. I can't be the eternal candidate for prizes that flit past me one after the other, it finally gets to be grotesque.

Aside from that, my sweet, after so many jolts yesterday, nothing new today,

---

[1] Nickname for Simone Jollivet, a friend of the couple and Sartre's first love. Originally from Toulouse, she moved to Paris and worked in the theater as an actress with her lover, Charles Dullin.

[2] Henri Troyat (b. 1911), Russian-born French novelist and biographer.

which is to be expected. I worked at the Center all morning on that thing about Guillaume II, which was becoming a pain in the neck. I finished it and will get on to other things. I read *Guillaume II*, conversed with Pieter and, I don't know why (ah yes, because Pieter had stuffed me with cake), I didn't go off for lunch. I worked till two o'clock at the Center, where he came to join me, pleased as Punch, because, seated at lunch, he had threatened a lance corporal that he'd smash his nose and kick his ass. The guy, behaving like so many around here, had raged that he'd been refused two reserved places by the proprietress, "Alsatian pigs, Prussians every damn one of them, and to think we're fighting for them." A strange remark since, actually, in the first place, we've wanted to have Alsace badly enough, so what's there to complain about? And in the second place, we're not fighting for *them*. After expanding on this theme, which made Pieter boil with indignation, he added following his own logic, "For them and for the Jews." Upon which Pieter, happy to have at last a pretext to butt in, "Well, here's a Jew for you, what d'you want from him? A punch in the nose, etc. etc.?" The other shut up. I for one duly congratulated Pieter, then we were kicked out, and I went to read in the café. Because on Sundays the cafés are open, but we're forced out of the Center because of the army movies. At five-thirty, there were so many people in the café that I went back to the Center, but there they were announcing another showing of the film. Exhausted, I sat glued to my seat and saw a charming little Harry Langdon, silent and without titles, and half of *Un'oiseau rare* [A Rare Bird] with Max Dearly and Brasseur, text by Prévert.[3] It held together more or less, on the dreary side—but for a wartime production it was about as good as any. It was preceded by documentary on the front lines, clearly intended—judging by the commentary—for the home front and winding up here by chance. It struck me as odd to hear them talk about "our valiant soldiers" in front of all those guys, the majority of whom had spent two or three months on the front. But they didn't flinch, they ignored the text and concentrated on the details of daily life; for instance, when they saw ten guys pushing a car that had skidded off the road, they hollered, "Heave-ho, Heave-ho!" and laughed in sympathy.

All in all a very good day. Besides which Hang left last night, and in two weeks it's my turn. I so long to see you, my sweet.

My sweet, my dear little one, I love you so. In two weeks—18 days at the most, I'll be holding you in my arms.

---

[3] Pierre Brasseur (1903–72) acted in over eighty films, often in collaboration with poet and screenwriter Jacques Prévert (1900–77).

⚜ *to Simone de Beauvoir*

March 11

My darling Beaver

Why shouldn't I show off my talents to you too? I've already typed a letter to my stepfather; one to Tania; if till now I shrank from doing it for you, that was because I was afraid the typed words might seem too cold to you. Besides, up to now, as I typed, I couldn't really concentrate; I wrote laboriously and poorly because all my energy went into finding the letters at the tips of my fingers: in that respect the letter to Tania was a model of infantilism, and I felt obliged to add a handwritten postscript so that she wouldn't think I'd totally reverted to infancy. But now it's going better, and my mind is freed, as you explain each year to your students—chapter on habit—and I long somewhat for admiration. I promise you I won't do it again except on your express request: I very well know that one loves to see the wretched scrawls of one's beloved and I too prefer your abominable gnarled letters to printed characters.

I got nary a letter today; insofar as you're concerned that was only just, since I received two yesterday. But it still made the afternoon longer, till I discovered a little idea on play and the spirit of seriousness. Then I wrote in my notebook for almost two hours and with a pleasure that I hadn't experienced since January. After that, Pieter came in, still full of stories, and Hantziger, who had talked with a disgraceful, hilarious naiveté about the reconciliation he'd worked out with his wife during his leave. Actually it was the same old story: when a person has a completed residence, it's a pain to put together another at the age of thirty-seven; so, for instance, he had a fine piano at his wife's place and who knows whether he could find another as good; besides, his wife earns her own living and isn't a spendthrift, and when a person is at the front it's nice, after all, to get a little package from time to time, and a little money order, too. As a matter of fact, he did come back from his leave in the chips; his wife had given him a thousand francs and he immediately bought some handsome clothes, which made good Pieter quite indignant. So you see, it's the usual, but it's entertaining to get him talking, it was all in the edifying tone of the Master who has just rendered unto morality what is morality's, and is assuaging his soul with a good deed. Furthermore it seems that the clerks gave him lively encouragement: every evening Nippert, the Jehovah's Witness, read him long extracts from the Bible dealing with conjugal fidelity. He returned very proud and told them: "Well boys, I have a pleasant surprise for you: I'm back together with my wife." And the others gave a lunch in his honor.

After that, Ping-Pong with the old redhead, whom I beat this time. And here I am. This morning I had put the finishing touches on my Jacques-Mathieu chapter, which I'll type up after this letter. I think it'll be more entertaining to read than it was entertaining to write. And that's all, my little one, absolutely all. It seemed a bit on the long side, but as though on purpose now that I could go to bed, I've been seized by an intense desire to type, and I'll be staying up till at least eleven.

My little sweet, I'm going to send you some books: *Le Siège de Paris*, *Bismarck*, and *Guillaume*. Before the end of the week, so you'll have them Saturday.

Till tomorrow, my little sweet; you cannot know how much I'm longing to see you again: nothing else matters to me. We'll certainly go for walks all over the place; I love you, my little flower, and long to kiss your little old cheeks.

You entertained me with that story about the Boxer. My darling, what a lot we'll have to tell each other.

I'm adding by hand that I love you with all my might so you'll have a word or two of my handwriting nonetheless. The letter has taken me three-quarters of an hour to tap out (composing as I go).

◈ to Simone de Beauvoir

March 12

My darling Beaver

This is the last time, I promise you, that I'll send you a typed letter. But keep in mind that I have nothing left to type, having finished copying my Chapter VIII today. And I can't stop doing it; remember my manic passion for the yo-yo? It's the same sort of thing. At the time you were frightened by it and irritated; right now you would be frightened and perhaps even irritated. They're incredible, these passions that possess me sometimes; do you remember the evening last year when we went chasing after an issue of *Verve*? I'll have to figure it out in my little notebook. Incidentally I am making progess.

Today there were two letters from you; you tell me that I won't have any tomorrow, but since I had none yesterday I sincerely hope I won't be without mail. There was a very long and entertaining one. I'm very put out by the scorn Sorokine has for me.

On the subject of money I'm somewhat embarrassed, like you; it must be too late to approach the Lady. Listen, do what you can for yourself and the Z's and if you can't find anything for the two of us, I'll try to put the touch on Pieter; though that presents some difficulties, due to the fact that we'll doubtless not be ordered back to Saint-Cyr at the same time and he might worry that his money could fall between the cracks; but it can be done.

Would you believe that we've just suddenly learned we'll be leaving within four or five days (I mean the whole division)? And where to? We're going back to our November billeting.[1] I'm delighted to be heading back to that spot. I have such poetic memories of it: breakfasts at La Rose; the Taverne du Boeuf Noir; you, my love; and that bizarre crisis from which, basically, my theory of authentiticy evolved. It's also linked to reading some powerful things: Shakespeare, Saint-Exupéry, *Spanish Testament*.[2] In fact, I'll hardly be there for more than a week, since Hang gets back on the 25th and after that I leave. When I return from leave I'll probably be called back from the front; I'm through with this division to which my destiny has been so linked thus far, I already feel it loosening its grip on me; around here they're talking about its immediate and distant future, as always, and that leaves me cold. Did I tell you that we'll probably have six weeks of instruction at Saint-Cyr, because meteorology has made so much progress since my time,[3] and that will be paradise, with who knows how many overnight leaves and even more, due to clever stratagems—in short, it will be like blessed peacetime.

The day passed, none too quickly, none too slowly: during the morning the Center was occupied by an officers' conference, so I came here and typed my novel; then I dragged a reluctant Paul to a new restaurant, which he harshly criticized, simply because it was new, and where in fact the food isn't any better than in the other, but it's quite charming, with wood paneling throughout, as in the lands of the North, and which ultimately looks like an Alsatian tavern; if I had known that earlier, it would have spared me those refined impressions of the Jesuit XVIIIth century that made young Bist laugh so. I'll go back there from now on.

It was Ping-Pong this afternoon, still with the redhead: for a moment I demolish her; then I wrote in the notebook about history; everything in the notebook goes by problem; for a week now it has been history, and refutation of Aron, of course. I also read a play by Léo Ferrero, which the Pitoëffs put on, *Angélica*, it's very bad, but for a brief moment it made me want to write a play; basically I'm itching to learn my limits—which involve drama and poetry. For poetry, I've lost all hope, but for theater I still have some. And that's were I am.

The things you tell me about T. explain her sudden silence, after extremely friendly letters, but in which I could detect the coming despair; as a matter of

[1] Brumath.

[2] By Arthur Koestler.

[3] Sartre had begun his eighteen months of required army service in November 1929 as a meteorologist at Saint-Cyr.

fact I had learned in one of her letters that the Moon Woman had fallen from grace; it seems that Poupette had explained to T. that the Moon Woman considered her a bit like a serpent she had warmed at her breast; beneath it all there must be some little story of "social" rivalry or a smile Dominguez flashed at T., which caused some comment, but it's just like the Z. sisters to go and move in with some woman when they were on poor terms with her. Because of their hatred for the Moon Woman, I'm forced to address letters to Olga's hotel.

Till tomorrow, my sweet; I've got to go to bed; for tomorrow I'm the one to light the fire: I haven't told you that after failing lamentably the first time, I triumphantly succeeded the second. This is the third time around, and the winner.

Adieu, kisses for your dear little eyes, my love; I love you.

I'll send the books tomorrow; but you really must send me a second package too, my little one.

⊶ to Simone de Beauvoir

March 13

My darling Beaver

Whew! I've just written *19 letters,* all along the same lines. I have one left over, which I'm sending you, to satisfy your curiosity. It was to the jury of the Prix Populiste. Armed with your authorization, I set to work immediately; I know of no more thankless task, in itself worth the two thousand. It was two o'clock when I began, and here it is a quarter past four. I'm writing to you to refresh myself.

About the cash, I'm a little unsure of Stepha.[1] Will she send it? And *in time?* Implore her to mail it punctually on the 20th. Or else, she should take a taxi at my expense and *go to leave it in an envelope with my parents' concierge,* which might very well be the best way, because it would allow her to dawdle for a day or two before deciding to do it. Meanwhile, I'll borrow 300 from Pieter; with the 125 they allocate me here, that'll "keep me afloat."

So right away today I wrote a very cool letter to T. (she's still not writing to me and must be in the depths of prostration) in which I tell her that very probably I'll be at the Dôme on the 26th at 7 o'clock.

---

[1] Ukrainian-born friend of the couple, wife of the painter Fernando Gérassi.

As for Saint-Cyr, you anxious little creature, don't worry. Just remember that I'll be seeing you two times for Tania's every one, and that of the 2 times, there will be *one* that's official, the other on the sly. This goes for the leaves and excursions around Paris. But daily, I mean every day at five o'clock and until eight—for I dearly hope to see you every day, that won't be so difficult. Or will it?

My little one, how I long to see your good face and to kiss you.

For today, nothing to report, as they say in the communiqués. This morning I read and this afternoon I did 20 letters and now I'm writing to you. That's all, my sweet. I haven't much to do but read because I finished my chapter and have almost run out of ideas for my notebook. I'm in a calm and pleasant mood, more comatose than sensitive, I'm waiting.

I love you with all my might.

⧉ *to Simone de Beauvoir*

Thursday, March 14

My darling Beaver

We're leaving tomorrow at three, I think I told you.

We hope to retake our little November habitat, but we're not sure. It is vacant but "requisitioned" and it's not certain we can stay there except with a billeting voucher. Otherwise, I'll simply take a room at the Boeuf Noir. That would perhaps be even more agreeable. Anyway, it wouldn't be for more than a week or ten days, since I'll be going off on leave then. And I surely won't find them there on my return, they'll be "in division sector."

Then, of all things, yesterday after I'd written 17 letters and yours, what did I see but the Salvation Army broad working her way into the room: "Among those of you who haven't just had shots, are there a few who would like to help unload some beer cases?" Dead silence, each counting on the other. I felt a solidarity with all the soldiers, and a vague shame, which must account for a lot of "voluntary heroism" at the front. It's ridiculous, and I was punished for it. I got up and went to give a helping hand, which meant carrying down cases of empties and bringing up cases of full bottles. It went all right till the last case, but this last (which was full and which I was carrying up) the truck driver wanted me to put on my shoulder, I obeyed and, on my way up the stairs, missed a step, and crash!, there were all the bottles on the ground and a sea of beer cascading down the steps. There were twenty bottles, and I broke eight of them, the others fell too but by the grace of God, didn't break. I had to undergo the condolences of a crush of people, the comforting words of the Salvationist, who gave me a great bowl of coffee "to get me back on my feet," and then I had to mop the stairs. I found myself quite pissed off at first by the shards: "silly meddler," as I said to that Greek on the *Cairo City*.[1]

This morning around seven-thirty, Lieutenant Ullrich was here, about to go off and assign lodgings in our new post, when a fat lady came in, tearful and self-important: "Monsieur, you must quickly alert the lodgers upstairs, there's been a serious accident." She repeated it twice, and as we were about to decide to do it, she added, "M. Jean Chiappe, the chief of police, is gravely wounded, he's in the basement." Upon which we understood and led her out with consoling words. She is totally off her rocker and wanders freely around our house. The other night she came in while Pieter was in the WC, opened the door, which he had neglected to lock, and held a long discourse without budging. Actually, we've been persecuted these past days by a mysterious vandal who smears the walls of the john with shit, and I strongly suspect it's she.

This afternoon, mail. Long letters from you. You know, I absolutely forbid Sorokine to bruit it about that I'm impotent—tell her that I'll play some abominable trick on her if she keeps it up, for instance I'll *speak to her* the first time I catch sight of her. On the other hand, I authorize her to label me a phony genius.[2]

I also received an enormous package: the 1st third of my typed manuscript, and spent the afternoon rereading it. I'm both pleased and disappointed: it's good *in detail*, it's even the best thing I've written, but what Lévy said earlier is somewhat true, that the chapters aren't linked, it fades off into the fog somewhat, and the subject isn't clearly presented. I'll have to go back over all that and give a clear framework to the early chapters. In particular I'll have to return to one old detail: Mathieu looking back; otherwise that character has neither consistency nor unity. The reader must know where he comes from, where he taught, how he knew Boris and Ivich, etc. All of that can be brief, but one must know it *right away*; in a general sense, it lacks roots, whereas all of your characters are so deeply rooted. It doesn't have to be heavy labor, but it's delicate.

Still no letter from T. On Friday or Saturday I got the last, she never goes this long without writing. Is she prostrate with despair, or what? Do you know? For the moment it actually leaves me rather unmoved.

And there you have it, little one. Everything has the smell of departure here, for even with soldiers a departure is a departure. Specifically, I'm like a bird on

---

[1] *The ship we had taken to Athens. (SdB.)*
[2] *Sorokine would say, drolly, "Your Sartre, who takes himself for a phony genius." (SdB)*

the branch; already I'm no longer in Bouxwiller, but in other ways I no longer feel linked to this division, since I'm going to be recalled, and after all, my leave draws me out of the war and toward yourself and Paris. In short, a wandering soul. I'm playing Ping-Pong, that's what I'm doing. Starting the day after tomorrow, I'll get down to patching up the novel. I'm not yet about to touch Marcelle,[3] but I'll try, as I was saying, to *situate* my chapters.

Till tomorrow, my little one, just reflect that when you get this letter we'll be *one week* away from seeing one another.

Kisses for your beautiful little old cheeks.

❧ *to Simone de Beauvoir*

March 15

My darling Beaver

So here I am back where I was four months ago. We bundled and tied all morning with brief respite at the Center, and then after lunch in overcoats, loaded down with satchels, gas mask and helmet, we turned up at the main square, near the secondary school where my grandfather used to go but since then replaced by a heavy German building in white stone and the local red sandstone. We watched the trucks going off and the students going into the school—it's coeducational: pretty boys and chunky girls—and time passed. We saw the students leave school, and finally around three-forty, two buses showed up into which we piled. The trip was as short as the wait was long. Yet I had time to plot out a prologue to *The Age of Reason*, it's the best way to introduce the characters; it will be June 10, 1928 (just 10 years before the story), there'll be three chapters: 1st Ivich: we'll see Ivich and the nuptial bed. We'll learn that she's an émigrée, we'll see Boris. We'll see the mother. We'll hear talk of the father. It will be the story of the bed where she slept with her mother.—2nd Mathieu: he'll be in the midst of taking the *agrégation*, we'll see him young and appealing, with Brunet and Daniel—he'll explain that he wants to be free, it'll seem pretty good to see him again 10 years later, and it'll facilitate not having to present *simultaneously* the fact that he wants to be free and that he is not so anymore, which would be an error in technique.—3rd Marcelle: some story about Marcelle's youth that will make her attractive. You'll certainly get a better

---

[3] One of the major characters in *The Age of Reason*.

sense later of their growing older and of the age of reason. I'm delighted with the plan. What do you think of it? I'm not entirely sure I've made a strong enough case for it, but I assure you it seems brilliantly obvious that it has all the advantages: it will give roots to my characters, and that will allow me to lighten the text thereafter. I'll start in on it tomorrow.

No sooner arrived, than we had to undo the luggage we'd done up and unpack the packages. We're still at the school, but on the second floor, in a vast and beautifully bare room—for our predecessors had unbolted the seats and heaped them one on top of the other at the back of the room. It doesn't look much like anything anymore. One blackboard, one crucifix, one map of France, one map of Alsace, a chart of the metric system and, aside from that, our folding tables (Vézelise beer), our typewriters, our helmets, and a huge empty space in the middle of the room. That's where I'l be living till my leave. It's even where I'll sleep—since Pieter has gone off to look for rooms and we can't have the same ones back, he found a cramped alcove in the house of some wary old people and one bedroom in another house already sheltering the chaplain. In each of them you have to be in by 9 o'clock at night, which kills it for me; I preferred to volunteer for guard duty, as I've been doing these past few days; I have a tiny bed in the room, four plants and straw, I find it not bad at all.

With all of that taken care of, I went to get the mail. There was one letter from a Spaniard named Ferrer who wants me to send him *L'Imaginaire* gratis, so he can demonstrate just as he pleases that Lautréamont was joyfully moving about at the core of Nothingness. And one letter from you.

T. hasn't given me any sign of life for *eight days*. Can you fill me in? Is there some new hitch? Or is she simply having a sinking spell? You know, today I had an imaginary but strong fear she might be pregnant. That would be just lovely. Well, even if it should turn out to be that, I'd arrive in time to make her admit it.

After the mail, I dragged around a bit, and then went out for dinner at the Lion d'Or, to get reacquainted. It was full of officers, but pleasant nonetheless. And I ate better than I have in four months (my leave aside) and I treated myself to a little glass of kirsch as I finished *Guillaume II*, which I'll send you tomorrow along with other books. But I have nothing left to read, you know, bad little creature. What will I do? You promised me more books, and nothing has come. Perhaps I'll find one or two little things around here, and anyway I won't be here for long.

There you have it, my sweet. I'm rather tired because I've been dealing with packages all day, and I'll sleep like a log, if only the pigs who sleep next door cut out the racket they've been making for an hour. And, tomorrow, I'll set to work on the Nuptial Bed, melted down and recast.

I love you so much, my little one, I too have a terrible need to see you right now, a real need that's not a whole lot of fun to endure, I'd like to have your little head against mine, my little flower.

✇ *to Simone de Beauvoir*

March 16

My darling Beaver

No letter from you today.

Today I went to La Rose for breakfast. Of all things, the pretty little redhead is using makeup, wears suggestive skirts and has turned slightly whorish. The fat brunette, on the other hand, got married. According to Naudin, who'd received her favors, "Plenty there for the cuckolds." After which I came back to work here, and bravely began the prologue. The more I work on it, the more I feel the need for it. But it takes courage to rewrite fifty pages of a novel I had considered finished. It will move right along, actually, and now that I'm into it, I'm enjoying myself. This evening I typed two pages of it.

At noon I lunched at l'Écrevisse and, during the afternoon, from lack of things to do (I have nothing left to read and have sent you, general delivery, the *Guillaume II*, *La Siège de Paris*, *La Commune*, and *Bismarck*, it makes a very entertaining little whole), I volunteered to get some coal by truck in the city we left yesterday. On the way over, it wasn't so bad, I was in the back with a Parisian from the Rue Lepic nicknamed—not unreasonably—Nimbus. We were feeling the wind like knives and being jostled about more than reasonably, but it was rather pleasant. Except that on the return, the speed kicked up cyclones of coal dust and turned us, Nimbus and me, into bona fide Negroes, which made us laugh. Between times I paid individual adieux to the Ladies of the Center, whom I'd had forgotten to thank the day before. I got back at five, washed up thoroughly, worked a bit, went out with the Acolytes for a café kirsch at 7 o'clock and— back about 8:30—since then I've worked. It's eleven and I'm writing to you.

Kisses to you, my little one, my love, for your eyes, for your cheeks.

✑ to Simone de Beauvoir

March 17

My darling Beaver

I'm typing my letter to you once more since you like that; and yet I swear I've been typing today, but I want to have you benefit from a few little refinements I've recently learned: for instance I now know how to put the circumflex and the *accent grave* on the u: just look: ùùù, ô, ô, ô. Whereas, there'll be no exclamation points in this letter, because I'm writing on a new machine which doesn't include them. My parents have sent an entire letter of praise on my typing artistry; and naturally, as Poupette had written to me and I had to thank her for having typed my novel, I seized the opportunity and with the gracious banter of fellowship, I sent her six typed pages. I find it astonishing, by the way, that she considers my novel gloomy; what do you think, you who were telling me that readers would probably be disappointed by its mildness?

So, today was Sunday. There were Masses and weddings all over the place. I for one wanted to have at least the body, if not the soul, clean on this day of cleansing, and I went for a bath, something I hadn't been able to do since my leave, not from lack of will but because where I was there were no baths. Then around nine o'clock I came back to the school, where I worked till noon. At the moment I'm doing a childhood for Ivich, which I'm finding very interesting; needless to say I'm putting in everything Z. recounted in Rouen; the further I go, the more I believe that it will give roots to my characters. For instance, Ivich's exam, her horror of amorous relationships, will take on force if the reader knows her parents; particularly the story of the nuptial bed, which in novelistic terms will seem the cause of her attitude toward things sexual. In the same way, the reader will see Mathieu very young and sure of himself, he'll have just dumped one young woman because he was afraid she had designs on his freedom; he would scoff at his brother because he has an apartment, etc., and one will also see Daniel as a young man with the reputation of being a virgin, and M.'s friendship with Brunet will be more moving later if one has seen them together earlier in sunnier times. Obviously it obliges me to give up my opening, which I liked very much, but it will still be the opening of the first part, there will simply be a prologue preceding it.

At noon, I went for the mail, I was very impatient to know what had become of yourself. Last night I saw the people at HQ, and I very specifically told them they had to have me leave on the 24th, on Hang's return; they seemed willing. So Paul left this afternoon, overjoyed because it coincided with his wife's holidays. Before that, we celebrated his departure at l'Écrevisse, with fine food and a bottle of sylvaner. This afternoon I read a bit in a detective novel bought here, very bad (an old Masque) and got back to work. I'm beginning to type as I correct, I mean that the third and the fourth version are typed. It's more entertaining.

As for money, don't worry, my sweet, you have done everything perfectly. Listen, Paul loaned me 300 francs before going off on leave; Pieter will do something too, so I'll arrive in Paris with 4 or 500 francs. Once there, I'll put the touch on Gérassi or Gégé, and besides, my good mother would help me if need be; the essential part was to have enough to "get by."

So, T. wrote to me, in very friendly and very pitiful tones; if she hadn't written, it was from pure depression. I have one less weight on my heart. It wasn't emotionally that I was put out, but for no known reason I had lodged in my head the anxiety I mentioned to you; and I have to say that she wouldn't have been any different if that had been the case: silent, perturbed, and doing nothing to get out of it. You know, in my family we get strange ideas when apart; my mother never fails to.

How I long to see you. Do you remember those vows we made in Marrakech as we wove palm fronds? I thought about it again today, and it made me feel very affectionate. I love you, my little one.

This is less well typed than the last time, but the fault lies with the machine.

ᏻᎦ *to Simone de Beauvoir*

March 18

My darling Beaver

No letters today. It annoys me, because I know nothing about you, with all these uncertainties. I'd so like for this holiday to be pleasant for you.[1] But aside from that, I'm in a good mood. My last village vacation was sobering: nothing but the Center, the Center, in the end I was bored sick with it. The cafés weren't appealing. Here it's so charming. I took up my old habits, I go to La Rose for breakfast, to L'Écrevisse for lunch, I see the same people again. But it seems weighed down with memories, my God but it's weighed down with memories. Just to think that I already have "wartime memories." Well, as you know, they're strong and pleasant, I have no regrets about what I've experienced, it's one of the fullest periods of my life. I'd almost say, like the Boxer, who wrote to me

[1] On March 17 Beauvoir left Paris planning to spend ten days with Bost at Charmont.

today, that we had to have it. He speaks of you as an "exquisite friend" and never tires of praising you, but also accuses you rather craftily of having talked rubbish about politics. You could say as much, I believe, about him. He's a good fellow, and I'm going to write to him.

Aside from that, I work a lot. I'm not keeping up at all with the little notebook. I'm working on the novel and that last chapter on Ivich (prologue) entertains me enormously. I'd really like it to be finished or at least well along so I can show it to you. It's in the general genre of atrocities veiled by the charm of childhood. I do a draft by hand, I correct it, I type it, I correct the typed draft in pen, and I type that corrected draft. That seems to make the faults stand out and, at the same time, it varies the exercise somewhat. You know, after the war I'll buy a typewriter and type my own works, like Nizan. Betweentimes I play a few games of chess with Hantziger, whom I beat regularly, and I listen to Pieter's whining, he's extremely disturbed because the big showcase window of his store got smashed.

My little one, my sweet, how I'm yearning to see you soon; I love you, you know! I long to take your little arm and have us go for a stroll, I so long to spend real days of life with you from morning to night. I love you. Why did I go and tell my parents I'm coming? Because of my poor mother, who is touching and who is really deprived by my absence. I didn't realize then that I'd be going back to Saint-Cyr, or I wouldn't have done it.

Good-bye my little one. Kisses for your little old cheeks.

❧ *to Simone de Beauvoir*

March 19

My darling Beaver

It's ten o'clock, I'm alone in the classroom with Grener, who's bone tired and snoring loud enough to shatter the windows, stretched out on a cushion from a railway carriage seat. Whence the cushion?—a mystery. I got the books safely. I'm delighted to be rereading the Jules Renard, but the man's appalling. I'm going to write a bit about it in the notebook. But I'm neglecting the notebook these days, I'm so intent on doing Ivich's childhood, and it's not going badly. I think it will seem romantic to meet her again at 20. All day long I've done nothing but type, type and write and I also took a short break at lunch to read Renard's *Journal*, I've already read a hundred pages. It's tiring because of the conceits, which consist solely of taking the opposite of a currently-held formula.

He very seriously calls this "having ideas." How appalling that crowd of authors was in those days. I constantly remember, as I read it, that Piètre Bost[1] wrote something like, "The very human *Journal* of the great Renard."

And that's all there is from me. I got a third letter from T., slightly stiff, because I'd bawled her out, but flourishing. And I'm searching in vain for something more to tell you, other than that I love you so much, my little sweet, and that I'm happy, so happy to be seeing you again.

Till tomorrow. I love you with all my might.

✦ *to Simone de Beauvoir*

March 20

My darling Beaver

I'm the one who goes to fetch the mail in the morning. And this morning it wasn't yet sorted. First they gave me a letter from you.

And what can I say about myself? Nothing new, my little one. I'm doing a whole lot of work. I would so like to show you a whole chapter of the prologue (Ivich) so you could see it in perspective. I get up at seven o'clock, I take the tricycle, as in the balmy days of November, I dash over to La Rose, where I read Renard's *Journal*, and I think about it. Dense. I come back to the school and there, from 9 to noon, I pound it out on the typewriter. I've totally redone the opening of the prologue and I think it will go well. I've put lots of determination into it, but will that show? And there you are, working with determination now? Oh yes, my little one, it's a sign of age. Afterward, I'm going to lunch at l'Écrevisse with Pieter. There, you should know that we told Sophie, the waitress, that we didn't want her to serve us anymore, that we'd prefer to deal only with Maryse, who's an unwed mother and charming. And Maryse was ecstatic, because it would show a thing or two to Sophie, who is only 18 and calls her an imbecile, though Maryse is 22 and has a 16-month-old child. Sophie is a bitch. Incidentally Pieter said, "It seems that Maryse was booted out by her parents because she got knocked up." But I scolded him, and we're most fond of Maryse, who returns the favor. So much for l'Écrevisse. At 1:30 we go back, I read a bit of Renard, I write on him, then I type till seven o'clock. At seven my head's on fire, not because of ideas but because of the typewriter keys, the eyes have to chase after the fingers, it's enough to split my head wide open. So,

[1] *Pierre Bost, Jacques Laurent-Bost's eldest brother. (SdB)* "Piètre" means paltry, wretched.

I accompany Pieter to l'Écrevisse, where he has a substantial meal and I a light one. This evening there were some infantrymen—they don't hold a candle to the light-infantry men. One of them was rolling drunk and hollering, "There's only one Frenchman here, it's me. Vive the French army and French Alsace." Then we went home, and I wrote on Renard till 11 o'clock, talked about politics with Captain Munier, wrote again, and I'm writing to you; it's midnight, I won't write to T. tonight. Perhaps tomorrow morning.

I don't know anything more about my leave. But it won't be long now.

Till tomorrow, my little sweet, you write me little jewels of letters, and I love you with all my might.

ᓀ *to Simone de Beauvoir*

March 22

My darling Beaver

First, here are four little photos. Captain Munier took them in January, they're rather funny. This is where I look like a Jew, according to Pieter, who knows about these things.

Next, I must tell you of my anxiety: it's two days now that I haven't had a letter from you. It certainly must be the mails from your wretched *bled* which works in fits and starts. Perhaps you'll hold it against me that I use the word "bled," which for you must join *toubib*[1] as the worst neocolonial slur. I excuse myself on the grounds that it's freely used here and has a very precise function: for instance, the place where we are isn't a *bled* because there are cafés, razor blades, and darning needles. But the artillery guys of X battery, 10 km from here complain of being in a *bled* because they're deprived of these things. All of which means that the mail is badly handled at your place, little one. To the point that this morning, with T. grumpy at me because I'd bawled her out for her eight days of silence, *precisely*—you'll note the lack of tact—at the moment she so longs to have me right there with her, I found myself a complete idiot because it was I who'd been to get the mail, who'd brought back buckets of it for the others, and there was nothing for me. But at this point it doesn't matter a whole lot to me, because *the day after tomorrow* under the most favorable circumstances—and in three or four days if things work against me—I'll be going off on leave.

---

[1] Slang for "doctor," from Arabic. *Bled* is Arabic for empty countryside.

My life remains empty and diligent; today I went on with my reading of J. Renard, whom I hate, and I worked hard on Ivich, I think I'll show you the chapter finished or very nearly so. I lunched at l'Écrevisse and went back to work for the whole afternoon. I'm going to write to my parents too and, in about an hour, I'll be in bed. You wouldn't believe how the time, which stagnated in my next-to-last billeting, rips by here, one would think it's a property of the air here. I'm hardly up when the day is done.

At the moment Grener, who is waiting for the officers to leave the next room, is snoring away on a bench (he's the one who accused me of whistling in my sleep). He's a beast who belches, farts, spits in constant floods; he's a smelter from near Strasbourg and dazed with beer. When he comes back from leave, he rubs his stomach and says, "I jumped the old lady" (which means: "I slept with my wife") and he tells how he went about it. And yet I grovel for his good opinion, simply because he's a worker. I manage, actually, because you have only to buy him a drink for him to think well of you.

There you have it, my little one. I so hope to have at least two letters tomorrow. I love you. Before a week is up, I'll see you.

⊷ *to Simone de Beauvoir*

March 23

My darling Beaver

I got your letters of the 21st and 22nd together, fortunately, so that now I'm quite reassured. I'm back at my former billeting and feel well and rather poetic about it. The time is going by with a rapidity that frightens me, I get up and it's evening. It's that I'm working nonstop. Ten hours a day on a prologue to the novel. I see you already frowning. But this prologue is indispensable. Otherwise the characters lack roots. It will have 3 chapters: I: Ivich—II: Mathieu—III: Marcelle. It takes place 10 years earlier, in June 1928. I'm in the midst of finishing the first chapter, Ivich, which I'll bring you. This will allow me to trim Mathieu's interminable monologues. Don't gripe, I swear it's a good idea. Ivich is a whole little short story in itself and, for once, my little one, you'll read a factum of mine from beginning to end. These will be three snapshots of the characters ten years earlier, with their youth (or childhood) and their hopes. With all of this, I'm not keeping up with the little notebook. I received your books and am reading the Renard with interest and disgust. A studious life, devoid of all stories (mine—Renard's too, for that matter). Pieter will soon be ordered back to Saint-Cyr, that's the first step. I lunch at l'Écrevisse and have breakfast at La Rose, of course. But I'm grateful, I haven't yet set foot in the Boeuf Noir. Perhaps I'll go there on a pilgrimage.

Aside from that, what can I tell you, my little sweet? That from time to time I wish to see you and to live a less austere life? That goes without saying. Today I was at La Rose beside a soldier who had his woman with him. The guy had an honest, open face, the woman had the face of a sow and she lisped, just to seem carefree, with an Alsatian accent. No matter, it moved me anyway, because there was this guy seeing his woman again here. It brought back memories. I drank a second mug of Alsatian wine in their honor, which meant that on my return I whistled *Caravanne* and decided that the moon was beautiful indeed above the path. We are still in the school, but on the second floor. I volunteered to sleep there so as to have a bit of solitude, but I scarcely have any, because Grener, the snorer (who accused me of whistling in my sleep) sleeps there too. I stashed him in the room reserved for the officer, but that doesn't help—he stretches out on a bench at eight o'clock and snores straight through till eleven o'clock. At eleven the officers leave, I wake him up, and he trundles off bent beneath the weight of his mattresses (railway carriage cushions), and then I have five minutes of solitude, I'm wide awake and I hum as I unwrap my puttees, but since it's late, I go to bed. My letters also contained some of the saltier village gossip, but since I do hope after all that you'll get them someday, I'm not telling you a thing about them.

Earlier I wrote to Poupette. Tomorrow she's sending me the continuation and end of the novel. That's good. It will undoubtedly be finished in October and will come to *six hundred pages*, I've counted. I'm somewhat proud of the length because till now I was doing something more like brilliant trifles. I've always considered abundance a virtue. But what a lot of work there's still to be done to make the six hundred pages right. Did you get the letter in which I said that on rereading, the details satisfied me, but that I was beginning to share Lévy's view, finding the whole somewhat choppy? That's why I'm doing a prologue.

There you have it, my sweet. Add that I love you very much and that I think only of seeing you, of holding your dear little hand in mine, and that you are my darling Beaver, my love.

✑ *to Simone de Beauvoir*

March 24

My darling Beaver

No letter from you today. But that doesn't matter at all, I'm going to be seeing you very soon. To tell the truth, I'm not altogether sure when—give or take twenty-four hours—I'll surely be leaving after Hang's return, but perhaps not *immediately* after Hang's return, because there are delays with the return of some men. As I said, it's a matter of a day or two, and it scarcely worries me. I'm in an excellent mood and I'm working nonstop. I've written every bit of 17 pages in 6 days, which is a record for me, the old tortoise. Now what do you think of that, it's all on paper. I'll also bring you the 100 first pages of the novel, we'll talk about it together. There's some good stuff in it, but it doesn't hold together well enough.

Aside from work, nothing. I got a letter from Kanapa[1] of which I'll copy you a page (I had authorized him to use a chapter of *Psyche*[2]). "So as not to tire myself out, I read in class your typed text itself. After the class, M. Wahl came to ask me if I could lend him the statement. I loaned him the pages and only remembered later that these pages were numbered 46–47, etc. For myself that didn't bother me. But I knew that the ideas that Wahl would read were yours no longer, and he would have considered they still represented your current thought. So I immediately wrote to him, 'I want to alert you that these notes are from M. Sartre, and that he categorically disavows them.' "

Don't you feel he's really all facade, this guy? What's he bringing on himself with this story about thoughts disavowed or not by me? And what a weird idea to ask to give a lecture if it's simply to *read*, word for word, someone else's ideas. And why doesn't he see that I don't give a damn whether Wahl thinks that I still believe those theories now or not? Vacuous and self-important. It seems a bit sinister, in fact, because it's so flimsy. I'm convinced that his accident last year did him in. He wasn't like that two years ago. Ultimately that group of old school friends is holding on to something that's a facade. Strange folk. No other letter. Yes there is, one from Saillet, Monnier's protégé, to ask me for *L'Imaginaire*. Yesterday, one from Paulhan confirming that the book is out, the thesis affair dead, and that he, personally, is "very upset." I doubt it. He's going to send me Malraux's *Complete Works*, so I can do an article on him. I like the idea, sounds like fun.

---

[1] Jean Kanapa, former pupil of Sartre.
[2] *A psychological study that Sartre didn't want to publish, except for the chapter on "The theory of emotions."* (SdB)

I'm still eating at l'Écrevisse, I'm reading Renard. Of all things, I found here and bought the Goncourts' *Journal* of 1870–71, which will complete my reading on the Siege of Paris and the Commune;—and Renard's *L'Écornifleur* [*The Scrounge*], which I wanted to read at the same time as the *Journal*. I bought the whole lot. Also found, for one franc, Schlumberger's *Le Camarade infidèle* [*The Unfaithful Friend*], pages uncut. I read it yesterday. It made me laugh to discover that the long-eared homosexual whom I observed ducking away as I was introduced to him is a fan of Corneille. It's actually not absolutely bad—but not at all as good as I'd expected. Martin du Gard, Gide, Schlumberger, they emit a distinct feeling of period. And Renard, the elder Goncourt, etc., too. Just think, along with others, we too will represent a period. I can feel the dust accumulating already.

But the essential thing in my day, my little one, is my work. I work and type so much it splits my head open. Tonight, I was completely disgusted, out of fatigue, with what I had written since Saturday, but generally I'm rather pleased, and I feel a real craving before getting down to work.

And there you have it, my little flower. It's a very literary letter, but what else can I tell you? There's nothing military going on in my life.

I send you a big kiss, my dear little Beaver. If all goes well, when you get this letter I'll be four or five days away from you.

I love you.

❧ *to Simone de Beauvoir*

March 24

My darling Beaver

No letters from you today. Here's what Jules Renard has to say about Beavers: "The Beaver, which looks as though it is giving birth to a shoe sole." Which strikes me as somewhat obscure. Perhaps you can figure out what he means? Unless he could be referring to your lovely little shoe,[1] which I'll be delighted to read in a few days.

This morning I had a close call. Naudin came in to alert me that they wanted to have Hantziger leave before me, on Nippert's return, or the 27th. As for me,

---

[1] *A name we gave to our writings, an allusion to [James] Stephens'* The Crock of Gold, *in which the leprechauns make little shoes.* (SdB)

they simply figured they'd have me leave after Paul's return, who knows when? (Paul will get back on the 31st.) The most painful part is that Hantziger has every right to leave before me. Age, among other things. I also had as pretext if he were to leave before me that 1st there would be *one solitary* clerk for the Division HQ (with Nippert off). 2nd, I'd have to leave with Paul (we being last). And there would be only one member of the weather unit at Division HQ. But those arguments would be turned back on me, because I was not leaving after Hang, and Paul was gone: with Nippert back, there would be two clerks at Division HQ after Hantziger's departure—with Paul gone, if I left there would be only one weather reader at Division HQ for a few days. My chances didn't seem good. But I *wanted* to leave. At exactly 8:30 I tore over to HQ and said, "But it's my turn to go! And in fact Hantziger agrees." "Ah! if Hantziger agrees, you don't need to get all worked up, we don't boss people around unnecessarily, you can switch with him." I had only to get around Hantziger. Which I did, pretending I was furious, which saved me from having to explain: "Hantziger! you sneaked over to complain to HQ! A week ago I was the one who'd be leaving first, and now it's you they want to send. You're a bastard, you could have asked me, I'd have worked something out, etc." Hantziger, disconcerted: "But I didn't go to HQ. Of course you can go first." And I: "You give me your word you didn't go to HQ, and I can tell them you agree to leave after me?" "Of course." "Good. Then I'm going to telegraph home." Act three, the captain. I go to him to have him countersign a telegram to T.: "But Captain, Sir, it depends upon your approval of my departure date. HQ tells me the 27th. Do you have any problem with that?" "No. We'll try to replace you if need be, but don't say too much about it." Upon which return to HQ: "Hantziger agrees and the Captain is willing." I'll leave the 27th and be in Paris on Thursday the 28th.

I spent Easter Sunday working, and you'll see a finished "Ivich." I already have some ideas for the 2nd "Mathieu." But Marcelle remains very hazy. I lunched with Pieter at l'Écrevisse, and I dined alone at the Lion d'Or, reading the J. Renard. Paulhan sent me *La Condition humaine* [*Man's Fate*], *Le Temps du mépris* [*The Time of Contempt*], and *L'Espoir* [*Man's Hope*] so I can do an article on Malraux; that gives me plenty to do, as you can see, with the thousand pages of *Don Quixote* and the Baudelaire I still haven't reread.

And that's that, my sweet, yet another day in my monastic life. Soon it will have been nearly 7 months of this life. At the moment it's a good time, quiet and productive, I'm working well, and I like this town very much. It seems— did I tell you yesterday?—that Pieter is going to be permanently recalled. That's the first step.

My sweet, I love you so much, for the moment you seem fragile. I would so like to hear from you. I love you.

✺ to Simone de Beauvoir

March 25

My sweet

Do you see my lovely envelope with the festoons? It's not altogether my fault, it came that way and I managed to make use of chance. That, so they say around here, among the officers, is the mark of French genius. Not on the subject of these *astragales* but about the battle of the Marne.[1]

My little darling, what a nice letter you sent me, and how much you seem to love me, you who live in "fear and trembling." I love you so much, too, my little one, and I so long to see you again. When you get this letter, you'll be three days away from me. For I believe that I'm really leaving on the 27th, perhaps the 28th at the latest. I'll know tomorrow, in any case.

What to tell you? I've absolutely settled the leave question by returning this morning to HQ, where they're finding me somewhat hard to get rid of. I finished "Ivich," you'll have 35 pages of it to read, plus 23 pages of "Mathieu-Jacques," which makes fifty-eight. (And four notebooks. But for a week now I've written absolutely nothing in the notebook. I'm entirely dedicated to the novel.) I worked again this afternoon, and this evening I had a conversation about politics with Captain Munier. That's all. And nothing but studied, orderly thoughts on Ivich, plus lots of joy about leaving, and lots of affection for you, my little darling.

And there you have it. I'm about to drop a line to my parents. It's late and I'm headed for bed. I'll write some more tomorrow. I so long to see you. I love you. I send you enough kisses to cover your little face.

I'm eager to read another 100 pages of your novel.[2]

✺ to Simone de Beauvoir

March 26

My darling Beaver

Tomorrow morning I'll have my physical, and tomorrow night I'll be going off on leave—at the latest the day after tomorrow (but that's not very likely). I'm so glad.

---

[1] In September 1914, the French army took advantage of a sudden gap in German defenses at the Marne River and stopped the German advance on Paris, only thirty miles away.

[2] *L'Invitée* [*She Came to Stay*]. (SdB)

train. It's nicer that way, I don't know why, probably because of the rhythm. At Port d'Atelier I had met two fellows from my division, a senior corporal and a man from the Engineers, and we joined up with a Breton from Quimper, with a very Breton face—he looked like Herland—and we did the trip together. It wasn't at all bad, though we were packed in like sardines, one out of three had a seat, and we took turns sitting; I stood for four hours in the corridor, but I never felt better, despite the horrible odors belching out of the toilets, though that didn't impair my appetite for dinner. Yet I was able to catch four quick hours of sleep on an awful pallet, in the cold, so I was in a daze all day today and won't write you a very good letter. (I ought to write two to T., who has written about my silence, but I'll only do one, I haven't the energy for more.) I read the Dostoyevsky with great interest, though it's superficial (no more so than Maurois's *Shelley*) but aims for the "picturesque" and gives masses of information on that extraordinary life and all in all the trip passed very quickly. At 3 o'clock we heard about the invasion of Denmark and Norway, and it gave a romantic rhythm to our trip, we spoke of nothing else, and then at 12:30 A.M., as we got to our billets, we heard an English program in French, and this morning just before leaving, at six-thirty and while drinking a hot cup of coffee, another program. You *must* read the papers, this could well decide not our fate in the war, but its length. The men weren't sad, this time. Just somewhat introspective but pleasantly so, and besides, from 4:30 on, we were completely taken up by the extraordinary adventure, and for the first time we were in a hurry to get there, to hear the news. It made rather a strong impression, that huge train with its dark blue light, packed with soldiers, so slow, and with no talk from the head car to the last, but of a mysterious naval battle off the Norwegian coast. Today is radio day, I heard 3 programs, that hadn't happened since September. The rest of the time, I was in a fog and more or less happy. I have such good memories, my sweet, you were so kind. It warms the cockles of my heart to think of our mornings at the Rey place, and all our serious, heavy conversations at Le Delfourt and Le Mahieu. To flatter yourself, little flower, just listen to what Dostoyevsky wrote and thought from the depths of his soul: "Each of us is guilty before everyone, for everyone, and for everything." But, my little one, on the contrary, how heavy and rich and full and happy it makes me to think about what we are for each other. I love you so much, my little flower, my darling Beaver. You know, you were every bit as moving as last time, waving on the platform, and I was every bit as moved, and the two images, yesterday's and the one from last time, become one. How I long to see you again. We don't know anything new here, on that score, except that the business with Pieter is going to drag on for the better part of a month. As for the rest of us, Paul—nothing. But it's a nothing that's not at all bad, quite the opposite.

My love, my head's abuzz with fatigue, I think I'll collapse if I keep on. I'm going to write six lines to T. then go to bed. I love you with all my might. Tender, devoted kisses for those little old cheeks of yours, little paragon of Beavers.

1) Don't forget THE CASH.
2) Don't forget to send the books to the Spaniard and to Saillet.

ஒ *to Simone de Beauvoir*

Thursday, April 11

My darling Beaver

This morning, there was a real little miracle: I went to the post office with Pieter, and there was your letter. My sweet, how happy I am that you are happy. I too am so pleased and so steeped in you and in our love; I don't think we've ever understood one another better, and it was somewhat agonizing and so pleasant (for someone who fears future responsibilities) to see you take up my concerns so well and make them yours, sometimes following them, sometimes far outstripping me and steeping yourself so much in all that we were thinking together. My dear little one, I don't think I could do without you; I have thought, unsentimentally but with dry precision, that if you were to die, I wouldn't kill myself, but I would go completely mad. So let's stay completely alive, my love. Have you heard? The war news is good, the Germans have blundered badly and are paying for it. My guess is that it will soon grind to a halt either here or there (but probably not in France) and I am starting to hope that the war won't go on as long as I'd feared.

Last night I slept very soundly, like a log. The moment my head hit the pillow I was snoring. I slept nine hours, and all day I was still wrapped in sleep. Yet I worked on the end of the Brunet-Mathieu chapter, though not too well. Tomorrow it'll be finished, and things will be better. And, as always happens the day after returning from leave, I had a thousand little errands to do all over the place, to HQ, to the Medical Officer, etc. Then we listened to the radio at La Rose, at noon and at seven. It's pleasant, there's a mob of wrought-up soldiers hollering for silence, drowning out the sound of the radio, and the pretty little redhead makes the rounds on tiptoe, and there's another pretty waitress, and the news comes through with those barbarous words—Skagerak and Categat—and we listen to it all intently, then the moment it's over there's a terrific hubbub of commentary. And then it's fascinating, as in a detective novel, to watch the truth bit by bit breaking through the false reports, which are denied, confirmed, denied again. Right now our days are full and lively: radio at 8:30—mail at noon—radio at 12:30, radio at 19:30, it sets up a rhythm—and between times, work. I'm as perky as a flea—or rather I would be if I weren't still dragged down by drowsiness. Another day or two and I'll be completely silent.

T. writes me religiously every day, charming little letters. From Olga you've probably heard the lamentable tale of her identity card. Now of all things Olga is taking offense because I put "for T.Z." on the envelopes addressed to her. I find her slightly crazy, though you told me it's pointless. She claims to be annoyed—that she'd never have opened the letters, etc. "The thing is," so T. tells me, relaying her fury impartially, "you're furtive, always slightly erring on the side of taking precautions." All's well.

Till tomorrow, my sweet, I love you with all my might, you are my sweet Beaver, my little flower.

1) I'm not keeping up my notebook at all anymore.

2) Be a dear and negotiate for the money as soon as possible. I get the impression that Paul needs his back.

❧ *to Simone de Beauvoir*

Friday, April 12

My darling Beaver

It's really late. Grener has just been holding forth for an hour and, faithful to my tactic of humoring him, I listened right to the end, nodding somewhat distractedly but enough to show I was taking it all in. He told me that in 1922 he'd been orderly to the son of President Millerand during a trip taken by the president-father and son to Morocco—and that set up relationships à la Dos Passos between people, because I was a schoolmate of the same Millerand boy at Henri-IV. It's true that such coincidental intersectings seem rather too many-faceted, and it feels a little odd though pleasant to hear someone say, twenty years later, of a former classmate, "He was stingy, by the way; he never gave me so much as a sou." And during the same trip, he was orderly to André de Fouquières. He charmingly related how he would shave himself with A. de Fouquières's razor and use his toilet water after the latter had washed and dressed, and how he would wash the mirror and windows with the man's bath sponge. Poor de Fouquières would have a fit if he knew.

Aside from that, I slaved away all day long and finished the Brunet-Mathieu chapter (beginning and end). Mind you, I don't know whether or not I'm pleased with it; we'll see tomorrow. We've cooled a bit to the radio because they scarcely give any more news, I haven't been there except at noon, we'll see what tomorrow brings. It's been raining here though from time to time the sun breaks through the clouds, however faintly. We do one reading a day in the morning for the antiaircraft defense unit around 9 o'clock. This morning I did one, with Paul, and it made me feel a fool because it was my first since February 3rd. But eventually you get the hang of it again. Did you know that Paul will have the good luck to serve as a physicist? The Minister of the Navy is asking him, for the duration of the war, to become part of a physics Research Center set up in Toulon. In his place you would have leaped at it. But if only you could have seen him: he was terrified and hesitant, his hands shaking. For him emotional shocks go on for more than three or four hours, it takes him that long to realize that something that happened to him is good. He wanted to telegraph his wife to ask her opinion, but I took it upon myself to make him accept. With Paul in Toulon and Pieter recalled to the rear, I'll be all alone here for a while, with some newcomers. It seems odd. I think I'll miss Pieter, who was likeable, a real bon vivant.

My sweet, I got a short disenchanted letter from yourself. You weren't sad but reeling from lack of sleep. You were waiting for a little click of change to come the following day. And that click didn't get there, my poor little one. It must have been my letter, I wasn't able to write to you on Tuesday, as you now know. It seems so strange that the days you're telling me about have *gone by*. I'm very pleased that the notebooks interested you (but why haven't you read the *Guillaume II?*), but as you know, I'm not keeping up with them at all anymore. I'm in a hurry to finish the novel. And yet I have rather a lot to put in; but I don't have time.

My sweet, my dear little one, how I love you. I feel you so near, in all you do, in all that worries you. You are my love.

&ofe; *to Simone de Beauvoir*

Saturday, April 13

My darling Beaver

I'm going to see the "Maginot Boys" tonight, just imagine! Lots were drawn and my name was chosen. I'm pretty amused by the thought. Mistler, who's with the Army HQ, spoke to me about it with some melancholy, saying, "Now those are boys with really cushy jobs." Of course they're professional dancers or singers. They go from place to place within the Army zone, to entertain the officers and, incidentally, as many privates as they can accommodate. They drew my name and Pieter's, and we'll be going in an hour, it's in the big room at the Center in Brumath.

Aside from that it was a literary day. It so happens that the work of patching up seems to be going *very* rapidly. Am I too self-indulgent? (since the business about the Prologue,[1] I've had a complex) or else, isn't it rather that the work was almost done and needed only a little push? Today I'm working on Lola's death. A dashing Captain showed up—War College, dines with the general—and he said to me, "Now this one who's looking all distraught, what's he up to?" I didn't look in the least distraught, I simply looked the way I usually do when I'm working. "Some personal work, Sir." "What exactly?" "Some writing." "A novel?" "Yes, Sir, Captain." "On what?" "That would take a bit too long to explain." "Well, I mean, there are women who get screwed and cuckolded husbands?" "Of course." "That's fine. You're fortunate to be able to work." Upon which I went off to buy some rolls for dinner, and he told the clerks, not without a touch of melancholy, "Authors should not be seen up close." "It's his uniform that doesn't fit," said good Pieter, indignantly.

Aside from that, yet another cloud on the horizon: our salaries are under scrutiny again, and the Chamber of Deputies will give a decision on the matter in May. They're talking of reducing our salaries by 2/3rds. That will mean another 1,000 or 1,200 francs, won't it? The latest news was that the danger doesn't seem so imminent, but well, we must be on our guard. You are sending me 7 or 800 francs a month; in this case I wouldn't ask you for more than 200. Could you get along on 1,700 francs instead of 2,500? Of course we'd have to impose economies on the two Zazouliches.

The radio is really funny: when we send Pieter to listen, he comes back beaming, there's nothing but massacre of Germans, with German corpses floating in Oslo harbor. When we send Paul, he comes back with a long face and declares, "No news but it doesn't seem to be going too well." And he paces with his hands behind his back, looking finicky and woebegone.

I'm reading *Man's Fate*, and I can see quite well what he wanted the reader to feel: fate accepted and willingly acknowledged. That's rather Heideggerian, after all. But there are ridiculous passages (Ferral's "eroticism") and others that are deadly dull. I think I'm simply going to explain that on the one hand there's a sort of philosophical grasp of the "situation," which is very laudable, and on the other hand an artistry achieved through old procedures, which is simply unacceptable. That way I'll mingle praise and criticism. But I won't write any-

---

[1] *I had found it very poor, and Sartre had deleted it. (SdB)*

thing about it for a long time. A lot of books are being announced that I'm really very eager to have. Kafka's *Amerika*, Clemence Dane's *La Vaque qui passe* [*The Passing Wave*]—Samuel Pepys's *Journal*, volume II (while we're on that topic, would you buy me volume I, in early May?). Be a dear and keep an eye out for it. But if they cut back our salaries, instead of such ruinous purchases, you could negotiate a subscription at Monnier's for me, which should be possible.

That's it, my sweet. There was a letter from you, and you were telling me that you were very disappointed to have gotten nothing from me on Thursday. But I know that, my poor little one—and by now you know the reason. How I love your little letters, my love. I'm happy you've renewed your interest in Sorokine (and happy she's content with simply exiling me for three years). But, in fact, that's what's happening right now.

My dear little Beaver, my sweet little flower, I love you with all my might, you are my dear love.

☙ to Simone de Beauvoir

Sunday, April 14

My darling Beaver

What do you mean you didn't get a letter on Friday? I did write on Wednesday. It's true that letters leave on Thursday mornings. But they generally arrive on time. It saddened me a little to realize you'd been left without letters, but eventually I realized it was old news. What an odd life without simultaneity we live. Which is truer: What I learn each day and you don't feel—or what you're feeling at the moment I'm thinking of you and which I don't *know*? I'm neither here nor there. At any rate, you *were* worried on Friday and there's nothing to be done about it. Little one, you were left for so long without news of me. And yet I was loving you so much and writing to you. That's the worst of it, as you say, you couldn't bawl me out. You know, I was somewhat moved as I read the boring dialogue between Kyo and May in *Man's Fate*. Not because of Malraux; but I was thinking that, without making too much of it, you and I were so strongly linked, and in just the right way. I love you, my little sweet, my little flower.

So, I went to the stage show yesterday. But I quickly left. It wasn't all that bad, it was just terribly boring. To tell you the truth they were professionals in civilian life, but fourth-rate. They came out in uniform (khaki knee pants, latest military style, soft khaki shirt, khaki tie), minus jacket, minus makeup, it was all very dreary. And they presented Max Maurey's inevitable *Asile de nuit* [*Night Sanctuary*], then a few songs and a few jazz tunes. We were packed in like sardines. Because Pieter almost passed out from the heat and I was standing, we left at the intermission and I went to bed around ten, quite content.

Today I worked well. I redid the whole passage on Lola's death and other bits and pieces. The lovely part about it is that I redo this or that as the spirit moves me; if something isn't going well, I take up something else. It's pleasant, and I'll be done in two months. At that point I'll send you the manuscript by registered mail, you'll reread it and take it to Brice Parain if it reads well. It's astonishing to think that this magnum opus will be finished. At noon one letter from you, nothing from Tania. It's the 3rd day of silence. I'm rather serene but nonetheless I'd like to be sure it's inertia or calamity, and not that she's found out something. You believe, don't you, that Z. would cut you dead if she had any reason to suspect deceit of any kind? On the radio I listened, with that strange enthusiasm I hate because it has to do with the lives of others, to news of the English victory at Narvik (seven German destroyers annihilated), then lunch, work, chess with Pieter. Lieutenant Z. came to borrow a book from me and to ask for information about Nietzsche. He wears perfume and paints his toenails red but doesn't wash. Now I don't wash either, but I don't put on perfume, so I was justly indignant. All the more so in that he departed bowing low like a hypocritical old hag and without even shaking my hand. There's talk of departure, perhaps we'll be going a few kilometers away to a barracks camp, but I don't give a shit, there'll always be an office for us. It sounds like this week. This evening we went to La Rose to listen to the news on the radio—but there was nothing new here so I am, writing to you.

My little one, send some cash, they're quietly asking for it here. There's no reason to be scared about our salaries, it was a false report from a right-wing newspaper concerning a vote that *overruled* a proposal to reduce them. Somehow we'll plug along till the end of the war. I got a letter from Duhamel, I'm sending it to you so you can get a little chuckle out of it: the contents are of no interest, but the signature's worth its weight in gold. The writing is halfway between a medical prescription and the autograph signature of a famous man.

Till tomorrow, my little flower. Kisses for your little cheeks, your little mouth, your eyes, my sweet, and a great big hug. You are my one and only charming Beaver.

◈ *to Simone de Beauvoir*

Monday, April 15

My darling Beaver

There was no letter from you today. I'd been happily anticipating hearing that you'd finally received the first of mine, and then nothing of the sort. But I'm not very anxious about you, and I feel so at one with you that for one brief day I can get along without a letter. I'm completely and always in contact with yourself, little sweet. The whole time when I'm working on my novel you are present as a strict little critic, and it's *for you* that I correct much more even than when I'm inventing—and that's easy to understand since the corrections are on imperfections that you have pointed out, and it is my goal to satisfy you in your role of little judge. I believe I'm working fast and well, these days. But you'll soon be the judge of that. And the rest of the time I feel you so close to my heart, oh, my charming Beaver. I hope you received a few of my letters before growing morose, and that the click, as you called it, came in time.

Aside from that, what can I tell you that's new? This morning I went to listen to the radio at La Rose (I don't eat rolls anymore; simply a cup of black coffee because I haven't any money left) and the news was good. For the moment I think, along with lots of others, that the end of the war is closer than we dared hope (which, alas, doesn't mean tomorrow or in three months). After that, work till noon. Lunch at the Lion d'Or with Pieter, increasingly appealing and not far from endearing. We talked for ages about the legs of a waitress and then women's legs in general. Then we came back, and I beat him four to one at chess. After which more chess and, because I'm on guard duty, I stayed on here alone and they went to listen to the radio at La Rose, I took advantage of it to work an hour longer. I finished *Le Temps de mépris*, which is profoundly abject. Really miles below *Man's Fate*; I don't know whatever possessed him to write such a thing. But there are really rather good passages in *Man's Fate*, and I strongly approve of his anti-psychologism (explanation below), which is totally inaccessible to others: There's only a single character, one and the same (Malraux himself) in various "situations"—and (explanation above) from the idea that human reality is a totality defined by its being-in-the-world. He is really very close to us. To the point of saying that "man wants to be God."

I received a totally friendly letter from T. and *Liens*, the new magazine put out by Saens, Dumartin, Tchimoutchine, etc. They've really progressed since *Trait d'union* and it's not so bad. I'll write to them. Would you buy me (on

May 1st) *Quatre mois*, Chamson's journal.[1] I read passages of it in *L'Oeuvre* and it looks terrible. But one's got to keep up.

This is a very austere letter, my sweet. Though that's not in the least what my life is like. It's all serene work. Since I got back, since I saw you so happily, and found you again, and with the novel ending, I feel a profound inner peace. I'm really happy. You know, this novel is a stage in my life. And I was so scared of never finishing it. Well now I'm beginning to feel I'm almost there. Just two or three months to go, and I won't have to cling to it. I'll rest awhile and then I'll begin *September*.

I love you with all my might, my sweet, my dear little flower. You're a good three-quarters of my serenity. You are so sweet and tender, my little flower. You know, this time you were entirely sweet enough, and you told me so well how much you love me.

᪣ *to Simone de Beauvoir*

Tuesday, April 16

My darling Beaver

It's ten o'clock. I worked quietly all day, and Grener poured a good bit of home-brewed kirsch into my cup. It's delicious. Now he's asleep and snoring, and I'm writing to you; I really want to write you and at this very moment, it's so poetic. I'll write to you only. Truly, I have fun only when it's you I'm writing to. I have just reread my corrections, and there are some that are good and others that need to be redone. I'm up to the Mathieu-Daniel conversation at the end. I'm into it up to my neck, and I think it'll be good, but it's difficult. I've regained all the eagerness I had last year for my factum, I'm obsessed with it all day long. That, you, and Norway: principal themes. Norway, I want you to understand that I'm not getting sentimental about the fate of the invaded country: they sold out to the Germans, and I'll weep for them some other time. But I dearly hope the German troops get a good licking, because that would probably hasten the end of the war. As for yourself, I haven't really definitively left you since my return from leave. It bothers me that you feel our leave was stolen from you. As for me, it seemed short but full, and I have lots of little memories of it: Ducottet, upstairs at Le Mahieu, the Café d'École Militaire, the quay along the Canal de la Villette and the Café de la République where we were both dead

[1] André Chamson, novelist (b. 1900).

tired. How rich and pleasant it all seems to me. Wait, I have another lone memory: a Café des Invalides that was overflowing with officers, and where I waited for the time to meet you at the École Militaire. I love you, my little one. So now you've gone and dropped the heel off your shoe again, just the way you did in the Jardin des Plantes, almost ten years ago by now. How it made me laugh. In my heart you are just as young as you were then, you old junk pile, and I care a thousand times more for your little self.

But all this is more or less sweet nothings to fill up the page, because I have nothing else to tell you: 7:30–8:30 La Rose after sweeping up. I had thought I'd enter in my notebook what I'm telling you now instead (my notebook is in abeyance): I sweep with malice, in the belief that I'm playing an excellent trick on the officers, *making them think* I've swept. And I put such love into my finicky job that eventually their office is splendidly swept. After that, La Rose and radio. Then, due to drizzle, no readings. Writing till noon and a game of chess with Pieter. Then lunch (from tomorrow on I'm not going to do that, because I'm without a sou and don't want to borrow again. I'm waiting till you've been able to find some cash, poor little pauper.) It was blanquette de veau, which I don't much like. And then, after that, work. I get a kick out of writing, and I hope the work shows it. At this rate I'll be finished by June 1st. I'm reading *Man's Hope*—which isn't good. When you get some money, sometime this month, you could still send me the Van Dine (*Meurtre au jardin* [*Murder in the Garden*]) and the Chamson, because I'll soon have nothing left to read except for *Don Quixote*, which scares me. Then I ate two rolls and went to La Rose for a mug of wine and to listen to the radio news. Then I went home, I worked some more, ate Hantziger's dates, Klein's kugelhof, drank Grener's schnapps while I smoked Paul's cigarettes, and here I am writing to you. I'm sorry your Sunday had no letters, my sweet. Yet I'm writing with clockwork regularity. I love you so much.

Au revoir, old beaten path, old derelict, this evening I feel a strong, strong longing to hold you in my arms and cover your dear little face with kisses. I love you.

❧ to Simone de Beauvoir

Wednesday, April 17

My darling Beaver

You send me such nice long letters, such sweet ones, and I send you hack work. Yet it's not for lack of affection or goodwill, but material, my good little Beaver! Nothing is going on either outside or inside my head. Outside, it's La Rose, it's the schoolroom. And yet it's rather amusing, when you think of this sort of phalanstery we make up, ten strong: three clerks, two orderlies, two drivers, three weather guys—plus the 2 from the SRA [Artillery Intelligence Service], Naudin and the 1st sergeant who come and go. Each of them hates the others, of course, but they're all united nonetheless by common pastimes, in small groups. Chess links Pieter, Hantziger and myself, while it's cards for Pieter, Grener, Klein and François, etc. This evening it was pretty sidesplitting: Grener, Klein, Courcy and Beaujouan were playing cards; Paul, in the grip of a new frenetic passion, stooped, scowling, mouth drawn, was struggling with a typewriter to increase his speed; Pieter and Hantziger were playing chess, and I was working on my novel. I don't exactly know what to compare it to (office, phalanstery, nursery, invalid hospice) to portray for you the strange impression it gave me. But one tires of it—I mean of looking for exact impressions in all of it, because it's not a bad way to live—and I'm not even laboring on my notebook anymore. Because my head's empty, my little one. To tell the truth, it would fill up again if I wanted, I get the feeling that I could simply turn on a tap and that would do it for six months. But it barely interests me anymore: I'm completely involved in patching up my novel, I do nothing else, I think of nothing else.

At noon I had no lunch, for lack of cash. I was perversely waiting for the *pay* they're giving out tonight. And tonight, in possession of fifteen military francs, I went out for a pair of sausages at La Rose, listening to the radio. Tomorrow I'll do the same and, above and beyond that, I'll take a bath. The day after tomorow, I'll take up the field kitchen. Don't worry about me. If you could send me a little hundred-franc note, that would be fine. If not, no matter. As for the Acolytes, I'll try to make them wait patiently till May 1st; after all that's not so far off. You can simply send me a mail order as soon as you draw the pay.

About the salary, it doesn't seem to be too serious, and you won't have to gnaw away at your own little living expenses, my sweet little flower, which would break my heart.

What else can I tell you, my little one? That not only is *Man's Hope* very bad, it also reveals a decay in Malraux's thought. *Man's Fate* had another tone to it. Someplace in *Man's Hope* he says of an anarchist who has turned communist, "I became a communist because I've aged. When I was an anarchist, I liked individuals much better." That could be applied to him, word for word. So much for him. I think that will be the topic of my article: from *Man's Fate* to *Man's Hope*. Basically, *Man's Hope* is like a bad Soviet novel, you know, those novels where cardboard characters ooze materialism. But for the moment I don't have time to write the article. Let's get the novel finished first. I suppose I'll have Pieter bring it back to you on his next leave. It will probably be finished by then. I'm so pleased, my little one, that you're working so well on yours, and that you're having a good time doing the Xavière-Françoise chapter. I've been thinking, on my side, that Mathieu isn't *interested* enough in Marcelle, that a reader doesn't feel strongly enough that he is fond of her. And to show that, it's not enough to make Marcelle more interesting, he himself must seem more taken with her. I'll work on it; Marcelle must be like the symbol of that whole life of intellectual and moral comfort where he isn't free.

Till tomorrow, my sweet, my little dear. How you moved me yesterday, with your little heel askew. I love you so much, my love. You are my darling Beaver.

❧ *to Simone de Beauvoir*

Thursday, April 18

My darling Beaver

This evening I'm completely groggy. Playful but groggy. I've just won three games of chess at Pieter's expense and am incapable of working, my head keeps nodding, I don't quite know why. And yet I had dinner this evening, in fact I ate very well—an omelette and potatoes for 10 francs. Pieter loaned me five of it and now I have just forty sous for breakfast tomorrow morning. After that . . . If you can send me fifty francs, it would be most welcome, I'll cut corners on everything to get along on that till the end of the month. If you can't, never mind, I can wait till the 1st with no great pain, I have some tobacco and apparently the field kitchen is very good at the moment, so it's time to take advantage of it. And I've just found a hoard of paper and ink cartridges. It's only books that I'll soon be lacking. If you have the Van Dine, send it. But it isn't books that are providing my entertainment, it's chess. I taught Pieter how to play and he's beginning to beat me, which spurs me on. From that to playing ten games a day is only a step. I've become rather good again, calculating five or six moves ahead. It's really nothing, but it gives one the feeling of possessing the chessboard, which is nice.

Aside from that nothing, of course. And T., who writes today, "You're not telling me much about your life." It's a terrible bore, but I'll have to write her a letter filled with detail. How to make it picturesque? A table, a typewriter, some paper, surrounded by jerks: that's all there is. And then a few little miltary details: yesterday they came to reclaim on the spot all the army sweaters issued this winter. We gave them up with much grumbling. Upon which today we were summoned equally urgently to take them back. That's how time passes. I also used a numbering machine to print the numbers on the officers' tickets for the Army Theater. It was pure benevolence on my part and for the sole purpose of operating the machine. The radio has lost its attraction since it stopped announcing a massacre of destroyers every day, the newspapers too. I absolutely don't think anymore. And yet I put in a very lively day—though with all illusion of waging war now gone—because of my novel. The big last scene between Mathieu and Daniel is done, and I think it's good. Much better at any rate than what I did the first time around. Now I'm going to take up Marcelle, which will be a lot of fun. I'll certainly be done in June, if we keep on doing nothing at all, which is quite likely. About our recall to Saint-Cyr, no news. But Pieter's wife writes that it's well under way. You ask, my little one, if I'm still bearded. Well, up to now indeed I was, somewhat, but when I got your little letter, I thought that you'd surely prefer to imagine my face just as it was when you saw me leave, and I ran to take a bath and shave. I'm writing to you in a state of total physical purity (the moral side is not in question). But God knows what state I'll be in when you get this letter, because my razor blades have been stolen. All the same I'll tend to my appearance a little. Being clean will change things. There are some gestures I didn't dare make, my hands were so dirty: shake hands, hold out money on the palm of my hand to a young waitress, etc. Even the military salute filled me with shame for I was displaying to my superiors the palm of a coalman. Today I held my head high, pushing the pride of being clean to the point of delusion: I fancied myself a dandy.

That's it, my sweet, that's all there is to say today. It's not much. This letter is made up of nothings, and it's intended to rekindle our taste for letter writing. But don't worry, I won't do anything about it.

My sweet, how your own little days seem poetic to me, how sensible you are, whether at the Mahieu, at the Dupont in Montmartre, or a thousand other places around Paris and always so poetic in my eyes, with your little papers, your students' assignments, your novel. I love you so much. I would so like to be with you, you know, and you'll take me to the tiny Montmartre restaurant without customers on the Rue Lepic—and also to the singing café with its bathroom odor. I love you with all my might.

❧ *to Simone de Beauvoir*

Friday, April 19

My darling Beaver

Today I'm typing my letter to you, so you can see my progress. I truly think it's going just as fast now as when I write by hand. But I'm humiliated, because Paul, with his new passion for it, is beating me. But then he's using unfair, ridiculous, grad-school methods. Now tell me whether that's a good description or not. Would you believe that he knows a few of Jaurès's speeches[1] by heart? Now that's strange enough, but true. Well then, he types out the speeches, always the same ones; he had first written them out longhand, watch in hand if I may put it that way, and he clocked the time it took. Then he set to typing the same speeches and each time he notes the time it took him; since he types them on scrap paper from the readings, the room where we live is filled with strange pieces of paper bearing on one side a graph of ballistic winds and on the other Jaurès's inflamed prose, with always the identical exhortations, since Paul always copies the same passages.

My sweet, I got the gloomy letter in which you tell me of our financial disarray. I immediately alerted the Acolytes without getting much response. And at the same time I negotiated a loan of 100 francs from Pieter. So don't worry any more about me. The hundred francs will get me through the month pleasantly, sometimes eating as usual, and sometimes not. All the more expensive than the Lion d'Or, and more fun too because of the radio and all those semi-whores—I should dress it up and say: demibeavers—who get pawed by the soldiers, endlessly complain about love, and weep into the drinks they serve. The other day a fat forty-year-old joined the fray; her enormous bosom began to jiggle then she burst into tears as she served our soup. Actually we'll soon be moving on. The proposals and rumors I repeated to you the other day have already dissipated into thin air (these misplaced blanks that you'll find scattered throughout the letter arise from a defect in the machine and not from my inexperience). So, concerning money, everything will go well this month. I'm in a bit of a quandary about next month. But, my little one, I have to admit to a guilty pleasure at seeing you struggle with financial difficulties this time. You did rather taunt me, though not spitefully, last year. I suppose I'll simply have to win the Populist Prize, but I don't really know what that would take.

Today was like any other day: simply nothing happening. As I mentioned yesterday, I wrote a long letter to Tania to explain how nothing was happening and how I had nothing to tell. Then I went to bed. I was awakened in the middle of the night, not by a nightmare but by the feeling that I was about to have one.

[1] Jean Jaurès (1859–1914), French socialist leader.

I was in the midst of a very innocent dream about London, when from within the dream I felt the atmosphere changing without anything terrible happening; it was the sense of the objects that had changed. It was still London at night with deserted streets, but by an odd contradiction that seemed dubious and disquieting, that dark night had something of the torrid echoes of early afternoons in June. I wisely woke up before I could witness the arrival of the assassins or the rabid dogs that should be the obligatory accompaniment to such a meteorological phenomenon. But then I discovered I was harboring an absolutely pure bubble of anguish, which even seemed to have an actual location in my body. Precisely at the top of my head to the left. There was nothing metaphysical about it; rather, it seemed quite physiological, but what we ordinarily call the body was not in the least involved. One could have thought it supported the Messieurs Dumas and Cannon, concerning their much-touted cortical sensitivity. Then the anxiety locked onto the word: Crazy, which rapidly grew intolerable, without images or representations of any sort. Have you heard of anything like this? Whereupon everything dissipated, the bubble burst and I went back to sleep. I'm telling you about it because I think I see in it the proof that nightmares don't arise by chance from progressions of images, nor from a general disposition of sensibility, but come instead from the fact that within the dream, affectivity *also* dreams; with images or without, little affective bubbles of dream form to which images become attached.

This morning, I hung back on the Mathieu-Marcelle chapter, the first one. I have a lot of problems with it: first, if Marcelle is really sick, that's going to complicate the question of the birth: she's in danger of losing her life over it, and I have no need of additional difficulties. Next, to what degree is her new character compatible with her little treacheries? All of that is obviously a matter of adroitness, but it's a real bother. So I worked without much enthusiasm. Ah yes, and besides, there's this: if she is really so anxious to have a child, is her gloom in the first chapter explicable? From one sigh to the next and from one chess game to the next, by the end of the day something was nonetheless accomplished on the novel. Basically what needs to be found is more the right *tone* for talking about Marcelle. I'm on the right track. Aside from that, I got a charming little letter from you, good little one, it pleased me greatly because, the money question aside, you seem on the cheery side. How wise you are, dear little Beaver. And oh how much you deserve your happiness. I love you. (It seems odd to be writing that on a typewriter.)

Till tomorrow, my sweet; here it is, almost ten o'clock. I'm off to bed. Today the weather was fine, and this first day of spring almost broke my heart. I thought of the Paris streets, of the quays, and I would have liked to be with you on the terrace of the Café de Flore. Kisses for your little old cheeks, my love.

๑ *to Simone de Beauvoir*

Saturday, April 20

My darling Beaver

You'll only get a quick note today: it's midnight, and I've been to the Army Theater, the real Army Theater, a troop of "civilians," as the soldiers say. I was counting on getting out by ten-thirty to write to you. But we were packed in like sardines, I was standing all the way in the back, and I couldn't get out. Tomorrow I'll write you a long account of this festivity which was entertaining on more than one score. I got a letter from you that moved me very much, my sweet, I'll speak of that tomorrow too. I love you with all my might. You are my dear, dear love.

๑ *to Simone de Beauvoir*

Sunday, April 21

My darling Beaver

Yesterday I wrote you a wretched little note and I'm somewhat abashed about it, because I know what my letters mean to you, as yours to me. But I was dropping from fatigue, I'd been on my feet the whole time. Dearest, I am full of remorse. It's odd, my little one, you tell me in this morning's letter that reading my letters you don't find yours nice enough. Well, my gentle flower, these last eight months the same has been true for me, I find yours so tender and so pleasing that I feel completely humiliated to be writing such trash. And yet I love you with all my might and I feel very tender when I'm writing to you. But you should be beside me, your little arm in mine. Well, here's the thing: it must come from the fact that they are the written word. When we write them they seem like dregs, we feel we're scraping them up off our feelings, like scraps of meat off the bone (still the phenomenon of quasi-observations, on which you would be knowledgeable little scoundrel, if you had read what I wrote). And quite the opposite, when we read them, there's meaning behind them, it's real observation and they seem just right. "There's still some duplicity in it," you'll say with your distrustful look.

You gave me a very flattering account, my sweet, not of my character—we're too old for that—but of my being-in-the-world. Of course, it was deeply intimidating because that manner of being tells its story through thousands of tiny peccadilloes and psychological deficiencies, and when we speak of the one, we of necessity think of the others. But it's important just to think that one really is *that* for someone. And the point is, there's nothing necessary left in it, it's well beyond the necessary, but it must be *you* who thinks of me in that way, no one else in the world could do it.

To make a long story short, you should know that on Tuesday the 23rd, or the day after tomorrow, the Populist Prize will be awarded. For now all my dodging has vanished, I really and truly want the dough, otherwise how will we live in May? It amounts to 2,000 francs net. I don't think it brings in one additional reader. Read Wednesday's papers—and, if there's nothing, because it's a modest little prize, buy *Les Novelles littéraires* on Saturday, because, even in the case of a happy outcome, I won't know anything until Saturday. Of course, if I win, I'll ask them to send you the check *without the bar*.[1] Let's just hope we win. On the list is René Lefèvre with *Les Musiciens du ciel* [*Musicians of the Sky*], who seems to be dangerous competition. Perhaps (though it's shameful to say it) the fact that I'm a soldier will count in my favor; it did in the last war. There's also Georges Blond: *Prométhé*, which had been pushed for the Goncourt.

So then, last night I went to the Army Theater. All of us at Division HQ, because we'd all inscribed numbers on the tickets with a beautiful device that warms my heart, and they wanted to reward us. It was the real Army Theater, with civilians and women. They must be making tours of two weeks or so, and it must be wearing, because in all their monologues they complained they'd lost their voices on the tour. They didn't stay here but in the large neighboring city, and a bus brought them here about eight o'clock and took them back around three in the morning after a reception at the general's. They had performed all afternoon and gave the evening performance before an absolutely packed and smoked-filled room despite the efforts of officers and MPs to prohibit smoking. I'll tell you right off that the level of the skits and songs was perceptibly lower than those at the Petit Casino in Paris. They were the lowest of the low. The female star was Pierrette Madd, a movie and operetta actress, who was a hit in 1920 and played Constance Bonacieux in *The Three Musketeers* around that time. Actually most of them were middle-aged. The women were, as they say here, "rejects." And the men, limited to those released from all military duty, were bald, obese, or deformed. The *paterfamilias* performance. Around eight-fifteen I got to the small square room, a movie hall before the war but now serving as the Salvation Army Center; the show was scheduled for nine. The officers had the balcony to themselves, the men were stashed below. It was already so full that there wasn't even an aisle between the chairs, and you had

---

[1] The bar signified "pay to designated payee only."

to jump across the backs of the seats, getting a foothold on the backs of those already seated. From row to row and shoulder to shoulder we reached the back of the room, not without collecting copious insults. We—meaning Pieter, Mondange and I. Mondange is a new guy, who replaced Mistler who's gone off to the Army HQ. He's 38, shy, appealing, a bit flighty, but with a touching goodwill. He'd just had his mobilization instructions and was called up three months ago. He was sent as Clerk of General Staff to Mont-de-Marsan where thousands of clerks wait for assignment. One day a senior sergeant called him: "I've got a cushy job for you: clerk near Laon, 150 kilometers from Paris. If you take it, you'll surely get your twenty-four hours a week." "You bet," says the guy. He takes it, travels for six days: Bordeaux-Poitiers-Paris-Laon. At Laon they tell him: "You're not there yet, you've got to go to Vesoul." And at Vesoul they told him: "You're going up to the Sector, to the front" (meaning, to us). The men (there were four of them in this case) feel they've been taken for a ride, spend the gloomiest of nights on the train; finally they get off here and for two days now Mondange has been spending his time sniffing for bombs and poison gas, quite surprised to see houses still intact. It gives us back some sense of drama to watch this guy look at us a bit like ghosts. And it does no good for us to say, "No, no, you'll see, we're much better off than at the rear"; quite honestly we were all extremely flattered when he said, "You poor suckers! How I've pitied you, with all your bad luck." Well, Mondange set off general stupefaction in the packed hall when he said, with a sweeping gesture that included all those suckers, "Just one bomb in here, and it's devastation!" Everyone looked at him, as though they found that rather strange, and he said, "It's true: you don't give it a thought anymore, but I for one still think about it." As a matter of fact, apart from the first ten days, had we ever given it a thought? We felt vaguely abashed, a bit like when you describe my existential nature. And we call him "the Rookie" with a tender and ever so vain cordiality. Of course, Pieter took him in hand. If I hadn't put a stop to it, he would gladly have given him to understand that our lives weren't free of danger. But he's disarming, good Pieter, for he told me this morning, "You see, I recognize my faults: I tried not to show off in front of Mondange." Well, there we were all the way at the back of the hall, heated up to forty degrees, stifling, gasping like carp, swathed in odors—particularly the odor of wine, since most of the guys were drunk. They had come to get in line, just as we do for the Théâtre Français, as early as seven o'clock with their canteens, and they took little sips from time to time to keep themselves company. At nine the show began. Overture: selections from *Snow White*, by the regimental musicians. You can just imagine. Then male singers, female singers, monologists of both sexes, acrobats. I was in seventh heaven, all the way back, and I finally understood that famous sense of fraternity you hear so much about from the old bourgeois who were in the war of '14. As a matter of fact, it should be noted that the bourgeois still talk about it and explain how the classes ceased to exist— my captain, for instance, gives me handsome speeches on that score—as did your former lover[2] of the Équipes Sociales. But never do workmen or peasants talk about it. I believe that feeling of fraternity derives from wearing the same clothes as everyone else, from never—no matter where you go or what you do— having to pay for your clothes. Yesterday I was strongly aware that we were all dressed alike and that the first reaction of each person was a sympathetic reflex for his neighbor because he was wearing the same clothes. And we feel tremendously at ease together, because people *aren't thinking anything* about you. It's something you can hardly imagine, it seems really like a tremendous change, in such a way that you don't worry about defending your physical individuality. We have only inner individuality (because it's not at all an osmosis or some sort of collective phenomenon), one is simply unencumbered with one's body. Well then, there were perhaps five hundred guys in a hall built for two hundred. And many of them had come to see "some women." It's not that there's a total lack of them here—or that they're not very generous with themselves; but since their last leave the men had lacked *the actress* in terms of symbolic representation of woman, who guides them and serves as theme for their desires. It was clearly visible when a dresser suddenly hurried past the curtain. There was a howl that rose from their chests, "A woman! A woman!" Applause and whistles. It was rather odd, because basically they aren't shut up in the fortresses of the Maginot Line, they merely have to walk down the block to see one. But it was *the* woman, though they only had a glimpse of a back and chestnut-brown hair. They're not badly off for available women to sleep with, but what they lack is the sanction bestowed by art, in peacetime, to their sexual encounters. Upon which a fat man appeared to announce the program, pretending to address the buck privates alone, but winking toward the general and, toward us, discreetly paternal. He was oily and transparent as head cheese. He didn't go down too well with the soldiers. And the soldiers weren't too likeable: they sulked because they were dealing with civilians, from the home front. With the people from around here who live the same life and would be under fire, just like them if it came to blows, they are thoroughly unpretentious. But in this case there was a sort of negativism: the resistance of a guy not to be understood and who knows there's a chasm between himself and the home front. When the comic, a great bald devil with a crown of white hair, came out and said, "Hello. I'm fine, how about you?" one soldier shouted, "You're not a soldier?" and everyone laughed

---

[2] *Sartre was joking. He was referring to Robert Garric, whose courses I had taken at Saint-Marie-de-Neuilly, and who had fascinated me for several months. (SdB)*

with vengeful satisfaction. They also pretended to see the actresses' charm exclusively from the physical point of view. One neighbor said, "I'd do this to her, I'd do that to her . . ." and the raw details were a kind of vengeance. But it was superficial sulking, like Sorokine's, they wanted to be eased out of it. And when they saw a snake-woman wriggling out from a giant dice, the ice was broken. Yet when the actor recited a few poems about them, they remained aloof. As a matter of fact, they were terrible. There was one that was supposed to be the advice of a veteran of '14 to a recruit of '40. "Feeling blue? Load up your pipe." Upon which they explained that a pipe dissipates the clouds of gloom, according to the Chinese. But the man could just as well have chosen the poems as symbols of what they felt—along with what they used to choose in peacetime—*A Love Like Ours* by Lucienne Boyer—as a symbol of their affectionate feelings. But they didn't want that, they were stubborn. Aside from that, the actors did with them as they liked, and the men took up the chorus each time they were asked. They considered it "not bad," except for the strong-minded like Grener, who thought it ridiculous. The funniest part was the women, particularly Pierrette Madd, who lustily led the crowd and vaguely imagined herself among the generals with a martial air and a touch of the well-behaved child. They were very obscene, of course, and *certainly* excited by this round of singing given before an audience composed exclusively of *men*, and men they imagined as starved. Pierrette Madd, who is a ridiculous old bag, jiggled around indecently, with suggestive gestures, alluded to bromides, imagining the feel of wolf eyes upon her (as a matter of fact the guys were unmoved. The thing that charmed them was this contact with "feminine elegance" in general). And it was all the crazier because after this plunge into the violent odor of men, she would go drink champagne with elegant officers. No orchestra, except the military band. All the songs were accompanied by a wretched pianist who had been allowed, so she could have her own little personal success, to perform a Chopin *Prelude* at the opening, which she played with shoulders hunched up around her ears from the emotion. They left me contemplative on my way back, these third-rate barnstormers, who certainly reap a vague harvest of glory from that applause. It mustn't seem too great inwardly: generosity, patriotic affection and finally— after so many years—the old bodies can go out on stage again.

And that's that, my sweet. I went home to bed. I wrote to you.

Till tomorrow. I'm going to copy out—I give you fair warning—whole long passages of this letter in mine to T. (everything to do with the theater). You'll forgive me in that I have only that to tell and, if I didn't copy it, the same words would come regardless. Today, nothing to mention.

My sweet little flower, I love you with all my might. You are my dear, dear love. Till tomorrow, my little sweet.

❧ to Simone de Beauvoir

Monday, April 22

My darling Beaver

I received a letter from you that moved me to tears. Alas, my poor little one, there you were running around in search of fifty francs that you're going to send me. I won't hypocritically tell you that I don't need them, that would be untrue, and anyway the letter would get there after they've already left. But I'll remember it. My little Beaver, when you remind me of the Fomento del Torismo in Palma, where you found me so endearing, I'll retort with these fifty little francs that you chased down for me on April 22, 1940, when you were so poor. They will come in very handy, you know. I'm cutting back my standard of living, with no extraordinary squeezing, to 10 or 12 francs a day: a big bowl of coffee in the morning (without rolls), so I still have the pleasure of breakfast. I eat some army bread on my return to the office. At noon a *plat du jour* and a piece of cheese for seven francs at La Rose (tip included) or a pair of sausages and a split of wine for five francs (Pieter gives me half of his vegetables) and in the evening three rolls for 18 sous, and still I can have a split of wine at La Rose and hear the news. I'll keep to this level next month. I'm just as happy, and it's a great saving. Actually there'll be some changes next month. We're leaving for a larger city 20 kilometers away, one celebrated for its Beauty, that played at the Vieux-Colombier.[1] We'll be in the state police barracks. But that's not so bad: there'll be an office and a dormitory set aside specially for the weather unit. So we'll be by ourselves. Naturally all latitude to come and go as we please. And I imagine that the police had beautiful barracks. Ordinarily they're well cared for. I finished the 1st Marcelle-Mathieu chapter. How I need you, my little one. How I would love to have your opinion. Ultimately you won't be able to give it to me before June 15, and if there are corrections to be made, that will delay things tremendously. Following that I've had several ingenious ideas. Tomorrow I'm attacking the big Marcelle chapter, the 3rd, which has to be entirely redone.

I got a letter from Bonnafé, who admits he has signed up as a reserve officer candidate and says he'll back out if I disapprove. I won't openly, and I think I'll just say he was a bit hasty. Taking the matter on purely concrete grounds without political overtones, why was he in such a hurry to be with worn-out second-rate intellectuals, he who claims to love the peasants so much and who gets along so well with them at Gaillac? I'm amused that he's at Gaillac; do you remember it, my love? What happy memories we do have (there was a park, and we strolled along beside the water, and then an open market where we ate some very bad cakes).

---

[1] Allusion to the town in the title of Jean Variot's 1922 play *La Belle de Haguenan*.

The weather is splendid here, summer weather, very still and lovely, pregnant with memories. It changes everything, and I went out for a little bike ride, in the evening, for the sheer pleasure of traveling around in the reddish light. I felt appreciative and happy. I love you.

And that's that, my sweet. I'm calm and happy, I'm working well, and I love you. My novel has me all enthusiastic again, and I sense that you're rather placid in Paris, all's well.

I love you with all my heart, my dear little flower.

✎ *to Simone de Beauvoir*

Tuesday, April 23

My darling Beaver

Here's a little letter that's typed for a change. It will also be a literary letter, be forewarned, due to certain concerns of mine. But first I want to thank you for your nice little fifty francs, which I found indeed in your letter this morning. It stirred my heart, my sweet. Actually, while you were feeling guilty for not sending anything, I was feeling guilty for having you send me something. When you—by which I mean you and the Z's—when you have no more cash, it means you have nothing to eat. Whereas I still have room and board. It's shameful of me, Pasha, to take your poor little sous, all the more so since, casting aside my deference to other people's good opinion, I could very well have borrowed them from Pieter. In short, I feel guilty. For who would judge me if not myself, when you my little conscience are not here? Thank you, my sweet, thank you for your poor little sous, they'll serve me very well and very neatly till the end of the month.

As for the literary torments, here they are. They involve Malraux, of course. He annoys me because he's too much like me. He seems too much like John the Baptist to my Jesus, if you see what I mean. In one scene, which is by the way abysmal, in *Man's Hope*, he writes:

"The age of the fundamental is beginning again . . . Reason must be *founded anew.*"

Of course, that's what he would have liked to make you feel all through his novel, but fat chance. From my present point of view, however, I too would like to have my novel make people feel that we're in the age of the fundamental. That's what I think, as you know; these days I think that it's only just now that we're going to feel the consequences of the loss of faith. But in the first volume of the novel, none of that shows through, and it's very sad. It doesn't come from a technical flaw, but lock, stock and barrel from the bogged-down situation I was in when war broke out. It's a Husserlian piece of work, and that's a bit demoralizing when you've become a Heidegger zealot. Also, I'm finding my novel slightly distasteful. I'll try to have what I can of this show up in the Mathieu monologue, which I've got to redo, but I'm afraid the whole doesn't seem at all existential. Fortunately it's finished. But I envy the courage of guys like Kafka, who can coldly say to their friends, "After my death, burn my writings." As for me, dissatisfied as I am, there's no question of the factum not appearing, since I finished it. And that's crazy because I'll be letting it go to press with an essential flaw, whereas I wouldn't tolerate having it appear with a technical flaw.

In other respects I've done practically nothing today because I'm beginning a chapter in earnest, the Marcelle chapter, and that is altogether different from doing a patch-up job. I was snared all over again in that discouragement you know as well as I do. Any pretext—including personal hygiene, which is not ordinarily even a consideration—sufficed for me to desert the work. And so, at three in the afternoon I abandoned my task and went for a bath. After that I did nothing but play chess, on the pretext that one is more lucid in the morning. And then I went to La Rose, and there I experienced a moment that was tremendously poetic, existential, what you will. It's summertime, my little Beaver, a crazy April fool's summer. A mob of the guys were there, wiped out by the heat. The room was dark, as it is when you close the shutters in summer to keep out the hot weather. And that's it. No: of all things, right there, while I was eating an omelette thanks to your poor little sous at a long long table, the taste of the country in that omelette, mixed with the taste of the crumbs of fresh bread, brought back an old memory: those times when in the summer heat at Saint-Germain-les-Belles[1] I would eat country omelettes with a woman teacher from Limousin in the evening at the end of an identical long table. What a long time ago that was, my little flower! I was very moved by that. I love you, my sweet little Beaver, I love you with all my might, and it seems like such a young feeling and, at the same time, an old warmed-over love with a lot of baggage. How young we were then, how young we were.

Till tomorrow, my sweet. Tender kisses to you.

---

[1] When Sartre came to see me in Limousin during the summer of 1929, after the agrégation. (SdB)

❧ *to Simone de Beauvoir*

Wednesday, April 24

My darling Beaver

A blizzard of good news. First, we've got the prize. This morning I bought six newspapers at La Rose to see the results, but there was nary a mention. Upon which I adopted an attitude of noble defeat: "Well how could that be, but well all right, I didn't get the prize but that's quite natural, etc." On returning by bike, I saw Paul inflating a weather balloon; he said to me, "Congratulations." Hirsch of the NRF had sent me a telegram: "Happy to congratulate you on your success. Best wishes." But I still don't have official confirmation. It all left me unmoved, except that now we'll have the wherewithal next month, my sweet. I don't know why; perhaps I'd made myself too sophisticated as concerns the prize, perhaps my attitude of noble failure embarrassed me. And besides, that's my personality: the good fortune that I expect and that comes my way gives me a hundred times less pleasure than the annoyance if it doesn't come. It's not only in sentimental stories that this happens. And by the way I was instantly stabbed like an insect on corkboard by a piercing anxiety of the "deference to public opinion" sort: should I thank someone, and if so whom? the 17, as Pieter advises me—or simply one (Thérive, for instance) delegating him to thank the others for me? What do you think? In any case, you'll have the chance to give me your view for, in any case, I won't write before getting the official notification. I know nothing about the method of check payment.

Another piece of news: today the home leaves were reinstated. There's unofficial but serious talk of beginning our 3rd round on May 1st. In that case, I'll go at the end of June, even if Saint-Cyr doesn't recall me.

Finally—but this is completely personal—I've just had a little boost to my self-esteem, which leaves me far from unmoved: you know that I play six or seven games of chess a day. I've made huge progress, and I've timidly plucked up my courage to have the local champion told that I'd like to have him play with me, merely to give me a lesson. I'm exaggerating; actually, he's not the champion, he's number two. The number one champ works at the post office, and he has international standing. But mine beat him once. He comes by and says, "Tonight at eight-thirty if you like. Bring your board, because I'll play two games at the same time." Upon which, glancing at the chessboard, he says to me, "Let's do one quickly to feel each other out." We get right down to it and, just listen to this, my little flower, *I beat him.* But it was nothing, rather like a surprise attack. What I realized is that the guy doesn't play a very different game from mine. Perhaps he's more studied, more calculating, but he lacks that mysterious, innate chess ability that had made me apprehensive and piqued my curiosity. I committed a stupid blunder—not too obvious and which I immediately spotted—and he never even noticed it. If I beat him again this evening, I swear I'll ask the champion to play with me. You have to realize: this guy has been playing his six games a day since he was 14! He was as vexed as a flea, but, being a good sport, when he left he said "Bravo!"

That's all for the good news. Aside from that, Lieutenant Z, to whom I'd loaned Jules Renard's *Journal*, held forth for one hour straight, at once mysterious and professorial, explaining that Renard is a sweetheart. Then another lieutenant, a university man, who had been lurking about yesterday while I was doing readings, came to ask me to lend him my philosophical works. Therefore, my sweet, would you *send him by mail on receipt of this letter two copies of* L'Imaginaire?

This morning there was a short letter from yourself, in response to my note of Saturday. But if you want to be fair, you'll send me a sheaf of pages in return for my enormous Sunday letter. You're being nasty with Sorokine, my little one. Don't protest, I'm not getting mixed up in it, but I do think it must have hurt her not to spend the night with you. A letter from T. It irritates me, my little one, to admit that I'm jealous of that young person; she writes every day, and extremely nice letters. But the Moon Woman has undertaken to get her back together with Dominguez, of whom she's had enough as a lover and would like to keep as a friend. Dominguez has her come to his place on the pretext of teaching her how to paint, and of course he explains her personality to her. She is strangely flattered. It's nothing, you might say, and nothing will come of it, but it's unpleasant. Not terribly unpleasant, it didn't ruin my afternoon, or depress me—but I don't much like it. And this is nothing new. Before, when she would write me her charming little letters, so well-intentioned, I could just sit back contentedly. I really don't know how to love people. Except for you. Oh, on that score, it's very different with you, my little one. At least in that respect there will be this in my life, that I'll have loved someone with all my might, not in a madly passionate or supernatural way but *from within*. But it had to be you, my love, someone so closely mingled with me that we no longer know what is yours and what is mine. I love you.

Till tomorrow. Tender kisses to you, my little flower.

Pieter, to whom I said, "I'm so proud of beating the pants off that guy that I'm going to write my friend about it," replied: "Would you let me add a few lines to say there's nothing to be proud about and the guy's a pushover?" I said, "Go right ahead," handing him a sheet of paper, and he answered, "No. I'd lay myself open to criticism of my style."

Marcelle is taking shape (old, cynical, harsh—in that vein).

✧ *to Simone de Beauvoir*

Thursday, April 25

My darling Beaver

After the Army Theater, I give you Army Justice. This morning—and to tell the truth it took some coaxing—I went to a session of the military tribunal. They dispatched four cases in three hours, and I arrived in the middle of it, around ten, for the third. It was held in a chamber of the Civil Court. Not many in attendance, the guard, helmeted, bayonet fixed, and then a dozen privates behind him, myself among them. Six jurors—colonel, major, etc. down to private (because there must be a juryman of the same rank as the accused) and in addition a government commissioner, a captain serving as prosecutor, a clerk of the court and a lawyer. Everyone with helmet close at hand. A helmet served as the magistrate's toque. After the deliberations, the colonel came in wearing his helmet, which he removed to read the sentence. The colonel lisped and didn't seem too nasty. At his side, a silent major looked dyspeptic and terrible. In the corner the prosecutor, a fat guy with a mustache and pince-nez glasses and wet lips, was replenishing his reservoir of anger. I could see the back of the accused, a private. He was a cyclist ten kilometers from the front lines, and his job was to carry messages to the commander of batteries set up 10 kilometers away. Charge: desertion before the enemy. It's the most serious. He had a pregnant mistress in a nearby town (it's annoying not to be able to give the names, it drives a person to periphrasis à la 18th-century poetry) and he lived with her before the war. Gone from September on, he wanted to marry her, but there was a mountain of red tape, the papers were waiting at the city hall of the town in question. One day, on a dark and properly drunken impulse, January 7th to be exact, he takes off on his bike, arrives in the town, searches out his mistress and spends ten days with her without being too conspicuous. Nonetheless he did go to a restaurant quite often, since he had a fair bit of money. One fine day he runs into a private from his regiment who tells him: "You better come back. Or you'll get screwed." "All right," he says. And he goes back. One would like to know what was going through his mind while he was there in X. with his fiancée, knowing that each passing day his case got worse, and yet he lingered. But the Court didn't worry about that. The colonel interrogated him in fatherly tones, with the sole aim of destroying his defense— which was actually idiotic; the guy would say, "I went there to get my papers, I wanted to get married." He said it softly, unintelligibly, and from time to time they made him speak louder. To which they replied: 1st, if you went to get the papers, you didn't have to stay ten days with your mistress—yet, 2nd, you know quite well that you can get married in absentia without leaving your post.— Irrefutable. Yes, but what was going through his mind? I could only see his dark hair and from time to time a large red nose. Finally he began to sob. Examination of a witness: the lieutenant who had declared him a deserter. A stony officer, terribly intimidated, who muttered a few phrases with great difficulty. He says that the accused was nonetheless a good soldier up till then, when he wasn't drinking. The prosecutor made a brief charge, the atmosphere tended toward indulgence. But it's really something to see a large man shaken by an anger of equal proportion. Between acts he was benevolent and gay, he joked with the lawyers, but when he spoke, his eyes bulged. And it was stranger still in that he accepted the extenuating circumstances and was the first to ask for the lightest sentence. The point is, I suddenly realized, that anger for them is an *art*. It's sincere, but you have to know how to ladle it out in just the right dosage, open the escape valves carefully, little by little. And you must frighten, it's a sorcerer's dance. You must close your ears to moderating arguments, pretend you're blind and deaf, adopt the set look of a graven image. The best part was when, after duly alerting the court that the general would surely defer sentencing till after the war (which in practice amounted to a reprieve because, if the man behaves, they'll strike it when peace comes) he made a symbolic gesture of almost getting down on his knees and said, "I *implore* you, Gentlemen of the Jury, I *implore* you not to grant him a reprieve." This lack of conviction was conveyed not by a show of kindness or indulgence, but by a sort of slackness in his anger; it constantly seemed on the verge of slipping away, and he stammered slightly— which made me all the happier because for the last case, where he didn't ask for indulgence, he spoke eloquently and faultlessly. All of this took place in a strange blue light, due to the paper of that color plastered over the windows, because of the airplanes. The lawyer got up. It was a woman, a friend of the accused's family. A blond, no spring chicken, who looked the quintessential Alsatian, the sort you might see with a big black bow on her head serving *choucroute* at "l'Alsace à Paris." She was really something, alone in front of the imposing helmeted military types, with the bayoneted guard behind her. She was substituting for the soldier's male cousin, also a lawyer but called up, so he couldn't be there. She began a rather clever, scholarly little speech on the concept of "desertion in the presence of the enemy." As a matter of fact there are two types of desertion: desertion at the rear, if the soldier, for example, fails to return from leave on time while his unit is stationed in such-and-such a place—and desertion in the face of the enemy when the soldier abandons his post at the front. And it was amusing because it clearly shows how modern war empties the meaning from notions as simple as *desertion*. Had the guy deserted in the face of the enemy or not? In 1830 it was simple: desertion when there was a battle on = desertion in the face of the enemy. But in this case the regiment was on line. Yes. But it had neither fired nor received gunfire. Next, given the depth of the disposition of the units, he was ten kilometers from the lines in a little town *that had not been evacuated*. Exactly as I am here in short. In short, *he* was at the rear and yet he belonged to a combat unit. "Neither geographically, nor militarily, nor psychologically did he desert," she said. To which the prosecutor limply replied, "Distance plays no part in this. In the air force a man is declared a deserter at 100 kilometers from the enemy." A new subtlety in the notion of desertion due to the fact that the unit of distance differs according to the weapon. And he drew upon himself this rather clever response: "Then a man in the antiaircraft units of Nevers or Tours should *always* be reported a deserter *before the enemy*, because nothing guarantees that on that very day enemy planes won't fly over that part of the country." Complete collapse of the notion of desertion. Always the same dodge: the old concepts of war no longer apply, except in a very few particular cases, just as 3-dimensional geometry is a particular case of 4-dimensional geometry: the one in which one of the four dimensions $= 0$. But after that she launched into a character analysis of the accused that was precious to me but very awkward: "Gentlemen, I beg your total indulgence. This man received a very poor education; he always had too much money, he has absolutely no will, no sense of duty." She did not realize that these "excuses" can mean a lot in the civil courts where a man is taken *as he is* and where his action is explained based on his history. But that they were aggravating circumstances for a military court which takes the man *as he must be* (in their view), or in other words based on minimum *standards*. To put it another way, the notion of a soldier is ambiguous: it is both a fact and an ideal. So the judges, well-disposed as they were, knit their brows. It would have been better to maintain that he was a *good* soldier. In short, the man had lived with parents who didn't get along. The father, a rich merchant, was pure indulgence toward him and didn't have the time to raise him. The mother drank. At 14 he stole all the money he could and fled to Paris, where he stayed for six years, hanging out with "unsavory characters." The father died, and he didn't come back for the funeral: "See how weak he is," said the lawyer not suspecting that she was shocking all the buriable fathers among the judges. Then he came back to Alsace, set up housekeeping with this woman, a large hearty soul who held onto him but couldn't keep him from getting drunk. The guy sobbed throughout the whole lovely statement. Of course he had asked the day before to enlist in the commandoes, they all do that the day before their trial. The lawyer spoke as though her lips were swollen; she was Alsatian and her French was rather bad; it rolled heavily off her tongue. Anyway, one became thoroughly convinced that none of this—prosecutor, female lawyer—made a particle of difference. The decision had been reached. Upon which she sat down again, they asked the soldier if he had something to say in his defense, and he simply said, still whimpering slightly but in a moderately firm voice, that he hoped to pull himself together. The Magistrate left the room, returned helmeted while the Guard presented arms, and the colonel read the decision, with exaggerated mumbling and lisping. The accused drew a year in prison, without reprieve. Obviously he'll never serve it. The soldiers in the audience found that not too terrible. They said, "He's a horse's ass" or "He acted like a jerk" and the personality of the soldier, crushed and crying, wasn't even under consideration; it was strange that the guy could have *meant something* to his father, for instance, who adored him, to his lover, etc. Just as strange as when you reflect that the naked body of some jerk at his recruitment physical can have aroused a woman, can be loved for his specifics. You get a wholesale impression from a guy seen at a distance, like that, and through the refracting medium of a court. It requires effort to think that he has a *human condition*, and that explains, without excusing it, the imperviousness of judges and politics.

At noon here I saw an orderly from Division Headquarters who'd been in that guy's regiment before coming here. He had a few details to add: as a matter of fact the private—the Court didn't know or didn't retain this—would go to town by bike *every evening* to see his woman and come back in the morning. His buddies covered for him. And then one evening he left as usual and stayed for ten days without coming back. For four days his buddies covered for him, doing his work for him. The fourth day there was a roll call and that's when he was caught. But the buddies said that he left that very morning. The 10th day, when he came back, they were on the lookout for him, and they told him, "You've been declared a deserter for only six days. We covered for you, don't give us away." But feeling low, he said, "Oh, I don't give a shit!" and he came right out and told the colonel he'd been away for ten days. Other soldiers held that strongly against him, because his friends got detention because of it. The orderly lowered his voice and asked: "Well, and . . . they didn't say anything about his woman?" "No. They held her blameless." "Oh? Well, fine. Because she's not entirely on the up and up." "How do you mean?" "I've heard people talking . . . She was putting out some strange sort of political propaganda. And then I want to ask you, just what could they have been doing for ten whole days?" I asked, "What was he, politically?" But the orderly clammed up and I couldn't find out a thing. There's the story, my sweet. There was also another curious and entertaining trial, but just think, where would we be if I started to tell you that one? Tomorrow perhaps, because all in all, tomorrow there'll be nothing happening.

I know an appealing soldier, a real grumbler, a Parisian with an awful drawl and a finger missing on his left hand (a whole finger, not just a joint). I said to him "But you're in the armed branch, right?" "Yeah. And I gotta tellya, my old man wasn't born yesterday, he hustled plenty. No dice." "But why?" "We're Reds in Ivry, so to get even they make us pay through the nose." I see him at the café. He disdains me, but cordially, because I'm from HQ. He's infantry. Yesterday I asked him, "Going to the court-martial tomorrow?" He said, "Hell no. To see Justice at work . . . ? That's revolting, pal."

It's not revolting, it's the dregs.

I'll have you know, my sweet, that after my lovely victory ode yesterday, my champ-opponent wiped me off the chessboard three times. But just wait, that isn't all. The good Pieter was fuming, kicking me under the table, and finally he said, "You gotta stop playing, you're playing like a dope tonight: I don't know much about the game, but I'm taking your place." And he got whipped too, heroically, so I could get back in the right mood. But when I had, it was ten-thirty and the guy showed us the door.

And that's it, my sweet. *Le Journal* has announced that a 5,000-franc prize has been awarded to M. J.-P. Sartre, author of *La Rangée [The Column]*.—I'm afraid that makes for *two errors*, and in so few words.

We'll be leaving in three or four days. For our winter residence.[1] They say it's charming in spring. I'm delighted to be going back again. We'll be back at the Hôtel Bellevue. Consider this a *good* piece of news.

Au revoir, my sweet, my little dear. I love you.

❧ *to Simone de Beauvoir*

Friday, April 26

My darling Beaver

An uneventful day, as I'd foreseen yesterday. The weather rather nice and cool, the hours gentle and empty. I went to La Rose and learned via the radio that the Allies took a drubbing in Norway.—That's actually unimportant, it's the totality of the operations that counts and not success or lack of it on a local scale. I read the papers and saw in *L'Époque* that the Populist Prize had come to me by nine votes. The sentence is worded in such a way, incidentally, that it's impossible to tell whether it was by a nine-vote majority—which would give me 13—or by nine votes in all and for all. In any case, I found out the following:

[1] Morsbronn.

Duhamel is chairman of the Jury, and I'm going to write him a letter that will cover all of them. I find it rather distasteful to write to the man, but I absolutely will not thank him *personally* (particularly in that he probably didn't vote for me; Paulhan says he's totally hostile toward me). I'll thank him *for the populist jury*, and as President. Isn't that the thing to do? Incidentally I'm still waiting for official notification. In the mail this morning I got only your letter and one from T.

After La Rose, weather readings and then work. This afternoon I was expecting the champion of champions in chess (the real champion) but he must find us kid stuff and didn't bother to show up. So I worked for quite a while, and soon I'll have finished the Marcelle chapter. I think her character comes through better. In the sense that I'm making it less elaborate and more sentimental. All in all, the first Marcelle was a composite role with comical traits. Now Marcelle is more a situation: a sickly, aging woman, who feels herself a failure, obliged to stay home because of her health, and she—without being a feminist, but simply reacting against her condition as a woman and a sickly one at that— doesn't want to let herself be dominated—and above all, passionately wants a baby to give meaning to her life, but she is trapped because they had long ago agreed to do away with it if there were one. In addition to that, she's disgusted by her own illness, the knowledge that she's ungraceful, etc. And above all because her life is absurd. She too, in her own way, has a *dark* sort of character, and it's not superficial. Besides, she is tied in knots: she cannot speak about herself. She is very fond of Daniel because Daniel is the only one who manages to make her take an interest in herself. It seems to me that with the pathos of the situation, this character, though more *typical* than particular, should suffice. What do you think? You'll undoubtedly tell me that you'll have to read it and see. I'm also keeping a scrap of conversation with her mother, but their relationship is very different (I don't exactly know what it'll be, it's not perfect but in any case it will be very short: six or seven pages). And all told the chapter won't be much more than ten. Sounds all right? Except that I'm now putting in two telephone conversations between Marcelle and Mathieu during the course of the novel to bring her back to mind (I've already done one of them) and also, in the 1st chapter I emphasize the Marcelle-Mathieu relationship (their plan was to tell each other everything, but he built up his lucidity by himself because he was inclined that way, without realizing that she was not following). This will fix things up somewhat. But I'm pleased that this novel is finished: I wouldn't write it this way again. You impressed me the other day, my little one, when you said that you saw how my desire to think the world through on my own is illustrated throughout my life. It didn't much impress me, I must say, insofar as it concerns me (he says modestly), but it did impress me as what was lacking in Mathieu. He was not historicizing[1] himself. I well understand that: 1st, he is in the throes of a crisis—2nd in succeeding volumes he will historicize himself. But the thing is, it's the general concept of the book that's in question. Basically you have to take heroes from childhood—or use devices. Yours historicize more than mine.

On the subject of yours, I'm so pleased, my sweet, that you can soon hand 400 pages over to Brice Parain. Would you like me to write to him for you? Don't forget that he is serving in the Army (a cyclist in Paris) and that one can see him, I think, from 5 to 9 only and on Sunday. If you dig around in the heap of letters I brought back to you, you should certainly find his military address. If not, write via *NRF*. You'll lose only a day.

This evening I worked a bit more. Of all things, I went back for a short stint at the notebook. Merely to set down, concerning Malraux, that the cardinal categories of ethics are *being, having,* and *doing.* And that subtle dialectical bonds exist between them. Example: Malraux; one has to choose between *being* and *doing*—Rougemont on the subject of Don Juan: he lacked enough *being* to *have.* At rare intervals I slip in a little note. But there may be ten pages of writing since my return from leave. But it's very good. I'll take three months of vacation and complete the novel. And then after that I'll go back to the notebook. I'll go back to it completely refreshed, and the XV already written will be in the past. It's really odd how life is more natural when there isn't a notebook around, how incidents melt away the moment we've lived them and how, in a sense, authenticity is the affair of an intimate journal (which, however, you mustn't think I scorn).

There you are, my little one, four pages made out of nothing, like *Bérénice.* I could have told you about the second of yesterday's trials, it would have been worthwhile, but to me it seems a little stale.

Listen carefully, little flower. When you get the lycée paycheck, you'll have to send me fifteen hundred francs immediately. That's cutting it close, because I owe 1,000 of it to Pieter and Paul and need five hundred to live on. Also, here's a book to add to the list of those I asked you for (about a week ago): Maurice Muret's *Guillaume II.* I'd like to see that after Ludwig's. I really need some books, my little one. I'm dragging myself through *Man's Hope,* which is full of ideas but terribly boring. He lacks almost nothing, that man, but, my God, how much he lacks it.

My sweet, I've really enjoyed writing to you. Even more than yesterday because yesterday was anecdotal and, basically, I like nothing so much as writing

---

[1] "To become involved as a concrete existent in an actual world so as to have a 'history'." Hazel Barnes, glossary to her translation of *Being and Nothingness.*

to you when I have nothing to tell you. That's a vice, you'll say. No, but it does remind me of our rambling discussions, it makes me feel as though I'm talking to you. I love you so much. I told you I'd be in Paris on July 15 because they're going to reestablish the leaves again, and the 3rd round begins officially on May 15th. Since it takes about two months before I leave, you can reach your own conclusions. Till tomorrow, my sweet. I love you with all my might.

ༀ to Simone de Beauvoir

Saturday, April 27

My darling Beaver

A little go at the typewriter for variety's sake, but also because I'm going to write official letters of thanks for the prize longhand. I got a very appealing letter from the director of the journal that's coughing up: *Les Cahiers de Paris*. Alas, also the March number of *Les Cahiers de Paris*. The laureate of the Populist Prize for poetry had given them some of his poems. If I'm the prose equal of that belaureled poet, I swear I'll dedicate myself to Industry the moment peace returns. And the journal itself is terrifying. You'd think it was a journal of pharmacist patrons of the arts who pay to get published, like Church, but with nothing but Churches. All it lacks are ads for Midy suppositories. It saddened me somewhat because ultimately I am compromised, and politeness requires that I, too, the laureate in prose, give some scraps to the journal that's slipping me the dough. So be it.

Meanwhile, in that very friendly letter, M. Picard utters not one word about the money. It will come in its own good time, I hope, but when? In short, we have four thousand francs of *hopes*, counting your supplementary work.

Aside from that, I have absolutely nothing to tell you, except that I love you with all my might, my little flower. We're still set to leave for the Hôtel Bellevue, and we're pretty excited. The idea delights me. I'll have my own room, where I'll be able to shut myself in when I like, and we'll get our place again after it has been inhabited for three months by other rodents, I'm curious to see in what state they'll have left it. And we'll see Charlotte again, who said in February as she saw us leave, "Alas, I won't see my handsome little fliers anymore." I'll give her a short ration of platonic flirtation, if you think that's compatible with authenticity. She was decent, and we're somewhat anxious to know what the Bordeaux Division that succeeded us will have done to her.

I worked all day, and then near the end of the day I went over to be wiped off the board by the chess champion. The work is going well. I think Marcelle will stand out as she should. In any case I think a reader will understand why Mathieu is fond of her: it's her virtue. In spite of herself. This evening, at La Rose, there were a dozen or so English from the Marines, who are stationed a few kilometers away. All of them drunk, not knowing a word of French, and most appealing. And the French soldiers were nice enough to them. They were a bit protective of them and explaining things that the others didn't understand at all; and at the same time they were amazed, like children, because they were English. One of the Englishmen was at our table. He was praising the merits of our Bordeaux. "Yes," said a French private, "but then the next day . . ." And he pretended to have a terrible headache. "No!" said the Englishman. And he drew from his pocket, with an air of wide-eyed wonder, a small box of aspirin. Everyone was charmed, including the waitresses, and we passed the box of aspirin from hand to hand saying, "So this is the famous English sense of humor." We came back and found Paul absorbed in a game of chess with Courcy. He too has a hateful identity complex toward me. Typing, chess, he learns everything two weeks after I've taken it up. But it's simply because he only has his *licence* and I've got the *agrégation*. Yesterday, we argued on a point of typographical detail: I was wrong and he was right. He put on such a look of beatitude that the clerks, though they have no feeling for facial expressions, went on and on and about it.

That's that, my little sweet. What meager gleanings. But I can't do any better, unless I invent. Anyway, you've had long letters these last few days. I love you, my darling, I love you with all my heart. I long so to see you. I'm impatient to know what Brice Parain will say about your little novel. Till tomorrow. I love you with all my might.

P.S.: We'll probably leave on Tuesday. Perhaps you won't get a letter that day.

ఞ *to Simone de Beauvoir*

Sunday, April 28

My darling Beaver
Yet another uneventful day. I worked and I played chess. This morning I tried two games *at the same time*, and I won them both. This evening, on the other hand, Hantziger beat me easily three times in a row. You were very reasonable in your letter, little judge. Now, how did it go? Something like this:

either your champion is a true champion and you don't beat him. Or else you win and he's not a champion. To be quite honest, my dearest, he *isn't* a champ and he *beats me.* I flattered Pieter infinitely by reading him the brief passage in your letter concerning himself. Straight off, today he called you "Mademoiselle de Beauvoir" instead of his usual "your girlfriend." He too believes I have no cause to feel proud. As a matter of fact, I beat the man just once and that by surprise. Since then I've been walloped each time. I don't want to leave the subject of chess without mentioning a surprising reflection by Mondange, the new clerk, who is a fine fellow but not very bright. Within the last few days he has laboriously learned the moves of the various pieces and the rudiments, and he watches our games with interest. This morning, while I was playing my two simultaneous games against Hantziger and Pieter, I said: "Give me the whites, I certainly deserve that much." They answered, "Yes, you do." And Mondange, surprised; "What advantage does that give you, getting the whites? Of course they *do show up better.*" I find that rather wonderful.

I was overjoyed at your little letter regarding Brice Parain. So it's as good as taken? He doesn't doubt it for an instant. After comparing yourself to Claire Francillon, you'll be able to compare yourself to your heart's content in your hours of gloom to Marie-Anne Comnène, who is a great authoress of the *NRF* and who has written a *Grazia* that's every bit as long as your novel. It would tickle me so much, my little one, to see a fat volume "Simone de Beauvoir—and the title." What title? It doesn't matter in the least, the *NRF* will find one for you. They always came up with the title for a person's first novel. That reminds me: would you like me to entitle (you'll shriek. You might like to know that I've got a sneaky, sheepish look on my face and am flipping you a sidelong glance). . . . Would you like it if I named the complete Mathieu series "Greatness"? I know it's madness and nonsense. But all the same, give me your opinion without bawling me out too much. Because ultimately it has to do more with authenticity than freedom per se. Send me the clipping from *Paris-Midi:* here we never get *Paris-Midi.*

I received a letter from Léon Lemonnier, from the populist Jury, who is going to send me the 2,000 francs. Pieter says he would never want to send them to you. So I'll have them sent to me, and I'll immediately send them on to you. With this business of sending and forwarding, count on the money around the 10th. He says: I will send you the money by postal check or order on your personal account if you have one. I of course do not. So it will be a postal check. But clear up one question for me: can a postal check be cashed immediately?

Marcelle is coming along, I think she will be touching and slightly repellent. It seems to me that it's quite good, but I made such a mistake with the Prologue that I no longer dare swear to anything. It does me no good to be away from you, little adviser. I had one idea on simplification at any rate: the mother will know nothing. Why go complicating things without rhyme or reason. And actually the mother will appear only briefly at the end of the chapter. I made myself nauseous last night through describing Marcelle's bouts of nausea. I pulled my tongue back and thrust my lips out, to verify the movement.

As for Saint-Cyr, well, my little one, Pieter's arrangements seem to be progressing very well (you have to count on three months for a recall. It's slow). Except it's impossible to decide whether Pieter's arrangements are *ours* or simply his own. Neither he nor his wife have any idea. If you want to set your mind at ease on the question, go to see her at 255 Rue des Pyrénées. There's a senator mixed up in it.

That's all there is, my little one. Tania hasn't written for several days, I've made an inner break, and I'm not writing either. So I don't know the story of the couple who took her for an American. Tell it to me in twenty-five words or less, if you please.

> Samuel Pepys: *Journal*
> Muret: *Guillaume II*
> Kierkegaard: *The Diary of a Seducer*
> G. Blin: *Baudelaire*
> 2 *Imaginaires*
> Chamson: War Journal (*Quatre mois* [*Four Months*] is the title, I think. Flammarion)
> Charles Braibant: *Lumière bleue* [Blue Light] *War journal*, August 24– December 39).

That's all I can think of for now. But with my novel and *four* readings a day, it will surely get me through a month. Oh yes:

> the Van Dine: *Murder in the Garden*
> and then see if L'Empreinte has come out with something good this month, I'd like a couple of detective novels.

Till tomorrow, you whom I love. Your little letters are jewels to me, they give me back all of Paris and our little life that I loved so much, and yourself. You are still living *for me*, you know. I'm at the Flore with you, or else at Sacré-Coeur, like the other evening (certainly we'll go, I'm delighted about that). You are my little flower. I love you.

෨ *to Simone de Beauvoir*

Monday, April 29th

My darling Beaver

Now we know, we're leaving in the morning. Clear the decks at four-thirty in the morning, load baggage till five-thirty—it's a real house-moving, furniture and all. Then at six-thirty we leave. We're rather pleased, really. The schoolroom from which I am writing is a veritable battlefield, the tables have disappeared and in their place are parcels, crates, packages piled one on top of the other. We went to say good-bye to the town, but on every street corner we could already hear "Adieu, té" with the Bordeaux accent, we could see the dark, fat little privates with blue cheeks, instead of the tall strapping blonds who usually hung around (we're a half-Alsatian, half-Parisian battalion), and the town no longer belongs to us. The Bordeaux troops are strolling around checking out this town that they don't know; curious, they ogle things that half repel us from overfamiliarity; they're still timid with the redhead from La Rose, and they don't know that the big blond seal who serves dinner is named Anna. Besides, they're all half drunk because they're just in from the front lines and have seen neither cafés nor women for almost three months. That surprises us, and we feel the town is no longer ours, they'll get used to it bit by bit, they'll—at first slyly, then brazenly—pinch the redhead's bottom, and eventually they'll feel at home. I for one already have visions of the landscape one can see from the Hôtel Bellevue, and it makes me feel poetic. Besides, the mosquito season is upon us and I'm very glad to put an end to that.

Apart from that, my little one, do you realize that I got no letter from you today? There was an immense one from Tania, narrating at great length the story of the couple who took her for an American. So don't you tell it to me, unless you've already done so. And a sour note from Catinaud asking why I haven't written to him. And that was all. It's a real little vacuum. All the more since tomorrow we'll get letters very late, because of the move. But I'll get two.

We'll be doing 4 readings a day: 8:00, 11:00, 16:00, 21:00, and there are only three of us; that means work, but I'll still get my five or six free hours a day to do my novel. We'll cut back on the chess games, which are finally getting to be hallucinatory; you know, it's like an old refrain that keeps at you all day long. Today, I played *nine* games (because this afternoon my novel was packed up). I'm really saturated with it. No more breakfasts, no more radio, but that's all to the good. It'll be like the country. I'll just need a few books to be completely happy.

That's that, my little one. Inch by inch, I've completely eliminated Marcelle's mother; she has no role at all now, in fact, since no one says anything to her.

The chapter will seem densely packed, but I hope it holds up (8 pages). It's done. Now I'm going to work on chapter 3 (Mathieu-Sarah-Brunet) which I find lots more fun.

My sweet, I love you so much, it's a real loss to go without a letter from you. But I know it's traveling along somewhere, little irreproachable, and I rejoice in advance at the thought of having two tomorrow. I love you, I send you kisses for you little old cheeks. I would so love to see you and take you in my arms.

❧ *to Simone de Beauvoir*

Tuesday, April 30th

My darling Beaver

Here I am comfortably installed in the Hôtel Bellevue again after an uneventful trip. Why is that good news? Well, there's no mystery to it: it's simply, can you believe this, because I have a room all to myself where I can stay all day. Today I scarcely did anything but doze because I hadn't slept much last night, but, you know, it's terrific having four walls around me and nothing there but me. It's been eight months since that's happened to me. It's an attractive little room, with marbled wallpaper, a bed, a small table, a water pitcher and basin, a bedside table and a flower vase. I'm in seventh heaven. I did after all manage to write for a very short while during the day, for the pleasurable sensation of being at work alone. Well, it's really marvelous; the constant obligation to create a barrier between my work and the guys' noise was so enervating. It's delightful here, and I've already made several auspicious little discoveries.

So we left at seven by bus, after lugging packing cases from five o'clock on. I had a mild liver attack, not painful but a bit worrisome, gone at present. We got in at 8 o'clock and again lugged boxes around all morning, then I shaved really close and washed, to show my best side to Charlotte; I didn't yet have my room, I only got it by late morning, I was exultant. The windows look out over the park at the Thermal Bathhouse. It's really something to see the countryside I'd left snow-covered now green and smelling verdant. More than ever before in my life, I am feeling what seasons are. It really affects me. There is no set age for discovering first truths.

So off we went to Charlotte's. But there, a bitter disappointment: instead of showing the joyful eagerness we'd expected, she barely gave us a smile, and besides, she looked quite ugly, with pinched features and a bitter expression around her mouth. We imagined that she'd let some man from Bordeaux steal her heart away and, to further torture ourselves, we went so far as to imagine that it was some meteorologist who, building on the esteem that we'd been able to instill in her for this military corps, had transformed that esteem into more tender feelings for his personal benefit. But, according to the latest news, it is because for three days she's had a terrible toothache and hasn't been able to sleep for three nights.

I came back around two o'clock, I played two games of chess, began to work a bit on my novel (I wasn't on duty), and dozed on my bed. Pieter woke me up, bringing me two letters from you, a long and a short one, I was delighted. My little one, 1,200 francs will do, because I'll deduct whatever I need from the Populist Prize money, and send you the rest. Count on 1,600 francs, which you'll receive around the 5th or 6th. Soon I'll send you Jules Renard's *Journal*. I'm undecided about the *Dostoyevsky*: I had promised it to T., but if I give it to T. when will you get it? Perhaps the best idea would be to send it to you, for you to read it quickly and pass it on to her. Of course you should buy Kafka's *Journal* the moment it comes out.

That's all for today, my little dearest. Not very well thought through, but I'm dropping from fatigue. Oh yes: would you *immediately* send me two packs of envelopes and two or three pads of paper like this, because I can scarcely stock up here and have almost none left, I don't even know how I can wait for the arrival of your package. When the Kafka comes out, you'll have to add *Fear and Trembling* and *The Treatise on Despair*.[1]

My darling, my sweet little flower, I love you with all my might. Till tomorrow. Tender kisses for your dear face.

∞ *to Simone de Beauvoir*

May 1st

My darling Beaver

Today I'm writing to you early, it's not yet six. That's because I've just finished touching up Chapter III and will type it this evening at nine, after the reading. I'm surging ahead. If it keeps up like this, I'll certainly be finished by June 1st. Pieter will bring it to you when he gets to Paris on leave, and you should give it to Parain right away so he can give it to Gallimard and Paulhan. Not before rereading it, however. And criticizing it. As for your criticism, it will undoubtedly

---

[1] *By Kierkegaard. (SdB)*

be of two sorts: on the one hand the words—or passages—to delete. You know there always are some. You can act on those right away on your own. You have carte blanche to cross out, erase, strike anything you like. And then there are the more important ones and the vaguer ones about passages that "don't work." About those, I propose: it would be nice if you explained your reactions in detail and sent them to me, and I'll make the corrections on the proofs to save time, because if we had to wait for my presence in Paris then lug the manuscript back again, correct and send it off again, we'd never be through. By this means the book should appear in October and probably start being serialized in the *NRF* by July or August. I only have some fifty pages left to do or redo: the Mathieu-Daniel chapter—the Daniel-Marcelle chapter—the chapter on Marcelle alone—the Marcelle-Mathieu chapter. That's it for the month of May.

I received the short article from *Paris-Midi*, sent by *Lit tout* to entice me. But he probably doesn't lure many clients if he uses the same procedures with all prospective subscribers that he did with me, I mean if he sends the most amusing and scarcest articles to nonsubscribers by the bundle and always with an eye to enticing them. It would suit me just fine to have *Lit tout* send me the curiosities of journalism this way for the rest of my life. The article is really something. But who wrote it? Who could know firsthand about the Notebooks? Chonez? I found it intriguing.

Here there's a great hullabaloo about our bedrooms; they want to provide space for some noncommissioned officers, and I'm afraid I'll ultimately have to share Pieter's. It would absolutely break my heart, I was so happy in this one. I'm not being attacked directly, but Pieter, being too wily and wanting to keep a room with two beds for himself alone, runs the risk of being turned out and replaced by two noncommissioned officers. In which case he would ask me to come join with him so he can keep his room (it's still more complicated than that, there have been blowups between the first sergeant and the radio-sergeant, but they're totally devoid of interest. The only important thing is that we're in danger of finding ourselves in that room with two beds). I'll defend my position to the death, never fear. Incidentally, it's curious how I—who was M. Plume[1] in civilian life—have become a really fierce wangler in military life. They're all a bit scared of me and I play it up as much as possible.

Aside from that, what have I done? Readings—but for now they've put the telephone in our little office and that's nice, we call in the results to the batteries without having to move. We don't leave our quarters anymore. I'm writing to you in my room on a half-moon table, with the window open onto the park of the Thermal Bathhouse; I can see green, gray, and violet trees, and I see passing

---

[1] A *character of Michaux's.* (SdB)

cars and motorbikes, and I hear the sound of voices, it's most pleasant. Pray to God, my little sweet, pray to God that I can keep all of this! It's true that, when this letter reaches you, my fate will be decided. But then, for the moment, I swear that it's a pretty remarkable life: with the telephone and the little bedrooms, it's becoming absolutely monastic; we don't see an officer anymore, nor even a soldier, we scarcely see one another. And then, the single worldly element: lunch at Charlotte's. She was more agreeable today and told me in a sulky tone, "So you miss Brumath? Because there are women in Brumath?" There was a slight advantage for the taking, but Pieter wanted to play the gallant and ruined everything.

Ah! I meant to tell you: how hard you are with that deaf-mute,[2] my little flower, you and Sorokine. The passages in your letter when you speak of her sound awfully hard and cruel—it really gets to a softhearted guy like me.

Nothing else. It seems that things in Norway are going badly. But it's Paul, the eternal sourpuss, who heard it over the radio. I'm waiting for tomorrow's papers. That would be a very bad business.

And what else, my sweet? Nothing. How I love your letters, my love, and how I need them. I love you. I too, and very often, have such a need to see you that I feel it isn't possible I won't be seeing you soon. But the moment that happens I try to be reasonable. It has to be no, my little flower. Hardly before July 15th, I'm afraid. And the Saint-Cyr prospect seems rather remote. Only, I believe that on July 15 we'll be leaving this monastic life for the long rest session, and then you'll be able to see me.

Till tomorrow, my dear love. Now I'm going to write to Catinaud. Not to T., who isn't writing to me. Do send me some books.

Kisses for your little cheeks, my love.

✿ to Simone de Beauvoir

Thursday, May 2

My darling Beaver

Don't be too put off by this paper: I'm waiting for your package so I can start using human stationery again. This is the *old-style* readings analysis sheet. By now we have prettier ones, and each has an individual little diagram.

---

[2] *A deaf, unbalanced student who was pursuing me. Soon after, she was institutionalized.* (SdB)

My dear little one, today I had many little blessings bestowed upon me. This morning, first of all, a little financial blessing: the NRF finally paid for my article on Giraudoux: 500 francs. So you will have the 2,000 francs *in toto*, and you'll be able to get through the month. I'll send back the 300 francs you are expecting to send me if it has already gone off. Everything is working out, and you won't have that miserable little end of the month that you had in April, poor little flower—and which breaks my heart. It was something like, "I've got 14 sous in my pocket," or "I had only a rice cake to dine on." No, my pet: not this month, this month it will be steak and a good little Esaü du Dôme from Toulouse. I love it when you tell me about "succulent" or "delectable" meals you've eaten. The one thing above all that brought tears was the day when you said you "did myself proud" at your parents'. And knowing all about your mother's cooking, I inevitably had to think of you as miserably starving. Second little blessing: your Tuesday's letter, so tender, my dearest love, so tender and so moving. My, how I "mourn your martyrdom and rejoice at your love, my luscious Beevour." I agree that it's an eternity till July 15. But, after that, if Saint-Cyr is no longer a possibility, at least it's *sure* that we'll be going to rest camp. And you could certainly arrange to come for a good long time. My little one, you too, you are my universe. I do not think any other two could be as one more deeply and more variously than we. We've been lucky. Third little blessing: the books. I immediately began the Muret, it's less intelligent and more stupidly partisan than the Ludwig, but it tells stories that aren't found in the other, and therefore I'll have an excellent knowledge of William II. Are you reading Ludwig's? You must. I'll send back the Muret in good time. Tonight I'll light my candle on the bedside table and begin the Van Dine. Why a candle, since I have electric light? Because I like to read by candlelight before going to sleep, it seems to intimate and rustic.

You know, you're really very wrong to pity me for my lot, my little one. I am deprived of you, which is a torment. But not more than you are of me, we're equal on that score. And otherwise, first, I think that I'm the last guy in the world to suffer from all the minor deprivations (lack of entertainment, of conversation, etc.) because of my sangfroid, and besides I've always cultivated a poetic little reclusiveness à la Silvio Pellico (he was moved by a flower, I think, that he saw in the prison courtyard). And in addition, it's amazing how well off we are here. First—knock on wood—I think I'll be keeping my room. A single contingency: the officers had reserved the beautiful rooms at the Bathhouse, leaving us this second-class hotel. But it turns out that their place has bedbugs, and they spend the whole day scratching. We're afraid they may began to eye our rooms, more rustic but sans bedbugs. So as they pass by scratching, we pretend to scratch too. Besides, you know, spring is pouring in from all sides.

You'd be moved to see small groups of soldiers chatting in the hedgerows, sitting on top of doorsteps, in a bosk, with that meditative patience that you admire in the Arabs. It touches and delights me, and I am *happy*. Besides, my novel is keeping me entertained. Today I worked on Mathieu's everlasting monologue, when he leaves Sarah's place. I'm going to try to "historicize" it a bit. I have some ideas.

Today I got up at 6 and I wrote to Magnane. After that, weather reading, then from 8 to 10 worked well. From 10 to 11 weather reading. From 11 to 12 work. At 12 o'clock, lunch at Charlotte's. On return—1:30 your letters and I'm alerted about a package at the postal clerk's. I go there and en route I meet the chess champ who leads me off for a game and clobbers me. On return I worked. At 3 o'clock another reading. From 4 to 8: work and typing. At 8 o'clock I dined on jam and cheese, reading the Muret. Then, did a quick reading and it's nine o'clock, I'm writing to you. Tomorrow is my day off, I only have to go for the coffee and grub. I'll have twelve hours of work, of chess and reading.

Till tomorrow, my little dear, my little flower, I so wish for you to feel how I love you. If there's any justice this letter will touch you even more than Sunday's, because I'm all besotted with good feelings for you.

I long to kiss your dear little face.

Nippert, the little Protestant jackal, is toadying to the noncoms, who treat him like the garbage he is. Yesterday Sergeant Courcy said to him, "Nippert, go get my wash from the laundress." He gets up and prepares, all docility, to go. Then Mondange, not deliberately, coincidentally: "Well now, that reminds me I've got some wash to be fetched too." Nippert spins toward him and says with hatred, "What the . . . ? I'm not *everybody's* coolie."

๑ฅ *to Simone de Beauvoir*

Friday, May 3

My darling Beaver

For me, here, it was an ordinary day. I was "off duty." Meaning, I went for the coffee and rations, period full stop. I took advantage of it to forge ahead on my work, and besides, out of laziness, alas, to move ahead in my reading of the Van Dine. Aside from that, nothing new. I got a wildly enthusiastic letter from a certain Marcel Berger, member of the Populist Prize panel: "Céline merely stutters in comparison to you, etc." *Except that* I learned from another member of the Jury that this delirious admirer hadn't bothered to get there on time for the meeting and showed up when the vote was done and signed. If I had needed one vote, I'd have been screwed. Nonetheless I will answer amiably. A letter from the cashier of the Prize—it was inevitable—asking for a paper on behalf of their journal. He modestly explains that he simply wants a scribble, since the journal pays nothing: "Perhaps could you give an abandoned fragment, or a fragment of a book now in the works . . ." So I'll give them the passage from *The Age of Reason* on the bombardment of Valence. It's the only one that can be excerpted. Finally a dignified letter from Dr. Catesson, asking why I have not replied (he's the doctor who wrote on van Gogh and on *Nothingness*). I replied.

Till tomorrow, my sweet, my little flower, my pure little flower. I love you with all my might. It's not obvious in this factual letter, but it's true and deeply *felt*.

๛ *to Simone de Beauvoir*

Saturday, May 4

My darling Beaver

When was it that I sent you such a short letter? Tuesday evening probably, but I don't remember that it was that short. I'm sorry. You yourself write to me at such length and so sweetly.

I'm happy to say that *Lit tout* sent me the short piece from *Paris-Midi*. As for Sorokine, like you I find her instability a bit irritating, but you must bear in mind that there are any number of gestures of affection that even a respectable man, however, cannot allow himself at a dance hall with a woman, and that a woman with another woman must avoid completely. It must be somewhat irritating for her. Though she may love you in her rough-and-tumble way, my dear, this affair makes me laugh. How nice and pleasant you remain amid all this, little pampered darling. Not overly in relation to your merits, of course, but in relation to what you'd like.

Today the monastic life, supermonastic. Pieter, though he's not sensitive to atmosphere, said, "It was no damn good, this Saturday." I asked, "Why?" and he said, "Dunno," with a vague shrug directed toward the sky. And Hantz was totally undone (Hantz is Hantziger). All afternoon he sat on the front steps, gazing out of great pink eyes at the park of the Thermal Bathhouse, and morning and evening he ate at the restaurant to console himself. But I was rather insensitive to this sadness. I can see very well what it was: the weather was muggy (furrowed altostratus, fair-weather cumulus, wind out of the West, sky 9/10 overcast, visibility: 20 to 50 km. 16°C—Pressure: 740 mm³ and gray with a dark sky, not even threatening, the kind that seems eternal. The men didn't know what to do with themselves. I knew very well what to do with myself. I worked, and had the excellent surprise, having typed five shapeless draft pages so as to see a neater text, of finding them good and definitive. Tomorrow I'll finish Mathieu's monologue, which I'm making determinedly existential. In short, he'll take up from the point where Roquentin left off. The order of the day: this morning got up, breakfast, weather reading. Two hours of work, weather reading, one hour of work, lunch at Charlotte's. After all there is some impalpable and tender something between Charlotte and me: she laughed heartily on seeing me come in, walking briskly with my gas mask across my chest (an officious idiot had told me that a very strict new order required us to carry masks). But I don't think it will ever go beyond that. I have a few such memories, hyperplatonic idylls of the eyes. Do you remember that girl in the Le Havre Library who moved me so because she looked a bit like you? Then, work, and around four o'clock I went to town, after all, to get the paper on which I'm writing to you because I was sick and tired of using ballistic analysis sheets for my correspondence and literary writing. I did a reading then typed. But while I was typing with a feeling of slightly morose emptiness, I saw my literary reputation under an extremely desolate light. Yet I was satisfied with that because in spite of it I was eager to write and to type, for the sake of the novel itself, for the fat volume it will become. I dined on a chunk of bread and a piece of chocolate, then I played a game or two of chess, and here I am. Wait a moment: Paul's back, I can hear him, I'm going to go and poke some fun at him. I'll tell you why in a while. There, it's done: I poked fun at him, and into the bargain I drank a bit of wine. But I won't tell you why because, on reflection, it would bore you terribly. Roughly, here it is: as a matter of dignity, he didn't want to have meals with the clerks. On the quiet I told the clerks to invite him, which they did. So now he's going to have dinner downstairs. I feigned huge surprise, asked for an explanation, and razzed him for changing his mind.

That's all, my little one, my dear little one. I would really like to be with you at this moment, at the little Café Rey, for instance, just before going to bed, commenting very tenderly on the events of the day. I love you so much, my little one. I had a short bout of faintheartedness today because I was so far from you.

Till tomorrow, my dear little one. I would so like to cover your little face with kisses and hold you in my arms.

⚭ *to Simone de Beauvoir*

Sunday, May 5

My darling Beaver

I should be writing to you on your handsome paper, which arrived today, but yesterday I bought this ugly striped stuff and for economy's sake I really have to use it up. Thank you too for the books. *Baudelaire* looks interesting—Pepys too, but I've just read Chamson, dreadful and grandiloquent, and the Braibant seems devoid of interest. On the other hand I find that *Solitude en commun* [*Solitude in Common*],[1] which I'll send back to you, my sweet, with the *Dostoyevsky* (Pieter is reading it at the moment, it will be Tuesday or Wednesday)—recalls some of the charm of *The Constant Nymph*. Not all the charm: the subject is less appealing—but still and all I was completely charmed this morning at the restaurant as I read it.

I won't tell you what I did today because I scarcely did anything (chess, readings, work). Tomorrow I'll give you a word or two about the letters I've received and about my work. Right now I'm going to bed, because somehow I'm rather tired tonight. With a slight headache, I don't know why.

My little one, my sweet little flower, I really wish you wouldn't worry too much. I don't like it at all, at all when you are unhappy. Kisses for your little mouth, my love, and for your little eyes.

⚭ *to Simone de Beauvoir*

Monday, May 6

My darling Beaver

You won't be getting a very long letter from me today—and I'm writing only to you—because I'm feeling pretty doleful: I don't know why, but last night all the colics and cramps in the world were visited upon me (I probably caught a cold in my stomach) and I woke up at four in the morning with a fever—a very slight one that gradually lessened as the day wore on but still left me feeling dazed and unwell. Tomorrow I'll be all right after a good night's sleep. What have I been doing? Well, I stayed in bed almost all day, sometimes I read, sometimes I closed my eyes and a tide of memories came back, memories with yourself in them. Particularly of when we went back to Bourg-Madame by bus,

[1] *By Margaret Kennedy. (SdB)*

last summer. Ah, my sweet, how I loved you, this whole afternoon long, how the slightest memory of a moment spent with you seems instantly precious and poetic. I was feeling a *great tenderness*, my sweet, and don't you start thinking it's because I was under the weather. I also discovered some old memories that have nothing to do with you: the look of my grandmother's bedroom on the Rue Saint-Jacques, etc. You know how pleasant it is to be stretched out on a bed, ailing, dozing in broad daylight. But wouldn't you know, there was no letter from you. Only a note from my mother and another from M. Durry (remember that fellow?), congratulating me rather inopportunely for my article on Giraudoux. I say rather inopportunely because though it came out two months ago, Durry allows as how he "can't resist, etc." A note from Nizan, who got himself transferred to the English army, which is right up his alley.

And that's that, my dearest, I certainly wasted my time today on the factum: Mathieu's monologue was no good, I should have started it again from scratch, but was too groggy. I'll set to work on it tomorrow, there's basically not too much to be done on it. I still rather like *Solitude in Common*. It's less appealing about halfway through, but it's terrific the way she has you feel the evolution of both the whole family and each of the individual fates that make it up. She's graceful, and a real professional. Sometimes it's a bit facile, that's all.

That's that, my little one, the life of an invalid. I didn't go to see Charlotte, and I'm very annoyed because Paul went instead, and she mistook him for me. Right now it's nine o'clock and I'm really going to go to bed. For the moment it's slightly cold in here.

My sweet little Beaver, my little flower, I wish you could feel the tenderness with which I've written this pitiful little letter and the *need* I have for you. I love you so much, my sweet. I'd so love to see you clumping in, and to hug you in my arms.

৵ to Simone de Beauvoir

Tuesday, May 7

My darling Beaver

I've completely recovered, except for a few little cramps, and I received two letters from you. An embarrassment of riches. Because I'm happy to be healthy again, to feel my old self again, relishing life's simple pleasures. I was happy all day long. How hard you are, you two harpies, with poor little Nony who, though she may not be mute as I'd thought, is nonetheless deaf and hunchbacked—

that much you told me—and half crazy. On the other hand, of course, you're charming with each other, like all tormentors. Your little Sorokine seems very appealing.

Your picture is very beautiful, you know, it moved me very much. My little dearest, how sorry I am not to see the handsome little coat, which seems to suit you so well. But perhaps I will. Or else we'll take it to the Hôtel Mistral, if the right season for it has gone by, and you'll put it on once in our room for me alone. This is the first time in our eleven years of marriage that you'll have gotten a pretty trinket I haven't seen at all.

This was a day of dead calm and the bliss of convalescence. I finished Mathieu's monologue. It isn't graceful but it is solid, and without being too weighty it asks the essential questions; I think it will put the whole novel into perspective. As for gracefulness—what can I do?—no dice. I ate—a real pleasure after forty-eight hours' fast—I played chess and did readings, and above all I was blissfully aware of health flowing within my body. I got a nice little letter from T., I will write to her after all—not tonight, but tomorrow at dawn (I'll get up at 6 a.m.).

Your finances I don't wholly grasp. You'd said that things would be fine with the 2,000 francs from the Prize. I cashed it today, I'll send it tomorrow. But one piece of advice: *except in the case* of final notification before garnishment (I don't know what it's called: demand, I think), do not pay the taxes. If I were you, I'd quietly wait for the end of the month and send half. If you have even the slightest qualms, *write* that you will send half at the end of the month; they'll be able to handle that. It should get you off the hook.

My little dearest, you don't know how much I love you. Or rather, yes, you do very well know it in general terms, but what you don't know is how much I love you now, at this moment—and when this letter tells you so, it will already be two days later. I would so love to have you here in my arms, for you read it on my face. I would so love to see yours, and to give it a kiss. I love you.

❧ *to Simone de Beauvoir*

Wednesday, May 8

My darling Beaver

Now listen, about your novel, I'm extremely anxious to know what Fairy Godfather Parain (I wrote that to annoy myself, and I'm delighted to think it will annoy you prodigiously), will say to you. My sweet, how I want him to be all enthusiasm. Look how idiotic this is: I'm writing as though it isn't yet done, while in fact it already took place yesterday, and it's just that your letter hasn't reached me yet. And if you've had a slight disappointment, how stale this will seem as you read it. But I'm sure there was no disappointment: your little novel is *excellent*, and that must be obvious to even an ass, and he's not such an ass as all that, it's more that he's cracked, with two distinct areas of mania: language and generations. On festive days he synthesizes the two, but I don't think your novel could provide him such an occasion.

Till tomorrow, litte flower. Here, nothing worth mentioning. Yes: Charlotte's in love with someone else, I think. She giggled and nudged another waitress when she looked at me (which, dear God, could well be not in the least flattering to me, particularly since I've got several days' growth on my cheeks and am tripping over my beard), but to him, a lovely little chasseur, she handed a bouquet of lilies of the valley.

I love you, my little darling, you are my dearest.

৵৹ to Simone de Beauvoir

[Thursday, May 9]

My darling Beaver

I'm feeling a bit sheepish about T., because now she's writing me charming, very upset letters *despite my silence*, something she's never done before. Today's elicited tears: "Please start writing to me again, I'm doing all I can to deserve it. Every day I try to work even when it bores me senseless, and it's terribly hard going . . . I'm constantly afraid of falling behind." By tonight I'll be melting (I'm writing to you at five in the afternoon, and there's a lovely warm sun, and my windows are open. I'm so happy, so pleased).

My little one, I love you so much. When I hear that you're in a bind, my heart begins to thump. I was so impatient to know what Parain would say. On the whole it's good: he feels that the essential passages are of the highest quality— he's sure it will be taken (if the second part is as good as the 1st, of which there can be no doubt, since there's no further need for exposition or anything). That's the best we can expect from him. There are parts that drag a bit, well so be it— even if there are more than I saw—they'll be cut; you wouldn't have wanted me, either, to cut the first 50 pages of *Nausea*, and yet with time, that has proven to be sound advice. As for the critique of general tendencies, that leaves me absolutely cold. First of all he failed to understand the subject. Next I find it amusing that he thinks of the dress rehearsal as stodgy (or perhaps it was the other rehearsal, I'm not sure, no matter). Doubtless the surrealist get-together in *Gilles* doesn't seem stodgy to him. He doesn't like the milieu, that we know. If he were in politics he could try to restrain or destroy it, but ultimately he's a publisher's reader, the milieu exists, your novel describes it, and there's nothing he can say. Obviously you could write a novel on a father, a mother, and a daughter. In the country, at Lons-le-Saulnier. Only that would have been a different novel. Pay absolutely no attention to it. In this his judgment reflects his personal tastes, not even those of the firm of Gallimard. And I'm convinced that he wouldn't have allowed himself that judgment based on general intentions unless he had some sort of affection for you. I think it's addressed to the woman you are much more than to the novel. With an unknown he would have been more impartial. I'll drop him a line.

What's new? Nothing: a day *off* today. I went for coffee at 7 a.m. At 4 o'clock I went for an extra allowance of tobacco that we received today, and that's all. The rest of the time I worked. The Boris-Ivich chapter is touched up, and it's good, I think. It may have lost a bit of that pretension to "toutounier"[1] language that it displayed early on, but it is better situated, and it seems to me—it happened almost on its own—one constantly feels that Ivich has done a lot of thinking about Mathieu. Aside from that, I received and read *l'Éloge de l'imprudence* [*In Praise of Imprudence*]. My little one, for the first time in my life I believe that you are wrong and Bienenfeld right. This comes, I think, from the fact that you discussed the book without reading it, as I often do. In fact, I don't know what Jouhandeau[2] is all about and I don't want to know if a person can will Evil—those are other questions (though on that last point, I agree with you, it's very complicated) but it's true that in the book itself Jouhandeau begins by defining Good and Evil, the values and antivalues of current morality, then he substitues his own morality without embellishing his values in the name of Good or his antivalues in the name of Evil, so that in fact, while rejecting accepted morality (in the name of *his* Good) and obeying social antivalues, he can say that he seeks out Evil and rejects Good. This gets more complicated because there is God. But what he means to say is so clear. All this is simply words. Or rather, there's a stoutness of heart there that should lead to a reversal of values and a new table of the Law, but minus the strength of mind necessary for establishing such a table. Now I have no idea at all what was said between the two of you on that subject, and perhaps your discussion was on the general question. On the other hand, she is strangely wrong when she claims that no great painter ever painted a still life. Basically, I see the problem: it's the anyone-but-a-fool-

---

[1] *An allusion to Colette's novel,* Le Toutounier. *(SdB)*
[2] Marcel Jouhandeau (b. 1888), essayist and fiction writer.

can-do-that thinking of people who confuse the magnificence of a subject with the painting. It remains an odd sort of realism, with a classification of the world's objects into objects "worth the trouble" to paint and objects not worth it. It is the primitive person distinguishing nameable from unnameable objects, it's the idea of the Neck and the Dirt that alarmed Socrates. Except that B., being an intellectual and abstract, should instead go all the way in the other direction, so as to declare a priori that the subject doesn't matter. But there we are, it struck me, in Proust, on the subject of Albertine; we aren't the same age for everything: she's thirty for bridge, twenty for philosophy, thirteen for painting. There are compartments. With Aron there are compartments too. He was a fifty-year-old in everything, but that didn't make one single fifty-year-old, you'd have to add up all those fifties to reach his true age. I wonder if that's not a Jewish intellectual flaw, and at any rate it explains the lack of authenticity, because authenticity is being the same, a single projection through all situations.

There you have lots of things to mull on, my sweet, which will get you nowhere. I'll stop there. Kisses for your dear little cheeks. I love you with all my might, and I love your little photo, too, you know.

Faint hopes for Saint-Cyr. But nobody knows when anymore.

You'll have to send me the 2 copies of *L'Imaginaire*, my little one, you've forgotten. And would you include Claude Mauriac's book on Jouhandeau; the word Hell is in the title.

ᕤᕥ *to Simone de Beauvoir*

Friday, May 10

My darling Beaver

How strongly I feel your tenderness, and how it saddens me that it is also slightly sorrowful. I so want to see you, my little one, you who are passing from the anguish of Abraham to the pains of absence. I love you, little one living too intensely, little one burning her candle at both ends. I would so love to hold your little self in my arms and simply kiss you, with all the time in the world to do it, and then after that we would talk and talk. So now you feel "seen from the outside" and that distresses you. On that too there's a synchronism between us, and when I got your letter telling about your talk with Brice Parain, I was annoyed because I felt he was aiming at me *too*. In my novel Mathieu et al. also have that "slipshod" way of talking, philosophical, slangy, what-have-you, that's basically ours. But to begin with it makes no sense to say it's Montparnasse talk, first because we don't see anyone in Montparnasse with whom we could forge a common language, and then because Montparnasse has as many languages as it has little groups, and there's nothing much left in common between the languages of the Boubous[1] and company, of the Magus and the Moon Woman, for instance, or I suppose Youki's, and finally because our language goes much farther back. But it is true that the language is *us*. There's obviously something of our bourgeois origins in it. You were a little girl of good social position, I was a little boy from a "liberal" family. And for me the jargon of students and the Normale was spliced onto that, plus the "secret" langauge of the same type that Nizan and I first constructed, then Maheu, Guille and I, then the Lady, Guille and I. Then you came along, I brought you all of that, and we rebuilt it together, and finally Z. slipped in a few little affected touches, such as "je veux tout bien" ["I'm awfully willing"] etc., or rather we gave it some affected touches to use with her. And there you are: this is what it produced. And certainly the "student jargon" side that's dominant—because it is neither professional nor family jargon—was able to last for us because we are in fact "set apart." I've written on and on in my notebook about how democracy, bureaucracy, centralization, combined with my type of pride and my profession as an intellectual and writer have made me a rootless individual, closed off from everything. And yourself, by living our life—you the Parisian, a civil servant like myself, you too are very much set apart, particularly if in addition you are, as you say, enclosed within our world and accustomed to settling for *my* opinions of you, as though they were the Ten Commandments (it's the same for me). All of that is perfectly true, and I understand how that horrifies Sorok., who obviously has a madcap language that she's put together all on her own, which must also have a singular émigrée history, countryless and quasi-homeless. Incidentally, ours must be particularly ghastly (however we try) for her, who is so jealous about anything in it involving insinuations and allusions. Actually, she's analyzed it very poorly, according to what you say—but she *cannot* analyze it well because she does it through her own language. But what could we possibly do about it? At our age—and with the painstaking will that we put into forging the instrument, that symbol of our own relationship—truly our language *is us*. So we must take ourselves as we are or else, if we aren't as we should be, change ourselves from within, and the language will follow. We've been too conscious of the words we use—banishing some, accepting others—for the words not to reflect something of ourselves (do you remember those interminable discussions with your sister about "*dégotter*,"[2] which we rejected, "*des fois*,"[3] etc.). For

---

[1] Fernando and Stépha Gérassi.
[2] To knock away an opponent's marble, unearth, discover a person or valuable find.
[3] At times, now and then.

example, if Françoise said to Elisabeth, *"Tu as de la peine"* or *"Tu as des ennuis"* or *"Tu as du chagrin"* or *"Ça ne va pas"* or even *"Tu es embêtée"* [all roughly, "Something's bothering you"] instead of *"Tu es emmerdée"* ["You're pissed off"], then that would be a different Françoise. *"Tu es emmerdée"* for you—and for me—conveys "warm sympathy with inner playfulness." The vulgarity is there both to hide and to symbolize the tremolo of the tenderness. And we toss this right out in front, plainspoken and clean-cut. It's downright stupid to say like Parain that it's "slipshod"; quite the contrary, it is the preciosity of coarseness with undeniable influence of the pathos found in American novels. So there it is, it represents the sort of sympathy for others that we play around with. At the same time, it's an appeal to objectivity: *Tu es emmerdée:* you are assured of my warm sympathy but please, play it very close to your chest, you too, etc. Now, it so happens that we *put* ourselves in our novels. In your first,[4] which Parain has read, there were women who were not in the least *you*, but also yourself when very young (and already some of this style came through: the *roundabout*, which is one of our favorite ways of expressing ourselves). In my case, Roquentin barely spoke in *Nausea*—and in *The Wall* there were only bastards, jerks, and outsiders. But in this novel as in mine, we spur ourselves onward, we talk about ourselves, our petty affairs, the kinds of people we love, so what can we expect, we're defenseless: people will be able to think whatever they like about us, talk about intellectual slang, about snobbery, Montparnasse, etc. We may as well let it happen. As for changing the least bit of it, don't. I know: they'll say—my stepfather and perhaps even the Lady—that the language is artificial and there's an affected coarseness. But if you write, *"Tu as des soucis?"* or *"Ça ne va pas?"* no one would say that it's artificial, when in fact it would be much more so. Much more *regarding* Françoise and Pierre, and Mathieu, in other words regarding us. The people who ask us to change are the people who are superstitious about the written language (as B. has a superstitious hatred of the still life) and who think that in writing one must transpose things. But we think, you and I, that *we must write the way we speak.* Consequently, the only way is to write the way we speak. Consequently, the only way is to write the way you write and let us be the judges. That's what I think, my dear little one—and I really believe I'm right. As for your letters—incidentally, I find Sorokine a little idiot—I know of none more charming, free and spontaneous. And that's not just my opinion, as you well know, my sweet.

So then, today, the invasion of Belgium and Holland. We learned about it via hazy rumor this morning, and then it was confirmed by our neighbor's radios. They kindly invited us, incidentally, to come and listen at their place

---

[4] *Quand prime le spirituel* [*When Things of the Spirit Come First*]. *(SdB)*

every hour if we want. But we went only at noon and at 7 o'clock, the way we did at the redhead's two weeks ago. The impression we get here is strange and very different from the one that prevailed during the attack on Norway: it seems almost a relief. The impression of being in contact with reality—even if it's sinister—after eight months of "rotten" war. As Goebels puts it, the impression that finally *this is* war. For us, actually it doesn't represent much of a change other than that we're forced to wear our helmets everywhere for fear of bursts of antiaircraft fire, an order that will fall into abeyance within a week, most likely. What do you hear from Bost? That's my only worry. Is he in the North or the East? And how are you doing, there in Paris? In a mood of agitation, of foreboding, or that happy indifference you sometimes feel? In any case it isn't the same war anymore.

In other respects for me the day has been all peaceful work; I did a draft of Daniel's anger after his talk with Boris and half of the Marcelle-Daniel chapter. For the moment I'm going to work on that, there's enough to keep me busy for a good week, and I'll be glad to spend a week without typing, which was getting to be tedious. And that's all for today, little one. Right now I'm going to do a weather reading, and then I'll write to T. and then I'll go to bed. I'm fully recovered and in fine fettle. But I'm eating *absolutely nothing* anymore in the evening, to lose weight (I've been doing it for four days now).

I love you, my sweet, my dear little one. I love you *passionately* and if I allow myself to write that, it's because here it's true.

⚭ *to Simone de Beauvoir*

Sunday, May 12

My darling Beaver

I'm wondering whether you are really in the Auvergne, with all this ruckus. Your minister, Sarraut, issued a circular enjoining "members of the teaching profession not to leave their domiciles." That would sadden me, my little one, the weather's so fine and it would be so good for you to stretch your little legs and take a stroll. I'll probably know today.

My little one, I was completely worn down yesterday; I received a totally lunatic letter from Tania, who's going to be X-rayed. "Dear God," she writes, "how I wish you would come, come at any price." It's easy for her to say, but she wouldn't want me to desert, after all. All the same, I find it *very* disagreeable to know that she's panic-stricken, as only a Z. knows how to be in the face of illness—and this time perhaps for good reason (I don't think she's gravely ill, but she could have a small lesion) and completely alone. It also shook me, from the point of view of authenticity, that she turned immediately to me (though she'd received no letter from me) as though it were *natural*. It seemed both silly and right; I've accepted the responsibility, but I'm regressing to the Anguish of Abraham that I suffered on my leave. Besides, I'm anxious about her illness. She had told me nothing about it, what do you know, my little one? It's odd, she is becoming more and more "my child," as Z. was at one time for you. This time, I've had enough of brushing her off with sweet talk each time she needs me. I've just written to her that if she wants it, and if the delays aren't too great, I was ready to marry her to get three days of leave. I don't imagine that will be very nice for you; though it's purely symbolic, it does make me look committed up to my ears. I for one don't like it at all, not so much because of that, but because of my family, from whom I must hide it and who'll surely hear about it someday. But I've told you and my mind's made up: I want to do everything I can for T. from now on. In exchange, I'll still take a little day to see you. If the illness isn't serious or if she's reassured, I'll beg off on the excuse that they don't give marriage leaves anymore since the Dutch business or because the delays are too long and so it's not worthwhile. In fact I actually do think it must take at least a month and a half. And in that case the project goes up in smoke anyway. What do you think? Do you think it's wrong of me to do this?

You must be annoyed, with leaves canceled again (they even called back those who were home). Yesterday was an odd day of waiting, we had a gray cotton sky overhead, the air was watery and it was very hot, real spring weather, sap and buds. In the morning the planes dropped a bomb on a town 15 km from here, everyone knew about it immediately, at 6 thirty—an alert, and the anti-aircraft banging away; from my window I saw the chase, the little mosquito glinting from time to time, and then lost in the sky again, and then the great white plumes chasing after it—without making contact, however. The bomb did no damage at all, I think. Then that was the moment when the sky grew overcast. "From the point of view" of events, a pause: around noon a lieutenant announced that a huge battle had broken out in Luxembourg between the French and the Germans, but we've had absolutely no confirmation. News is scarce. Then the letter from T. You can imagine how strangely dislocated it made me feel. I worked rather well nonetheless, but I'll have to redo all of Daniel's monologue. I wrote to T., and then went to bed, I set the alarm for 6 o'clock, and I'm writing to you, my sweet. The weather's delightful, and I'm unaccountably reassured— no doubt because it's beautiful out and it's morning. And besides, today's my day off. It's six-forty-five, I'm going to hop on my bike with a canteen slung across my chest and go get java and rolls at the bakery. Good-bye, my sweet. Till tomorrow—or rather till this evening, because I'll write to you this evening. I love you with all my might, my darling Beaver, my love.

✤ *to Simone de Beauvoir*

Sunday, May 12
Evening

My darling Beaver

You sent me a really pathetic little letter, so distressed, my dearest. What to tell you? That here there's no distress at all, and that people are saying, "That's war, it had to break out sometime." But that won't reassure you at all. That perhaps with luck this will determine the outcome of the war? As for that, yes, that might give you a bit of hope. But we have to be quite clear: behind the Belgian and Dutch frontiers lie the German Siegfried lines. So at best we can hope to stop the Germans at their frontier but not penetrate behind their lines. Except that would give them an immense front to defend, which would be so much to the good, because their manpower reserves aren't inexhaustible, and their materiel reserves are far from it. Where exactly is Bost at the moment? You didn't say. Is he part of the Army of the North? I don't think so. If I remember correctly, he was at the Alsatian front? In that case there's little chance after all that they would send him over there. Think of it this way, at the Belgian frontier there was a whole army, completely ready. Nonetheless, I'm glad not to be thinking of you at Clermont-Ferrand—you know that it was bombed. Ultimately Paris seems better defended and more difficult to reach, but I'm beginning to get anxious about you. If ever I read, "Bombs fall on Paris, twenty victims," despite the minuscule chance that you might be among them, I would cease to live. How are you going to get through these four short days, my little one? The wisest thing would have been to go to La Pouèze. But I understand that you feel "closer" by staying in Paris. The Parisians are aghast—I know that too from Pieter: his wife who had been bringing in five thousand francs a day with the business, *didn't make a single sou* on May 10, need I say more. Here people are very calm, except for a few professional pessimists who already see the Germans in Paris. I think the men have forgotten their civilian lives. I have, in any case, forgotten mine, as I was thinking this morning. Mind you, I haven't forgotten *a single one* of the people I was fond of, but the war doesn't make you lose them, it's simply that there are new relationships between people, war relationships, another way of seeing oneself, thinking of one another, more meditation, more ceremony on meeting again, more patience during the waiting, more solemnity, a clearer sense of hierarchies, etc. Well now I'm so used to them, that I see the world through those relationships. I no longer know what it's like to *live* with people I love, and it doesn't seem natural to me either: what is natural is that we see them from time to time with ceremony and a little frenzy, and that we think of them all the time from afar. I limit my wishes to going on leave more often. And yet, even that's impossible since, as you know, for the time being they are canceled.

I suppose it's this totally forgetting about peace that helps one endure the war. At this point bombs could fall all around me and, of course, I'd be terribly scared, but as though in the face of a *natural* disaster. And that's why too, and not from lack of imagination, those huge massacres that are about to happen in the North move us so little. I remember the sinister and sacred impression I had when I read in a September 3rd or 4th newspaper, "The first French blood has been spilled." It was still a civilian's emotion. As of now not much has been spilled, God be praised, but we've gotten used to the idea that it's made to be spilled. It's no longer the sacrilege it was in the beginning. I understand the problems that the men of 1914 had in returning to civilian life—and yet we've been in it only eight months, and thus far it's been only a quasi war.

I had my day off, and I worked. But it seems to me that everything I do is artificial, slipshod. I think it's because the heart of the novel is finished, I know too well what I want to say, and it doesn't interest me much anymore, there's nothing but touching up left. It's time for it to be finished, and actually in a month it will be. I'll feel totally besotted after that, most likely. I'll get back to my notebooks and then, after a short rest, I want to work on a philosophy book about Nothingness. That would be rather fun. Perhaps I'll make a thesis of it. I read Brabant's *Lumière bleue*. The man's deplorable, a big lug from the North, self-satisfied, radical, facile about his emotions, sanctimoniously self-satisfied (he calls himself "poet" because he's written novels, and when they requisition his country house, he deplores the fact that he doesn't live in a town that could put a placard on his walls saying, "Here resides a poet, Army steer clear"), terribly family minded, as French as they come, but it's still entertaining because it shows Paris from September to December. For you it wouldn't seem like much, but I missed out on all that. I got two letters from T., one the evening of the very day that she wrote me about her anxieties. She'd just gotten my scolding letter which, contrary to my fears—I felt very guilty—had the effect of a touch of the whip. She drew herself up in all her little dignity and on the spot her health was relegated to the back burner. She writes, "I bitterly regret the stupid note I sent you this afternoon. It was panic and nervousness on my part. I don't know how to wait. In any case I'm far from dying." I'm not fooled; what she means is, "I turned to you for help. But that's okay, you're not worthy of it. Well, it's nothing at all, no really, I'm not sick." But the best part is that the next day, totally reconciled with me—and very pleasantly so—she tells me about everything and alludes only vaguely to her illness. I'm going to slam on the brakes about marriage, because she's quite capable of saying, "I'm fine, but marry me anyway, so we can have three days together." Meanwhile, find out every last detail about her health. You can do it *officially*, I told her I was keeping you abreast of it to whatever useful ends. I must tell you that I'm astonished at T. She has shown touching goodwill and, all things considered, during these eight months of war she's been perfect. It's true, it's always the same thing, that the other has been perfect with you, and that I'm also *you* for T.

Aside from that nothing new, my sweet. It's ten p.m., and I'm writing to you. Tomorrow morning at 6 I'll write to my parents and to T. I lunched at Charlotte's and played chess. I'm not the least bored, and I'm happy to be alive, and I'm *interested* in what's going on. I would so like to pass on a little serenity to you. It's true that I would lose it completely if Paris were bombed. My sweet, I love you so. If I could see you again for a couple of days, no more than a couple of days, I'd be in seventh heaven.

Till tomorrow, my little one, tender kisses to you, little world-charmer.

I'll send you the money and the books tomorrow at 1:30. I wanted to take care of it today and then I forgot. Incidentally, I'd love to have you send:

1st some *books* (I'm running out—do you have a list? Have you read the Pepys? It's charming. I'll sent it to you when I'm through).

2nd two packs of ink cartridges—blue or blue-black, doesn't matter which— but not South Seas blue.

3rd more paper (but that can wait a bit, whereas the rest is urgent).

Thank you, little sweet.

෨ৡ *to Simone de Beauvoir*

Monday, May 13

My darling Beaver

Today, a day without letters. Just one, a brief one, from my mother. My guess is that for a while there will be some slowdowns in the mail. Here, to the right and the left of our sector, there's constant cannon fire, dull and steady pounding from our side (we say, "There goes one"), sharper bursts preceded by a whistling (we say, "Here comes one") from shells fired by the Germans. These days it's one continual bass rumble, and it seems *an object*, I mean it rises against the distant landscape like a line of individual trees, but melded, cutting off the horizon. We listen to it *when we want to*, in other words from time to time we lift a finger and say, "There it goes" or "Here it comes." The rest of the time we live as though nothing at all were happening. Aside from that, of course, there are the planes. From dawn to 10:00 a.m. today, the curt ripping of the antiaircraft and the putter of machine guns blankets the bass notes of the artillery fire, and then from time to time a beautiful full roar, much more regular than the sound of a car: it's an airplane. And when we're lucky, we can see it. We were very lucky this morning, because there was one that banked in very low over our heads, a thousand meters up, a beautiful black, followed by the little creamy spatterings of the shells. Everyone was outside, eyes on the sky, the cooks, the officers, our readings unit, the colonel's driver. But Pieter, who had just blown up a balloon and was standing there, head raised, with his handsome red balloon in hand, suddenly took fright and said, "I'm going to let them spot *you* with my balloon," upon which he took off up the steps and went into the house, just the way he did that day with the cows.[1] Meanwhile, 10 meters away, a nest of anti-aircraft machine guns—very familiar to us because day after day the guys with nothing to do would come to see our readings, and we would hand them the balloons—began to give off the crackling smoke and the firing that we were expecting, upon which the plane fled, one machine gun jammed and wasn't able to fire more than two shots, the other gun pursued the plane with a salvo, and we cried out, disappointed, "Missed!" But, meanwhile, the cook of the field kitchen, two hundred meters further off, forgetting to give Paul his coffee as he watched the plane through binoculars, cried out, "He's on fire" and swore that he'd seen a reddish flame coming from the fuselage. Paul denied it. At noon we learned that he'd fallen in flames ten kilometers from here. It remains to be seen whether it was *our* machine gunners that got him. It's a question of self-esteem. One supposes that they didn't, but more or less through an honesty of feeling. Of the five occupants, two were killed, two were taken, the fifth is still at large. So much for my pleasures. But you wouldn't believe how *natural* it seems, in the misleading sense of "a natural curiosity." You remember how one day in Catalonia I'd put you on your guard when you wanted to see a great pile of rock salt, and all that we had to say that day about natural curiosities? Well, the same goes here. I don't know how to explain it: reading what I've written, you'll believe we were at a performance, and yet it has to do with the hesitation, the contingency and the slowness of this spring and the grass all around us.

---

[1] On September 22, 1939, Sartre wrote about rounding up some rampaging cows. Pieter was no help then either. See *Witness to My Life*, pp. 258–60.

Here, meanwhile, great hubbub. One entire part of the Artillery Division is going off to subterranean confinement with people from the Infantry Division and the HQ in an underground defense closer to the lines, fifteen kilometers from here: it was foreseen for the moment when things began to heat up a bit. One of our captains left with the colonel and the general, a lieutenant and two clerks. As for us, we're staying here with Captain Munier—or perhaps we'll move into a little farmhouse not far away. Therefore *no increase in danger at all* (i.e. zero danger: all of the planes flying over our heads are absolutely not thinking about us, they've got lots to do elsewhere). But the hilarious part was the moment when they chose the clerks who would go. Hantziger volunteered. They only had to choose one other. The choice was between Nippert and Mondange. Nippert, the little Protestant rat, Mondange, the stalwart new guy who came from the far reaches of the Landes, where things had been extremely peaceful, thinking he'd found a cushy spot and coming to roost at the front. He glows with modesty and charity and all the gentle virtues, but most definitely not with courage. Each of them began to protest, Nippert saying that he had hemorrhoids and children (the hemorrhoids came first, it suits him so well to have hemorrhoids) and Mondange saying that he's from an earlier class. Finally Courcy said, "Well then, let's draw straws." You should have seen Nippert's face while they were drawing straws. He had undone his collar and sat down on a chair, white as a sheet, his throat so tight he couldn't speak. The lot fell to Mondange, who's leaving this evening—and Nippert sat on his chair five minutes longer, limp and speechless. Finally he said in a hoarse voice, "That's fair." The first sergeant is leaving too. Last week, listening to the gunfire, he'd said, "The voice of the gun is calling me." But his lips trembled strangely all morning long. In actual fact they have nothing to fear. Guns are going off quite close to them, and a shell fell 80 meters from their blockhouse, but they are ten meters underground. The problem is rather the life they're going to be leading: express prohibition of going out into daylight, awful odor, gas lighting only, 100 men crammed in there. I thank my lucky stars that I'm a weather reader, in other words doing work that requires the open air. With my asthma, I couldn't have stood it. There's the news, my sweet. Aside from that, I worked very well this morning and particularly this afternoon (the Marcelle-Daniel scene); this time it was fresh, new, it didn't seem like a patch-up job, and it simply poured out, I had fun. I'd really like to get a letter from you, my love, from you who are making me ever so slightly anxious this evening.

I love you *passionately* (always in the full sense of the term). I won't say it again because the word irritates me, but remember it well, my sweet, my little flower. Tender kisses for your little cheeks.

*   *   *

It's easy to see that the war is really getting under way. My mother added in a postscript to her letter, "*JO*[2] (she underlined it) sends you a kiss."

Hurry up and send some books, little flower.

❧ *to Simone de Beauvoir*

Tuesday, May 14

My darling Beaver

Today I had two little letters from yourself, and they contained some surprises. In one was the madwoman's sonnet and in the other your sister's letter. I found Poupette's letter very interesting; her trip had been weird, and her three companions met along the way seemed very romantic, the fat gentleman, the customs officer, and the soldier. Spain is looking ominous.

Listen to me, little Beaver, here's something supremely important, while I think of it—and it's making me write to pretty much everyone, it's a real bother. On the *20th* they're changing our postal sector. They do this from time to time. So the letter you write on the 20th should be addressed thus:

Private Sartre
Meteorology Unit—A.D.H.Q.
Sector 14459 (fourteen thousand four hundred fifty-nine)

I sent the money this morning by money-order card, so you'll get it the day after tomorrow, the 17th or at the latest the 18th. Alas my little one, right after that I received your little letters crying poverty; through my negligence you'll have yet another day or two of starvation. But in all good faith I thought you didn't need it till the 20th. Forgive me, my darling Beaver—it breaks my heart when you are a little pauper. I sent only 1,950 francs so as to be able to finish the month without borrowing anything from Pieter.

I'm pleased to know that you're less anxious, my little one. As for news, well, it's neither good nor bad. At best we'll be able to hold the Liège-Anvers line and probably Liège will fall, but all in all that's to be expected. If it doesn't happen, so much the better. In any case they have the advantage of first strike. *In the long run*, the battle must turn to our advantage, it seems to me. Read Pierrefeu's columns in *L'Oeuvre*, they're still the best. The most reassuring thing I can tell you is that now there's a chance the war will be over before the

---

[2] Her husband, Sartre's stepfather, Joseph Mancy.

winter of '41. But all that I'm saying here will already seem old hat by the time you get this letter. This time lag in anxious public or private moments is annoying.

As for me, my sweet, for the present I'm little more than a laborer in the fields of my novel. I do nothing but that, and I'm about to be done with it. And dear God, what a gaping void after that! I think the Daniel-Marcelle scene will be good, I'll have finished it by tomorrow. I'm doing nothing but that since I have nothing left to read, and then I slept a bit this afternoon, I don't know why. I made an exception and went out for dinner at Charlotte's this evening; on the way back the weather was extraordinary, mild and calm, with a lovely pale sky and all the distant country sounds, a sharp scent of green, except that you could hear coming from a nearby village, whose steeple we can see from the road, the alarm siren's wail. It seemed strange, and it made this whole calm countryside sweetly venomous, rather like a sour ball. The place is deserted, at least half the troops have gone off to that noxious cellar. Apparently it reeks and it's damp; the colonel's driver, who came back to get his things this afternoon, says that the guys pulled really long faces when they saw it: you've got to go down 95 steps underground, they have electricity three hours a day. The rest of the time it's kerosene lanterns. No going outside. All the officers eat together in one room—all the men together in another—the same food for officers and men. That's the only advantage: it's good. But as for us, we're still here, and here we'll stay. Their departure gives these days a slight flavor of summer's end, you know, when a few obstinates stay on in the empty hotels but three-quarters of the country vacationers have already left. The officers sit in their armchairs with nothing to do, there are only two clerks left, and we weather readers are entirely alone in our annex. Until further notice, I don't much fear the bombing for you: they're not bombing civilians, they bomb military objectives (essentially, the airfields) *without worrying about* sparing civilians. The difference is not slight, because it excludes all bombing of Paris. They're not worried about reprisals in that quarter.

My sweet, how it bothers me to think that your little head is astir with worry (and I understand you so well, as you know). I would so like to *talk* with you about all of this. Alas! Home leaves are canceled and will undoubtedly remain so as long as the major battle has not been resolved. Be patient, my little one, be very patient. I love you so much and am so at one with you. Till tomorrow, little flower, many kisses. I love you.

❧ to Simone de Beauvoir

Thursday, May 16
P.S. 14,459 (from the 20th on)

My darling Beaver

No letter from you today, nor from anyone. The mail was actually very late, probably because the bombing raids have destroyed part of the railway between Nancy and Lunéville. The papers don't get in till four o'clock now, the officers' radio was working badly, so I spent the whole day cut off from the world. To tell the truth, it didn't change things for me too much. We feel isolated and powerless here just as though we were civilians: somewhere in the North, not just the country's destiny is being decided but my own and yours as well; but here I am, placidly doing readings four times a day, I am not in any danger whatsoever, I'm useless; we have to make for ourselves states of mind to correspond with this condition: we close ourselves off, we wait with a sort of profound resignation. It's actually odd how many different mental attitudes the war can demand: it wouldn't be at all the same way of seeing the world if I personally had to undergo bombardments, and there would be another way to keep a firm hold—and yet another if I were a pilot or in the commandoes. But as it is, I can scarcely be asked for more than a sort of obstinacy about making my garden grow, which I do. I've made good progress. The Daniel-Marcelle conversation will be finished tomorrow at noon. There'll only be the Mathieu-Daniel scene, which you had me add, plus the last Mathieu-Marcelle scene and finally a ten-page chapter on Marcelle waiting for Daniel's telephone call. And I've given myself another month to do all of that. I'm reading little—the *Baudelaire*, which is appalling, with academicism à la Brichot signifying nothing, but nonetheless a bit better than the Porché. The Pepys, which charms me and which I'll send you, and then after all *As I Lay Dying*, which I found again and which I had never read, wretch that I am. As entertainment, of course, they offer us daily airplane chases. But the antiaircraft always misses them; we see stupid little puffs of smoke in the sky racing vainly after the plane, it's as irritating as can be, and eventually we don't even budge (it happens seven or eight times a day). The beautiful part is the noise, the beautiful regular noise of the motor, which seems to swell in the sky and to trace a parabola from the horizon, and the spitting of the antiaircraft embroidering on it and sometimes the cough of a machine gun. It fills the day. Since parachutists have fallen in the environs, they posted a requirement that we go out armed with rifles, but the requirement came up against our passive resistance. There's only one man from Brittany, the son of a major, a private and clerk to the Infantry Division, who's scared shitless and hurtles down cellar stairs when he hears a plane and gravely walks along the roads, his gun under his arm, looking as though he's out on a hunt. It seems there's no more thought of evacuating the 2nd zone, and for a while we'll still be able to eat lunch at Charlotte's. From time to time we get news of the interred of the Division HQ: It seems they're getting acclimated to their lot, they have electricity longer now and only complain about the dampness. If something can reassure you, my little flower, on my personal state, you should know that the other night the enemy attacked our sector—forcefully enough for us to win favorable mention in a communiqué—and that we were *absolutely* unaware of it, no more than yourself in your little bed. We didn't even hear the guns. This, to tell you that we're still far from the operations.

From time to time I'm stirred by the desire to take up my notebook again. Ultimately, I kept it during the doldrums of the war and dropped it at the good part. But I'd rather finish the novel as soon as possible, and then we won't speak of it again. I was counting on sending it to you via Pieter. But alas! who knows when Pieter will leave. This third round was to begin on May 25. In ten days, as a matter of fact. I fear we may have to wait a long time. Poor little Bist, it's for him particularly that it breaks my heart. Nonetheless we mustn't be too discouraged: obviously there's no question of restoring the leaves as long as the "Battle of the Meuse" is going on. But it wouldn't be possible, either, for the battle to last indefinitely with such intensity. I know they cite Verdun, which lasted six months; but here the conditions are quite different. Either they'll break through—which I don't expect at all—and we're screwed. Or they'll stop for a breather and the war of positions will begin again. In that case we'll probably see the leave-takers timidly reappearing. We must be patient, and above all tell ourselves that this proves that Germany wants to be through with it before winter. So the chances are good that we won't see the interminable three or four years of war that were first foreseen. My little dear, I would so like you not to be too anxious, that you be patient. I don't too much like being without a letter from you.

Other events, nil. Except for an electrical breakdown, in the evening, which obliged us to carry out the reading by candlelight—and a crisp and sudden cold, which gripped us right to the bone; wind tonight and eight degrees. We were less cold last winter because the cold is pursuing us right to our bedrooms. Fortunately mine is the warmest.

My sweet, I still have buckets of little memories of our sweet bygone days. The state of war develops the sense of rumination, and it's very true that we become more profound. In our feelings anyway. The mute unreeling of memories recurs day by day. Today it was Siena with your little arm in mine. Remember how we made fun of M. Suarès. Yesterday it was Spain, because of Poupette's stationery. That's what is pleasant and abnormal about our meditative state, the slightest little act falls as though into a pond, and afterward there are concentric circles that grow dimmer but wider and wider. And you are always there within. My life is filled with you, my love.

Till tomorrow, little Beaver. I love you with all my might.

✢ to Simone de Beauvoir

Friday, May 17

My darling Beaver

Today no letters or papers. There was no mail at all; by 8 p.m. the train scheduled for 8 a.m. hadn't reached the station of the large city where they go to get letters. So that makes two days now that I've been cut off from the world. Add to that the radio news, which is inherently confused and choppy, but all the more so because it's listened to with ears glued to the speakers (the officers' radio). We hear snatches, at times "great success," at others "desperate situation," and we often don't know *either* who's talking (Radio Stuttgart, Italian Radio, the BBC) or what they're talking about. Of course there are also the rumors going around—generally defeatist rumors because of this long wait. And the men from the North who are desperate because they've been without news of their families for four or five days. The curious thing is that the money orders are still reaching them but not the letters. From this I conclude that Censorship netted all the letters from the North in one fell swoop and stopped everything. Weather gray and cold, raindrops, 8 degrees in the morning and evening. The whole thing, to be completely honest, seems completely ominous. All of this, it goes without saying, with the steady accompaniment of cannon fire. It's obvious that *this* is what war is—at least for the most fortunate, who aren't suffering in body: the waiting, the total absence of news and the false rumors. Pieter's robust optimism was sorely tried. Mine too, this evening. Pieter was charming. Suddenly he said, "But what if it's *they* who win. *We never think about that.*" That describes him. And then, suddenly regaining his optimism, "Oh, but in any case they won't treat France like Poland: it will be livable." What still disconcerted me was those snatches of news heard on the radio. The Italian radio announced—or at least I'd thought that's what I caught—"The Germans had broken through the Maginot Line along a *hundred* kilometers." As they were said to be near Rethel, that gave me a slight shudder, though it was rather incredible. In actual fact, it was about a pocket near Sedan, the one they've been talking about since the day before yesterday. The '14 war proved that we could live for a long time with similar inroads. This evening we're somewhat reassured, we've asked Captain Munier, possessor of the aforesaid radio, and we know for sure—as sure as the communiqués allow—how matters stand. Of course Paul is the most serene. He gets cheerfully indignant about the organizational faults of the French army and judging himself to be up to his ears in a catastrophe to which he feels equal, he digs away peaceably in his little garden or else he pecks away fitfully at the typewriter, occasionally uttering his little schizophrenic's song. In the midst of it all, I work. I've finished the Daniel-Marcelle chapter, but I'll have to do it over once I've let it sit awhile because it is "complex," as Gégé would say. And then daily life: weather readings, Charlotte, chess. For the moment we are keeping track of our daily victories and defeats. I've beaten Pieter 9 times while he's beaten me twice. There's a slight nervousness in the air, and this morning we bitterly raked over each other's faults. For the hundredth time I told him, "The basic thing about your character is that you're a huge shit fly, buzzing and clumsy." And for the hundredth time he said, "You're hard on others, Sartre, very hard, but very indulgent toward yourself." But by afternoon we had reconciled. With the telephone downstairs removed, there won't be any telephone operators either. So we'll have guard duty one night in five, but it essentially consists of sleeping. Whereas the unfortunate men of the Infantry Division stand guard duty, through their captain's whim, on their feet and with a loaded rifle at their side. They pass the time by listening to jazz on the radio. I don't know whether you can appreciate the charm of the scene: a guy in the dining room of an evacuated hotel, his loaded rifle on the table, listening to "J'attendrai" as sung by Tino Rossi.

And that's all, my little one. I'm afraid you too might be anxious and nervous. I fervently wish that my letters aren't delayed as much as yours, because it's annoying. Particularly for yourself, you can get ideas. But what can we do? We're smack in the middle of a war. Now we'll be going through our worst time. It won't last forever, my dear little one. Surely not. I love you with all my might. At this moment the war has heightened my sense of hierarchy to where you're the only thing in the world that matters to me; more than ever I think only of you.

Kisses for your little cheeks.

∞ *to Simone de Beauvoir*

Saturday, May 18

My darling Beaver

Today the weather has been beautiful and I got two letters from you, and I won't say that the news was better, no—but at least there was news: on a large map in the officers' room I saw little flags marking the front. So I'm somewhat reassured. But how somber your letters were, my little flower, they broke my heart. My God, how I would love to see you, be it only for an hour, and talk with you and hold you in my arms, it makes me so anxious to feel you off there, absolutely alone, and with nothing more than stubbornly untroubled letters from me which arrive three days after they're written. On top of all that, I know that you're getting all the recent ones with additional delay. Research reveals that it isn't the effects of bombing raids that delay the trains, it's the necessity of sending long convoys of men and munitions to the North. So what delays your letters must similarly delay mine. I hope that a rhythm will set in: the train expected yesterday at 7 in the morning got in last night at three o'clock. 20 hours late. I hope this margin of 20 hours holds up. In that case you'll have had only one day of disappointment. Little one, I sense as you do the temptation to lose my individual fate in an immense collective destiny and dilute it therein, but I believe that's a temptation we must resist. What we feel most forcefully, and that it's most precious to feel, is how much a country's fate is something individual and unique—just as for a person—and bounded by death—just as for people (I don't mean by this that we will lose the war, but it is enough that *we are in danger* of losing it)—and how much our own fates are *situated* within that perishable fate of the nation. But that doesn't matter, the nation is a situation, and besides that there are millions of free beings, and for each of them victory or defeat will be an individual story, the death of the nation would be one of those, and so would a return to a secure peace. That's why my little dear, I think of *your* destiny and of mine, and I can't help thinking that is the one, and not some other, that we'll live out to the end. I am absolutely not separated from you, quite the contrary, I've never been so united to you, and we will be so in any case, my love, for better or worse. I love you. Don't take all of this for the depths of pessimism. I think of it only in terms of *possibilities*, because they are more sensitive and more alive today, but basically we should be thinking this way from the beginning of war on and even, in fact, at all times.

So today the weather was fine, it was warmer and it was a day off. I worked, finished a chapter. It's absorbing nonetheless; I can delve into it, though I'm afraid there's a certain sort of inventiveness in the *words*, particularly, that's stifled by worries. Lunch at Charlotte's. During the afternoon I played chess, and then I took a bath. The Acolytes talk about the news. "I'd like to be two weeks older," said Pieter, the incorrigible optimist, and Paul responded admirably: "Who knows whether in two weeks you might not wish to be twenty years older." This evening I heard Paul Reynaud[1] on the radio, and now here I am writing to you. Two letters from T. who isn't, it seems, so sick. Under these circumstances I think there's no use marrying her, I'll write her that it would be pointless.

Till tomorrow, my sweet, my little flower, I wish you could feel how much I love you, how much I care for you with my whole being. We are *inseparable*.

❧ *to Simone de Beauvoir*

Sunday, May 19

My darling Beaver

I have just learned that the Germans are at Laon, and I am terribly anxious about you. What are you going to do? Are they going to evacuate Paris? I want to believe in an improvement, but I fear that a repetition of the Marne isn't possible. That one came from a big mistake on Von Kluck's part, and I suppose they've learned from that error and won't commit it twice. My little one, this letter will reach you very late—in three days. Where will things be then? If there's still time, I urge you to leave. Send the 2 Zazouliches to Laigle and you, if you can, if the government doesn't require (which it certainly won't) faculty members to stay in Paris or follow their lycées to the country, *go to the Lady at La Pouèze*. Do it for me, my love, my little flower. Think how excruciating it would be for me to know that Paris was being bombed, under siege, or surrounded, and know you were *in it*, without any news at all of you and alone, terribly alone. I can think of no one else save the Lady who could put you up. Go there, that will be my only consolation. To my way of thinking, you should immediately send off the two Z's to Laigle. I'm going to write to T. with that thought. Even if you still have to stay on a few days because of your work, send them off. Don't forget that you run the risk of *having no money left* for leaving yourself. I hope that you've finally received my money order. At the Lady's you won't need money, she'll feed you and will lend you a bit. I'm in despair at the thought that the letter you write me today will take three days to reach me. My

* See end of letter for more optimistic thoughts.
** Take Sorokine along with you if you don't want to abandon her.
[1] Paul Reynaud (1878–1966), French premier, who was trying to prevent German occupation of France.

little one, my sweet, I care for you from the very marrow of my bones, it tears me up to think of you there *absolutely alone*. Never have I felt so painfully how much I care for you. I am afraid only for you and, whatever happens, if I find you again—and that's certain, on the condition that you leave in time—life will still be livable.

That's that. Here things blow hot and cold. At eight I listen to the radio and hear that the German advance has slowed. At noon Lieutenant Ullrich, who has heard the radio, says, "We're beginning to put the brakes on them." At one-thirty, having lunched without a care at Charlotte's, we come back and meet up with a frantic radioman: "We've just listened to the news, they're at Laon." Upon which Paul declares, "Well then, it's all over. Let's hope we'll be German as soon as possible." We bawled him out some and then here I am, writing to you. I can't tell you anything about the situation, I don't know it; I have some two-day-old papers, and I can only see the officers' map with the ribbon and the pins, and the bulge that's swelling, swelling inordinately. Soon this map won't be enough, it'll take a second. For the moment you certainly know better than I what's up. I don't in the least believe the game's lost. But I do think you must be careful. For the moment you're more exposed than I. And then I think that the Lady is the only person who can help you if things take a turn toward tragedy—which we do have to contemplate after all, even if we don't believe it.

My sweet, I have nothing more to tell you, except that I love you as much as possible, and that you are my dear, my only love. When I contemplate—out of intellectual honesty, you can be sure—a life in which it would no longer be possible to write, to publish what I write, and in which we would have many material privations, if I think that I might possibly lead such a life with you, it seems to me that I could still find happiness in it.

Till tomorrow, my dear love.

I add this—two hours later. Even at the worst (Paris occupied) the war is not lost. It's the fleet that makes the blockade, and the Germans have no fleet. So long as we have an intact army (the one in Alsace) and an air fleet and the English can make a blockade, we're not at all lost, and many reasons remain for hope. No one defeats what Romains refers to as the "millions of men" as they would a regular army—and no one occupies an *empire* with a fleet and immense colonial resources as though it were Holland. Except that Paris *can* be occupied (you know that Joffre in '14 contemplated doing battle on the Massif Central), and that's why you must leave as soon as possible. I love you.

ᘿ *to Simone de Beauvoir*

Thursday, May 23

My darling Beaver

No mail today. But I mustn't complain: it was the letters from the North that got through; there are some poor guys who've been waiting nine days for news. Paul, whose wife is up there in an area that's actually well protected by the Maginot Line, got seven all at once. As for news, it's neither good nor bad, just confused. The Germans are at Abbeville and near Boulogne, but the Allied troops coming down from Belgium have retaken Arras and are holding onto the outskirts of Cambrai; I scarcely fear anymore that the Belgian army will be cut off in its retreat, since it is now in contact with a necessarily small German force in the North. Which doesn't prevent us from still feeling a chill up and down the spine as the news blows hot and cold. There's little we can do but wait. But it's rather irritating to be waiting *here*, with nothing to do but those innocent readings four times a day. But on the whole the day was cheerful. It was around six o'clock that the news slightly sobered us—much less than the day before yesterday. The weather was beautiful and mild, I played chess, read some in a detective novel that I'd brought back from my peregrinations yesterday, and worked a while too. But I feel less hurried right now about finishing the factum, for if it were finished, I wouldn't know how to send it, because packages are suspended in both directions. I am hoping, my sweet, that you had time to send books and ink cartridges, but I'm not overconfident. So much for that. In any case it will be reinstated someday and I still have snatches to read, the end of several of the books that I'm chewing over and spitting out without swallowing, a habit for which you've often scolded me. It will teach me to finish books.

We're leaving Charlotte and Morsbronn tomorrow. But don't worry, it's simply to go four kilometers away to another village where we'll be just as comfortable. It leaves us completely unmoved; rather it'll be fun because it will give us a change. Incidentally, there's a military co-op in the village where we'll be able to stock up. And, since the village isn't evacuated, we'll still have a restaurant. The reasons for the departure are unclear: this morning, orders were given here to evacuate the civilians, followed by counterorders. Upon which two buses showed up and a large number of civilians suspected of espionage were stuffed into them, among them the town hall clerk and a nurse who was sleeping with a radioman, who rooms next to me. Upon which, finally, they are having us leave for that new village, where we will meet up with the clerks and all the officers who are back from their blockhouse.

Another reversal: as I write, a radioman called us and gave us the most recent bulletins: we're holding Amiens and Cambrai and, while still cut off, the Belgian army has only thirty kilometers to go in order to turn about and cut the Germans off. So ends a day well begun, but it is truly strange to follow like this at three-hour intervals a battle that's been going on not forty-eight hours, as heretofore, but days and days with many alternating successes and disasters.

My sweet, through all of this I am constantly with you. How I would love to be with you to share it all. I love you with all my might, my sweet, my little dearest, my little flower. I send you kisses for your sweet little cheeks, you are my love.

Sorokine annoys me, the way she keeps at me and calls me Shrimp. Tell her she's a pain in the ass.

✑ to Simone de Beauvoir

Friday, May 24

My darling Beaver

An uneventful day. The mail seems more or less back to normal, after the surge of refugees and the troop movements. I got your Wednesday letter today. And yesterday's newspapers. But your Tuesday letter and papers from the day before yesterday are missing. Your little letter was so depressed, my sweet, my little flower, it broke my heart. It seems absolutely gloomy to imagine you running around Paris with that anxious headache and palpitating heart and that nervousness. My sweet, I hope you're less gloomy today: yesterday the news was better, today it's unchanged. Don't pay too much attention to the names of the cities when you're told that the Germans "are" at Boulogne or at Abbeville. It's very true that they are simply raids that would be important if the infantry and heavy artillery could follow, which they are far from being able to do in any case. What can be said is that today we're merely engaged in a battle, under conditions that are much less favorable than they might have been if stupid mistakes had not been committed but which are in no way tragic. With also a certain inferiority in materiel, compensated by the German shortage of gas. One shouldn't think of the Belgian army as cut off from the Northern army: in the first place the situation is so tangled that we are encircling the Germans, who have encircled us. Next, the two Allied armies are in fact separated—between Saint-Quentin and Cambrai—by some thirty kilometers—precisely the region where the worst of the fighting is happening. For the moment we must wait and not get too anxious, my love: it's something else that's beginning—something other than what's just been happening over the past ten days, and this time it's a real battle.

I understand perfectly the cowardice you speak of: the tendency to reach for even the most slightly optimistic false report, the tiniest, most unfounded reason for hope. But really what can we do? What throws us off track is that everything is going on outside ourselves. One is absolutely passive, which is not a human attitude in the face of danger. All of that would disappear if we had decisions to make on our own. It's in that light that this evening I saw men, who had just come from the front lines this morning, completely befuddled and feeble and groggy from the week's news, which they'd only now heard, and open to all those little compromises of men who'd just held out for eight days under intense and precise fire, been without food for four days, except for an occasional sardine on bread, and had, among other things, endured a *fifty-hour* bombardment without flinching. It's that these two attitudes are so different. For my part I was somewhat protected from such compromises, not by my nature—which might so incline me—but by the fact that the rumors propagated up to now have been *uniformly pessimistic*, right up to the last few days. The internal process was not the same; it required mending, patching up, stuffing each fissue, saying at every turn: That must be the tip-off (a word that denotes both the inside dope and a hoax), like the officer on temporary duty with the Division HQ who heard me announcing the taking of Saint-Quentin to a clerk and turned on me, pale and nervous: "Where did you hear that? It's baloney." "I heard it on the radio, Captain, Sir." "Ah! Oh là là!" and, with a thrust of his chin, "Bah! It must have been the German station." And then he ran down the stairs so as not to allow me the time to reply that it was a French bulletin aired by a French station. That's more or less the kind of thing I did for a week, looking at places on the map ten times over, using a pencil to measure German advances in order to minimize them, etc. One of my favorite exercises was to convince that pessimist, Paul, that things weren't so bad. I applied all my bad faith and dialectic to the argument, so I could tell myself afterward, "Since, pessimist that he is, he agrees after a presentation of the facts that the situaiton isn't all that bad, etc." But none of that prevented a real Heideggerian anxiety, without the nervousness. T. wrote, "It's amazing how people seem like squashed bedbugs to me right now. Only you are a person." Well, that's what I was feeling, that contradiction—which is of course the human condition—of being at the same time a 100% free person, master of one's desires and also, 100%, a squashed bedbug. For a day or two I envisaged the question only in a very distant future: how to live *afterward*—and that gave me cold sweats. At this very moment I'm reading *Hitler m'a dit* [*Hitler Told Me*], I've read an article on the systematic depopulation the Germans are practicing in Poland (in the May 1st issue of *La Revue de Paris*;

to be read if you see it in the library at Camille-Sée[1]), and that did nothing to gladden my heart. But for two or three days now it's been very different. I am definitely and profoundly tranquil, with quasi-retrospective nervous jolts. Here there's been a lot of depression. Paul and Pieter have been sympathetic and decent while others have been not at all so, but I can scarcely talk to you about it. I'll get back to my notebook in a few days and tell it all in detail. There's much more to say about it than I'm telling you here.

Today was very neutral, I had the day off, till tomorrow at noon I won't be doing readings. I read—a detective novel from the Empreinte series that doesn't look half bad, and an article on Russian propaganda methods in Bessarabia—and I worked; I'm finished the Mathieu-Daniel chapter (where Daniel admits he's secretly been visiting Marcelle). There were some interesting people at Charlotte's: they were just back from the lines, where they'd been subjected to intense shelling. In particular I saw Civette, the spotter, again, that softly handsome young man who left at the same time as I did on my last leave. His observation post had been liberally sprayed by the Germans, and from there he could see the Germans sprayed by our artillery, according to hints he gave. I said to him, joking, "You have lots of dead men on your conscience" and he answered, "And I accept them gladly, buddy, gladly." And there is one other who was truly chastened by the life he was leading out there. He's not at all so handsome, but he is full of a fierce pride as he considers from here what he endured out there (artillery fire of such perfect precision and so directly aimed at their observation post that, in the opinion of many, it was a miracle they escaped). I left him hollering at a fat, peaceable Jewish guy who was protesting gently as he ate some preserves, "The instinct for self-preservation, old boy, should not even exist!" "Hey!" replied the other, "you can't do a thing about it, it's bigger than you are."

And that's all for today, my sweet little flower. Though the immediate danger has been averted completely, you did the right thing to send the Z's back. I only regret that Tania didn't take the time to have her X rays taken. Aren't you going to feel completely alone? It's true that you'll have Sorokine, who certainly must wish in her heart of hearts to have Paris surrounded so she'll have you all to herself. She'll obviously be charming because she'll have no grounds for jealousy; I really hope you'll be able to hang onto her.

My little flower, I love you so much. It really upsets me to think of you there, bathed in anguish. I so hope you can regain some semblance of peace. I love you.

---

[1] One of the lyceés where Beauvoir was teaching.

✐ *to Simone de Beauvoir*

Saturday, May 25

My darling Beaver

I got a good little letter from you today, quite serene again. Which makes me happy. And in fact, we here are so reassured (without the slightest trace of optimism) that we're not even bothering to listen to the radio except at noon. Events seem to be slowing down somewhat; it was about time. You must get back to work, back to feeling a bit cheery. My little flower, my sweet, how I would love for a little peace to settle on your passionate little soul. I can picture you so clearly, gnawing your little knuckles, poor darling Beaver.

As for the Z's, it's a great pity that they aren't leaving, particularly if T. is hauled off to the cooler every day.[1] But what can be done about it? I'm going to follow your instructions to the letter, tell her to leave the minute you decide there's danger, and instruct her to be in Laigle by July 1st in any case. I'm rather sorry she didn't get the letter I was stupid enough to send to the Rue Vavin, because I explained to her that it was impossible for us to get married, and I'll have to find another way to explain it to her again. But you could do nothing other than what you did. She'd have gone out of her mind if she had thought that you had read her letter, and that would have come back to haunt me. So we'll blame the mail, which is actually quite erratic, since I haven't yet received your Tuesday letter. I'm so sorry that you're facing such a difficult month, financially speaking. And what can we do if T. can't get a travel permit? Yesterday I wrote telling her to try for one and to leave before the 1st of June if they refuse it. Otherwise she'll molder away in Paris indefinitely. But will she do it? You know her.

Here there's a lot of commotion. Spies first of all. They're all over the place, they're arrested in bunches and then a few are shot here and there. Not infrequently, you hear, "You know the stationmaster of———, you must have seen him as you went by the other day? Well, he's been shot." Etc. Everybody has seen a spy, has been on the verge of nabbing him, and then of course the spy got away. But the fact is that there are some, and no doubt their existence is not unconnected to strange reshufflings going on in our division. I suppose that censorship wouldn't let me say anything more, so I'll only tell you that we're on our way. In three or four days. Not very far from here. Nonetheless it'll be a real brouhaha. Meanwhile, though still here, we're no longer "in sector." For us this means total freedom. From 19:00 this evening on, we have no further readings to do till our departures. So I'm going to work conscientiously. It's been

---

[1] To get her identity card checked.

a pleasant day, quiet and vacant. First readings, then lunch at Charlotte's then I read a bit of the detective novel and then I worked and then this evening there were confabulations of all sorts about the spies and our imminent move, there was whispering in every nook and cranny, with very serious requests on all sides not to pass on to anyone the scraps of information. A rumor was also making the rounds that General Gamelin[2] had committed suicide, but the radio has just denied it.

And that's it, my little sweet, that's it for today, an uneventful letter, from a happy man. I would so like to get an identical one from you.

Now I'm on my way to bed, and I'll read a brief history of Norway, to bring me up-to-date, by candlelight. And tomorrow, nothing to do, it's simply splendid.

Till tomorrow, my sweet, I send you heartfelt kisses, I am constantly preoccupied with you, my dear little Beaver.

Watch the papers to see when packages for army personnel are authorized again, I imagine it won't be long, since mail delivery has gone back to normal, and then you can send me books and some *ink cartridges*.

ꙮ *to Simone de Beauvoir*

May 26

My darling Beaver

For now I'm getting your little letters right on time. Yesterday around two o'clock I got Friday's, which is very nice. All the more so since it's much gayer and you've resumed living again. Since Friday the news hasn't been bad and I imagine you've had three days of tranquillity. My sweet, how much I prefer to know you're content; it's disastrous for me when you're unhappy. You really surprised me with your enumeration of the books you're going to send me: did I really ask for a Fabre-Luce? I must have been crazy. I consider both Fabre-Luces jerks. And then, my love, above all do not send me *some* Verlaine: I would like *the* Pléiade Verlaine (complete poetry) or nothing at all. And add to that Claudel's *Le Soulier de satin* [*The Satin Slipper*], which I'm more eager to read than the rest. You have time, alas, because packages still haven't been reauthorized.

---

[2] Maurice Gamelin (1872–1958), French army commander in chief.

I was amused by the little story you told me about the horrible fat blond who told Sorokine to read *Nausea* and would have been even more amused, my love, if I were not honestly convinced that Sorokine invented it out of whole cloth. That girl often lies just to entertain you. Besides, there's something fishy about the story. Particularly the end—where she says, "Do you know what he did to her?" shrugs, and buttons her lip—smacks of Sorokine's juvenile perverseness a mile away. Well anyway, that's what I think. As for the Moon Woman, now there she is being quite Machiavellian. What is she driving at and why is she wasting her time speaking ill of us to T., acting sanctimonious with her, doing her real favors and then, the moment you'd think them on the best of terms, coming to you to rail against her? But you never said *how* the Moon Woman managed to read my letters. Was it by digging through T.'s things? Tell me a bit about her and explain her psychology, particularly this: since she takes you for a vile robber, bent on the loss of others and hostile to her, why does she come to reveal her plans for T. (having her stay in order to teach her a good lesson)? That expression, "Teach her a good lesson," is exactly, do you recall, what she used when she thought that T. had gotten a good thrashing from some guy last year. "That'll teach her a good lesson." In all of this there's the superior attitude of a woman who has tramped on a customer as prone to tramping as herself, but it also seems to me like a trace of cruelty resulting from an inferiority complex. I'm guessing that the Moon Woman, having so many reasons to think herself better than T., constantly stumbles up against that unfair grace, T.'s "class," and is irritated by it and thereby particularly likes to see T. enraged, humiliated, and dejected. T. once told me naively, "She's never nicer to me than when I'm drunk and vomiting." It goes with a vaguely homosexual and very irritable feeling, it seems to me. At least that's what I glimpse in that obscure soul. Yesterday I wrote eight pages to T. I bawled her out for her hesitation about leaving Paris, I pointed out to her that she's not courageous at all, she's afraid of blood and the dead, and, in case of danger, she'd end up wailing uncontrollably. I renewed my exhortations: 1st to get herself a travel permit; 2nd to leave before the 1st of June if she can't get one; 3rd to leave in any case the moment you told her to.

As for my day, dearest, it passed without too many headaches. As I said, we had no readings, it disturbs us a little to be living on unearned income. We wander around, we play chess, I worked a bit but nonetheless there was the sense of arrested momentum, I'm not doing much these days, I mostly play chess and read. The air was heavy and stormy, and during the afternoon I stretched out on my bed to read a detective novel that wasn't bad: *Mort à marée basse* [*Death at Low Tide*]. Spy-itis is still rampant here. Rumor has it that the most unexpected people have been shot, and a while ago, around eleven at night, as I was on my way downstairs to urinate, Sergeant Naudin took me by the arm and said, "Come see the lights." He'd been alone for an hour on an embankment watching "the lights." In fact I did see a brilliant dot appear and disappear in the distant fog. He said to me, "It's three days now that I've been watching 'them.' It goes on all night, you know." He watched again for a moment or two and then he said, "Morse code."

And that's it, my sweet. Still no news about our departure, though rumor has it we'll be holding down a nearby sector that's *extremely* quiet.

I love you, my little flower, I'm so reinvigorated, knowing you are reassured. You are my dear love, I send you kisses for your dear little face.

❧ to Simone de Beauvoir

Monday 27

My darling Beaver

The news isn't very good today, but you won't hear it till tomorrow, I learned it via the American station an hour ago: there's fighting at Calais, and Hénin is surrounded. And yet it's not as bad as at the worst a week ago: even if the Belgian army, surrounded, finally had to surrender, we have a continuous front from Montmédy to the sea which is constantly being reinforced—and the Germans will certainly have lost in men and materiel as much as they might take from the Allies by the capture of that army. But the fact remains, by the way, that we're not to that point yet. There seem to be relatively few French in that army: particularly Belgians (about 600,000), a good proportion of the British Expeditionary Corps (2 to 300,000 men), and perhaps 100,000 French. It's the Belgian regular army that's there. A reserve army of a million Belgians will form up in France. Pierlot announced it officially. I think that Weygand[1] is essentially contemplating reorganizing and fortifying his front. There must have been terrible routs at first. My mother writes that the son of her neighbor in the next apartment turned up dusty and exhausted with nothing but his uniform to his name. He was looking all over for his unit. And today the brother of a soldier from here, we've just learned, showed up abruptly in Rambouillet, back from *Belgium*, where he'd been in the very first days. There must have been some

---

[1] Maxime Weygand (1867–1965), army officer of World War I recalled on May 20 to assume command of the French army when France was already overrun by the Germans. He advised capitulation.

real horrors, and it will be no small matter to reorganize everything. But it seems to me the situation is far from hopeless. Things get worse every day for the Belgian army and better every day for the army of the North. That doesn't mean there aren't nasty moments still to come.

As far as I'm concerned, I've had my lucky break for the day: *three* letters from you. Actually, mostly three envelopes—because one of the letters was written by Poupette. Another was dated Tuesday the 21st, I'd never gotten it. I also got T.'s from that same day. Very friendly and making me regret the extremely stern leter I'd sent her this morning. But above all there were *your* more serene letters; you're working, you're getting some pleasure out of life again, which means so much to me, and now from day to day I *know* from the radio what days you'll be feeling somewhat placid. For instance, all of today. Tomorrow and the day after I'll receive rather serene letters. Only it's something of an ostrichlike hope, because you might be anxious again by the time I get them the day after tomorrow, and yet they're all I want to keep track of, as though they were the emanation of your present, instead of a small fragment of a past that's already dead.

As for me, I've been leading my studious little life, I've beaten my crowd at chess, Pieter, Paul, Hantziger, and I get beaten by the champion. I also resolved a little chess problem from l'Empreinte and reconstructed a master game according to the information given in that same Empreinte. When packages are allowed again, you'll have to send me a little treatise on chess, I want to perfect my game. I also worked on my novel, which went well. I've just reread it with satisfaction, though with a critical eye. Add to that the news programs: BBC at 6:15, Radio PTT at 7:30, New York at 21:00 and Radio-Paris at 21:30. We have maps, like the old men at the Café du Commerce, and resume our running commentary between programs. I also typed ten pages. This novel, through so many avatars—peace, the "phony war," and the real war—is gently inching its way to completion. There are moments when it seems to me, as it does to you, maniacal and obstinate to be writing it while men are dying like flies in the North and when the destiny of all Europe is at stake, but what can I do? Besides, it's *my* destiny, my specific individual destiny, and no grand collective bogeyman should make me renounce my destiny. So I've kept at it these last days, except in moments (around the 18th or 19th) when I was truly too gloomy to write. I still don't see any future for it. I'm interested in it for the present. To think that it will be published, or anything along those lines, that people will read it, that's all a thousand miles from my mind. No, but here's the thing: it's got to be finished around June 15th. That's all. That's its only future. After that, it doesn't depend on me any longer. Of necessity, I'm more or less pure now as I write— I lack those petty vanities and author's little hopes that I couldn't avoid last year.

I'm as pure as when I was writing *Nausea* or the first short stories in *The Wall*, completely unknown and without even knowing if my books would be taken. But this is something else again, it seems more "existential" and more somber, after all it's *against* the failure of democracy and liberty, against the Allies' defeat—symbolically—that I'm doing the act of writing. Acting to the very end "as if" everything were to be again as it once was.

Aside from that, my sweet, nothing very new. On what topic was it that I was thinking of you with such love? It made my heart skip a beat. Wait. It was on the topic of travel, of course—places come back to me just like that, out of my head, and then you are right there in it and it gives me a terrific longing to hug you. I've forgotten exactly what it was. Anyway, my little flower, you cannot know how *moist* it makes me to think of you. You too, my little one, you are my flesh and blood, my skin and bones, my marrow, anything you like. Take extra special care of yourself for me, my sweet Beaver. No news about our departure. It's imminent, I suppose, but ultimately it certainly isn't for tomorrow, for we would know about it already. Anyway we won't be going far. Perhaps we'll even go to rest camp or to the backup position. So have *no concern whatsoever* about me.

Till tomorrow, my little flower. Tender kisses to you.

෨ *to Simone de Beauvoir*

[May 28]

My darling Beaver

The beginning is missing.

You remember the notorious C.S.A.K. and the attempt near the Étoile? That guy was mixed up in it and was challenged about it. He's a case. A tall sad guy, and ugly, with an interminable, sinuous nose, and an ill-starred look to him, stubborn in his somber pride, bitter and terribly nervous, in furious anguish right now because his mother lives 30 kilometers from Rethel and she's ill. He hasn't had any news in a week. He sleeps one hour a night, gorges himself out of anxiety, and exaggerates everything, saying, "The Germans are at the gates of Paris, it's politicking that's gotten us into this fix, we're done for," listens to stations transmitting in languages he doesn't understand, leaps in terror like a rabbit when he hears Dutch words which he misinterprets (the announcer was saying approximately: *d'esten van Cambrai*—and he jumped, "To the West of Cambrai, they've overrun Cambrai!") and he declares, "My brother, who's a captain in the army HQ staff, wanted to have me posted near him, but when I saw that things looked rotten I asked to stay here. I couldn't stand not to be at the front like everyone else." To which the good Pieter remonstrated, "Yes, only you chose to stay on a front where things aren't looking so rotten." And yet that's just the sort of lie which is consuming him inch by inch, altogether like a paranoid. I'm delighted: I'd certainly been thinking that those guys from the C.S.A.K.—not the bosses but the others—had to be like that. He's a radioman and through an exchange of friendly services we lend him our bike to go to town and he calls us so we can listen to the bulletins. It's invaluable.

Aside from that all is calm. Last night we were mistaken for spies: we were making a night reading, which requires us to use a pocket flashlight every thirty seconds to read the azimuth and inclination dial. Apparently from a distance it looks like a regular alternation of darkness and small bright flashes that can be taken for signaling. We did the reading, packed away the theodolite, and as we were peacefully going home, Captain Lemort, the captain with whom I'd already had a run-in about food, appeared before us: "Who's there?" he cried. We didn't recognize him. I said, "Readings." "What?" "Weather group, we've just done a reading." "Names?" "Pieter and Sartre." "Ah? Sartre . . ." and with a gentle, terrible sort of irony, "But look here, Sartre, it's awfuly unwise to be traipsing around with a flashlight, it could be taken for signals." Meanwhile I was walking up to him and saw that he had his revolver in his hand. I said to him, "We have to do it, to read the figures." "Ah! But couldn't you read without a flashlight?" "No, Sir, Captain." "Ah! then couldn't you do that under cover?" "With great difficulty, Captain, Sir. The balloon would bump into the ceiling." "Ah! very good!" and he let us go, disconcerted. This morning we told this to our officers, who had a good laugh over it.

There you are, my little one. I'm totally serene again, and I suppose that at this same moment you must at least feel the lifting of a great weight. Don't get it into your head to fear for me, my foolish darling; I remind you, I'm a vestal of the Maginot Line, I tend the sacred fire and that's all.

My love, I love you so much. I told you so last night, full of emotions, and I tell you so tonight in all serenity. You are my darling Beaver.

᪐ᕉ *to Simone de Beauvoir*

May 29

My darling Beaver

I was rather stunned by your letter: it seems so shocking to have that happen to poor young Bost. But on all due reflection, it's the best possible news.[1] Since he was able to write to Z., it mustn't be too serious. One month for the wound to heal, he says, a month for him to get back on his feet while convalescing, and then ten days of leave, that means two and a half months pulled off the lines. That's terrifically valuable in a fast-moving war. Be sure to tell all that to Z.

My little one, I love you so much. Today I put a cartridge in my pen (the next to last, alas) and thus stripped, with the tip of the glass tube sticking out, it looked like your sick little pen. It didn't take more than that to put me on the verge of affectionate tears. It so resembles you, your poor little pen, and then you are so good to use it gravely and to love it somewhat like a child in disgrace. My dearest, how I would love to kiss you.

As for me, the day would have been almost uneventful without the home visit paid me by the ignominious little Nippert. He had brought the *New Testament* and made me read a dozen or so prophetic passages to convince me that Hitler is the 1st beast of the Apocalypse, the one with a deadly wound that heals, the one who prepares the coming of the 2nd beast or the Antichrist. In general, here's what's in store for us. First there will be the First Coming of Christ. "Which many believers confuse with the Last Judgment," he said with a scornful laugh. Christ resurrects those of the Just who are dead and leads them away with him. And the Just who are still alive he takes away too, still completely alive. As for the unjust, they fend for themselves on earth. I was charmed by that brusque draining off of the Just. I pictured it as Kafkaesque and almost feel like writing a fantastic short story about it. But the fantastic side was eliminated by Nippert, who one day asked a man of rare expertise, "But in our scientific and economic (sic) century, how could that be done?" A charming question for a believer, for ultimately he's quite willing for miracles to have been miraculous in the barbaric times of the early Christians. But, in our Age of Enlightenment, he wants them to have a positivist veneer. And the expert replied, "The Lord will remove the Just living in our midst, but we won't notice because our spirits will be turned elsewhere." For instance they could remove Poupette at this very moment and we wouldn't learn until only a very long time after that she had disappeared. After the Coming of Christ will come the Great Tribulation. Those

---

[1] Bost had been wounded and evacuated from the front.

who tribulate are the Jews. They'll all be reunited in Jerusalem. (Imagine the look on the Arabs' faces.) And, hold on, they'll begin to be persecuted as *Christians*. For their misery will have converted them. And the Lord will have a certain soft spot for them: "Because, you understand, with their intelligence and their commercial spirit, if they take up wanting to convert others, they'll succeed better than anyone else." After the Great Tribulation will come the first beast. Then the second, and finally the Lord, having killed both of them with one breath, will render the Last Judgment. All of this will take place in a very short period, still according to Nippert: "We're in the century of speed." About Hitler's personality he's uncertain: everything seems to indicate that he is the first beast. But he also says that, under the reign of the second beast, each person will be marked with the sign and no one will be able to engage in commerce or fill a job if he isn't marked. This mark of the beast is obviously the swastika, which would lead one to suppose that Hitler is the *second* beast. Except, on the other hand, it is specified that all this will come about after the Coming of Christ, whereas the Coming of Christ has not yet occurred. I told him, "What do you know about it?" If you suppose that he has already come, everything clears up: the Great Tribulation is the persecution of the Jews by the Nazis, the first beast is Hitler, the hail of iron is the war and the second beast is Stalin." He lowered his eyes, blushed like a young girl, and said with a saintly look, "Oh, I for one know that Christ's Coming hasn't yet happened." "But how do you know that? When you yourself told me that we won't notice the removal of the Just." Still looking at the ground and wearing his inner smile, he said, "I just know." "Oh, come on now, why?" Then he whispered, "Because he'd have taken me along with the Just."

Thus I have the rare good fortune of being able to speak on a daily basis with a guy who has the *certainty* of being raised *living* to Heaven by the Lord. There mustn't be too many of them like that, if you leave aside the old guys in institutions. He isn't the least bit crazy and his certainty doesn't prevent him from having an atrocious fear of bombs, shells, etc. It seems he was most satisfied with that conversation and at dinner he ranked me among the unjust whom the Lord will save at the eleventh hour.

And there you have it, my sweet. The rest of the day was chess and work. Would you believe that Pieter beat the champ. He's bearing up under his glee. I got a letter from my stepfather which contains these words: "I won't congratulate you on your high morale, because that would irritate you, but I can tell you that I'm very happy about it." I could die laughing.

Till tomorrow, my sweet, my little flower. I love you with all my might.

❧ to Simone de Beauvoir

Wednesday, May 29

My darling Beaver

It's six in the morning. It's not such a bad system to write you in the morning because anyway—for eight months now—we've always mailed our letters in the morning. Because the last collection is at 7:40 in the morning and there's only *one* mail a day going out: mornings at eight. The delay in my letters came from congestion of the rail lines.

Yesterday we heard about the capitulation of the Belgian army. The evening before we had premonitions of very bad news on the way for the following day: the bulletin was very delayed, the commentary vague and disturbing and, for the first time, I'd been fidgety but not anxious (on previous bad days I had instead been anxious but not fidgety) to the point that I slept very badly. At six-thirty the following day comes the announcement of a speech by Paul Reynaud for eight o'clock, and things looked worse and worse. Finally, at eight o'clock, the address. I'll tell you, it meant *nothing* to me. I had already been resigned for several days to disaster for this army. Let me be very clear: I cannot contemplate without horror the fate of the English Expeditionary Corps and the French divisions that are surrounded between Dunkirk and Calais, and the idea that they were there—for once I felt the simultaneity—cast a sinister pall over the day, like the one I felt, for example, the day Barcelona fell. But it was more in things and the mood of the moment that the gloom resided. I for one was thinking that this capitulation could hardly influence the course of the war. Now everything depends on the resistance of our Aisne-Somme front and on the possibilities remaining to us to transform the war of movement on that front into a war of position. Nonetheless, we played a great deal of chess yesterday, and played it artlessly. Incidentally I won 5 games out of eight.

Aside from that, nothing. What's happening to us is rather strange and powerful: our days are well filled and engaging, we're not bored for an instant; it seems as though we're in an *adventure* but our personal life is reduced to the vegetative: eating, sleeping—working a bit too, and from that point of view nothing distinguishes one day from the next. It's an odd state: I don't think incidentally that it would be possible for me to push the sense of the collective any further. For yourself it's rather different, because you still have a life, with affairs, affections, rages, arguments. Things seem more of a mix. But as for me, since for the moment I'm reassured on both your fate and T.'s (you're right, you must make her leave) I really have no more than collective worries.

I worked rather well yesterday. Of course, no readings, which contributes still more to the absurdity of the life we lead here. I got one very slim little letter from you, and I understand so well, my little one, that you scarcely feel like making it long, lacking fullness of heart.

What more to tell you, my little sweet. I too lack some slight fullness of heart. But I have never loved you so much, when I think of yourself it is almost with tears in my eyes. Till tomorrow, my little one, I would so love to kiss you with all my might.

What strikes me in all this is the sort of historic luck of Hitlerism, which you might think the nations *deserve* through a sort of profound and irremediable disintegration.

ᗢ *to Simone de Beauvoir*

Thursday, May 30

My darling Beaver

I'm terribly anxious about yourself, you'll get sick if you worry so much, I can see you so clearly, striding along, terribly upset, constrained, with the nightmare city all around you. I was hoping, as you must have seen from yesterday's letter, that you would be more comforted today, but it's almost worse. The thing that's true is that two months from now *either* the Germans will be in Paris and the war will be over (which I do not believe at all) *or else* our positions at the Somme and the Aisne will have held and for a rather long time it will be a war of positions. Because, remember, exhaustion is beginning to get to them, they've lost hundreds of thousands of men, 2,000 tanks out of 5,000 and 2,000 airplanes. It's between now and July 1 that this battle will be decided. It's not shaping up too badly for us, incidentally; I mean that for the Germans it will probably be the fatally costly three-quarters success that they wanted to avoid at any price. Expending unlimited men and materiel to secure a front that's more vulnerable than the Siegfried Line—surely that is not what they had in mind. So for the last two or three days I've been rather optimistic—and mightily relieved concerning Bost. I'd hate to have something really bad happen to him. I've set my alarm clock for six to write to him tomorrow morning (since T. isn't writing to me anymore, and according to a tacit law of retaliation, I'm not writing to her either). There's only one cloud on the horizon: Italy. It would be a nuisance if it got into the war. A real nuisance. But ultimately it wouldn't aggravate the situation terribly. I'm saying this to you in advance so you won't carry on too much when it does happen, because we can now foresee bad news a couple of days off. The good news, if there is any, will have the added charm of being unexpected.

Mind you, don't get it into your head to worry about me, that's too generous. I'm no more in danger than if I were a crossing guard at Romorantin. *You*, in Paris, are in much more danger than I. I'm sorry about that, I would like to be interesting too, but in all honesty I have to tell you: in effect I was prudently removed from circulation, upon declation of war, so nothing evil would befall me. And that will continue.

Today, nothing new: seven games of chess, newspapers, letters, one from yourself, and some rather good work. And naturally the radio seven or eight times during the day. I've definitely made a hit with Charlotte. Today Nippert went to the restaurant for lunch because the army grub was inedible. He was with Paul, Mondange, and Courcy, with his back to me. As it happened I still had his *New Testament* which he'd loaned to me. Since he's scared of the women, I had the idea of asking Charlotte to return it to him, thanking him as though he'd loaned it to her. Meanwhile I was winking at the three merrymakers who exclaimed in shocked tones when she returned it: "What's all this, you're using the Bible to seduce women," etc. It aroused some lovely indignation, he turned beet red, and then Charlotte, returning to the attack on my urging, went over and ran her fingers through his hair, and poured him a glass of schnapps (he never drinks alcohol) saying, "This one's on me." The whole thing was accompanied by a thousand little gestures and nonsense between Charlotte and myself. Nothing will come of it, but I'm rather proud, because she's difficult and very much sought after and if you could see me, my Beaver, you would be surprised that I could excite anything but derision and horror. My filthiness has become legendary but, so Paul was telling me, it is accepted by everyone, "almost affectionately." Those are his very words. I'd be very wrong to feel embarrassed. Only good Pieter rebukes me, saying, "No, you're definitely too filthy." And when I ask him to lend me certain ordinary objects, like nail clippers, etc., he answers, "Once you've washed."

That's it, my sweet. I'm not bored, and my life isn't as austere as you think. First, for chess I've been seized by one of those barren, manic passions that overtake me sometimes and that you hate. Then, that battle we're steeped in via the radio has something morbidly gripping about it. And I still have books: I'm reading Samuel Pepys drop by drop, and at the local tobacconist's I'll find two or three Empreintes I haven't read.

My love, I await tomorrow with impatience, I hope that I'll have a little slightly calmed-down letter. I love you with all my might, and I'm with you completely.

Kisses for your little cheeks.

I'm afraid that Nizan, who "cleverly" had himself transferred to the English Expeditionary Corps, might be in Belgium.[1]

&ro *to Simone de Beauvoir*

May 31

My darling Beaver

This will be a very short letter today. It's not the heart that's lacking, but the matter. Yesterday there were no letters, no bad news—nor good news, no work. The day seemed slightly long—but only slightly: particularly from 4 to 7; on the other hand from 7 to 10 it went by like a dream. All the same I did work a bit, but for the moment my novel disgusts me, I see all the tricks, all the repetitions, all the faults. And then I have nothing more to say, all the chapters are pegs. They've got to be there for the story but they don't add a whole lot that's new. This is what I've been thinking: I'll polish it as much as I can, then I'll send it to you. (It seems that *we here* can send packages, we just can't receive them.) If it works, you'll correct the mistakes and remove the badly done parts. If you decide that it's still too imperfect, you won't take it to them. You'll keep it in your own custody till the end of the war, I'll begin the other and the two will be published together, after a general revision. What do you think of that? You're going to shriek about the responsibility.

It bothers me not to have received a letter from you. Yesterday when I left you, you were in a very sorry state, poor little Beaver, and I'd so like to think that you'd bounced back. Yesterday I wrote to Bost. You're going to face another blow: Italy's declaration of war—it seems imminent. They still might hold back at the last moment (Roosevelt is putting pressure on Mussolini), it's also possible that they'll limit themselves to a big diplomatic maneuver. But in any case it will be, I think, the final blow, we'll have hit bottom. After that, we can only wait for good news, which in the end will surely come.

My sweet, I have nothing more to tell you: I've played chess—won, lost; mostly won. I finished the Mathieu-Daniel chapter and then, taken with a sudden need to *talk*, I carried on an hour's conversation with the Acolytes, who were surprised and flattered. And that's it.

[1] *In fact he was there, and killed [on May 23] by a German bullet. (SdB)*

My love, I love you with all my might, I think of you constantly, you are a painful little wound on my heart because I sense you're so sad. I long to hold you in my arms, my little flower.

✢ to Simone de Beauvoir

June 1st

My darling Beaver

Today I got a letter from you that was much cheerier, and my peace of mind is completely restored. I'm also reassured to know that Fabre-Luce is actually Lucas-Dubreton; I'd been afraid I'd asked you for some strange work in a moment of aberration and was denying for all I was worth. Tell me, my little Beaver, I was thinking yesterday, after I got your letter, what's become of my notebooks? Are they somewhere underground in bits and pieces?[1] If they're lost, well then that's that, what can I say, they just weren't meant to see the light of day, I won't be too broken up about it. But if by chance they were safe, I'd like to know it. What I'd particularly regret losing would be my most recent philosophic things, rather than my ruminations about myself. But basically there must be quite a bit of it in the notebooks that stayed at your place and I could work out something. Don't worry too much about it.

I worked only a bit yesterday. On further thought, I'm keeping Mathieu's efforts toward the civil servant's loan, but condensed: 8 pages instead of 18, because it's not bad, after the Daniel-Mathieu conversation during which we can seriously imagine that he'll marry Marcelle, to suddenly see the guy tearing off to a moneylender to ask for money, without any comment. I think I'm right. But you be the judge. An idea came to me: my last volume will be set entirely *during a leave* of Mathieu's. What do you think of that? There'll be plenty of others to describe the war per se.

Aside from that, I played chess but extremely badly, I lost six times and only managed to salvage one draw with Pieter. At that point I had an argument with Hantziger, who doesn't play correctly, and I took it upon myself to forbid my Acolytes to play with him. They obeyed, Paul somewhat sullenly, for as he said, "Basically we're using force." And I said to him, "Yes, but it's *moral* force." Thus we are exercising a blockade against Hantziger, who can't play chess at all anymore and seems sorely tried. I want him to crawl back saying he's sorry about

---

[1] *Those that I had lent to Bost on his last leave (three or four) disappeared when he was wounded and evacuated. But a number of others survived and have been published. (SdB)*

the errors of his game (you find his black bishop on a white square when he believes he could be more effective there, or else his tower suddenly goes off on a diagonal. We call the chess games we play with him pancratiums).

And that's all. Nothing on the news; it seems they'll save most of Blanchard's army, it's really a tour de force. A piece of news today that's still ambiguous, the resignation of Gafenco, Rumanian foreign affairs minister. Here the mood is calm again, and life goes on in a very ordinary way. Already we're listening less to the radio: mornings at 6:30, at 12:30, and evenings at 7 o'clock. And yesterday I didn't even listen at seven. We're still on very cool terms with Munier because of incidents I haven't related to you, out of prudence, and which naturally concern "responsibilities."

Would you like to know about the task I performed yesterday? I looked for words or combinations of words consisting of 10 letters, with no letter repeated. For instance *"vertugadin"* [farthingale]—actually, that one I did for the cryptographers. Then I quite rapidly found 33 combinations: (*Doux baiser* [sweet kiss]—*Jambon cuit* [cooked ham]—*Vénus à Milo*—etc.). It's fun.

And that's that, my little dear. I'm still completely bound to you, I can feel you up against me, you populate my days, you are here, more than ever. I love you with all my might. Many times a day I too have humble little desires, so individual and uncomplicated, to be next to you and to kiss your little cheeks.

I love you.

✎ *to Simone de Beauvoir*

Sunday, June 2

My darling Beaver

This time it was an entirely good letter, so cheerful. Watch out for the Italian delcaration of war, my little one. It's almost upon us, but don't let it get you down, and besides I want to believe that it's our last blow for a while. I so love to hear the echoes of your serenity again in your letters, and then too the little worldly echoes of your life. Sorokine, Zaz., Gégé; when I don't hear you speak about them, it's because things aren't going well. But now, yes everything's fine, there were big arguments with Sorok, little overcherished, and then Zaz. had bared her soul. Do you know why T. hasn't written to me for six days now? I'm having my little springtime flirtation (in war it's permitted) with Charlotte. Oh, it's nothing at all, merely platonic and reserved, and that's the way it amuses me. There'll never be any more than smirks and glances. She's well behaved and I'm being authentic. But I'm gently advancing in her good graces. And it's fun persuading Pieter that it's he who's progressing. Finally he's beginning to believe it slightly, all the while protesting, and today he told me, "No, my friend, if I deceive my wife, and I'm not saying I will, it'll be a thing of the flesh not of the feelings. I want to remain faithful to her in my feelings." I want to give you a clear picture of the thing: she's at the counter with her fat sister-in-law, and we're at the opposite end of the room, at a table. She never leaves her counter or we our table, everything passes from one to the other across the full length of the room and in the midst of an infernal hubbub. It goes on for an hour, approximately, every day, during lunch. And yet, from time to time when she serves some schnapps at the next table, she does come over for a quick aside at ours. That's all, but it provides a little distraction and it breaks up the day, we have our "Charlotte's hour."

Aside from that, I worked a bit today. Only a bit, but rather well. On *L'Angoisse d'Abraham*, because I really have to get to it. I think that after a day or two it will be all set, but it's rather difficult. I have to make it clear that if we are free, we are free not only to choose our acts, but to choose our Good, though, in other respects (Kafka, Kierkegaard), the Good is not arbitrary and a person is always responsible in choosing it. Since the example is precise—whether to marry Marcelle or not—it will be rather clear, after all, and not too philosophical.

And then what? I mostly won at chess today. But we're maintaining our dignity vis-à-vis our positions, Hantziger and I. In any case he's wavering somewhat, he'll show repentance in a day or two. The Acolytes are a bit flabbergasted that I forbid them to play with Hantziger, they realize that I'm in command. But all in all they don't mind. I seriously began *Don Quixote* and read a hundred pages. Well, you know, it's very entertaining. I won't need too much of it, but I think that three or four hundred pages out of 800 must be delightful. Incidentally, it has a very modern way of telling the story that's not too much spoiled by the ironic grandiloquence of the style. So, I've got a bit more to read, and then from what I could see there are two or three Empreintes at the tobacco store, I'll buy them when I get your money.

This time it's really all, my little one. We're completely serene for the moment, but with a certain something drifting and hazy that surely comes from the hard knocks of these past weeks. Well, all in all, things are definitely better than last week.

My little one, my little flower, I'm every bit as one with you in serenity and calm as in catastrophes, you know, and I wouldn't have it any other way. I love you with all my might, and long to kiss your little old cheeks. I love you.

❧ *to Simone de Beauvoir*

Monday, June 3

My darling Beaver

This time around I'm anxious about you, I never thought it would come, and here it is. This evening the rumor was going around that Paris had been bombed, at first I didn't believe it, all the more so in that the Germans had dropped tracts saying, "We don't want to bomb Paris, we want to enter it." But the French radio spoke of a 2 to 3 hour alert for the Paris region with bombs dropped, without any precise information. Thereupon London said a bit more at 20:00, and finally at 10:00 in the evening the first sergeant came back with the news that someone had heard the New York radio: 1,000 bombs dropped, 80 fires started, 40 dead, 150 wounded. To tell the truth, there are contradictions. It would be surprising for 1,000 bombs to cause only 80 fires. But in any case it's enough to make your heart sink, I'm really worried. This isn't the same kind of anguish as in past days when your very fate was in the balance. It's not as difficult because if there were truly 200 persons killed, that makes about one chance in 15,000 that you were among them, which is to say practically nil. Nonetheless, I'm really frightened, my little one. Besides, I think this might have frayed your nerves. It's true, I say to reassure myself, that perhaps you might have heard it through the grapevine, as I did, if nothing happened in your neighborhood. You would have heard the familiar sound of the antiaircraft guns, and then some louder bursts, and you would have learned a few hours later that some real bombs had been dropped. But that's not certain, you might have been very close to one of the explosions. Besides, it isn't so much this bombing raid that scares me as the others, the ones that will soon follow. My little dearest, do be very sensible, go into the shelters, that's still the best course. And the moment it's possible for you to leave, go for a little trip to Angers to stay with the Lady. Fortunately you don't have long to stay in Paris, the vacations are coming soon. My love, it's infinitely more disagreeable to fear danger for another person than to be in danger oneself. There's a good chance you're feeling plucky, which gives me the jitters. I'm impatiently waiting for your letter, but I won't get it before the day after tomorrow. Make the Zazouliches leave immediately, of course, paying no attention to the stubborn set of their chins: they have to be put on a train, period. I haven't been writing to T. (law of retaliation), but I'll pick up my pen again and urge her to take off immediately; I actually hope she'll be gone by the time my letter reaches Paris.

I'm writing to you from the clerks' room, downstairs, the large glassed-in room—the veranda. It is very dark, only two lamps are lit. The mice are scampering around as though it were theirs, I can see them running up a broomhandle, nibbing at boxes without paying any attention to us. Pieter and Naudin are watching them, there's nobody here but them: Pieter, a bit punchy too, is also waiting for it to be 22:30, for the latest news on the radio, but it's likely that the radio will adhere to the orders of discretion it's observed thus far. It's clear that we'll have several more difficult months ahead.

Aside from that, nothing. It was a rather happy and uneventful day up to this evening. On a lark, I went for a bath and a shave. Everyone found me twenty years younger. I played chess and beat the champion one time out of three, I was conceited as a pig—yet all the same he does give me a knight. I didn't beat him by surprise, but by trickery and concerted action. He said to me—which I found charming—"My congratulations," when he was checkmated. I lunched at Charlotte's, with no flirtations or feelings: she was busy, there was a crowd and it slipped my mind. And then afterward I played chess again and worked as I should till evening, then came here because it's my tour of guard duty and I'm waiting for everyone to leave so I can go to bed. The last time I slept here, the Germans had just taken Abbeville. Today Paris was bombed: this veranda brings me lousy luck. Paul surreptitiously reconciled me with Hantziger. We were at neighboring tables and he called out, "Come on, now! Kiss and make up!" Hantz finally held out his hand and I took it, saying, "Stupid ass!" with which he considered himself satisfied.

Till tomorrow, my dearest, take good care of yourself. I love you with all my might and I don't know what would become of me if anything bad befell you. I long to cover your face with kisses.

๑๖ to Simone de Beauvoir

June 4

My darling Beaver

I'm writing to you with the window open, it's 8:30 p.m. but still quite bright out so I haven't yet turned on the light. It is a beautiful day, very balmy, very bucolic. As Pieter was saying the other day, "In weather like this, you get to missing things." "Well," I replied, "just where would you be on a summer Sunday, in weather like this?" "In the country." "Well, that's where you are." "Yes, but not with old farts like you." The same goes for me this evening, with this difference: if it were peacetime I wouldn't be in the country. I'd be on the terrace of the Flore, with you, I'd be eating scrambled eggs on toast and we'd be eavesdropping on Sonia, Prévert, or Agnès Capri.[1] As you know, I can say this without the slightest melancholy; I have almost completely lost any "feeling of peace," without gaining in return any feeling of war. Today I felt peaceful and idle, without much anxiety because the bombing raid in central Paris where you are doesn't seem to have claimed many victims at all. I haven't worked much, simply set to rights the chapter when Marcelle waits for Daniel's phone call—and I wasn't able to play much chess, because Paul and Pieter seemed to suddenly run out of energy. Pieter is bothered by the Paris air raid, which produced a gentle inner collapse, plaintive and caressing; as always, there was an inscrutable tenderness in his eyes, he licked his lips and then during the afternoon he threw himself on his bed and slept for three hours. I understood why he's disturbed actually: his wife has just had a minor operation and she's convalescing, it's frustrating to be helpless if there's some chance of being evacuated, and besides of course, since May 15th her business isn't bringing in a thing, because women aren't exactly in a hat-buying mood. On the other hand, lots of refugees came in to buy stockings at her other store. Paul took this bombing serenely—the one on Nancy scared him more. "Home turf," Pieter said, philosophically. But he wasn't playing chess either because he'd undertaken to wash his uniform. All day we saw him ferociously scrubbing his laundry on a wide board streaming with water. Seeing that, this morning I took my bicycle and went for a ride to the next village two kilometers away. It's a real expedition, because for now the roads are guarded by patrols, barricaded by log stockades at the entrances to villages, etc. But nothing happened to me and I had fresh impressions of the countryside. In particular, a stork, driven from cover somewhere, grazed the top of my head in his hedge hopping, his big wings spread out like a glider; it was all marvelous and ridiculous, but it's striking how much real storks resemble the wood storks they sell in souvenir shops around Alsace, leading one to believe, yet again, that nature has imitated art. Silly. I dismounted; Civette, the hero who wants to avenge his natural father (did I tell you about that?), also dismounted (he was coming from the opposite direction) and we gazed at the animal for a long time. Then I went home, I loitered around the place, I don't really know what I did, it was one of those times when one feels too bulky for one's own good, too material; without being sad one feels mild self-loathing, it happens to me often in civilian life, much less so in military life. I wound up reading *Don Quixote*, which is really excellent and sometimes makes me *laugh*, which is extraordinary because if admiration is retrospective, laughter certainly isn't. Besides, it's extremely poetic. There's one place where they're eating with some goatherds, and they drink some wine from a goatskin

---

[1] The singing proprietor of a small night spot favored by Beauvoir and her friends.

in a horn which they pass around, and then Sancho goes to sleep and Don Quixote keeps watch all night, it's as appealing as can be. This afternoon I received two letters from you, completely serene again but, it seemed, a little out of date in a mildly worrisome way, because some news yesterday somehow invalidated everything you were telling me. All the same it was very satisfying to have so many pages from you to read.

I'm waiting impatiently for tomorrow's letter. I only hope there is one; you have a habit now of adding a word in the evening. *That's* a bad habit, little wretch, now that one in three comes a day late. There was also a nice letter from Tania and one from my mother, who's doing what she can, poor thing, busy with an organization trying to reunite families broken up by the evacuation. I agree it's useful work. They compare cards that come in from who knows where and wind up finding similar names: the husband is in Limoges, the wife in Perpignan. But it very often happens that after working all day she hasn't managed to match up any family cards.

After that, serene like you, I played chess with Paul and beat him. Then I reread my novel from beginning to end. With satisfaction; not that I find it good or bad, I'm not at that stage anymore: it's done and I accept it without further comment. But I haven't many details on my revisions left to correct. It will be truly finished in ten days or so unless we learn that Paris has been taken between now and then. I imagine it's a weird underground life people have been living in Paris all this time. They'll be fleeing again after this bombing raid.

My little one, from the latest news (New York, 21:40) I've just learned the *true* figures on the bombing: roughly 1,000 people wounded. Anxiety is getting the better of me again. Not that there's any chance of your being involved since it's pretty well established that the Germans were aiming—though very carelessly—at military objectives. Hence toward the outskirts of Paris, not the center. But that drives home a sense of the real danger you would run if it happened again. My love, do go along with evacuation if someone suggests it to you. Be sensible and virtuous, I beg of you. How could we rejoice together about peace, which will eventually return, if you had one of your little legs missing, or perhaps all of your head?

I love you, my sweet, my little flower. My thoughts scarcely leave you. Except when I'm playing chess. I love you with all my might.

If I never speak of *Marat*, it's because I'm somewhat loath to read it. It's by an American, and I have only the greatest contempt for American learning.

I've concluded that the subject of my novel is slavery and the grandeur of democratic man. I won't forget to point that out in my review copy blurb, to give a contemporary flavor to this work which might seem too pacifist.

✿ *to Simone de Beauvoir*

Wednesday, June 5

My darling Beaver

So you're not dead. Your letter was even a bit strange, with the alert playing only a very small part—no more than earlier alerts—and not yet knowing anything, finding it all in all amusing, a pretext to see the people in Bienenfeld's hotel and to listen to more records. You must only have learned from the newspapers in the evening or the following day that there had been nine hundred victims, in terms of the news you were just as far away as I was. Almost all the letters are like that here, except my mother's, who saw the Citroën factory blow up, and one from an old woman who lives beside the Porte de Versailles and who knew that bombs had been dropped on the Lycée Michelet, Vanves and the Paris market. Now I understand the "marvelous sangfroid" displayed by the Parisian population thus: in 90% of the cases it was ignorance. I am—though I don't quite know why—slightly more reassured as far as you are concerned. First there was your letter, and then after all, despite a certain carelessness in letting bombs fall helter-skelter, it was still military targets that served as pretext.

My sweet, you mustn't in the least feel so embarrassed about my notebooks. You can't imagine how lightheartedly I contemplated their loss. After all, the most important part is still in my head, Nothingness—and that's more likely to be the subject of a book. As far as the war is concerned, many observations are no longer valid. Which leaves the work I did on my personality. But that's not lost either. And besides, what can we do? Right now we live so cut off from the future—particularly from a literary future—that little notebooks seem so futile. I may miss them someday, in the same way I miss that short story I lost in the Causses: poetically. But for the moment I don't miss them in the least. I would simply like to know if they still exist, in case I were to go on with that lesser work after finishing my novel.

You found Nippert amusing, and I'm very pleased, but one mustn't take him for a visionary or someone strange. The strangest part is that he isn't strange at all. He's a dull little twerp with base bigoted thoughts who can believe at the same time that the Lord will raise him from the earth along with the Just, and break out in a cold sweat from the fear of spending a week in a fortified bunker 10 kilometers from the front. As a matter of fact those strange notions he's got in his head are *social*. It is the societies of biblical research, the Jehovah's Witnesses, that stuffed them in. It's grafted onto the slightly pedantic and malevolent strictness of a straightlaced Protestant that's much closer to his true nature.

There's not much to say about me, my sweet. The weather's beautiful, I worked a bit, finished rereading my factum and played some chess. I have to struggle against a seasonal sloth. You know that in the spring I never do much of anything. I'm in a hurry to have this novel finished. Captain Munier has indicated his hostility toward us by advising Courcy to prevent anyone but the clerks from using the typewriters from now on. It's all the same to me, at the most there will be thirty handwritten pages out of 650. And incidentally on my nights of guard duty, who could keep me from typing if I want to do so? But it's a slight lack, as Olga would say. Nothing from T. today, which was the day when she should know the results of the X rays. Could they be bad? You must know. It would be too bad under the present circumstances, if she had something; I don't see how we could have her cared for.

The Germans are on the offensive again. We heard it this morning on the radio. Which suggests new blows and somber days like those in May. But we're beginning to get used to it. We've had no other bulletins, and we've taken the opportunity to steel ourselves against the bad news that might come tomorrow. Keuris, the chess champion, came by to play, he beat me but only by a hair. These days I hold him to the fire each time around; I've made great progress. He brought me two books. His reading is surprising. The last time it was *Le Pape* [*The Pope*] (a history of the Papacy would have interested me, but this was pure hot air). This time it was the private life of Abdulhamid. There's also a life of Law. That's more entertaining, but it's done by a hack who tarted it up with mincing descriptions and gallant speeches. Nonetheless I'll read it.

And that's all, my little dearest. With this life of leisure, I sleep rather little at night (from 11:30 to 6 o'clock) and quite often I take a little siesta in the afternoon. It's altogether voluptuous to sleep in broad daylight.

My love, I long to kiss you with all my might. I know that you're equal to it, that you're serene, that if the need arose, M. Bienenfeld would put his car at your disposal, all this contributes enormously to my personal serenity. I don't like it at all when you are not happy, my little flower. I love you.

I haven't yet received my monthly cash. Did you send it, my little one? If not, do so quickly, for five days now I've been sponging off the good Pieter. The good Pieter, I forgot to tell you, is in the grips of a tragic dilemma: he's fond of his wife but he's also fond of his shop, through which, and contrary to what he'd been thinking, he's just learned that he's doing great business. Now, if his wife leaves Paris, their store must be closed. He's doing his best to persuade himself that the danger is not too great. "Besides, down there (in Perpignan near their son) the inactivity would gnaw at her, " he told me with a sneaky look that you had to see to believe.

last village, completely dead, too, still neat but with gouges everywhere on the walls from the shelling. But it must have been a quick battle, because you cannot imagine the quiet of that affluent hamlet, with small manicured gardens that still looked well tended, very clean streets and alleyways, a large deserted factory on the outskirts, and naturally a beautiful clear blue sky above. That's where we were going to hunt down the packing case, and the lieutenant informed us incidentally that we were two kilometers from the lines. Once again it seemed like a war out of Kakfa, with that impalpable, silent front, which they call a "line" as if the better to demonstrate its abstraction and which is no more perceptible when you approach close enough to touch it than it is at ten or twenty kilometers. It seemed very strange, watching the soldiers going about their garrison duties, cleaning, sweeping the courtyard, peeling potatoes, lazy and slow like old-timers in military service, to think of all the young men who, at the same moment under the same sky were getting their mugs shattered in a real landscape of war. As for the story of the packing case, it ended mysteriously, just as it had begun, because when we got there they told us, "Ah! You've come for the case? Well, a car came to pick it up." "Yeah, what car?" "A car . . . ," they said vaguely. And since the lieutenant persisted, they said, annoyed, "Well, you know, that's none of our business." Which was entirely correct. So there's a case of meteorological stuff that lay there buried for at least three or four months without anyone knowing who had left it and then, a few days only after its discovery, a mysterious car comes and takes it away. For a moment we watched the rapid flow of a little stream, then we climbed back up on the truck, sat down again on our chairs, and got back, without a hitch, by noon. From there to Charlotte's; she's friendlier now and she and I exchanged a few gibes, then I slept for two hours because the weather was sultry, and I worked. But I grew irritated because it was bad work, sliding toward the glib. Beneath its apparent simplicity this chapter is difficult, and I'll have to get back to it tomorrow, and find another angle. It was terribly hot in my room and around seven o'clock we went to eat a couple of eggs at Charlotte's restaurant, outside in the courtyard, which in peacetime serves as a dance floor. Pieter went for a dip in a stream while I slept, and I'll go tomorrow, you can even swim a bit. Well, my sweet, I do hope you'll get in some swimming during the long vacation fast approaching. What are you going to do? It's not possible that plans aren't already floating around in your little head. After dinner, chess: one game with Paul, which I won, two games with Hantziger, a draw and a victory. And here I am, writing to you. As you could see, I somewhat anticipated the enormous disproportion between the printed words "Paris bombed" and the way the people who weren't directly bombed experienced it. That doesn't mean you shouldn't be prudent, my little flower, and prudently go down to the shelters for the length of the raid.

You saw that an air raid warden was killed? The others must be all puffed up with self-importance.

Till tomorrow, my sweet Beaver, my love. I love you with all my might.

᪥ to Simone de Beauvoir

June 8

My darling Beaver

Might you not by chance have inadvertently sent my money to the previous sector, 108? Yesterday Pieter received a mail order sent from Paris on Monday, and here we are past the 7th and I for one haven't received a thing. Where do we stand, my sweet? Listen, just send 100 francs by telegraph, I'm tired of borrowing a sou at a time from Pieter. But in any case don't worry, I'm not dying of starvation. My guess is that we'll have a good June this time. With the Z's at Laigle, you'll be less encumbered. Where will that put us? I'm always pleased when you have some cash. You're so touching, my little one, with your modest little pleasure in music. You'll soon be an expert, you'll explain to me all your ideas on romantic music when we see each other again. When that will be I do not know. My guess is that we're going to have a rather hot June. At last the news is more or less good. You know, I'm beginning to feel a bit like an old-timer when I hear that "our valiant soldiers are holding on" and I get cheered up inside when I hear they've "*stoppé*" the Germans at such and such a point. Finally I feel "protected" just as you yourself might feel. It's not much fun, but what can we do?

Today I feel rather relaxed. With the Z's at Laigle, the news not bad, Bost out of danger, and you tranquil, my entire little world is safe. From T. and from you I learned that the radio had been reassuring, everything's going well, but what a lot of uproar since May 5th. And it was piling in on you day after day. There was a day or two when I felt very gloomy, and then I steeled myself little by little, Still, today we were looking rather askance at one another while waiting for Reynaud's address, because his specialty is announcing grave developments, the way Proust specialized in deathbed vigils. But here he belied his reputation. Aside from that, nothing but sultry, sultry heat that hasn't let up since early morning and absolutely scorched my room. A beautiful clear sky, a very tolerable world. I'm *having fun* writing the last meeting and big scene between Mathieu and Marcelle; it's a long time since I've managed to enjoy writing something. Chess: I beat everyone except the champion. My flirtation with Charlotte ended, we're eyeing each other warily, like a pair of China dogs, I don't quite know why. There's a "gang" that's come and spoiled everything: they are coarse and overfamiliar with her and she's really scared of them—and what's worse, they often have lunch with us, so she thinks we're in cahoots. Who cares. I'm reading *The Life of Law* written by a jerk but it's awfully entertaining—and then from time to time, *Don Quixote*. The virtue of classics is realized afterward, in that they *mark* the period during which one has read them. Thus in January there was the Shakespeare period. And now it's the *Don Quixote* period. Quite naturally, without a person's giving it any more thought than to other works, nor that they move you more than others, but rather because they're almost natural phenomena by virtue of being rehashed, they eventually accompany the day like the rain and the wind.

I don't know whether Alice Masson[1] was Belgian, but she certainly seemed so. Try to find out if she really left for America as she claimed she was to do last May—in which case she would be recently returned—or if she was pulling my leg. From what she says, she isn't nearly as rich as is thought and she was actively looking for work in New York. It gave me an odd feeling to read that; in a roundabout way, though an insignificant event, it very perceptibly recalled my life all last year, and that bothered me for several minutes.

And that's all, my dearest, my little flower, absolutely all, other than that I love you with all my might and that I've experienced a slew of little *Erlebnis*[2] for you, as though you were right here. I reflected on how you made a wish in front of a palm tree in Marraskesh that I would get the Prix Goncourt, and that really brought me to the brink of tears. My Lord how nice you were, and how well we got along. I long to kiss you with all my might.

৬৯ *to Simone de Beauvoir*

Saturday, June 8
evening

My darling Beaver

This evening the news looks a bit better. Italy is hesitating and the Germans are marking time at the Somme. I also heard an optimistic bit of information

---

[1] Sister of the surrealist painter André Masson (1896–1988).
[2] *In the phenomenological sense, "lived experience"; Sartre used it to mean "emotion, pang."* (SdB)

"from a very highly placed source," which censorship forbids me to pass on to you. You may wonder how the information came to me; well, it was pure chance. In any case, right now things have a completely different look about them from only two weeks ago. Besides, I feel that Weygand's deep placement of troops—what the Swiss call an "elastic front"—is the best way to wear down the attack without losing too many men. It really seems like an attempt to "think through the war" as Reynaud says—to carry out a "directed battle" as Weygand himself says.

I found Bost's[1] letter extremely interesting. The thing that particularly impressed me was that the rout of fleeing soldiers lasted *twenty-four hours*. It must have truly been a disaster. What he says about the fortification of Sedan has been confirmed by numerous guys from the North and the East who can't understand how they gave up in three days, even allowing as much as possible for the incompetence of inexperienced troops and plain bad luck. Here, from that point, an anxious but calm day. What you write me about the strangeness that would exist if the worst should come to pass, I had felt very vividly during two or three days between the 18th and the 20th. I truly lived the worst, I *prepared* myself for it. I was particularly haunted by the idea that it was *possible*, and that all those ideological barriers of ours that helped us think of Germany as totally crazy and base would hold no weight at all against historical necessity, which would demote them to last year's fantasies if Germany should prove victorious: instead of helping us to think about reality, our ideologies would become outmoded objects of historical thought. So they lost their hold on me somewhat, and I had nothing left to cling to but authenticity pure and simple. And that, incidentally, was giving me strange advice, which I'll tell you in person and which might well be ranked among the temptations. After two or three days, with no clear improvement in the situation, I was armored, I mean that the worst had lost its strange nature, it had become a normal possibility, like death, integrated among all *my* possibilities. Nowadays it is so well integrated that all hope seems impudent. I'm no longer at the stage of hoping *positively* what we'll win the war (nor do I think that we'll lose it: I simply think nothing, the future remains blocked), I limit myself to nurturing the negative hope that we won't lose his battle. You'll tell me that the one cannot exist without the other. And that's true, because if we don't lose this battle, we'll be very close to winning the war. Still and all, it's a speck of logic, and I'm telling you how I feel. When this letter reaches you, for that matter, it'll be very much out-of-date. We'll be able to let ourselves go with true optimism, or else on the contrary we'll be

[1] Seriously wounded at the front on May 23, Bost had been evacuated toward Beaune, where he made a slow recovery.

plunged into darkest pessimism. I can well understand too what totally helpless freedom you are enjoying at this moment. You know, my little dear, if in practice it is possible, it's *absolutely necessary* for you to take Sorokine along with you in case of evacuation. Who cares about her mother's maledictions? I'm not thinking at all of the affection she feels for you, but you can do so much by taking her along: you will save her from the chaos of a forced evacuation and from a total lack of money, and besides she'll be with you; otherwise she might remain for months without being able to give or get news. Take her with you, and if that costs us a bit of cash, who cares, what can we do? Besides, above all we are privileged persons, and that will constitute the only concrete aid I understand and allow: complete aid to one individual—whereas my mother wears herself out in giving partial aid to several (I'm not saying that isn't necessary, too). There you have my thoughts on the matter.

I found it very amusing that Bost, in all simplicity, calls the Germans "Boches." How many times has he told me he detests that sort of epithet. But it's so natural. I generally refrain, but you know that from time to time I can't resist calling them Fritz or Fridolins, there are certain phrases that simply demand it.

For me this has been an uneventful but rather pleasant day. First, much washing and shaving, because I felt like having my picture taken. I want documentation of my current sveltness, obtained by total fasting in the evening. Three rolls in the morning, a full lunch at noon, often without meat, and in the evening nothing. Nothing at all—five times a week, the two other times a couple of eggs at Charlotte's. It works very well for me. So I had myself photographed by Paul, at Charlotte's. I had brought her some chocolate, and she was touched and blushed as she said, "How handsome he is, such a close shave!" And a bit later, when I was whistling, "Such a good whistler!" This represents the high point of the idyll. Even Pieter was struck by that. Of course not one further word, nor look, nor smile was exchanged between us the rest of the time. And here's something: today I worked well, I went back to my Marcelle-Mathieu chapter and I think I've given it the tone I want. I'll have to tinker with it, but the essentials are in place. Still no money, my little Beaver, what the devil does this mean? I for one believe that amid all these emotions you've simply forgotten to send it to me. Because I received some prospectuses sent to the old sector 108 on the 2nd and 3rd of June. So if you had made a mistake, the money order would still have come. If you're in the right, it would be worthwhile to inquire at the post office, because if you were paid on the 30th as I suppose, that makes ten days since the order was sent.

So, this afternoon I worked, read a bit of *Madame Bovary*—it is *ugly*—and then I went for a drink with Pieter around five o'clock. But Charlotte wasn't there. Then chess with Paul, chess with Hantziger. Four victories, of which two were achieved via beautiful, profound moves. These days I get a voluptuous feeling on *touching* the pieces, it's a sign of progress, I feel a sort of sensuous familiarity with those bits of wood. All of a sudden, it came back to me that when I was sixteen I set up chess matches with Chadel in all the Latin Quarter cafés, drinking cocoa (ah yes) into which I dunked croissants. That amused me. Chadel must have been killed in the war by now. And here we are, me writing to you. Why on earth, my little dearest, did that story about the stork move you so? I had nothing to do with it: I'd seen a stork and it seemed to be made of wood, but all merit should be ascribed to the bird. Anyway, whatever the reason for your feeling tender, I want you to know that it was just right, and it makes me feel happy and warm to read in one of your letters that you have indeed found me in one of mine. I for one feel you very forcefully in yours, and you seem romantic, my little flower. It's true, you're leading an odd sort of a life, which you will always look back on with satisfaction later, if all goes well. Did you read in the May NRF what Bernanos[2] wrote about the soldiers of 1914–18 (the first 10 pages of the article. There are some exellent things).

Till tomorrow. I didn't have much to tell you and now look, it's a long letter because it's so pleasant to ramble on this way, I almost get the impression that you're here. I love you.

⊛ *to Simone de Beauvoir*

June 9

My darling Beaver

Today I got from you a very poetic little letter, telling me how you spent the early morning at the Dôme, reading the papers without a thing to eat or drink. It delighted me. As for the money, my little one, here's the way things stand. The letter is completely lost. It happened at the time when I was complaining that your letters were reaching me a day late, because you were writing them at night. I remember that one was missing, and I was expecting two the next day and only one came, then another day without a letter and then came two letters at once. I got the count mixed up and thought that I'd made a mistake, that I

---

[2] Georges Bernanos (1888–1948), Roman Catholic novelist (*Diary of a Country Priest*) and polemicist; he opposed the Munich agreement and in June 1940 gave his support to Gen. Charles de Gaulle.

had my whole allotment. I remember the sort of slight disappointment I felt, as when one finds less money than expected in one's wallet but thinking, "No, that's right, I must have figured it wrong." The thing that increased my conviction is that I look at the date *on the envelope* and not on the letter. And in fact there are letters stamped on the 30th, 31st, 1st, and 2nd. But today, as I looked at the dates you put down, I saw that the letter of Friday the 31st was missing. So I *never received* it, and the mails are to blame. You'll have to complain. But now, what sort of an idea is that, to send me money orders in letters? That means I have to chase after the mail clerk to cash them and then, as you see, they are in danger of being lost. Up to now your system had been to send me mail-order cards which the clerk comes around to pay, and that's a lot more convenient. Particularly now that the post office has moved to a neighboring village where I'm not allowed to go. So I think that at most you'll have to inquire at the post office, stub in hand, they'll take the necessary steps, will learn from the mail clerk that I didn't cash money order no. X, and will reimburse you after stopping payment. You're the only one who can do that. I'll send you the books tomorrow. I'll send you *Dostoyevsky* and Samuel Pepys, and then I'll see if I have anything else.

So, yesterday we were completely optimistic. But the news last evening and this morning (heard on the radio at 6:30 this morning and at 11:30), without being alarming, properly speaking, is not reassuring. The Germans have crossed the Aisne, they've advanced in the region of Noyon, they're attacking in the Argonne, they have 60 divisions in the battle. Meanwhile as for us, we're missing that whole army we sent to Belgium and which will only be usable at some later time, we must also reorganize the troops that gave way at Sedan—and we also lack equipment. Not the sort of thing to fill the heart with joy. I'm ashamed, I have to tell you. Yesterday, I reluctantly assumed a defensive self-important air as I spoke in my letter of a mysterious reassuring bulletin, but it was a ludicrous self-importance. To tell the truth, it wasn't my fault. A soldier under direct orders from the general saw on his table a personal communiqué from *General Weygand* asserting that the Germans have reserves of ammunition and fuel for six weeks only and that if we hold out till then, the game is won. He came in and told us that, mysteriously, and begged us not to put it in our letters because if they were opened he could get in a lot of trouble, etc. My guess is he's a nitwit. In short, Pieter and I promised, and we kept our word. Very surprised, incidentally, that such comforting news was not communicated to the troops. And then, in the end they read out the note in question at roll call this afternoon. Paul, whom we had informed with due mystery, is laughing at us.

It's six in the evening and I'm writing to you, having worked well and finished the last draft of the Marcelle-Mathieu chapter, I'll only have to go through it once more. It seems to me that Marcelle is now alive, intractable, reasonable yet sneaky, passionate, sulky, sick, serious, beautiful and graceless, proud the way my grandmother was, somewhat negatively. You'll soon receive the manuscript, but I tremble slightly at entrusting it to the mails. I've read a bit of *Pour s'amuser en ménage* [*For Home Amusement*], by Max and Alex Fischer, found by the toilet, where it was designated for the ultimate use but pretty much intact, minus three pages already used. What else have I done? I've lunched, but without exchanges with Charlotte. We're all worried, with a sort of mutely chronic anxiety that grips the heart all day long, though we don't need that to make us think about the news to feel that way.

What else? The chess champion handed me his three daily thrashings in record time; the driver of the mails brought me from town a pack of blue-black ink cartridges (that may seem like nothing, but it makes me happy), and I finally wrote a bit in my notebook. A few pages on Nothingness, again. That's all, this time, my little dearest, absolutely all.

My little one, I love you with all my might. I'm happy that the *bachots*[1] are starting tomorrow: in eight or ten days you'll be completely free. That's nice for you and, also, reassuring, in case of possible evacuations. I'm filled with little *Erlebnis*, and feeling most tender, I would so like to stroll with you, anywhere at all. But that will surely happen one day. Hardest, tenderest kisses to you, littlest of all charms, little all-charm, little charm-all.

๑๖ *to Simone de Beauvoir*

June 10

My darling Beaver

Today just a short note: we're moving out but I'm afraid the mail will leave before we do, which is why I'm writing to you in haste. We're not going very far—just eleven kilometers away, to a rather large evacuated town. I haven't much of an idea where they'll put us. The news isn't very good. Narvik abandoned,[1] Italy declares war—then a disquieting item on the radio at 6:30: battle raging "north of Paris." So has there been such a significant retreat as all that? All the way to Compiègne? We'll probably hear at 7:45. That's the way it's been

---

[1] *Baccalauréats*, national examinations for secondary education degrees.

[1] Norwegian town and ice-free seaport seized by the Germans in April 1940, recaptured by French-English forces in May, but retaken by Germany on June 9, due to the collapse of the front in France.

going, and day by day the news gets worse. Nonetheless I worked well today; the Mathieu-Marcelle chapter is done. And aside from that, nothing. I think we'll be missing our Hôtel Bellevue slightly. At this very moment I love you tremendously, my little one, you are such an immediate part of my anguish, I am with you.

✺ to Simone de Beauvoir

[After June 10]

My darling Beaver

Tomorrow will probably bring the armistice and peace soon after that. That throws us into a weird state of simultaneous despair and relief. As God is my witness, I'd cheerfully have sacrificed four years of my life to avoid this particular peace. And more than that. But there it is, it has happened and already we're wondering how to live with it. I think that life within it will be possible, my dearest, if we truly have the will and the courage, and that it will be possible without cowardice (and yet with an abundance of humiliations). Still, I am thinking too I'll see you again soon. In a couple of weeks, in a month perhaps— and for a long time. And that brings me, in spite of myself, a sort of joy.

Here everything is in retreat. A slow and lazy retreat, but a retreat nonetheless. We quietly slip away in stages, to avoid being cut off by the Germans, who are at Saint-Dizier. The officers remain arrogant on principle, but their hearts aren't in it anymore. The light-infantry men jettisoned their spare shoes all along the way, to lighten the load a little. The road was littered with shoes. And German airplanes flew lazily over our convoy too, which was an easy target. But they didn't drop any bombs. We felt it was the end. As for us, the readings unit, they simply forgot about us—at Haguenau, where we'd been for three days. "Get up at 6," our captain had said. "You won't leave till the second group, at 6:30." At 6:30 we were in the courtyard of the boys' boarding school, but the truck didn't come back; at the last moment they'd decided there would be only one departure. We wandered around the evacuated town, had a good solid breakfast, and then we just barely stopped a truck that took us to within 5 kilometers of the village where we were supposed to go, but not before that unfortunate Paul had his foot half crushed by a slab of metal that fell on him during a sharp turn. Here it's complete rout. The guys heard over the radio that we're on the brink of armistice (no one has any confidence in America) they're likeable enough, they joke around, but as Pieter said, "They've had it." Pieter himself is holding up well, but he's petrified because he's Jewish. We're falling back on the center gradually, I suppose, to avoid being encircled. The general walks the streets, stooped and grumbling. But I sense that the officers haven't quite taken in the situation. That will come. We had a charming lunch in a farmyard, where a crazy young woman was killing sick chickens by hurling them onto the ground as hard as she could. And then, at present, we're in limbo. The Swiss radio station has just announced that the first German detachments have entered Paris. It makes me somewhat heavyhearted, though I've been resigned to it for three days.

I love you with all my might. With you, my love, life will still be possible. And I'll soon see you again. Give very fond greetings to the Lady for me.

❧ *to Simone de Beauvoir*

June 28

My darling Beaver

I'm fine and will see you soon. Go back home to Paris and prudently await me.

I love you with all my might.

❧ *to Simone de Beauvoir*

July 2
Jean-Paul Sartre
20th Column
16th Group
Temporary Prisoners' Camp #1
Baccarat

My darling Beaver

I'm a prisoner and very well treated, I can work a bit, and I'm not too bored, and besides I think that before long I'll be able to see you again. I so long for that, my sweet little Beaver. Listen, you can write to me at: Private Jean-Paul Sartre 20th Column—Temporary Prisoner Camp *Number 1*—Baccarat. If you're still at La Pouèze, the best would be for you to go back to Paris in a week and await me there. Write to me right away and tell me everything that's happened to you. I love you with all my might, I think only of seeing you again. Give my best to the Lady and the Gentleman.

I long to hug you in my arms and kiss your poor old cheeks, my love.

Send me a package of *grub* really soon, because I'm slimming down somewhat here. I've got a trim waistline, but I don't want its curve to go concave.

๑ *to Simone de Beauvoir* [1]

> July 2
> Jean-Paul Sartre
> 20th Column
> 16th Group
> Temporary Prisoners'
> Camp # 1
> Baccarat .

My darling Beaver

I'm a prisoner and very well treated, I can work a bit and I'm not too bored, and besides I think that I'll soon be seeing you again. I love you so much, my sweet, but I'm afraid that without news you might fret. Write to me.

Private Jean-Paul Sartre. 20th Column. 16th Group. Temporary Prisoner of War Camp #1—Baccarat. Send me a package of *grub* because we're losing a bit of weight here.

I love you with all my might and long to kiss your dear old cheeks.

๑ *to Simone de Beauvoir*

> July 8

My love

I am a prisoner and not at all unhappy. I hope to be home before the end of the month. Write to me.

[1] *Sartre had sent duplicate letters to La Pouèze and Paris. (SdB)*

Temporary Prisoners' Camp Number 1—9th Company. Baccarat.
I love you with all my might.

❧ *to Simone de Beauvoir*

July 8

My darling Beaver
I've been a prisoner since June 21st, my birthday. But don't worry: I'm very well treated, in excellent health with all members perfectly intact. If I'm writing in pencil, it's not that a shell shattered my pen, but that I lost it yesterday. At the moment I'm stretched out under a tent flap and, all in all, my captivity has been limited to camping. I'm have high hopes of seeing you again soon, and everything is fine with me. Of course, Pieter and Paul are prisoners with me.
I love you with all my might.

❧ *to Simone de Beauvoir*

July 22

My darling Beaver
I still have no letter from you and I don't know whether you have received mine, which is why I'm taking advantage of the opportunity to tell you again that I'm a prisoner or rather "detainee," by which I mean treated with respect and with the hope of early release. I would like you to know that I'm not at all unhappy and that I look upon the present and even the future with tranquillity. My sweet, so long as we two are together we will be able to live. I love you. You can write to me at *Baccarat* (Meurthe-et-Moselle). Prisoners' Camp Number 1. 9th Company.
I love you with all my might, I'm afraid you might be feeling very anxious. I only hope you haven't left La Pouèze. I long to hold you in my arms, my sweet little Beaver.

❧ *to Simone de Beauvoir* [1]

July 22

My darling Beaver

I still haven't received any letters from you and don't know whether you've received mine. That's why I'm taking advantage of the opportunity to tell you again that I'm a prisoner or rather, as they say, "detainee," meaning I'm treated with respect and with the hope of early release. I'd like you to know that I look upon the present and even the future with tranquillity. My little sweet, so long as we two are together we will be able to live. I love you. You can write to me at *Baccarat* (Meurthe-et-Moselle). Prisoners' Camp Number 1.

I love you with all my might, I'm afraid you might be very anxious. I only hope you haven't left La Pouèze. I long to hold you in my arms, my sweet little Beaver.

I've begun to write a metaphysical treatise: *L'Être et le Néant* [*Being and Nothingness*].

❧ *to Simone de Beauvoir*

July 23

My darling Beaver

Yesterday the mail from Paris suddenly arrived, in obscene diarrheic abundance, 4,000 letters for Baccarat, and it seemed like an intestinal attack, there were *seven* for me from you. It seemed marvelous, my love, my life was turned around. I'm so happy to think that you're safe and that you know I exist and that I'll come back to you. I love you, it seems that I'm resuming a sort of consistency again now that I am back in contact with you. I'm going to write to you every day, the difficulty comes from the fact that I have to go by the civilian mails, because for the moment they only accept open cards at the camp post office (*coming* from prisoners, of course—in the opposite direction unlimited volume is accepted, and not one of your letters was censored). So one must be crafty and make use of civilian visitors. So don't be surprised if there are days without letters. Actually I guess you'll get several at a time and in fits and starts. My sweet, I'm going to quickly reassure you about me. It impressed me so much

---

[1] *Sartre had sent duplicate letters to La Pouèze and Paris. (SdB)*

to think of you so sensible and relatively tranquil, that I want to hurry to give you some good news. I'm *absolutely not* miserable. I've gone through various states: the liveliest interest, a drowsy stupor which makes the hours go by like a dream, linked to a slight physical weakness, due at the outset to insufficient nourishment. For the time being the food is about normal, I've regained my strength, I have a few books, I'm writing a metaphysical work, *Being and Nothingness*, and I'm finishing my novel. There's a lot of impatience and, at times, tender moments to the brink of tears, deep inside, but none of this *ever* rises to the surface completely. I'm neither stoical nor authentic but under lock and key like one of Freud's patients, without the least effort. And time goes by as it does for convalescents, and we have absolutely puerile outbreaks of gaiety, as de Roulet[1] saw among tubercular convalescents. As for my future, I still have the same incorrigible optimism, which is not the same as simple levity, you can be sure, because from May 25th to June 20th I've had the time to think it all over. I'm convinced that we will survive, my love, and I've not at all given up on my destiny. I'll even try to publish Mathieu—in large measure, this will depend on agility and tact. But I obviously cannot expand on that idea here. The thing I might most suffer from here—but without being pained by it—is a loss of both grace and openheartedness. To all comers I display the expression I have when I'm out walking with my stepfather, plus a five-week-old beard. The beard is a mark of personal obstinacy, for we have barbers here, and anyone can get spruced up like a dandy. Which reminds me, why do you imagine me with my head shaved? All hairstyles are permitted here, and mine tends to resemble Joan of Arc's. But if I've lost that inner grace I still had at Morsbronn, it's not because of my captivity, which is altogether benign, but because of my French associates, who exhibit all you might imagine: beastliness, baseness, jealousy, stupid pranks, coprophilia, etc. I've assumed some authority over those around me, incidentally, but all desire to laugh is gone. As for life in general: we are entirely at liberty to do whatever we want in a huge barracks and within a vast enclosure. The day is broken up by coffee at 6 o'clock in the morning (5 o'clock German time)—it's roasted barley—victuals at 11 o'clock: German bread (a loaf for every 4)—barley or cabbage or bacon soup—and soup at 5 o'clock. For several days now we've had roll call at 6 o'clock, we line up by columns in the courtyard. At 10, lights out. Betweentimes we can do exactly as we please: read, stroll about, wash up, write, etc. When the weather's good, you could see dozens of completely naked prisoners sunbathing in the courtyard, stretched out on a blanket, you'd think it was the beach. Except, no matter what you do, you do it among men

---

[1] Lionel de Roulet, former student of Sartre, married during the war to Beauvoir's sister Hélène.

by the thousand. The operative unit is one thousand men. You cannot imagine a more closely packed, more charged social atmosphere. Of course the whole thing's extremely interesting. Particularly at the outset. I recorded it all in my notebook, because we were not simply captured at Morsbronn, my sweet; there was a ten-day debacle that took us to the environs of Épinal and is certainly one of the most curious stories of all those I read about or heard tell. I put it all down in my notebooks, which I'm still keeping up, even here, when there's something to say.

As for liberation, here's what I think: I was a bit too optimistic in the letter you received, but all the same I firmly believe that I'll be with you before September 1st. There's the strong likelihood that we'll be freed. They are making a very clear distinction beween prisoners taken before the 20th (beginning of the negotiations toward armistice) and those taken afterward. And I don't believe at all that the Germans are that eager to keep us, they've got many other fish to fry. Except that my guess is that the French government itself is in no great hurry to see us and for many reasons, among them that all evacuees must be sent home, which is the most urgent problem. Then there'll have to be reemployment, otherwise it will create hundreds of thousands of unemployed overnight. The railways and freight transport will have to be reorganized, the power supply restored in the factories, etc. All of that is happening progressively, and the news of each day brings a bit more hope. *From today on we are out of tobacco. My sweet, would you send me two packets—not by mail, but by the Red Cross, 12 Rue Newton, near the Étoile, go there yourself. 1st a package of grub and 2nd a package of books (the Louis-Philippe, the Verlaine, L'Imaginaire) and the tobacco.* That would be so sweet of you. If they only want to accept one, *first* send books and tobacco, and food the next day.

My sweet, I have so much to tell you, but I'll begin tomorrow. Paul and Pieter are prisoners with me, of course. There are six of us, welded together by misfortune, a delivery truck driver named Beaujouan, a metro conductor named Civette, an indirect-tax inspector named Longepierre, besides Paul, Pieter and myself. From tomorrow on, I'll do a daily account.

My love, I love you with all my might; as I've always told you, so long as we two exist, I'll manage to be very happy still. Getting your letters gave me back my joy. I love you with all the warmth that I needed to lament, you are my life, my little sweet, my whole life. Till tomorrow.

With the grub, *above all* send some gingerbread and chocolate.

Don't tell Z. that you've gotten long letters from me, nor above all that I'm writing to you every day, because I've only sent T. two or three short notes, which remain unanswered. To you I've written *five* times, and you've only received one letter.

✣ *to Simone de Beauvoir*

July 28

My darling Beaver

It must seem to you, my poor little one, that I'm not nice enough and that I don't write to you often enough. But listen, it's not my fault: we are officially authorized to write only open postcards at the rate of 2 a week, on Wednesday and Saturday. So to write to you at slightly greater length, I have to go by the civilian post office, and this requires some cunning and the right opportunity. So, my love, you won't get your little daily letter. Yet I yearn so to write to you, I think of you so much and I love you so much, my sweet. To me, that odd sort of life you're living for the moment in Paris seems so poetic, living on the Rue Denfert-Rochereau, which reminds me of an entire charmed past, so long past, when we were still only two little aspirations, and in that part of Paris which seems slightly like a cemetery to me. Do write to me, my darling Beaver, it's six days now since I've received anything from you (following 9 letters, the last from the 19th) and I'm so scared you might tire of writing to me, not knowing if I'm getting your letters. I still have received nothing from my parents, and that worries me a bit because little by little everyone here is getting letters from home, and not me. It's true that Saint-Sauveur is an isolated hole. I dearly hope that they haven't fled before the German advances and gone and taken refuge in the unoccupied zone, because it's the devil itself to get back in. And then too it bothers me that my poor mother is going so long without news from me. But I'm delighted to think that all our little group has been spared, from Bost to Sorokine by way of the Lady; what will become of us all? That's another matter, but anyway there they are. I suppose, incidentally, that we'll all live through what follows *together* and that we'll be bearing very heavy burdens in very hard times, my little one. But that doesn't discourage me at all, and I intend to be as hard as the times. I'm interested in the future and full of hope. What you tell me about universals and particulars interested me, but I don't think that way, it's too contemplative. I would so love to see you and talk with you about all of this. Well, you should know I'm waiting with tremendous curiosity and a sort of joy to see this new world.

My lot has much improved here (it wasn't at all bad) since I last wrote. I'm completely caught up in *Being and Nothingness* every evening, as at Morsbronn, and I eagerly await the following morning because the following morning will be a chapter on negation, or on the being-for-itself.[1] But there are little tricks I've been thinking of and which are in the notebooks. I've forgotten them. I like to think that perhaps they've been saved.

---

[1] Consciousness conceived as a lack of Being, a desire for Being, a relation to Being.

We have been regrouped differently—by professions—and I'm part of the liberal arts professions. I fell in with a little fellow with glasses and a very "Café de Flore" look, who is indeed a pillar of the Flore, knows Leiris, Caillois,[2] etc., like a fish out of water here, who came up and asked me whether I was related to the writer. I said that there's no writer in my family besides me, and he replied, "I admire you." He's here across from me right now, reading *La Revue des Deux Mondes* with a sober-minded air. He's the shrimpy sort, and it irks me to find the Flore here. I'd become accustomed to the earthy faces of the farmers with their long wailing farts, I got along well with them. This one's a surrealist. But he's discreet and innocuous. Two other guys opened the door and came in to peer at me curiously. With that, I shaved and washed up, a thing I do very rarely here, despite the danger of catching lice (a hundred or so have them here). It created quite a stir in the courtyard.

It seems that liberation has begun—not here, in other camps (in Seine, they say, in Seine-et-Marne, etc., but naturally that's just rumors). A little treatise could be written about the false rumors here. They're an extraordinary phenomenon here, as much for their exuberance and precision as the rapidity of their propagation. They have their own rhythms. They tend to cancel each other out, actually, by which I mean that an optimistic rumor is immediately annulled by a pessimistic story, and just as pessimistic as the other was optimistic. There are times when we "go to the rumors," I mean we go down to the courtyard. I'll have to tell you about this complete and extraordinary society, the prison camp. All in all, I'll just say it's very likely, at this point, that prisoner liberation has begun. I'm very hopeful. Take the bad patiently, my dear little one, I'll certainly be back before peacetime. I made some overly optimistic calculations in my first letter, but if you count definitely on the 1st to the 15th of September, you can hardly go wrong. But what's a month or a month and a half, when even two months ago we were afraid it might be three years? And we won't part again and we *will be happy.* For it's happiness, mostly, that will be left to us, my little dear.

Here are some errands:

In one card I asked you to go to 12 Rue Newton, to the American Red Cross, which sends off packages. I would like two parcels:

1) tobacco—chocolate—gingerbread (as much as you can, since we share everything);

2) books: Verlaine—Claudel—Louis-Philippe.

I'd also like a money order. Ask the post office if it can be done. That depends

---

[2] Roger Caillois, writer and teacher at the École Normale Supérieure. Michel Leiris (b. 1901), novelist, memoirist, ethnologist.

on your supply of cash. If you're rich, five hundred francs, since I have some debts, if not whatever you can do from fifty francs up.

My dearest, you are so right to say that our love has seen a bit of everything. But it is solider and tenderer than ever, my little dearest. The proof has been shown that it resists everything. I love you, I think of you all the time, without impatience, with a strong and tender certainty of seeing you again soon and forever.

✧ *to Simone de Beauvoir*

July 29

My darling Beaver

Alas, you're wearying of writing to me in the dark, you haven't yet received my letters and your last one was most uncertain and most despairing. Alas, my poor good little Beaver, it wrenched my heart, yesterday, to get yours of July 24th, in which I read that you had such great need of me. I too, charm of my life, I need you, need you so much. I've been days now, and months, without one moment of abandon or tenderness or just friendship vis-à-vis those around me and myself. I'm not at all miserable, I even have loads of pleasant moments, but I'm hard as a pebble. To melt into water, it's you, tender little Beaver, you alone I'd need to find again. If I find you again, I find my happiness again and I find *myself*. My little one, it will come soon, and we will be so happy, both of us. Perhaps there will be vacations again and summer, and with your little arm in mine, we'll walk about Paris together, that very changed Paris which I so long to see.

While I think of it, you say that at the Bursar's office they were *curt* with you? In these times of dismissals, that's not very reassuring. All the civil servants here are quaking in their boots. Give me some details: *whom* did you see and what did they say? I for one am actually not very scared, I'm beyond reproach and a soldier. But who can tell?

Family news is beginning to get through here. It's not always very cheerful. Some of them learn about the death of a child, others that their house is destroyed. As for me, I still have no news of my parents, I have no idea what they're up to. Something else: there are trains for Baccarat and people can come for visits, but I don't dare tell you to come: the latest has it that the trip would take 16 *hours*, and we can be seen for only 20 minutes at a time, in a visiting room. If I were to see you morning and evening, that would make 32 hours of travel in two days (since you have your classes and they might not let you stay here) in order to see me for 40 minutes in public. And, on top of all that, incidents often occur that provoke the suspension of visits for a day. If you have bad luck, you might find the door shut and nobody home. You decide, my little one. Of course I have no greater desire than to see you, but twenty mintues . . . ? You tell me: and 3 o'clock l'Acropole? Do as you like, I've alerted you. But *don't miss any classes* right now, I hear lots of unpleasant stories on that topic. A Sunday would be best.

I'd been repulsively dirty, by choice and semi-mysticism, I was repugnant. But suddenly I couldn't bear to be seen in such a state by a kid from the Flore, a cute little intellectual who has not a thing in his head except book titles. I washed and shaved the moment he recognized me. Now, I'm washing every day.

Word is going around that the liberation of prisoners has begun in the camps around Paris. Is that true? They also say that we here will all be freed in a month. Meanwhile, imprisoned officers and noncommissioned officers in the active service are leaving for Germany, but I think that is more good than bad.

My sweet, you'll have to go in search of *Psyché*,[1] to get it back and guard it jealously; I'm going to have great need of it.

What a wise little life you are leading, my dearest, it brings tears to my eyes. Don't argue too much with Sorok. The things you've told me about Toulouse, about Dullin, have completely disgusted me.[2] I want to see you alone and for a long stretch. The only thing we'll do is go to spend a few days with the Lady at La Pouèze. As for her, I'd realy like to see her. If you know something about Nizan, Guille, Maheu, Aron, etc., tell me about it in your letters.

Till tomorrow, my dear, dear little Beaver, I love you with all my might, you are my little absolute.

---

[1] In the autumn of 1937 Sartre began this philosophical book and wrote 400 pages before abandoning it to finish writing the collection of stories, *The Wall*.

[2] Simone Jollivet was expostulating on the blossoming of her career, with Charles Dullin "in the palm of my hand," and hoping soon to present a play of hers as well as her versions of Greek and Roman plays in Paris. *Letters to Sartre*, p. 339.

◈ *to Simone de Beauvoir*

August 3

My darling Beaver

I'm taking advantage of the fact that someone is going back to Paris to write you a quick note. It'll be short, because such opportunities appear at the last moment, and you have to rush to profit from them. Another letter from you yesterday; how they stir me, my sweet, how I feel your love; the thing that bothers me is that I'm writing to you all the time and you're still not getting anything. My little one, I would so like you to receive my letters, for you to know that I'm getting yours. Listen, my sweet, your own letters have changed my life, I'm so happy and peaceful, I'm waiting patiently.

Here, much ado. There were 7,000 of us and 4,000 are going to leave. For Germany, some say—to be freed, according to others. I simply believe that they're going to other camps. In any case, I'm staying here. And things are beginning to look good. They're already asking for some officials (railway service) who are leaving today, it might well happen shortly. The camp is boiling, lies and false rumors are circulating on their quick little feet, it takes your mind off things. I'm still writing my philosophical work, and also I've found a chess player at my level (pretty good, on the whole), which fills the day. My admirer from the Flore is a jerk. It's distressing, but that's the way it is. Pieter is completely overwhelmed and I scarcely see him, but I've found two from the Midi, Pomé and Commetton, whom I find absolutely charming. I'm surrounded by indirect-tax auditors. I live in a large, bright room, I have books (I'm reading Albert Malet's *Les Temps modernes*, a work for high school freshmen), and the weather is fine. In short, I'm in a good mood, and the work is paying off well. My little one, if only I could see you, I'd be completely happy. I love you.

Listen, you do amuse me, about Sorok. She's full of life. She makes me laugh, and she's appealing. I feel tenderness for you alone, my little one, the rest of the world doesn't even exist. How wise your letters are. The last ones were almost serene, you are always true perfection, you always do, think, and say just the right thing at the right time.

Till tomorrow or till one of these days, my little sweet. Do you remember? One year ago we were in Marseille, and perhaps it was the day of the bullfight. I love you. If something has counted in my life, it is certainly everything to do with you.

Advise my mother, if you see her, to go and see Monod, it's important.

✣ to Simone de Beauvoir

August 12

My darling Beaver

I can only write you this brief note thanking you for your long letters. Yet, my sweet, I would so very much like to be able to talk to you at length, but that will come soon I hope, things are very hopeful. Surely you'll see me show up one day behind Balzac's statue.[1] Perhaps I'll be in overalls, with a work cap. Everything's still going very well here, I'm reading Paul Bourget[2] (it was the favorite reading of the State Police, whose barracks we're occupying) and I'm still working on my philosophy book (76 pages written, it's shaping up). Right now the road scouts are putting on a show, in the courtyard. You see that we lack for nothing. But I'd really like to feel your little arm against mine, to go for a walk with you. *Do not come* if you had any intention of doing so. It's possible that we'll be leaving here. I love you.

✣ to Simone de Beauvoir

My darling Beaver

I got *nine* letters from you in two days, it changes my life. Write, my sweet, write as often as you can. I'll write to you as often as possible, but they only allow the open cards, and you can see that there's not much room on them. And yet I'd have lots of stories to tell you. For the moment I'd like you to know that I'm very comfortably set up in a State Police apartment, though without any furniture, just these four walls with tropical flowers on the wallpaper. Fifteen of us sleep on the floor and live principally lying down, I read lying down, I write lying down, and I imagine I am an ancient Roman. Otherwise, we're free to stroll about a vast enclosure, and only the constant rain prevents that; I'm not bored, I'm totally serene. Listen, my sweet: you must send me a package of books (Verlaine, Louis-Philippe, Claudel, etc.) and *some tobacco* and a package of grub (particularly gingerbread and chocolate) via the American Red Cross, 12 Rue Newton. I long to kiss you with all my might.

[1] From Beauvoir's memoir, *The Prime of Life*, p. 365: July or August 1940: "I sat outside at the Dôme and gazed at Rodin's statue 'Balzac,' the unveiling of which had caused such an uproar two years before, and it seemed as though Sartre was going to appear at any moment, smiling, walking toward me with that quick step of his."
[2] (1852–1935), critic and novelist who became increasingly conservative in outlook.

✧ *to Simone de Beauvoir*

The opening is illegible.

. . . and from there we have a superb view. My situation has definitively improved since Baccarat. I have a bed, a bedroom (for 3), a table, a wardrobe, a chair, I'm an interpreter in the infirmary. I've begun new work that I find fascinating, and every morning I do a half hour of exercises—and every Tuesday I give lectures before an audience made up almost entirely of priests (in collaboration with a Dominican). I lead an odd life, strange and pleasant, very full. I'm not giving up on my Disciples. All in all, we're well treated, and actually the Medical Staffers, to which I belong as part of the infirmary, are considered not prisoners here, but rather neutrals. But how I miss you, my sweet. Besides, I'm afraid you may be really worried, not knowing where I am. Write to me. Tell my parents that you have received a *card*. I love you.

✧ *to Simone de Beauvoir*

October 26

My darling Beaver

Still no letter from you, I'm wondering whether my cards have reached you. I'm in a camp at the top of a hill, at first I was on the infirmary staff, then I became "an artist"; I write plays which I produce and which are given on Sundays. My best friends are a Jesuit and a Dominican, I'm as comfortably off as can be. My love, it's our eleventh anniversary, and I feel very close to you. I love you.

✧ *to Simone de Beauvoir*

My darling Beaver, herewith some brief scrawls, since I mustn't encumber the mails with my prose, and I also have to write to T., who has received nothing at all from me, and to my mother. So kindly cut along the lines and give to each her due. How I love you, my sweet. I want you to know that all your letters are coming through without delay. But you really mustn't be so submissive. Write a little note every day, it's not against the law. My dear little Beaver, my love, it gives me so much pleasure to get your little letters. They're so minuscule, I have to construct a whole story out of a single word; it's like reading a French history book. But the concentrated stories seem poetic and mysterious. As when you say, "Bianca is marrying a young American." It made me laugh till I cried. Aside from that, our little group appears so unchanged, it's amazing. And you, my sweet, how wise you seem, how much you love me. You will have to be patient. In one letter you tell me I'll be set free in a month. I don't believe that at all, reason tells me how slowly these things move; think of a dab of tar stuck to you ever so slightly, the way it clings from inertia more than anything else and just won't let go, though eventually it will. I so yearn to see you, to take a walk with your arm in mine. But, my poor dear Beaver, you'll be very disappointed: I've come up with no new theories. Only tons of stories. Those I can promise you. At first, I fell in with an odd group: the camp's aristocrats, in the infirmary. There's also the powerful plutocracy of the kitchens, and the politicians or barracks bosses. I was ejected from the infirmary through intrigues and—aiming to avoid fieldwork, for which, till further notice, I have no great gift—found myself in the unoffending milieu of *artistes*, reminiscent of the cricket[1] and Racine, too, under Louis XIV.[2] Lots of bowing and scraping, right-minded citizens. Actually they're very appealing. The most appealing I've seen since the war began. They have a regular little theater where they put on shows for the fifteen hundred prisoners in the camp, twice a month on Sundays. And for this service they get paid, can sleep late in the morning, and needn't do a bloody thing the rest of the day. I live with them in a large room crowded with guitars, banjos, flutes, and trumpets hung on the walls, with a piano that some Belgians play throughout the day. The Belgians play swing in the same style as the pianists at the College Inn—this will provide the pretext for a little heartfelt note to T. I write plays for them, which are never presented, and I'm paid too. Aside from that, my usual company is priests. Particularly a young vicar and a Jesuit novice, who actually hate one another and come to blows about Marian theology and have me settle their disputes. Which I do. Yesterday as it turned out, I ruled against Pope Pius IX on the Immaculate Conception. They can't decide between Pius IX and me. And I want you to know that I'm writing my first serious play, and putting all of me into it (writing, directing, and acting),

---

[1] Referring to the fable of Jean de La Fontaine about the improvident cricket, who sang all summer while the ant was laying in winter supplies.

[2] Jean-Baptiste Racine (1639–99), retiring from the theater in 1677 and renouncing its promiscuous ways, became a paragon of idle respectability at the court of the Louis XIV.

and it's about *the Nativity*. Have no fear, my sweet, I won't end up like Ghéon,[3] not having begun like him. But take it from me, I really do have talent as a playwright. I wrote a scene of the angel announcing Christ's birth to the shepherds that absolutely took everyone's breath away. Tell that to Dullin, and that some had tears in their eyes. I recall what he was like when he directed, and I draw my inspiration from him, but remain much more polite, given that I'm not paying my actors. It will be given on December 24th, with masks, there'll be 60 characters, and it's called *Bariona*, or the Son of Thunder.[4] Last Sunday I also acted onstage, with a mask, a comic role in a farce. I get lots of fun out of it all, thanks to loads of other farces funnier still. After this, I will write plays. My love, I'm not bored, I'm very cheerful, I'm waiting patiently, resolved, if the heavens don't help me, to help myself. I do three-quarters of an hour of gymnastics every day with boxers and wrestlers. In addition, since last week I have been charged with organizing a sort of people's university here, and that interests me too. Incidentally, I have lice but, like all natural phenomena, lice have been a disappointment. They don't bite, you just feel them crawling, and they are notable only for being remarkably prolific. My old pipe has arrived. Thank you, that moved me to tears, my sweet, charm of my life. I haven't ceased being bound to you. My love, we prisoners are a little like old men, mulling over old stories, and you're in all of them. How happy you and I have been, and we will be again (but I don't want anything like Tennyson's life[5]). Kisses to you for your little face and little cheeks. I love you.

☙ *to Simone de Beauvoir*

December 10

My darling Beaver
    I am getting all your letters, and you can't imagine the pleasure they're giving me. You must write to me even more often, every day if you like, there are no set limits. And getting letters changes everything. I love you, my sweet. Your

---

[3] Henri Ghéon, pseudonym of Henri Vauglon (1875–1944), dramatist and poet who converted to Catholicism.

[4] Published in Paris in a limited edition in 1962; again in *Les Écrits de Sartre*, in 1970; and in English in *Selected Prose: The Writings of Jean-Paul Sartre*, trans. Richard McCleary, Evanston, Ill., 1974.

[5] In her letter of October 29 Beauvoir had wished him such a life—absolutely calm and uneventful—by her side. (*Letters to Sartre*, p. 345.)

last letters were very sad. You must learn to be patient and above all not think that boredom is a requirement of virtue. Remember, my little flower, that when I come back to you it will be for always. And remember too that I'm not at all unhappy. Quite the contrary, imagine what it must be like for a writer to know his entire audience and to write specifically for that audience—and for a playwright to put on and act in his own plays. I wrote a Christmas mystery play which is apparently very moving, so much so that the actors are moved to tears as they play their parts. As for me, I play the role of the Magus king. I write the play in the morning and we rehearse in the afternoon. Thirty characters. I've met two or three guys here who truly interest me, and I'm discovering a totally new form of theatrical art in which a lot can be done. I'm reading Heidegger, and I have never felt so free. I love you with all my might, my sweet.

ᐵ to *Simone de Beauvoir*

My darling Beaver. They scared you, and I spent ten days deprived of letters from you. It had me raging. I so love your dear little letters, my love. I am getting them all, you know, in bundles of five or six. It makes for a quick little report of your daily doings, but since I know like the palm of my hand the things and people you talk about, I embroider them. My lover, you mustn't dream that I don't love you anymore, if you only knew how untrue that is. I've never loved you more. Anyway, if you feel too lonely, just reflect that Poulou[1] wrote me that he'll soon be going through Paris and that he'll see you a lot. I hope that will come about. As for me, I can tell you that I'm still living with my priests and that I give them classes in philosophy, in exchange for which they stuff and house me. I haven't suffered from the cold at all, and I've often reflected that you're suffering from it much more than I, my poor little one. I'm becoming a sort of spiritual director for the many, it has to be done. My sweet, be patient and confident. I love you with all my might, you are constantly present for me. I'm not unfeeling at all, quite the contrary, you are my little flower.

---

[1] Sartre's childhood nickname.

ᥬᥬ *to Simone de Beauvoir*

My darling Beaver. How sad your dear little letters have been for some time now. I beg you, don't let yourself fall into discouragement, remember that I will soon be coming back to you, my love. Don't *feel* too solitary, even intellectually. I'm sure that it's only an illusion. Keep in mind that I love you, that I haven't changed at all, and that we are together in everything, my little one. Besides, it's all right to be full of hope. I want you to know that here I haven't for one moment despaired or felt downhearted. I am more and more interested in what I'm doing. Above all don't think that I'm cold or in poor physical condition. Not at all, we have as much coal as we need, and I've often thought, my poor little one, that you were much colder than I this winter. I lack for nothing, and besides, the priests have adopted me and they stuff me. As for my return, it will be soon since, as you know, they are repatriating the civilians right now. I've taken up Heidegger again, which a priest from Saint-Étienne bought, and I give three hours of class on him every day. The censors returned all my writings, my novel, my philosophical work, and my notes. That delights me, as you can imagine. I actually have little time to read, I'm doing so much. Don't worry about Tania. Since then she has gotten some of my letters and things have straightened out. My little one, I still love you as surely and deeply as ever. I live with you. Give young Bost my best.

ᥬᥬ *to Simone de Beauvoir*

My darling Beaver. Another little note, though I have really nothing to tell you. In fact there's a great deal, but I would have to write to you every day, and that's impossible. But I forget nothing, and I'll tell you everything when I get home. Incidentally, my love, don't go thinking that I experience anything at all that separates me from you and that will later give you some delay in catching up. When we see each other again, you'll see on what even footing we'll be, though you might well be surprised by my new projects. Remember what I told you about the things that must happen in a writer's maturity? Well, here it is happening to me, with good motives and intentions. You will see how fascinating it will be for *us* when I get back. My sweet, thoughts of you never leave me, and all of this interesting life that I'm leading here, I'm leading with you. We are not separated. There has been a release of incurables here and there's one, a friend of Nizan, who intends to go and see you and give you news of me. I for one, right now, have to set up a new theory of Time. It's going well. Good-bye, my sweet, till later. I love you.

1941

❧ to Simone de Beauvoir

[February]

My darling Beaver. I'm no longer getting your sweet little letters. Herewith a letter-reply form to fill out. But you know, you shouldn't believe what they say, please keep on writing to me on ordinary paper with an envelope. This form of letter simply takes priority over the others. Don't let yourself be disconcerted by the Post Office employees. But, look here, don't send me any more money. First because, I hope, civilians will soon be freed. But even if we should be held here a while longer, *keep all your money*, there's nothing I need. You will soon see Marc Bénard, an awfully nice nurse who has just been released. I'll tell you in detail everything I'm thinking and doing, so much so that I'll have nothing left to tell you when I get back. Do not publicize this visit. While awaiting my departure, I've gone back to philosophy and am laboriously constructing a theory on Temporality. But Heavens, it isn't as easy as working on Phenomenology, where everything simply flows. But it is coming along. I'm happy I'll have a philosophical theory to show you after all. I love you.

❧ to Simone de Beauvoir

March 2

My darling Beaver. Did you see Bénard? Breathe not a word of what he tells you except to Bost, and put that young Bost to work. Keep on trying to write me letters, my parents' ones are accepted. I'm still on the verge of leaving. My sweet, you must be joyful. I believe you have every reason to be. I myself love you most joyfully, and with all my might.

⊶ to Simone de Beauvoir

March 9

My darling Beaver. Be patient just a very short while longer. The first convoys of civilians are beginning to leave, and I expect to be among the next. I love you. T. writes that she is undergoing a treatment (or will undergo it) that will cost 3,000 francs. Will you see if the NRF has something like that to give me, from the sale of *L'Imaginaire?* You would give it to T. The weather's fine and I've written a whole theory of Temporality (200 pages). How I would love to be at your side.

⊶ to Simone de Beauvoir

[Mid-March]

My darling Beaver. We're leaving in a short while for France, where they will divide us into groups in a triage camp from which we'll be sent off to our respective domiciles. The operation will take two weeks *at the most.* Today is Friday. By the time you get this letter, I'll almost be there. Say nothing about my arrival, because I want to devote all of the first days to you. (Except for young Bost, of course, whom I'll be delighted to see again.) I received your card, and I'm pleased that you saw Billiet. It was a different man that I had wanted to send you, a nurse, but ultimately they came back here. Here the weather's fine and, as you can well imagine, I'm in a good mood. All my memories of Paris are beginning to thaw one by one, but tentatively. My sweet, is it really possible that I'll see you again soon, that I'll see your little smile again and your little old cheeks? I love you so much, my little dearest. When you get this note, make sure you stay in contact with the Hôtel du Danemark, because I'll telephone there the moment I get in to set up a meeting with you. I long to give you a big kiss.

๛ *to Simone de Beauvoir* [1]

My darling Beaver

I'm still here, they haven't kidnapped me and I still love you with all my might, just the same as on Sunday evening in the Luxembourg, when we parted. I don't know whether I've ever felt the temptation you mentioned, at any rate I've never gone farther than today.

Here's a very good piece of news, my little flower, which will make your little bones quiver with joy: the NRF owed us 12,855 francs; I said: twelve thousand eight hundred fifty-five francs. Spend, spend, my sweet, all your cash. It's too bad you didn't take more of it. I don't dare send you any, I won't cash it till Saturday. In one stroke all our difficulties subside.

I saw Parain, Gallimard, and Queneau,[2] who were very surprised that I'm not letting anything be published. They were acting as though something was fishy—I'll explain it to you. Incidentally they knew things concerning me that quite staggered me. I'll tell you all. I saw Merleau-Ponty and Wagner.[3] Cavaillès[4] is with us, and a manuscript of mine in the form of a journal (a notebook?) has actually been found on a train track; he is holding it for me.

My relationship with T. is perfect. She is absolutely charming with me, in a proprietary way; I feel like a beloved cat or Pekinese, which is pretty ludicrous. I feel great tenderness toward her, because she is touching and pleasant, but the marvelous Zazoulich has vanished along with 1938. Mouloudji[5] often goes out with us in the evening because he hasn't a sou, and accepts whatever he is given without a fuss. He doesn't seem to hate me anymore, and I like him. I lost your book on Hegel.

I know what T.'s been up to, I'll tell you, it is innocent and dangerous for her, but absolutely inconsequential at the moment. I've decided to have her give up painting, which she hates, and have her do theater work. I'll talk with you about that. Excuse this dry little note, she has gone off for fifteen minutes and I'm writing with one eye glued to the door, because she absolutely must not see this letter. My sweet, its dryness does not correspond in the least with the state of my feelings, I can see your dear little face again before me, and I do so want to be with you again. Have a good time, my little one. I love you with all my might.

---

[1] *Sartre was back in Paris.* (SdB)

[2] Raymond Queneau (1903–76), comic novelist and editor at Gallimard.

[3] *Liberal arts professor, an old friend of Sartre and the brother-in-law of Merleau-Ponty.* (SdB)

[4] *Philosophy professor who played a major role in the Resistance and was executed.* (SdB)

[5] Algerian former child film star, fellow acting student of Olga's; after the war he became a popular singer.

1942

to Simone Jollivet

Tuesday

Dear Toulouse

Yesterday Arnaud told me about your mother's death. We hadn't had much occasion to talk about her recently, but I vividly remember what she meant to you a few years ago, and I'm afraid it may have been a very hard blow for you. I'd love to see you, but I don't know whether you might prefer solitude just now. Send me a note at the Hôtel de Paris—or call me there—and I'll come to see you on the day and at the hour you choose, to remind you, better than by letter, that I sincerely and deeply share all that happens to you, the bad along with the good.

In all friendship.

1943

&ce; *to Simone de Beauvoir*

Saturday [summer]

My darling Beaver

How far away you are. I miss you, little dearest. Paris is so dull when you aren't here to see what I'm seeing at the same time I see it. To console myself, I keep thinking you're having a good time. But your brand of entertainment isn't the sort I can really enjoy; it's as though I were trying to mentally delight in imagining you eating a good little plate of mussels in tomato sauce.[1]

Here there are ups and downs. But the grounds of wisdom are unchanged. Of course, what gives pleasure to some gives pain to others: she says it's a botched vacation. She's out on the street the whole time, and if I see her for five minutes, I have to drum her lines into her, which doesn't bother me.

The good news is that the screenplay[2] will probably be taken. After a stupid sleepless night spent at Zuorro's place,[3] weariness had turned me gloomy, and I felt disgusted by this never-ending business; I went to bed, feeling already beaten and rejected. But by Friday morning the 9 hours of sleep had put me in fine fettle and I read out my little play with an insouciance troubled only by the fear of displaying the holes big as sunsets in my socks; my shoes, dappled with old white spots of soap and toothpaste, rested cheek by jowl next to handsome rough leather shoes belonging to Delannoy.[4] I read the part I'd done—roughly half of what needs to be done—and I bumbled my way through a telling of the

---

[1] She was on a cycling trip; he hated tomatoes.
[2] *The screenplay of* Les jeux sont faits [*The Chips Are Down*]. (SdB)
[3] Marc Zuore, a friend of the couple, a professor of humanities.
[4] *The presumed director of* Typhus. (SdB). Jean Delannoy (b. 1908) made *Le Retour éternel* (*The Eternal Return*, 1943, story by Jean Cocteau); and in 1947 directed *Les Jeux sont faits.*

rest, given that I'm not too sure what is coming. There was that cold silence that had disconcerted me the first time, and then Giraudoux made a few comments which boil down to this: that the personality of the characters was not brought out enough and that now the thing to do was to emphasize the psychological. But Borderie[5] immediately protested: he for one thought everything was fine, and incidentally managed not to understand very well though there was not one item to understand. The thing is that he has picturesque little schemes in his head and he'd like to assimilate what he hears into them. He said to me, "The woman is trash, isn't she? She's a completely fallen woman?" I said, "That depends." Carefully, because I wanted the dough but Giraudoux and [René] Delange[6] (who doesn't want his cookie playing a whore) interrupted to set things straight. Then he said with a sigh, "Too bad: it would be so amusing, a man who pulls himself together because of a woman who's a tramp." Phony irony. That's his level. But Delannoy seems satisfied, though he too is calling for psychological motives. He would like to make the film. We argued about the possible cast, which is a good sign; they paid me compliments without any qualifications. I don't know why but it's the death on the bus that really hooked them. To make a long story short, they asked me to finish it as quickly as possible (let's say by Friday), and I think they'll take it. A single hitch is that I'll hardly be able to cash the money they'll turn over to me then (37,500 francs, I hope) before the 17th or 18th. By the time they set up the check and the contract—and the check is endorsed by the post office—it'll probably be the 20th. But if that's the case, I'll put the touch on my parents against a postal check they can cash on the 20th. Don't worry about it. I haven't yet spoken about "My associate M. Smith."[7] I will on Friday.

Grenier[8] requested your manuscript.[9] I'm going to send it to him, asking him to bring it back to the *NRF*, where Parain will find it on his return in August. I took your galleys[10] to Festy.[11] But how *badly proofread* they are, my little one. I enjoyed the opportunity to reread a hundred pages but found rather a lot of errors, which I corrected as I went along. Well anyway, the screenplay is taken, don't worry: you'll need no work at all next year, we'll be on easy street.

I got a bawling out from the concierge of the hotel about your trunk. As I was telling him in dulcet tones that I had cleared everything out and left the room ready for the next tenant, he said, "But, good Lord, what about the trunk!

[5] *The producer.* (SdB)
[6] *A journalist, the publisher of the journal* Comédia, *influential in film circles.* (SdB)
[7] Beauvoir.
[8] *Jean Grenier, a philosopher and reader at Gallimard.* (SdB)
[9] *Pyrrhus et Cinéas.* Part dialogue, part philosophical response to Sartre's existentialism, with which she didn't entirely agree, and a circumspect variant of her own.
[10] *She Came to Stay.* (SdB)
[11] Chief of production at Gallimard.

What the hell do you think I'm going to do with the trunk! Mlle. de Beauvoir hasn't given me one sou in tips all year, I'm not going to haul that thing down." I left, undecided. Bost isn't here, I can't carry it alone and take it to the Louisiane all by myself. What to do? If I catch Bost tomorrow, I'll go back there with him.

This is nothing but a choppy little note, my love, to tell you that I love you and that the screenplay is shaping up well. In the coming days I'll write better, I'll depict moods and atmospheres. It's five o'clock, it's Saturday, I'm upstairs at the Flore, the sun is coming in the window, Tania is rehearsing at the Lancry. This evening we're to see Mavröidès.[12]

Till tomorrow, or the day after tomorrow, my darling Beaver, a kiss for your beautiful tanned face.

◈◈ *to Simone de Beauvoir*

Thursday, 8 [summer]

My darling Beaver

I have lots of time to write to you. I was supposed to go and watch Tania acting at the Théâtre Lancry (it's her third performance, she didn't want me to come to the earlier ones); but the cruel night watchman you sent me to refuses to go about reserving me a seat. Merleau-Ponty offered: he's leaving with me and will get off not at Uzerche but at Montauban. We'll travel together. Except that I can't find him anywhere, even though it's urgent. So I came back to settle down permanently at the Flore, where he will certainly drop by, since I have his identity card, and I'll wait for him here till eleven, occasionally ducking over to his place, 188 Bd. Saint-Germain. If that doesn't work, well, I'll get up tomorrow at five o'clock, and I'll be the one to line up for the tickets. I can't wait to see you, my sweet, my little dearest, and I'm terribly eager to wander about with you, *even* by bike. I miss you very much.

Delange, who is definitely a pearl, told me this morning that he was going to find something for you: 12 radio sketches, one a month, to arrange for next year (they furnish the idea, you do the dialogue—it lasts 10 minutes) for which you would be paid 1,500 to 2,000.[1] That in itself would be very handsome. It would take you all of four hours a month. I enthusiastically accepted for you!

---

[12] *An actress friend of Tania.* (SdB)

[1] Beauvoir had been removed from her teaching post in June 1943 after being accused by Sorokine's mother of corruption of a minor because she had refused to help break up Sorokine's relationship with Bourla. Delange helped her find work as a radio producer, making a series of programs reconstructing traditional regional festivals.

Tomorrow he's going to talk about it with the director of the radio station.[2] I'm having dinner with him and Crommelynck tomorrow evening after the after-noon's big reading: the screenplay is all set, it only needs to be adapted. And, so that it'll be more presentable, this same Delange looked me up the day before yesterday at the Flore to suggest he have it typed. I accepted, and entrusted it to him this morning. I don't actually know whether the typist will have the time to type the 70 well-packed pages. He told me he had seen Borderie again, who seems to be very keen on the subject. So there is a strong chance. Truly we'll be able to say piss off to the alma mater.

Dullin seems uneasy in his statements and planning. I got him on the phone yesterday—he's at Férolles—and he sounded embarrassed. I think I know the reason for this: he must have decided—so said Bonnaud—to mount *Pourceaug-nac* beginning August 15th for his September season opener and to put on *Les Mouches*[3] once a week only. I for one couldn't care less. But I'll advise Olga to refuse: she'd only get 100 francs a week and it will prevent her from acting anywhere else. On the other hand Picard, Aninat's dentist lover—who just signed a contract for three plays with Hébertot—got a phone call from Lanier,[4] most depressed: in a long embarrassed letter, Dullin has just let him know, more or less, that he won't use him next year. It's ridiculous when you think that three days before the dress rehearsal of *Les Mouches*, Dullin, carried away with en-thusiasm, turned around in his seat to say to Lanier, "He's a great romantic actor." Well anyway, I'll have an easy conscience about all that, because on Monday I'm going to Férolles with Tania. I'll be stuffing myself royally much of the time no doubt, but I'll have to give Toulouse her due for her work. If Dullin doesn't have a clear conscience on my account, it'll be charming, we'll all be uneasy.

So Tania is playing Molly Byrne in [J. M. Synge's] *The Well of the Saints*. There were nervous fits and tears on the day of the opening, though she insisted she felt no stage fright and was simply experiencing a coldness—but in the end, I think she is very good, insofar as the small part permits. The first days of rehearsal I had to play the benevolent old fogey in the wings; they treated me with respect and asked for a play: it didn't make me feel any younger. These days we must certainly resign ourselves to a place in the front rank. It's a very sad little troupe in a sad little theater. They are all excessively fragile, any trifle casts a pall over them, they each have their self-esteem, their proud but humble

[2] *Radio-Vichy. The CNE [National Committee of Writers] authorized the broadcasts in the Free Zone. (SdB)*

[3] Sartre's rendering of the Orestes-Electra story, with Olga Kosakiewicz (under the stage name Olga Dominique) as Electra.

[4] *Who was playing Orestes in* Les Mouches. *(SdB)*

dignity and, of course, they hate one another, despite some enthusiasts like Chauffard,[5] Darbon, Delarue. Leccia[6] complains that they're not paying her and that she comes in to play on an empty stomach; Vilar,[7] in the male lead, is leaving because he's been insufficiently appreciated. Cavé, the director and head of the company, borrowed in his own name the money he generously loses every evening. He's extremely sad about it; he actually has a naturally lugubrious air and has, for consolation, only the secret love of an ugly young woman named Odile who plays the minor parts and inadequately carries out the job of stage manager. Naturally Tania senses the smell of death; and, as you know, nothing makes her flee as quickly as misery, death, or misfortune. She clams up the moment she gets to the theater, and it takes the footlights to rouse her. The theater is on the Rue de Lancry, near the Place de la République. It is identified by nothing more than a little mangy, barely visible, yellow-brown poster, so narrow that they had to write the letters vertically. It is in the courtyard of a building that used to house trade union headquarters. You go in through an unremarkable door, with a poor excuse for a canopy, you go down a corridor, enter a courtyard, walk under an arcade, and reach a movie theater. It is usually all but empty, 80 people an evening approximately. It doesn't have the smell of just *one* death but of several successive deaths, beginning with the trade union halls, and it's in a neighborhood (Porte Saint-Martin) that's been dead since 1830. Every evening at about seven o'clock we hang around over there, drinking Vittel, either at the Rognon Flambé or the Louis XIV, shabby little bars that completely fail to live up to their brilliant names. After which my evenings are free, and I meet up with Tania again at the Flore or at her place around 10:30. So that means I see her from 12 noon to 7 p.m. She protested somewhat at the outset, I think there was even one violent scene. But her saintliness regained the upper hand and for the moment there is no problem. For the past few days I've been working on the screenplay in the morning (finished this morning) and then I'd see someone like Chauffard or Lescure[8] (the latter gave me fifty grams of blond tobacco that was specially sent to me in the diplomatic pouch by a Swiss admirer) or else I'd go out to shop for food. The noodles didn't appear, but at least 8 kilos of potatoes did. That suits me fine, because I have no more bread. Tania gave me seven hundred grams on her ration card, but alas it's not enough. During the afternoon I had Tania run through her lines, we would dawdle in her room and then go to the Théâtre Lancry on foot (but without much enthusiasm because the weather is gloomy, rain, gray and lowering skies,

---

[5] A *former student of Sartre who had finally opted for the theater.* (SdB)
[6] [*Darbon, Delarue, Leccia*] Actors, students of Dullin. (SdB)
[7] Jean Vilar (1912–71), actor-producer, student of Dullin.
[8] A *French poet and editor who published French Resistance writings in Switzerland.* (SdB)

cold). From there I would come back by métro to the Flore, where last night I saw Pasche, who had imparted very interesting observations about his patients and who'll take me next year to see some at Sainte-Anne. Day before yesterday I saw Lescure, tomorrow evening will be Crommelynck and Delange, Saturday I'm to have dinner at the Leiris'.[9] On Sunday afternoon I will see my parents, Sunday evening probably Zuorro.

Bits of news: Moulou[10] has a job here, at a German television company; Biran made me some interesting proposals; Oettly is taking a theater (l'Ambigu) and commissioned a play from me—I said neither yes nor no—Mme. Fiévet has been fired from Gallimard, but fortunately Winnifred Moulder is still there; Queneau came by to suggest on behalf of Gallimard a book of my critical articles, but I said it wasn't time yet; Violette Brochard is in Paris and will see Tania on Saturday at 2:30, yet another free afternoon; Lola won't be going to see Sarbakhane[11] and will spend Mondays with Tania in a nudist camp, Tania has agreed to go if she can keep her dress on. And then, would you believe that Zina[12] has gotten it into her head that she simply must have an affair with Chauffard. She even asked me to set up a date with Chauffard to which he would come, unsuspecting, and she would show up fifteen minutes later looking completely spontaneous as though she'd come on some errand for me. She would sit down, hold forth brilliantly for a half hour without paying any attention to Chauffard and leave with merely a meaningful look in his direction. Upon which, Toulouse would show up, invite Chauffard on some pretext to have a cup of coffee at her place later that same day. Tania, Zuorro, and I would then go over to Toulouse's and gorge ourselves. Toulouse would serve coffee, Chauffard would show up true to his word, drink the coffee, chat, and as she took him back to the front hall Zina would plant a kiss on his mouth. Fortunately circumstances prevented Toulouse from carrying out this astonishing plan. She left earlier than she had expected for Férolles, and the meeting is off till next year.

There. Zazoulich got a letter from you, luckier than I, who went by the post office yesterday and the day before in vain. I'll go tomorrow morning and, if there's nothing, tomorrow afternoon. I really long to see your nasty little hand-writing again.

Au revoir, my sweet little Beaver. Ponteau-Merle[13] came over, he took my identity card and my cash, and tomorrow he'll kindly go through the line for

---

[9] Michel Leiris (b. 1901), novelist, memoirist, ethnologist.

[10] *Mouloudji.* (SdB)

[11] *Sorokine.* (SdB)

[12] *Toulouse's (Simone Jollivet's) stooge.* (SdB) A gypsy who had been adopted by Jollivet's mother and raised with Simone, whom she adored.

[13] *Merleau-Ponty.* (SdB)

me. Things couldn't be better. I'll get there at the appointed time. I think I'll write you one more quick letter. Still to Clermont-Ferrand; have things forwarded if you aren't there.

I send you a big kiss, my darling Beaver whom I love with all my heart.

☙ *to Simone Jollivet*

7/17

Dear Toulouse

I've had the greatest of difficulty with the people at the Society of Dramatic Authors, who asked me for a registered power of attorney with my notarized signature in order to issue my money to me in my absence. To settle it, I'll draw the money when I get back (I was only admitted to the society the day before yesterday). So I would like to ask you, if it's no bother, not to send my check till August 1st. Then you'll receive all of my July paycheck. Thus all will end well. (Incidentally, I have enough money.)

I was sorry our schedules required us to part so abruptly the other day. I would have liked to tell you again how sure I am your memory won't give out. And then, on reflection, I also believe that I didn't tell you clearly enough that I *do not like* the "genre" of demoniac stories (the fantastic). That might also explain why I reacted somewhat sullenly. I for one expect something quite different from you. We should have spoken about that too, but if you like we shall, after the summer vacation.

We've been at Uzerche for 2 days, Beaver and I, we're waiting for a bicycle in order to take off for Brive, Tulle, and Clermont-Ferrand. The weather's superb, but I don't much like Limousin.

Warm greetings.

☙ *to Simone de Beauvoir*

Wednesday [end of '43]

My darling Beaver

It's three twenty-five, I'm at the Flore, I'm scrupulously writing. So here you are a *"metteuse en ondes"* [radio director], now what exactly is that all about? Nobody has been able to give me the complete story. Today, however, you're not giving a damn about waves; you're gliding from top to bottom. I thought a lot about you, about the trip, the arrival, I remember a slew of arrivals, in the morning—one at Saint-Gervais. Yet I do envy you slightly. Above all, have a great time.

On Monday I had a gloomy Tania on my hands, she has no idea why "It's much the worst pain, To not know why, Without love without hate, My heart holds such pain";[1] tears, wails, wringing of hands, long silences, I was bored stiff. To top it off, Zuorro showed up for five minutes with a package of tea. That was pleasant, helped her toward sleep. Yesterday morning I worked and had lunch with my parents. During the afternoon, work from three to five-thirty at the Flore, then I went along with Roy,[2] who's certifiably crazy, to Morgan's. From there to Tania, who, ten minutes after my arrival, was weeping and squirming on her bed hollering, "Go call the theater and tell them I will not be going on." Though I have no idea of the real reason for that flood of tears, I do know its immediate cause: she had taken eight capsules of orthedrine. One or two cheer you up, three can make you dreamy, with eight you can well imagine. I refused to make the call and made quite a bit of racket. Ultimately, I went with her, howling, into the métro, where she cried in spurts, as though her eyes were two severed aortas. She had me promise I wouldn't set foot again in La Cité's auditorium "because if I see you, I'll shriek, I'll leap off the stage." I wasn't that eager, I went to work at the Flore, it went well, till 9 o'clock, but at 9 Vitsoris and a friend came and talked my ear off. At 9 thirty I was at Dullin's theater. I found him in his dressing room as Jupiter, cold as October rain, spitting out his words, complaining of loneliness. I laughed and chattered away as though I hadn't noticed a thing. As soon as he began to brighten up, I left, promising to come back next Tuesday. It was because Nino Franck[3] was wandering the corridors asking for Olga Dominique's[4] dressing room. I saw him, he's very taken with her, he said that *things might turn out very well* for Typhus[5] and that he'll talk to me about it on Friday. I'll keep you posted. At 10 o'clock I saw Tania show up, smiling and gay, she'd played the young woman's part with real feeling. I took her home by métro with Zazoulich in tears because (so she said) she had played badly and Cuny[6] was in the audience. That didn't prevent Cuny from coming to find her in her dressing room to tell her that he intended to act with

---

[1] Paul Verlaine (1844–96), "Ariettes oubliées," from *Les Romances sans paroles* (1874), which opens with the familiar echo of Rimbaud, "Il pleur dans mon coeur/ Comme il pleut sur la ville."
[2] *A former student of Sartre. (SdB)*
[3] *A movie critic, influential in film circles. (SdB)*
[4] *Olga's stage name. (SdB)* She was playing Electra in *Les Mouches.*
[5] *A screenplay of Sartre's that was filmed without his name in a distorted version. (SdB)*
[6] Film and stage actor Alain Cuny.

her (though there's no money for it). She lent me one of Bost's pipes because I'd broken the beautiful one that was like a rubber teat. I stayed with Tania for five minutes, just time enough for her to sob a little about her lot. "I'm living so comfortably, boohoo!" she said, weeping. "And I've got everything I want, boohooo! And I have money, and I'm going to act! There must be something perfectly horrible happening to me for me to feel so gloomy under these circumstances." I stroked her neck a bit and left. Got to the Hôtel Louisiane, no key. Did you take it away with you? So the door will stay unlocked, so what. I greeted the kids[7] and ate three little eggs. I wrote the letter to Bourla's father and I slept like a god. This morning, four hours at the lycée, then 3 eggs and a package of noodles. I argued till two-forty with the kids, who don't like *Le Sang des autres* [*The Blood of Others*],[8] for rather stupid reasons, I think. But they're nice, every day I find my place set, a plate, a coffee bowl, a spoon and a knife, on the striped tablecloth, it's touching. And here I am. I'm going to work a bit before MerliPonte[9] gets here.

Till later, little one. I'll write on Saturday. Go up, ski down, get right in the swim of things. I love you with all my might and I send you a kiss for your good little cheeks (they'll surely be tanned when you get back, I passed some completely tanned people who were just back from skiing).

Toast the Yule Log for me.[10]

---

[7] *Sorokine and Bourla. Bourla, a former student of Sartre, Jewish, and whom we liked very much, was killed by the Germans.* (SdB)

[8] Beauvoir's novel published in 1945, and in English in 1948, dealing with the existential decision of a Resistance fighter to continue taking risks, despite the dangers to his friends and others. Sorokine's disapproval could have been personal, since the character of the protagonist's girlfriend, dying of a wound, was partly based on herself.

[9] *Merleau-Ponty.* (SdB)

[10] *I was off skiing, at Morzine, with friends and Bost.* (SdB)

1944

to Simone de Beauvoir

[early 1944]

My darling Beaver

If I hadn't already done it once, I would write in this letter that I'm sending it to general delivery and that I hope you'll go to pick it up there. But I think that you'll do it without that. To tell the truth, I do have your address, but as agreed I left the letter at the Rue de Seine, and it would be a waste of time for me to go and get it. I'm writing to you from the Flore, which is nice and quiet; your letter delighted me, I think you must be in seventh heaven. But has it snowed? And lessons? Tomorrow my guess is that I'll get another. This one, I wish to note, is my *third* letter.

Since Sunday there has been little going on. On the topic of work, I finished the Parain article[1] and returned to the novel[2] with pleasure. I've already written fifteen pages of it, and you'll find fifty when you get back, it's so much more fun than writing about language.

On the topic of moods: I was a bit put out to see my screenplays rejected, I'm so used to praise now that when I'm not given it, I get disoriented. I was in a rather black mood till Sunday night. Sunday night marked the paroxysm, for I went out in the rain to dine at Mistler's wife's place. Nothing could have been more horrible. She got flushed at the end of the meal and her face, which was already ugly, underwent a terrible change. There were two children there, a little girl in braids and the delicate young boy who'll become a novelist later on and who is slightly behind in his studies because of illness. Mistler, whom

[1] "Aller et retour" [*Round Trip*], *which appeared in* Situations I. (*SdB*)
[2] *The Reprieve.*

all his intimates call Edgar, was also there and a cat, the only pleasant element, who wipes his rear like a genuine human being, with toilet paper. You're going to say that's impossible, of course, because other people's marvels irritate you, and yet it's true, proven by the fact that we dined in the midst of a great rustle of paper, because the animal goes at it over and over, lacking the skill to match his good intentions. Dinner: splendid cabbage soup, steak, homemade cakes and preserves. Coffee and real kirsch.

I went home to bed at your place and woke up in an excellent mood. I saw Lefèvre-Pontalis,[3] still set on getting married; I went out to eat some eggs and noodles on the Rue de Seine, and then I went to the Rue de Trévise to watch the rehearsal.[4] It's getting better and better. Camus and Tania stand out, leaving Kéchélévitch behind. Jeannet will be given his walking papers tomorrow, he's not up to it. Perhaps Chauffard will take his place. I hate to ask him to give up Dullin while the Gallimard theater isn't a sure thing. Queneau will probably do a one-act curtain raiser. Which would be fine.

After the rehearsal we went for a cup of tea at the Flore, Tania, Kéchélévitch, and I. Then home and hearth till midnight. Tania's gentle as a lamb, because her sister has talked reason into her: What was she thinking about to go running after Camus? What did she want from him? Wasn't I so much better? And so nice? She should watch out. And anyway, was it all that much fun seducing guys? She, Olga, had done it for years but it didn't interest her anymore at all. Tania was drunk with rage, but she had been shaken up. In response, playing the coquette, she put records on the phonograph and danced around me lasciviously from 7 to 10. I was listening to the records. Tuesday: work till eleven o'clock. Chauffard and Roy from 11 to 12. Roy is altogether nuts. He gobbles up tales of the insane and falls into a dejected silence the moment something else comes up. Some misfortune will befall him unless, as I hope, his madness, like mine in years past, is merely that he thinks himself mad. In any case his face is gradually becoming distorted and looks strangely like those you see in institutions. He claims to have so well demonstrated to one of his friends that the insane are *right*, that the friend, convinced, had himself committed and is conscientiously delirious. Tania, het up and viperish—one hour all told for the day, from 1 o'clock to 2—then work, then Prix de la Pléiade[5] and jousts of wit, finesse, profundity, malice, irony. Mouloudji has a very good chance. We pro-

---

[3] *A former student of Sartre, who had become a very well known psychoanalyst.* (SdB)
[4] *Of* Huis clos [*No Exit*]. (SdB) In early 1944 Sartre suggested Albert Camus direct and play the male lead, with Olga Barbezat and Tania, but the play was taken up by the professional Théâtre du Vieux-Colombier, where it premiered in May with Tania Balachova, Michel Vitold, and Gaby Sylvia; Raymond Rouleau directing.
[5] Founded by Gallimard. The prize went to Mouloudji's novel *Enrico*.

ceeded by a preferential vote, a sort of elimination: assuming you were to vote, give 3 names in the order of your preference. There were seven of us. All 7 gave Mouloudji's name some spot, 4 the top one. Therefore the majority. Only Éluard, Malraux and Bousquet weren't there. As for Malraux, we'll have him, if we eliminate *Le Maçon*, whose homosexual aspects displease him. After the gathering, we talked with Camus, Groet,[6] and Parain. They're going to take the Ethics entry out of the "Philosophy" volume of the Encyclopedia and make a separate work of it in which we (you, Camus, Merleau, Leiris, I, etc.) will try to make a team manifesto—a position paper on concrete morality adapted to the circumstances. Camus, who had nothing else to do, followed me to the Flore, where I stayed with him till 9 o'clock. It's rather fascinating: he's lightly taken by Tania. The Russian soul, which we explored to the innermost, is still only slightly familiar to him. He speaks of Tania's "genius" and of her "human value." Meanwhile, she marks down in a small date book, tongue in cheek, the "points" she wins over Camus. It looks like this:

Sunday : III Monday : IIII, etc.

After he left I read. At ten o'clock I was on my way up to the kids' place; they're in quite a state over various little things I'll tell you about. I ate some noodles at their place and some of Bourla's chocolate and then, nearing midnight, I went to bed. This morning, four hours of class, with no alert,[7] alas. In the afternoon, Tania, and since six o'clock, work and reading of manuscript. And I'm writing to you.

They're progressively putting out the lights, my sweet. So I'm stopping. I love you so much: a good part of the minor anxiety of the first days came from your departure, my good little companion. By now I'm getting used to it, but I feel so idiotic all by myself at the Flore, when I was so happy to chatter away with you there. Adieu, my little one, I send you a big kiss.

Did you know that Zazoulich read *La Belle Heaulmière* in your last Monday's broadcast?

---

[6] Bernard Groethuysen, a philosopher associated with the *NRF*.
[7] Against Allied bombing raids.

1945

During his trip to America, Sartre wrote few letters to me, and some were in fact lost. Letters sent by boat arrived only after immense delays. His reports to Le Figaro *and to* Combat *were wired in, at the papers' expense. (SdB)*

ᏉᏇ *to Simone de Beauvoir*

[July]

My darling Beaver

Who is not as darling as all that because she hadn't written me even the tiniest little note to Cannes. Finally I did get one long letter here, and you are forgiven because you seem to have had a very good time. It makes me laugh that you're in Vichy right now—though actually you're not there anymore. I suppose you're going to wander around for all you're worth in Le Forez and in the area where we went in the summer of 41? Have a lovely time, you who haven't lost your youth (incidentally I haven't lost mine either). I have scads of things to tell you. Let's see, first of all, about those that might just give you a little pleasure. The August trip to London seems in the cards again. Passing through Paris I found a letter from M. Massigli, who is putting me off till fall, with no word of you. But I ran into Cohen, the director who wants to do *Les jeux sont faits* [*The Chips Are Down*]; he told me that an English company wants to do a film on the atrocities, that they have splendid documentary footage but that they are adrift in an attempt to establish a general approach. He told them, "There's only one man who can do it: Sartre." I replied that I would accept on the *express* condition that you be invited too, because you are my adviser. That the money was not very important: all my expenses would be paid there, and so I could pay for your stay. He said it's his brother who's assigning tasks for the film and that it wouldn't be any problem. It would only take agreement from the chaps there for a Frenchman to do their screenplay. He'll give me the answer around the 10th of August, and we would leave about the 20th. It's still uncertain, but there it is . . . By the same mail, I'm sending off a line from Dorian, of Euraméric, who is interested in your play.[1] Accept it: he organizes conferences in South America. That's the good news. Actually there isn't any bad.

Aside from that, Tania has been charming these past few days, except for the eve of my departure, when suddenly she told me with clenched fists, "I've come to discover that with nobody in the whole world do I feel so bored as with you." But it was only a hasty generalization, and she has returned to a more proper assessment. I didn't go and line up for my ticket, a mysterious individual gave me *for free* an admission slip. It was outrageously fake, incidentally, and the railway employee gave me such a hard time when he handed me my ticket that I didn't dare show it at the gate. So then I bought a ticket to Antibes[2] and went an hour and a half early to sit on a station bench with Tania. After which I spent 26 hours in a packed train, standing in the corridor, it's rather a pain in the ass. Besides, they heat up the locomotive to the limit, which covers the travelers with soot, I arrived done in and black as a chimney sweep. Nonetheless (while not having eaten a thing in 24 hours) I lined up for information at the Gare de Lyon to find out how to get to Saint-Sauveur.[3] It turns out, you simply don't. You could go by Auxerre, there was a connection in Auxerre itself (after going all the way across town), but that would take an admission slip, therefore another wait, and above all a four-day delay. For Gien, you don't need an admission slip: you take the 6:05 bus in the morning, except that at the precise moment you're getting on that bus in Paris, the only train for Saint-Sauveur is leaving Gien. And when you reach that grim city at 9:15, you have to spend 24 hours there waiting for the 6 a.m. local the next day. Nonetheless I decided to leave for Gien, but with the thought that once there I'd manage one way or another. Except that after traveling for 24 hours, getting up at 4:30 was a bit difficult, and I decided to spend Sunday in Paris and leave only on Monday morning. From there I dropped by the hotel. They naturally told me, "The key is at Mademoiselle Sorokine's." I went up and found her in the arms of the

---

[1] *Les Bouches inutiles* [*Useless Mouths*].
[2] Lacking a travel permit to Paris, Sartre bought the ticket for nearby Antibes so as to gain access to the train platform.
[3] *Where his parents had a second residence.* (SdB) His stepfather had died in January.

charming Moffat,[4] who is definitively set up in Paris until his repatriation and who is doing absolutely nothing but spending his days with her. I like him very much. The trunk[5] had arrived, and there was also some mail: a 2,000 franc tax bill for you; and a letter from Dolorès,[6] which pleased me tremendously. The letter's tone is very dignified, given that she hasn't received the letter I had Knopf[7] hold for her, and in short she's writing to say, "Stop diddling, write to me." That of course must be met with a studied rigor, but one can sense the fine, decent warmth beneath it all. I wrote to her last night, and I'm going to continue from here. The trunk was in perfect condition, your 6 meters of fabric and your two pairs of shoes are there safe and sound. I handed out chocolate and pâté to Sarabakhane, tea to Olga (who came back to give a final farewell to Bost, who is awaiting departure from one day to the next). Then I went to get some cash at the Postal Checking (1 hour and a half in line), then to telegraph a money order to Tania. I want you to know that from 2 o'clock in Cannes to 6 o'clock in Paris I hardly stopped to breathe. As a reward I went to the Pont-Royal for an hour by myself, then took Sorokine out for dinner, then spent the evening with Moffat and Sarba[8] at the Pont-Royal. It was a friendly evening but one requiring effort, because the language difference makes communication arduous. Around 10 o'clock Sorokine was giving signs of impatience, and I left them to go to the Cheramy,[9] where Astruc[10] bared his heart, leaving me at the same time with a hilarious little piece he'd written about money. "You are extremely lucky to be moral," he sighed, confessing to his arriviste propensities. Thereupon I went to bed. On Sunday I saw Chauffard, Nathalie Sarraute, Violette Leduc,[11] [Michel] Vitold,[12] I wrote some letters, drew up my review copy blurb, then toward evening, I brought Chauffard, Vitold, and Darbon with his phono to Sorokine's, and I played all the records I'll be taking to Duhamel.[13] From there I went to get my mail at the Hôtel Chaplain, where I ran into Olga, who I hadn't realized was in Paris, and whom I invited with Bost for lunch the next day. I have to tell you that I had just caught a terrible fever and such stomach

[4] A young American officer who later became a screenwriter in Hollywood and married Sorokine. (SdB)

[5] Which Sartre had sent me from New York. (SdB)

[6] Dolorès Vanetti, an actress whom Sartre had met in New York, became for a time a love second only to Beauvoir.

[7] Sartre's American publisher.

[8] Sorokine. (SdB)

[9] A restaurant-bar near Saint-Germain-des-Prés. (SdB)

[10] Alexandre Astruc (b. 1923), novelist and film director.

[11] The novelists Violette Leduc (1907–72) and Nathalie Sarraute (b. 1902).

[12] He played Garcin in the 1945 premiere of No Exit and the next year directed Men Without Shadows and The Respectful Prostitute.

[13] Marcel Duhamel, editor of the Série Noire [detective stories]. (SdB)

pains that I couldn't imagine getting up at 4:30 to catch the train again. As it turned out, I went home to bed and spent a painful, almost sleepless night. The following day, still very low, I saw Cohen at noon, then Olga and Bost for lunch, then Martin-Chauffier, who on September 15 will give us[14] some forty pages on the camps, which will require us to change the tenor of the Nov. and Dec. issues (because it is coming out in book form in January). Then once more Bost, with whom I spent the evening (till 10 o'clock). I went to say hello to Sorokine and Moffat, and I went to bed. At 4:30 woke up, set out on foot, rucksack on my back, to the Gare de Lyon, because the first métro doesn't leave the barn till 5:30. I was still slightly weak, but it's rather nice to venture out in the wee hours. I bought *Labyrinthe*, in which André Rousseaux devotes 4 columns to explaining that I'm a neo-surrealist and I lack Love. That certainly hits the nail on the head, for myself who has encumbered my life with too much of it. But we must not be talking about the same thing.

The trip went without hitch, I even had a seat for 2½ hours, then stood from Montargis on in a compartment without a corridor. Finally Gien. A massacred town, dying, no bread, no bus, hitchhiking is a joke because there are no cars to hitch. After much walking and inquiring I found an old Renault which, for 11,000 francs, took me the remaining 55 kilometers to Saint-Sauveur. And here I am, welcomed with open arms and leading the luxurious country house life in the midst of a crowd of people who are completely unknown to me but who let me be totally free. My mother is very worthy and very touching. Of course she was convinced I'd been killed in the accident in Saint-Fons (which had actually happened the night of my return to Paris and had been the cause of the 4-hour delay) and had wept the whole night through. I think she needs some imaginary worries. But I'll give you a better picture of the life here once I'm more used to it. I was very glad to find a letter from you here, good little Beaver, I was bothered by having no news of you, except for a stupid little scrap found at Soroquin's. I'm happy to know that you're wheeling down the roads with the violence of your tumultuous nature. How can the bicycle be a good one? Sauroquin insists it's terrible. Don't break your little neck.

Au revoir, my sweet, big kisses to you. I'm longing to see you again, I felt very lonely in Paris without you.

Send me posthaste (perhaps by telegram) an address if you wish me to still have a chance of reaching you by letter.

---

[14] *Les Temps Modernes.*

✍ *to Simone de Beauvoir*

[December 31]

My darling Beaver

Where are you? Surely in Tunisia and surely having fun. It's December 31st, and I'm still on this blighted ship.[1] Under the most favorable hypothesis we will debark on Thursday the 3rd, after an 18-day crossing. And at that, we spent 3 deadly dull days in Bordeaux, from Friday to Sunday, with the threat of not leaving till Tuesday or Wednesday. I have to tell you that a Liberty ship is a freighter, worse even than a military freighter. In addition, you must realize that it is too light to ride the waves steadily, and with each roll of any consequence at all, its propeller rises out of the water with a frightening noise, which does nothing to improve our speed, as you may well imagine. I put a few notes down on paper for you, but as I didn't know at the start whether or not I might do a short article on it—because ultimately it's rather colorful to cross on a Liberty ship and it's worth talking about—I kept the tone objective and said nothing about myself. Then I gave up, because you simply *cannot* write at sea. It's extraordinary, you get the impression that the wind and the rocking empty your head. You can't do a thing but chat endlessly or stare endlessly at the sea where the motion of the waves replaces the movement of ideas in your head. Twenty times over I tried to write my article on Materialism and Revolutions and each time was seized with an intolerable boredom before the blank page, a sort of nausea. I couldn't even read: I don't just mean Malraux, but not even the detective novels I'd brought along. I just can't manage it. Some are studying a bit of English. Others play solitaire. But mostly you go from one end of the boat to the other, successively assuming various stable positions. In the morning, up at 8:20 for breakfast in pajamas. Then you loiter, you make the rounds on deck, then you shower, shave and dress, which takes you up to noon. At noon, lunch. The afternoon hours drag by more slowly, you chat with this one and that one, you look at your watch: only a half hour has gone by. Finally at 5 o'clock you have dinner, and then after dinner, chess, or you go up to see "the ladies." We have bought some cognac, and we get drunk one night out of two. I feel so all-at-sea between heaven and earth that I scarcely remember I've left Paris and completely forget I'm going to New York. I think of nothing and no one. It's an extraordinary, languid state, sufficient unto itself. Which is fortunate, because if you had to live these eighteen days a captive of the sea's monotony with impatience or regret, it would be enough to send you overboard. In short, I want you to realize I'm no longer myself at all, and those who consider me "too

---

[1] A *"liberty ship"* taking him to New York. (SdB)

intense" have only to sail with me on a freighter. Incidentally, I haven't been seasick, though they stashed me away in the stern, which leaps and dances terribly. It's surely a matter of will. Simply, for the first four or five days I smoked, ate, and lived on the sickly sweet and nauseating surface. But eventually that too became the real and natural flavor of existence, one couldn't remember that there had ever been another. Afterward all that disappeared, or else I grew used to it, I couldn't say. I want you to know we had some heavy weather and storms, and a breakdown right in the midst of a storm, the captain almost sent an SOS, but eventually they were able to make repairs. Now, something you can easily imagine in Tunisia but they would scarcely believe in Paris: we live on the deck in our shirtsleeves. I can tell you, these are the Southern Seas, and most particularly the Sargasso sea. Tell Moulou when you get home that I've seen the Sargasso weeds in droves, and they look like bunches of raisins. I must be *truly* famous, poor little Beaver, because though I'm only identified by mangy tags on my suitcases, the whole ship knew who I was. They asked me to give a lecture on existentialism, and people fought for my books, and they really made a hash of them. They're *all* Pétainists and collaborationists, some are dreaming of a nice little dictatorship in France, they have ideas that would make your hair stand on end, and I ostentatiously left the table one day when one dirty little jerk from the Centrale[2] was telling anecdotes tending to ridicule and scoff at the resistance fighters in the Vercors.[3] We had forgotten that sector of humanity, my little Beaver. It is simply frightening. Nonetheless, one must live and talk. I'm getting along pretty well with a guy named Riboud who has been living in America for more than 10 years and is going to ask for naturalization papers. He has the American sense of democracy, which is already something. There's also a marvelous fellow in a blue and yellow striped shirt, blond mustache, and beret with a pom-pom, the dreamy Sunday painter type. I get along well with him. Angéli, whom I talk about in my notes, is a rather good sort, profoundly conservative but in a sailor's way rather than a property owner's. Add to that a doctor named Barthélemy, a giant who eats like fifteen, plays the benevolent curmudgeon, and at heart is profoundly malevolent and hypocritical. They're the best we've got. They call themselves the "Existentialist Bureau." And then there are the women. The wife of the Brazilian consul has been making passes at me all week. She's thirty-five and beautiful, with the pampered look of an Egyptian dancing girl. Stupid, actually, and terribly flirtatious, hoping to have the captain, Angéli, the painter Baudin, and the writer trailing along behind

---

[2] Prestigious engineering school.

[3] Jean Brullet—whose *Le Silence de la mer* (the first book published by the then-clandestine Éditions de Minuit) dealt with simple villagers silently resisting the German occupation— took his pseudonym from this mountain range.

her. I gave back in kind for a week, and that goes to show the extent of this vacuum, this boredom between sky and sea, this existence cut off from everything, in which one feels *caught up* in this ship for a whole lifetime and from the beginning of time. There was some agitation, promises made, exchange of handshakes and then on Christmas night I got drunk and bawled her out. I'm not too sure what happened, but I can see myself again in her cabin, and a little Cuban who sleeps above her saying to me, "If I were Madame T., I would smack you one." The rest escapes me, as always happens when I'm drunk; except that I slept for a while in a lifeboat while they were searching for me all over the place. Since then there has been a certain coolness, a renewed relationship, a coolness, though I'm convinced she wanted to keep me as aspirant #2, giving the greater portions of her favor to Angéli (I don't think she sleeps with anyone). So I definitely cut off a stupid flirtation that had no rhyme or reason, got me agitated without awakening the least interest for her, and would, if it had turned out well, have caused me nothing but trouble, been injurious for Dolorès, and threatened to end up with dishonor for me, or in any case rather pitifully. Which is to say that I adopted a distant and polite attitude. Meanwhile the lady tied some rather tender knots with Angéli and, after undergoing two days of coquetry to get me back, isn't paying me the slightest attention anymore and is billing and cooing with him. It's the typical sort of idiotic inopportune affair; I couldn't stop seeing myself with horror as an insect. The sea air must really turn a person slightly batty: we spent whole evenings in that lady's cabin and there was always a young homosexual curled up at her feet like a page. A gracious and curious guy, incidentally, very dark, very silent, who is going to Hollywood to try his luck and whom I find rather nice. He is twenty. This is what has filled the time. Three days ago I forced myself to get back to reading, though without much pleasure. But most of all, here we are with the end of the trip in sight. I'm beginning to sense New York. So are the others. We're beginning to tell each other stories about America, we approached Riboud about doing a lecture for us on American life (initiation of the French). Duhamel's brother is here. He's the image of his celebrated brother, but colorless. At the table he spins anecdotes. He is set on being part of our group, but we flee him whenever we can.

There you have it, my darling Beaver. Of course the whole thing includes many a detail that will be told to you. But note the simple act of having written four pages, and already the pen is dropping from my hand. There have been very funny moments: one night when we got soused at the lady's place, she made advances to me while I remained aloof. At three in the morning, we were on our way back to our cabin at the rear, and at that point, drunk, vaguely sensitive to the lady's advances, I close the door quietly and go back up to her cabin and knock: "I'd like to speak to you for a moment. Would you like to go out with me?" "Yes," she says, in friendly tones. She goes out on deck, myself behind her, and scarcely does she reach it but two guys (Baudin and Angéli) appear on either side of her and, without seeing the other and without seeing me, say softly at the same moment, "I'd like to speak to you for a moment." Then I stepped forward and said, "What a bunch of clowns we are!" and I went back down to bed, laughing, leaving them to untangle that one by themselves.

I hope to have letters from you on my arrival, little sweet. I'm annoyed that because the trip is so long, you get the letters and telegrams a week after the expected date. As a matter of fact, if we get to New York on the 4th, we'll be lucky. You'll already have been in Tunis for two weeks. Have a good time, my sweet, enjoy yourself. I love you with all my might, and I send you a kiss.

I'll add a few words between now and Thursday.

1946

[January]

My darling Beaver

I know less and less where to write to you. You tell me you're not leaving till the end of January. But are you going to leave? There are scads of letters for you in Tunisia. I'm sending this one to France. But have the ones in Tunisia sent back. There was a complete shipboard log, and also letters from here.

Your letters have warmed my heart. I'm so happy that you had a good time in Megève. I felt as you did while I read the articles by Las Vergnas that a black named Pélage passed on to me, how strange and ridiculous it is that everyone continues to concern themselves with us when we're both in another world. Like you, I feel we must make changes in our lives. Only my mother and Tania keep me from leaving with you to work anywhere at all for six months a year. But between that and the daily Café de Flore, there are intermediary positions. Here life is calm and uneventful. I get up around 9 o'clock and never manage, despite all my efforts, to be ready before 11 (bath, shave, breakfast), I go to some appointment, and I lunch with Dolorès or various people wanting to see me. After lunch I take a walk all alone till 6 o'clock around NY, which I know as well as Paris; I meet Dolorès again here or there and we stay together at her place or in some quiet bar till 2 in the morning. I'm drinking heavily, but without any problems so far. Friday night I'm going up to her place and I'm staying there till Sunday afternoon at 4 (because of doormen).[1] She calls me the prisoner. But this Friday we're going for the weekend to Jacqueline Breton's

---

[1] She was in the process of separating from her husband and wanted to be as circumspect as possible.

(Wednesday and Thursday: Boston—Friday to Monday: J. Breton in Connecticut). And from Monday on I have half an apartment on 79th Street; I'll give you the address. It's a friend of Dolorès's who'll let me have it for 15 dollars a week. As for dough, it's going badly, I have enough to live on but not enough to buy anything. I'm going to see a literary agent this very day so she can place some articles for me. There's a lot of commotion about me here, but they don't ask me for paid articles. And at the lowest estimate I've got 700 dollars' worth of presents to bring back (and on everything I earn I owe the State 25%). My lectures bring in only 50 dollars each, they take me all day, sometimes the night and the next day.

Incidents, none. Except that Dolorès's love for me scares me. In other respects she is absolutely charming and we never get mad at each other. But the future of the whole thing is very grim. I don't know how to write this to you without being rotten to her (because of the chilling effect of the written word), and yet have you get a sense of how things are. I'll talk to you about it at length. (I'm not making daily notes because there never is anything.)

Au revoir, my dearest, my darling little Beaver, au revoir. I'm at my best with you and I love you very much. Au revoir, little one, I'll be so happy to be with you again.

I'm thinking of coming back around the very beginning of March (3rd or 4th), sailing around the end of February (27–28).

ৰ৵ to Simone de Beauvoir

Monday [February]

My darling Beaver

For a month now I've been hoping for a letter from you and have received nothing. I'm not too anxious because letters take a long time to get here and because I've had no news from my mother since February 10th. I don't suppose you're both dead. I imagine that Tunisia[1] isn't particularly favored by the postal system. But what distresses me is wondering whether you've gotten my letters in Tunis. I've written a lot except in the past two weeks during which I really didn't know where to send you my letters. I think you must be home by now. I'll be getting back on March 15 by plane (I'm leaving NY on the 14th). I had

---

[1] Where she was lecturing on existentialism.

only a choice between two boats taking 10 or 15 days and leaving around the 1st, or a plane on the 15th (which still had one seat). *However*, it hasn't been easy finding articles or money. It's only now that the whole thing is shaping up. But I must write the articles and make the purchases. So I still need a few days. You will have lost your bottle of champagne, but I'll give you another with the 300,000 francs from *No Exit*. I'm going to give lavishly paid lectures in Canada, going by plane (Toronto, Ottawa, Montreal: three days the 8th, 9th, 10th). I won't be able to meet Sorokine.[2] But Dolorès will take care of that, will give her a bed and show her around. If she gets here on the 11th, after my return, I'll waltz her around New York. But how is it that you didn't even send me a telegram through the Consulate to alert me about her arrival? It was Moffat who let me know: all said and done, this silence doesn't make too much sense to me. Where are you?

I'm busy from dawn to dusk: articles, lectures, *No Exit*, it means I'm trapped. Farewell to my little walks. But I've got a thousand things to tell you re Jacqueline Breton, David Hare,[3] my visits to the country. For example, on the way back our car turned over on a highway. Hare was on the bottom, then Dolorès, then me on top. Nobody was hurt: just 300 dollars of repairs. Nonetheless, it was a serious accident. I'll also tell you about Dolorès, who is a poor and charming creature, really the best I know after you. At present we are involved in the agonies of departure, and I'm not having fun every day. Out of fear of the doormen we've emigrated to D. Hare's studio, downtown. She has a nervous fear of this neighborhood, the Bowery. You could scarcely imagine the odd mixture of fear and decisiveness, profound pessimism and surface optimism, passion and caution, diffidence and spunk in her makeup. Her passion literally scares me, particularly since that's not my strong suit, and she uses it solely to her disadvantage, but she can display the candor and innocence of a child when she is happy.

Here it is the same as in Paris: everyone is talking about me and everywhere I'm dragged through the mud. I suppose it's my lot. Lévi-Strauss pretending to be unaware of my relationship with D., said to her one day when she asked him if he liked me, "How do you think I could like him after reading *She Came to Stay?* He's portrayed warts and all, and he seems like a filthy bastard." Thanks a lot, little jewel, for the portrait. I'm struggling against the sharks who'd like to live off me and exploit me. Dolorès makes me discuss questions of money ruthlessly, claiming that it's obligatory to do so in America. I do it badly. I've just come from the lawyer's office, about renewing the contract for *No Exit*. I

[2] *She was on her way to join Moffat in America. (SdB)*
[3] *An American sculptor, Jacqueline Breton's second husband. (SdB)*

felt I had been perfectly ruthless. But it seems I behaved like a child. Here we go, here's one of my days: 9:30 to the famous photographer [Cecil] Beaton (the d'Harcourt of New York) for a photo for *Vogue*, and to *Vogue* to discuss an article I'm doing for them. 11 o'clock to Knopf to write a letter to Hamilton, my English publisher, to dissuade him from publishing *The Age of Reason* before *The Reprieve*. 12:30 to a restaurant with Oliver Smith, who is going to produce *No Exit*.[4] 2:30 to 4:00: to the lawyer's to sign the contract. 4:00 to 6:00 I'm writing to you and my mother. At 6 o'clock I'm going to a cocktail party at Richey's, my former landlord. At 7:45 I go to Saussure's, the Swiss psychoanalyst (you know, making eyes to ape the virile member) dinner. Tomorrow: 11:00 to 12:00 I'm seeing a guy from the OWI [Office of War Information]. 12:30 I'm lunching with Richard Wright—3 o'clock I give a lecture on theater at Carnegie Hall. I'm just back from New England, where I spoke at two women's colleges. It was really something. The day after tomorrow some French Canadians are rehearsing *No Exit* at the Barbizon Plaza Theater, and since they want me to authorize them to give it in New York, I'll go to see the play. *Huis clos* played with a Canadian accent, not bad. Aside from that, I yearn to go home, I'm half dead from passion and lecturing. I'd like to see you calmly and write *La Dernière Chance*.[5] I saw Picon's article: unfair and asinine. He claims *I don't have the right* to speak about heroism and he denies me the title of novelist because I know what my characters will do in the third volume. He really must be an ass. Yes, I do want to see you, talk with you, go places with you (Belgium, Tunis) and work. What's the story on *Morts sans sépulture*?[6] I'm now completely in the dark about it. Yet I must have written at least 10 or 12 letters.

Au revoir, my darling Beaver, I love you. When you get this letter I'll be three or four days away from Paris. Kisses to you, my sweet.

❧ to Simone de Beauvoir

[March]

My darling Beaver

Here's some cash. Welcome back, my sweet, welcome back. You're only a few hours ahead of me. Take this quick note as a first kiss on your dear little face (how peeling and tanned it must be).

---

[4] Directed by John Huston. See below, letters of 1959.
[5] The last volume, never competed or published, of the tetralogy *The Roads to Freedom*.
[6] Translated as *Men Without Shadows*, his 1946 play about torture, which premiered on a double bill with his *La putain respectueuse* [*The Respectful Prostitute*].

Here everything's moving along well—but what a lot of fuss! Particularly to do with the Théâtre Antoine. There's been every imaginable complication, and finally I have a play in one act on my hands. Tania is back—in a good mood. It seems she's made enormous progress and that Vitold told her, "You'll be excellent in *Men Without Shadows*." If only it's true. I've seen Bost, Olga, Giacometti, Annette,[1] Claude Day, Zuorro, Pierrette Laurence, Maheu, Guille, Rirette Nizan, Caillois, Etiemble, Lefèvre-Pontalis, etc. I had a good time, but fear that my poor mother missed Strasbourg and the Alsatian solitude.[2] [Jean] Genet has written an excellent play: *The Maids*—which he read aloud to me, alas. The *T.M.* [*Temps Modernes*] has committed a disaster in mutilating [Olivier] Larronde's poetry, he's raging mad.

I'll be there right away, little Castore, wait for me, I'm coming to take you in my arms.

I got your letter, I thought about you a lot and love you with all my might.

∞ *to Simone de Beauvoir*

Friday [summer]

My darling Beaver

I'm here. Rain and lack of money drove us out of Belgium. How I long to see you. Of course I was thinking that you love me, my dearest—and also that I love you. Italy was so lovely, we were so happy there.[1] Don't worry. We'll hide, we won't see a soul.

Around 10 o'clock (perhaps just slightly later) I'll be at the Deux Magots. I'll stay with you till noon. The catastrophe is that T. doesn't understand "till the 24th" as we do. To her it means *"including the 24th."* Which means that, to end things on a good note after all, I think we'd better give her that much. We'll thereby gain a period of good feelings—because she *is* in a good mood for the moment (the play, a new hotel). I'll meet you on the morning of the 25th and we'll go through Monday evening without seeing a soul (except a moment for poor Bost: Olga is having a pneumothorax[2] a 2nd time) or being apart.

My sweet little Beaver, things are so marvelous when I'm with you, I so long to spend a good while with you. The rehearsals [*Men Without Shadows* and *The*

---

[1] *Giacometti's wife.* (SdB)
[2] He had taken his mother with him to Switzerland on a lecture tour.
[1] He had been in Rome, working on the Italian production of *No Exit*.
[2] Treatment for tuberculosis.

1947

❦ *to Simone de Beauvoir*

[spring]

My little sweet, dear heart

I'm leaving almost immediately for Rome and haven't time to write you a real letter. I just want you to know that I'm filled with joy at the thought of seeing you again on the 14th.[1] I'll be at the Gare des Invalides at the appointed time. You'll have a reserved room at La Louisiane. And we'll go, the two of us, for a walk. I'm off on a trip—a farewell present with the little one; we'll stay till the 10th, on the evening of the 10th we'll be in Paris or on the morning of the 11th. To Rome, simply.

I'm so pleased to know you're in New York. Here everything is going well. With Dolorès, no change. The rest of it (financial problems, threat of a trial with Nagel,[2] etc.) seems to be working out. Nothing new, except for little anecdotes. We celebrated the 100th[3] all through one night at the Véfour. Was bored senseless. To wind it up I dragged Astruc through the mud (out of sheer drunkenness and perversity) and he had a nervous fit.

Adieu, little one: in 12 days I'll be seeing you again, and that fills me with pleasure. We'll get back together as though we'd parted the night before. I am so happy when I'm with you, my little one.

I'll write again from Rome, but nothing says you'll get the letter.

[1] *I was on my way back from America.* (SdB)
[2] Louis Nagel, Sartre's agent and one of his publishers.
[3] *Performance of* Morts sans sépulture. (SdB)

/ 279

1948

๑๖ *to Simone de Beauvoir*

Tuesday, the 18th [May]

My sweet

I'm still afraid that my letter to you in Cincinnati arrived too late, and when will this one get there? It is now the morning of the 18th, I'm calculating as closely as possible, but the thing is that on the 16th and 17th (Pentecost), no letters went off. I should have written on the 15th. That seemed a bit early, simply because I have no sense of the time right now: the days are too much alike; I'm suddenly reminded by the calendar to write to you. It seems so odd to me, my little one, that *at the same time* you are having days whose rhythms are absolutely set by boats, by airplanes, with no one of them like the others. In a letter from Dolorès I read, "So-and-so (one of those ciphers she describes at length and obsessively in her cheery letters) came back at top speed from Mexico because it's the rainy season." That made me think; you understand, he *lives* there, his work is there and every year he pulls up stakes and takes off as soon as the rains begin. Whereas you, in easy stages you're moving toward that atmospheric cataclysm. Our trips have always been slightly skewed toward solar catastrophes and atmospheric precipitations because of lack of money, academic vacations, etc. That hasn't changed. We have always seen landscapes at their most uncomfortable, most moving times, when they're chafing in the heat or going spongy from the water. But after all, that's the way Mexico is every year right now, and there's no privileged *abschattung*.[1] I so hope you'll have a splendid trip.

As for me, the same day starts over again each morning. Life is organized

---

[1] Successive appearances of the object in profile.

according to topics rather than anecdotes: the topics reappear each day scarcely varied, all the same ones as the day before. There's the topic of fine weather: same blue sky, same July heat in May, and everyone says: we're due for a storm. Which never comes, but they aren't resigned yet—nor am I—to accepting this heat for what it is. Everyone goes about in shirtsleeves and sleeps in the nude. The heat has taxis springing up all over, which is convenient. Besides, along with the good weather, we have the topic of elegance: Princess Elizabeth is in Paris. Which means approximately as much in the day's events as the death of Leclerc.[2] It moves clumps of humans from place to place, it blocks off streets, it fills the papers (headlines twice as big as those announcing the shameful news from Palestine[3]) and in the evening the Place de l'Étoile emits tricolored beams and its Arc is lit up. And everyone wonders, "What will she be doing this evening?" It brings to every mind the presence of horse races, dances, palaces, etc., where otherwise no one goes anymore. Background theme—for me and others, though few—Palestine. It's the kind of thing that makes one as indignant as the war in Spain and, in addition, there's that sort of malediction against the Jews that seems unbearable. If you think for instance about a certain Polish Jew who miraculously escaped the camps and gas chambers and English solicitude, who settled in over there after a clandestine voyage, to find the armies of anti-Semitism all over again, the country invaded, and despair. And then the UN, of course; it's *outrageous*. Here at least a few are saying as much; people are embarrassed. Well, luckily there's Elizabeth.

That's that. This will give you some slight sense of it. For the moment here are the personal topics in decreasing order of importance.

1) Work. As always in Paris, I feel I'm in a swamp and trying to wrench myself out of it. There's the telephone and the struggle against same (I sent Cau[4] away Saturday, Sunday, and Monday, unplugged the phone, and have never worked so well in Paris. I decided on the spot to limit telephonic agitation to the hour between 12 and 13, when I take my bath. Cau will come at 11:30.) There are meetings and dates. Always too many of them and seemingly unavoidable when I accept them and later, with bitter regret, find them pointless. For instance, *why* must I see [Manês] Sperber[5] today at noon? He has urgent questions for me. Fine. But urgent *for him*. Basically, I feel uneasy about him because we're doing the German issue without him. Nonetheless I tuck myself

---

[2] Jacques-Philippe Leclerc, 1902–47, general and war hero famed as the liberator of Paris. He died in an air crash in North Africa.

[3] *The English were using every means to prevent the Jews from creating the state of Israel.* (SdB)

[4] Jean Cau, Sartre's secretary.

[5] *A writer and friend of* [Arthur] *Koestler.* (SdB)

away, from 9 to 12, and in the afternoon from 3 to 7, but it's never uninterrupted work, it's not the royal road of Ramatuelle,[6] it feels more like driving a car in Paris: release clutch, apply brakes, change speed, jerky starts and stops, etc. The result is anxiety and frenzied efforts. I'm working on Mathieu: I've entirely redone the passage when they're at Padou,[7] waiting for the Fritzes, and I'll take it to the end before doing anything else. The advantage, if you will, is that instead of being immersed in a long dream (Ramatuelle) one takes a point of view that's perpetually reflexive. I read a bit: for the Ethics, the Bloch (*The Formation of Ties of Dependency*) which Cau found for me in the library of the ENS along with Calmette (Middle Ages)—for my pleasure; Mallarmé and books on Mallarmé (Thibaudet, Mondor, Noulet, Roullet, etc); I'm *dazzled* by *Le coup de dés* (a *rigorously* existentialist poem based on a Hegelian theme: Cause and the Intellectual Animal). All in all, I gripe, but things are going well enough.

2) Dolorès. Standstill. Friendly letters, almost gay at times, tender and confiding. I feel *very good* about her from within, and it makes me uncomfortable (also from within, of course) about my relationship with the little one.[8] Tell me, my little dearest, why didn't she get *Visages*? I had alerted her, and now she's pointedly asking for it. It must be at the bottom of one of your suitcases. Send it to the Gérassis so that they can have it delivered to her. She writes to me that I must *live*, that just because she sacrifices herself to T.,[9] etc., that's no reason for me not to live. I reacted vigorously: I don't think that's a good attitude for her to adopt. In any event she added her official authorization for me to go to Argentina. This comes at a bad time: still without news, which proves their hesitation and lack of great enthusiasm about my coming, I thought you would agree with me that we should pass up a trip offered with so little graciousness. In any case, with that much money and the points mentioned and argued, even if they were to retract them, the whole thing stinks, don't you think? So we'll go to Iceland, my sweet, since those bearded fellows pleased you, then to England and Ireland. (At first I misread that you were in Ireland, and I had trouble grasping the impression of strangeness and marvel that had quite clearly struck you.[10])

3) The little one. She is nice and amusing, I feel real friendship for her but, in one respect she kills me. There's a play by Porto-Riche[11] in all this, isn't

---

[6] *Where we had a quiet stay during the spring.* (SdB)

[7] *In Alsace.* (SdB)

[8] *A young American journalist.* (SdB) She was in Paris to cover Princess Elizabeth's visit.

[9] *Her husband.* (SdB)

[10] *During a landing in Iceland, on my flight to Chicago.* (SdB)

[11] Georges de Porto-Riche (1849–1930), playwright. Sartre is possibly alluding to *L'Amoreuse*, about a woman who tyrannizes her husband through his passionate demands.

there. I very punctiliously do as I'm told, but finally it becomes mere conscientiousness, doesn't it, it's boring. Here's my schedule: She lands at my place (Rue B.) around 5 in the evening, exhausted by her life as a journalist, her clothes in tatters, her calves scratched, her feet all blistered, her face spattered; she covered eight kilometers through the brambles of the Trianon to surprise Elizabeth at lunch, and she reached it dog tired, to find 50 journalists who had come in by the front door; or else she battled it out with the police. Following conventions adopted at the beginning, she collapses on my bed and drops off with the sleep of Sorokine, by which I mean that I come and go, cough, light my pipe over and over, and she only wakes up at eight o'clock when I shake her. Sometimes, at 7:30, she draws grating notes out of a violin while I play the piano. One piece by Schubert serves us as common pretext. Then she takes a bath at my mother's,[12] who tolerates her because she represents one more link to Paris. At 8:30, departure, search for taxi, dinner. (Yesterday: Place du Tertre, day before the Petit Chevreau—with the Bosts, Kerny,[13] and the Paglieros[14]— the day before, the Rouzier, outside. The day before that: the Escargot. She adores eating.) Then, at almost eleven, another taxi, where she loses some trinket (day before yesterday her bag with 30,000 francs, yesterday her hat). Then we search and take action, and we find or do not find the object (the hat found; the bag not). Then invariably, whether I go back to my mother's or sleep at the little one's place, I mount and submit. The mornings are pleasant: sun, the Arc de Triomphe in the distance, the greenery, the rooftops, her balcony, and then an American orange juice, American coffee, and departure: I get a taxi, go back to my mother's, drink some of Dolorès's American coffee and work. My feelings are sweet and cordial: she is altogether likeable; I particularly like her for her ties to her profession. She clings a bit, it's true, but is unstinting in assurances of future detachment. I think she'll have some trouble with it but she'll manage. There'll be yet another painful parting, but for you, my sweet, no painful return. No, no, little one. No painful return. I'm waiting for you, I would love to see you and tell you all.

4) *Dirty Hands*.[15] Every day it's sold out. The movie:[16] annoying, convoluted topic. Everybody wants to gyp me: Nagel despairs, Brandel wrings his hands, [Gabriel] Pascal foams, they insult one another, make up, blaming me, it's not

---

[12] Sartre now shared with his mother an apartment, partitioned in two, on the Rue Bonaparte.

[13] *An actresss, friend of Dolorès.* (SdB)

[14] [Marcello Pagliero] *Italian director-actor who had played the hero in* Les jeux sont faits. (SdB) In 1952 he codirected the film of *The Respectful Prostitute*.

[15] Sartre's 1948 play *Les Mains sales*.

[16] A project that eventually fell through, based on documentary footage of war atrocities.

progressing, they suggest delays, etc. Tomorrow I'm lunching with the 2 (Br. and Nag.). That'll be something. They're assailing me with letters that keep saying the same thing.

5) Bost, Olga, etc. I seldom see them, but they seem happy.

6) Merleau-Ponty. Gave Scipion *a punch in the nose* at the Leiboviczs'. Sober, claims the entire responsibility for that act carried out in a state of inebriation. Here are the facts: he was peeing (2 in the morning, fiesta). He hears Scipion's voice: "You're a bitch." He gets annoyed and muses: "Scipion, Astruc, etc., they're all like spoiled pets. They believe they can do anything they want with impunity. One should start treating them differently." He goes out buttoning up on the way, reenters the room and discovers that, his wife being the only woman present, it was, without a possible doubt, to her that Scipion had been speaking. He says, "You called my wife a bitch?" Scipion says, "No." Merleau-Ponty says, "You've got no memory" and smacks him one. Scipion goes off, a hand on his cheek and saying, "Oh là là!" Mme. Merleau-Ponty says to M. Merleau-Ponty, "It's true that he called me a bitch, but I'd called him a bastard twenty times in the last hour." "In that case, my dear, I deplore the fact that you put yourself in such a situation, and there's nothing for me to do but apologize to Scipion." He goes to do so: "Return the honor." "What?" "The smack." "No, naah! I couldn't." "Yes you can." "No." Finally he does reciprocate. Merleau-Ponty, his honor satisfied, takes Scipion off for a drink outside. They were parting as good friends when Scipion has the misfortune to conclude, "All in all, you were hearing voices in the toilet." Upon which Merleau-Ponty removed his jacket, Scipion too. They eyed one another interminably in their shirtsleeves, then each of them put his jacket back on and parted unreconciled. Merleau-Ponty declares, "After all I'm 43, I'm a professor of ethics, I have to teach them how to live." What a bundle of complexes beneath it all! Last year he had similarly punched Astruc, who had insulted Suzou. Mother Leibovicz commenting on the same business, said, "When Maurice is drunk, he wants to screw every hour on the hour and lets his desires be known to 3 or 4 different women, who refuse him— not that they don't like him, he's just too hasty—so he sees red and strikes out." As a matter of fact it's much more complicated than that.

There, little one, that's it for the essentials. I'm best with you, I haven't lost you at all, the Matriarchy continues, I'm neither out of my element nor unoccupied; I love you with all my might and I laugh happily thinking that you are on such a superb and rainy trip. You are my dear little Beaver and my soul.

1949

∞ to Simone Jollivet[1]

42 Rue Bonaparte
Wednesday [summer]

Dear Toulouse

I still feel all of the same friendship for you, though you didn't allow me the leisure to tell you so the last time we saw each other. I will do anything for you I can: you have only to ask, if you are still my friend; I am at your disposal. And first of all I would like to see you. Any time at all from Saturday on: you pick the day and the hour.

We send our best love.

∞ to Simone Jollivet

August 16th

Dear Toulouse

I received your two letters and I wonder if you even want me to answer the things you're telling me. I suppose that in writing to me you were clarifying

---

[1] Her lover and colleague, the actor-director Charles Dullin, had recently died.

things about yourself for yourself and that you wanted your thoughts to be told to someone (to me, since I am your *closest* friend) but that you excuse me from all commentary. All I could tell you is that I too know of that duality—though not in quite the way you do, and that it seems to me we always hesitate about accommodating ourselves to it, about gaining some profit from it (by that I mean for writing) or about replacing the dualism with a monism. When we would like it to be glorious, it is sordid, and when we want to limit it, we impoverish ourselves. I'm speaking to you about myself, thus a bit in the dark insofar as what concerns you: all of this should be the subject of conversations; so we can refine our aim. All that I know is I would like to construct an ethics in which Evil is an integral part of Good. Do you know Kafka's phrase, "Good is sometimes discouraging!" An intermittent taste for the "crapulous," an ethics that would not save it, would be a sad mystification. But, as I've told you, you're more the one who can talk to me about all that and about Loudun,[2] since they are one and the same.

I only hope the anchorite side is not too heavy for you—particularly the solitude, till our return. Your last letter touched me—in the sense that it was truly *on target*—and I'd like you to believe that your letters are very important to me. I'm pleased that you're going to Férolles; I believe the country is the natural habitat of anchorites.

I for one am more a practitioner of cenobitism. I'm living in a sort of community, this villa of Mme. Morel's, folk spread out around the garden, the bedrooms, it's rare when there aren't a dozen people hollering at the same time. They are people who get bored separately on the hilltops and come to be bored together by the sea. But my monastic cell is perfectly defended. Nobody comes in, and I work twelve hours a day. Juan-les-Pins is behind us, teeming with the owners of gyp joints, vulgar, miserable people, particularly so because the season hasn't been "a good one." All the clatter from the cut-rate attractions in every shop in town, the songs, sounds of sax, trumpets, violins, cries and laughter converge in the evening over the terrace of the villa. But at this distance they're no bother, it could easily be moving, in fact. We have dinner as night falls, it seems very 1880s, charming, and this comes from the fact that the villa, built around that period, is an anachronism which only the lack of funds has prevented the municipality from eliminating. Besides it's already a collective institution given the number of people that benefit from it. Mme. Morel's son, his mother-in-law and two brothers-in-law have just arrived. It's too much, and I'm going off for a few days (till Monday, to be precise) to a hotel in Menton. I think you'd

---

[2] Medieval town where a convent became possessed by demonism.

better write to me here, since I'm coming back. The Genet[3] is coming along (I saw him in Cannes, at his Lucien's place, coddling a three-month-old baby. "Maternal," was Niko the Abyssinian's comment) but not as quickly as I would like. All in all I'm more or less happy.

Dear Toulouse, I so hope that you don't feel *too* lonely: I haven't really left you; write to me.

⇚ *to Simone Jollivet*

[December]

Dear Toulouse

We wanted to see you on Saturday or Sunday, but then the Beaver was completely done in (with awful grippe) and in addition we had to run around for presents (we've reached the age when you give presents without getting any; I have two very young godsons and a flock of demigodsons). I called you on Sunday (Tru. 00-36) around 4:30, but the phone rang for a long time in a void. I wanted to apologize and tell you that the moment we get back (January 4 or 5) we would love to see you. Perhaps you could send me word to tell me how things are going there and if "our friends" ever showed up. Write: c/o Mme. Morel, La Pouèze, Maine-et-Loire.

I send you a big kiss.

[3] Sartre was working on a preface to Jean Genet's works, but the essay began to take on a life of its own, eventually becoming the six-hundred-page *Saint Genet: Actor and Martyr* (1952).

1950

❀ *to Simone Jollivet*

January 2

Dear Toulouse

Happy New Year. I know what you're wishing for: good work. I know that's what you want most. And, as you put it, *it's your turn*. I'm very happy you have recovered. Nighttimes: that seems quite natural to me. Ideas that reappear, rise, fall and bother us. It seems to me I've had times like that, but I don't remember exactly when.

Yes, rest assured, I'll be meticulous about orders and counterorders, or rather there'll be no further counterorders, but you have to realize that my wish to see you again was the sudden impulse of an overfull life. It deranged *order:* would you believe that by dint of disorder I'm driven to order or, if you will, the apparent order of my life is the sign of profound disorder: everyone and everything must be pigeonholed. There you have it, each new initiative is catastrophic: it causes turmoil. (I'm constantly taking on new initiatives, incidentally. Whence the passage of order to chaos then to a new order then to chaos again.) The last week of December was chaos. I do apologize, you know. And with the new year we are inaugurating a period of order, etiquette, and ceremony. Everything is in place, full to overflowing: no new initiatives are foreseen nor will they be tolerated before *at least* two months' time. (I'm saying 2 months because I expect to leave with the Beaver for Italy or Egypt around the beginning of March for 2 months.)

Here, all is work. I really do work 15 hours a day. On Genet. He decided to publish an expurgated edition of his clandestine works and I'm writing a preface for them. Working fifteen hours a day on a genius of a chiseler and homosexual is enough to make a person's head spin. He gets under my skin and gives me hallucinations. He wakes me up in the middle of the night. But it's fascinating.

I'll be back around the 5th. I'll give you a call immediately, and if the phone doesn't answer because it is ringing at the neighbors', I'll send a *pneumatique*. We'll come to see you, Beaver and I.

I send you a big kiss.

❧ *to Simone Jollivet*

Thursday

Dear Toulouse

For several days now I've been trying in vain to reach you by phone (it's ringing, but God knows where). Would *you* be kind enough to call me tomorrow morning, Friday, around 11 or 12 o'clock (Dan. 92.98). I have the tickets for Saturday, and we'll decide what time to come and pick you up.

I send you a kiss.

❧ *to Simone Jollivet*

Friday 15:30

Dear Toulouse

First, please excuse the pencil: I've lost my pen. Then, here we are back again, and we're very eager to see you. When? Tomorrow afternoon I'm discussing Marxism with some Indochinese communists, and Sunday I'm seeing Genet to ask him a few questions on his life. Would you like Monday afternoon around 3:30?

(I'm not calling you again, because it doesn't do any good, but *you* can call me around noon tomorrow to tell me if that suits you too.)

I send you a kiss.

๙ *to Simone Jollivet*

Tuesday

Dear Toulouse

Random thoughts (it's the best for correspondence in Tamanrasset, the most spontaneous, I feel) in reply to your letter.

Le Démon de la perversité. Yes, I've read it. And do you remember—slightly different—*Le Vitrier* [*The Glazer*] in Baudelaire's prose poems.

Your conflicting reflections: "How noble I am," "It's despicable to think that," etc. I've experienced all of that and still experience it without letup (I don't want to be a saint, but I do want to be moral. From the point of view that interests you here, it's the same thing). I think the answer is clear: the poison lies in the very will to be moral and saintly. If you want *to be* something, you certainly have to ask yourself: am I that? It's best to *act* without giving thought to being. To help someone because the object, the situation, cries out for help, without looking back on *being*. Rightly not wanting to be anything. One rediscovers the idea of spontaneity, in the immediate.

The attraction for the Toughs. You were quite right in Paris (1927) when you said, "I'm a homosexual." In fact I'm up to my neck in a study of that attraction *in Genet*. It must not be quite the same thing. But it's true that you have some traits in common: Demonism, Evil, etc.—and that all relationships to the Other pass through a relationship to oneself: the Other is the intermediary between oneself and oneself: as the means you use to see yourself as Other. And *above all*: the theme of your *Ombre*[1] is developed throughout in his work. Each character seeking himself in the Other. Love: "You are alone in the world, at night in the solitude of an immense esplanade. Your double statue reflects on each half of itself. You are solitaries and live in your double solitude" (*Querelle de Brest*).[2]

Reply to letter of August 15: I have no steel gray bathing suit, I'm not dressed in sailor garb; I'm wearing short-sleeved white shirts, almost the uniform here and best way to go unnoticed. Yes, why not try the company of the Corsican[3] for a while? it would be strange: but take care.

Dullin's letters: *do not worry at all, Toulouse*. It was the Beaver (I wrote to Chicago and she replied) who *locked them up at her place*. You'll have them the minute she comes back.

---

[1] A *play by Simone Jollivet given at the Atelier before the war.* (SdB)
[2] Novel by Genet, published in English as *Querelle.*
[3] A *young woman more or less in love with Simone Jollivet.* (SdB)

1951

۶‍ی *to Simone Jollivet*

[Summer]

The beginning is missing.

. . . [André] Masson for your stage sets: did you know that he decided, disgusted by Barrault[1] (at the time of the Marigny *Hamlet*), not to ever do another stage set? But for you (and perhaps for me) he might agree to do it.

What is Fandoar? I don't remember having heard you talk about it.

As for me: a cenobite for sure.[2] 15 people here nonstop. A superb terrace with a view of the sea and the Cap d'Antibes, but out of bounds due to the great influx of people who show up there, it gets like one of those moving walkways. All of it in an atmosphere of growing tension with exacerbating hatreds and, on top of all that, Guille[3] has come to weigh down the whole thing with his widower's mood and the sour urine smell given off by his children (morally and, alas, above all physically). Consequently I play the anchorite at the heart of cenobitism. The Lady, charming on my behalf, has trays brought up to me at varying times (here we eat when we think about it) and I never leave my room, where I work without letup on Genet and read a bit. Today it's ending. These people are leaving in an immense hubbub of contradictory wills, and I'm off to Sainte-

---

[1] Jean-Louis Barrault (b. 1910), actor, director, producer.
[2] *I was in America.* (SdB)
[3] Pierre Guille, a friend from the École Normale Supérieure days.

Maxime. I'll telegraph my address to you when I know it: Merleau-Ponty was to reserve a room for me in a hotel and tell me its name. He has not done so. I'm staying at Sainte-Maxime till the 15th then slowly wending my way back up to Paris via Marseille, Aigues-Mortes, Arles, les Baux, etc. *I won't have finished Genet in October.*

The article on O. W.[4] fascinated me. There certainly is something powerful and strange there: the dialogue with Dullin, dead yet so alive. What you say in your note about the *object* is the most interesting from the "constructive criticism" point of view. An objection: you take as *known* the contents of the production. In other words, you're addressing spectators who have gone to see the play. But in criticism the fiction is that you are talking about it to someone who hasn't seen it. You mustn't think of publishing it *for another reason:* your dialogues with Dullin, for you and those who know you, aren't a process but the prolongation of your life and your *real* way of thinking. A reader thinks of an operating procedure (cf. Mallarmé doing theater criticism, conversing with his soul). That's what you want to avoid at all costs. What's needed is to try a series of articles or a book that would reflect you and would have understood by the readers, in which one would have the time to get used to it and to see that *it's reality*. By itself the article shocks because the reader—theoretically—doesn't know you: for him you could be anyone at all who has chosen the gimmick of speaking to Dullin as a mode of exposition and (a bitterly ironic phrase) to "make it live." Tell me if you agree. (You'll tell me: but there are quotations from Dullin that come from the fact that I was intimate with him. Yes, but what makes you known to the reader, you with your fidelities? It will take patience and care, you can't abruptly start in with: "I meet Dullin at the café"; for you a simple sentence announcing a fact. For the reader who doesn't know you, it's a strange mixture of disrespect and familiarity: *shocking.* But understand what I'm saying: *not to me*).

I'm happy to know that you're at Férolles. That's where the cult of silence will be most natural.

I send you a kiss.

---

[4] Probably Oscar Wilde.

1952

꘎ to Simone Jollivet

June 4

Dear Toulouse

Here's a little greeting from Naples and Capri. A pleasant trip, no incidents, happy. Except that (you know I'm doing a book on my *last* trip to Italy.[1] Not this one, the preceding one) right now I'm struggling to write "Venice in the rain" in this South where the sun is shining. Except too that I can never recall the impressions I expressed and consigned to paper in that piece of writing; Rome isn't the Rome I saw (is it the difference between autumn and spring?), etc. Minimal differences, but irritating. For example in October I didn't see prostitutes in Naples (a city reputed to be very prone to prostitution) and I said so. That's all it took for me to see them this year. Not too many, but all the same I can no longer write with a clear conscience that "I didn't see any prostitutes in Naples." You'll tell me that in fact I didn't see any in October. Yes, but, you see: I *could* have seen them. And the hitch in travel writing is that if you say, "I didn't see any prostitutes in Naples" the reader understands that there aren't any. Small problems. But do you know what I was thinking on *your account?* I was thinking that you would like Naples (for a whole slew of reasons having to do with you and Naples; I'll lay it all out on my return) and I said to myself:

[1] Fragments of this work appear in *La reine Albemarle ou le dernier touriste*, Gallimard 1991.

/ 293

in this *active period* that Toulouse is inaugurating, why doesn't she make a place for travels *too*? I know what you'll say, Férolles and work are not nothing. But anyway, I find time to travel and I too as a rule am pressed for time. You could easily find a *month* during the coming year to go cavorting around this part of the world (or elsewhere: Spain) and I would be pleased to help set things up for you (as for the lira, I know good ways to get some). Don't be irritated. If you like we'll talk about it some more when I get back (around June 20) and if you don't like the idea, we can just forget I even mentioned it.

Are you working? Did Cau give you what you wanted in time? I'm asking questions but I have scarcely a hope that you'll have time to answer me: the Italian mails too are a relic of the XVIIIth century, and I suspect that they still transport the mail by coach. In any case, if you get this letter (mailed the 5th) before the 10th, you can write to me at general delivery, Bergamo.

I send you a tender kiss and wish your work as successful as my trip (and not as my work).

1959

[At the invitation of John Huston, who had directed No Exit on Broadway, Sartre found himself at the American film director's Irish estate, attempting to write a screenplay with him about Sigmund Freud. The collaboration produced several vast Sartrean scripts, which appeared posthumously in France (1984), and in the English translation of Quintin Hoare (1986); and a 1962 Huston film of more conventional scope, Freud, from which Sartre withheld his name despite his considerable contribution.]

᪥ to Simone de Beauvoir

[October]

My little sweet

Thank you for the articles and the letter. Yes, the articles are very good, and that makes me happy.[1] Really happy, of that you can be sure, little Beaver. I'm in a profoundly good mood, under slightly difficult circumstances—which I'll relate in a moment—and that good mood certainly comes from the fate accorded to The Condemned. To tell the whole truth, I wasn't expecting it—I had expected fewer reservations (never mind) and less true warmth. I tell you this so you'll really believe I'm delighted, so far away from you. And I'm very pleased that it makes you happy. Many thanks, my sweet, thanks very much.

I'm going to send you a telegram in a while (the bedroom phones don't work,

[1] On Les Séquestrés d'Altona [SdB]. [Paris 1959. The Condemned of Altona, trans. Sylvia and George Leeson, New York, 1961].

we have to make calls from the entrance hall) telling you to say yes to Cayatte, [2] particularly if it gives you a bit of fun. But you'll surely get this letter before Tuesday. I believe you must make the film, we must try everything, we poly-maths. Besides, it's almost a novel. Cayatte has no great talent, but he'll go just as far as you want him to. Only (apart from the successful outcome "from the cinematic point of view," as your mother would say), I believe you have to think that it will be seen by masses of people who've read your books and will want to find you in it: the story must be as profound as possible. That means: put yourself in it completely, as though it were the novel about the couple that you had felt like writing. If you believe that—and I suppose you *do* believe it, that you see it not merely as a meal ticket—I agree 100 percent. Three million: *of course*, and even more. For the adaptation of the Miller, [3] Borderie—they're loaded—paid me six. Well, you'll see. As for Rozan, have her take the 10% and tell her it will stimulate her enthusiasm.

Getting back to me, in two words I'll reassure you right off: excellent trip in two hours (7:30–9:30 p.m.) then an hour by car in the dark between low gray walls. I couldn't see anything else. Since then I haven't once left this huge barracks of a place though from my windows I can see vast green fields which, from all reports, must stretch for miles and miles. On the field I see cows, horses—sometimes one, sometimes another—ridden by the master of the house, wearing a cap, who goes tearing by his house in the afternoon at a trot, at a canter, followed by a stubborn little donkey that gambols about behind them, making a farce of the whole thing. Trees too: I don't know what kind. As for the house, nothing could be stranger: a hodgepodge of objects (pre-Columbian, African, Japanese, even French) *authentic* but uncongenial neighbors, each one reducing the next to the most radical inauthenticity. To cite my room alone: a wooden Christ from Mexico, Italian and Mexican lamps, a Hindu statuette (Shiva), Japanese screens, carved and painted wood panels (behind my bed, around the mirror)—rose and watery green—they seem of European origin to me (I could be wrong). Add to that a harlequin painting (vaguely cubist, a real fake Picasso) and comfortable, undistinguished furniture (large, deep armchairs in white—beige rug, gray walls, white ceiling—with Italian chandelier). I was forgetting to mention that you can get lost in it. The bathroom floor is similarly covered with a beige rug, which even goes under the tub. The toilet lords it over the rug. Across from that, with its back to the window, an easy chair permits me to gaze simultaneously at tub and toilet. Through a vast number of similar

---

[2] *He wanted to work on a screenplay with me. The project never panned out.* (*SdB*) André Cayatte (b. 1909), director of socially conscious films mostly in the forties and fifties.

[3] For the producer Bernard Borderie, Sartre adapted Arthur Miller's play *The Crucible* to the screen, as *The Witches of Salem* (1957), starring Yves Montand and Simone Signoret.

rooms drifts a great Romantic, sad and solitary, our friend Huston, totally vacant, aged, literally *incapable* of talking to his guests. There's an endless stream of them: day before yesterday Major Pickmill, "master of the hounds" (which means grand master of the fox hunt); yesterday an expert in Chinese and Japanese objects (who turned out to be a crook, according to Huston); today a producer and his wife. *Nobody*—mind you—*nobody*, neither Huston, nor his wife—a former dancer, 32 years old, rather pretty and quite batty—raises a finger for them. It falls to Mrs. Philips (Reinhardt's[4] girlfriend, you know her) to play the mistress of the house. Little Beaver, it's 5:30. Time to gather. As for Freud, things could be worse. As for drink, I'm not drinking (except one little dry martini, sometimes 2. No Scotch. Except for the first two nights). Arlette[5] can tell you better than I. Au revoir, my sweet. In two or three days I'll write another letter and will describe the illustrious couple who are our hosts. Ah! one more thing: I am not bored, and to tell the truth I don't know why.

A tender kiss for you, my dear little Beaver, a very, very tender one.

෧෨ *to Simone de Beauvoir*

Thursday [October]

My sweet little Beaver

What madness! What sheer madness! Such a barrage of incoherent fleeting thoughts! Everybody's got a complex, all the way from masochism to brutality. Still, I don't want to give you the impression we're in hell. It's more like a big cemetery: everybody dead, with their complexes frozen. There's very, very little life here. Except for the house, which is expanding beneath our very feet. Did I tell you it's a "work in progress"? Workmen run around overhead singing then come in and bang away in my room, paint the bathroom door and depart leaving a pink "wet paint" sign. Little refinements keep popping up: The day before yesterday found music pouring down the walls—a radio had just been installed (by the way, with sensational tone and volume). From time to time the long and lanky master of the house and his wife come into my room to take down a picture so as to change the frame (he wants gilt frames, she, "more sophisticated," wants something discreet), nobody cares about the picture itself, a mere pretext

---

[4] Wolfgang Reinhardt, who was producing the film. He was the son of the great theater director Max Reinhardt.

[5] In 1956, Arlette Elkaïm, an eighteen-year-old philosophy student, met Sartre. They became close companions and, in 1965, Sartre adopted her. She is his literary heir.

for choosing a frame, though they own what is surely the world's ugliest Monet (worth millions: 150,000 dollars—a vague sketch, *perhaps*, for *The Water Lilies*). Since all the guests understand this incessant coming and going (except for me, a registered Frenchman), they leave their doors open *all day long*. They're unbelievable, these imperial or regal rooms, all opening onto an imposing landing (adorned with two terrible idols), each room with its small human creature inside, which feels it is dying. As a matter of fact, there's an incontestable correlation between the extraordinary Irish countryside and the soul of the master of this house. Here's what I mean: 8 to 9 million Irish in 1900; today 3 million. The others have emigrated to America, from where they support the Irish who stayed behind. In addition, the Church and convention delay marriages (the women get married *after thirty*, the men after forty). Of course as soon as possible they produce six offspring of middle-aged parents, who proceed to die or emigrate. No misery, simply poverty and above all *death*. Just think: in the past 50 years 2 out of 3 men have left. You can just imagine this abandoned heath. Everywhere stubborn little walls enclose plots of land that still show signs of life while others are completely dead, repossessed by nature. Everywhere you go, ruins, which range with no warning from the 6th century to the 20th. A house in ruins (generally from the last century or the 18th) beside two lowly little houses painted with American money. The ruins are impressive, the facades usually remain standing, but you'd think a bomb had blown out the roof and insides. You can see the sky through the windows. Mostly they're small houses, but sometimes they turn out huge and quite overwhelm the little one-storey huts, mirroring the character of the countryside, where the dead overpowers the living. Add to that, strange round towers beside a dark and lifeless body of water, like a salt-water lake (Galway Bay) and other tall towers (which are naturally considered phallic) near churches in ruins and cemeteries (they are said to have been built by Scandinavian invaders in the 6th century); and then everywhere those stubborn, gray, useless little walls (the tallest were built as public works to employ the locals in bad times). You really get the feeling of a *dead* landscape: only the presence of grass proves that an atom bomb wasn't dropped there, killing all life with its radiation. The weird part is that the countryside seems profoundly *human* (with all these vestiges), and for that very reason in its death throes. You see the Irishman gazing at his land (which is extremely rare, Barrès notwithstanding).[1] It's the only way to see him, in fact, because otherwise he hardly shows his face. So there you have it: one step away from lunar. Which is precisely the interior landscape of my boss, the great Huston. Masses of ruins, abandoned

---

[1] Reacting against an education he considered too abstract, the novelist Maurice Barrès (1862–1923) developed a mystical affinity with his battered natal countryside of Lorraine.

houses, wastelands, marshes, a thousand vestiges of human presence. But the man has emigrated. I have no idea where. He isn't even sad: he is *vacant* except in moments of infantile vanity when he dons his red dinner jacket or rides horseback (not very well) or takes inventory of his paintings and directs his workmen. Impossible to hold his attention for five minutes: he doesn't know how to work, he evades reasoning. But I don't want you to think it's only toward us that he displays the gloomy stupor that shocked me that evening at the Véfour. Almost every night he invites the strangest people: the *richest* heiress in England, a rajah-cum-innkeeper (large hotel in Kashmir), an Irish "master of the hounds," an Amurrikan producer, a young English director. And he says *not a word* to them. Arlette and I went into the living room as he was languidly talking with the "master of the hounds," a broad-backed lad with a red nose, very much the gentleman-farmer. He introduced us, but the major said he didn't know French. Whereupon Huston tapped him on the shoulder with a "grin" and said to him, "Well then, I leave you to practice your French," and he disappeared leaving the three of us dumbstruck. In a panic, the major, his eyes darting about, finally declared, "Churchill is funny when he speaks French."[2] I let out a "Ha! ha!" and silence descended on us till they called us in to dinner. I must say that often after dinner we sit face-to-face, three on one side: Arlette, Mme. Philips and me (for the last two days Reinhardt has been in Munich), three on the other: the producer, Huston and his wife, and that literally *no one* utters a peep. In fact Huston seems physically exhausted. Yesterday, a four-hour excursion (the one and only, because today his wife is leaving for London), the wife drove, Huston—who *had seen nothing* of this prelunar landscape—fell asleep almost immediately and was out most of the way there. The other day they got hold of the two documentaries he'd made for the army and which he talks about all the time: San Pietro (a battle for a village, shortly before Monte Cassino) and *Let There Be Light*, about the treatment of shell-shocked patients by military psychiatrists. Very disappointing films. Mediocre and excessively propagandist. But when there was light in the living room we (particularly Wolfgang Reinhardt, who knows him well) noted that his eyes were brimming with tears. It seems, though, he settled here not to contemplate the state of his soul in the Irish countryside but to evade taxes, for in Ireland he pays none, or practically none. By a sad misunderstanding, he had admired the "gentleman's" life of the rich property owners outside Dublin but, unwittingly, chose this desolate heath 3 hours by car from Dublin. He rarely stays here for more than two weeks at a time and one is led to believe that he won't return once the house is done. It is a void purer perhaps than death. He said something odd, one day, in speaking

---

[2] In English, as written.

of his "unconscious" vis-à-vis Freud: "In mine there's nothing." And his tone hinted at the meaning: nothing *left,* not even any more old inadmissible desires. A vast lacuna. You can imagine just how easy it is to get him to work. He evades thought because it is depressing. We'll all be gathered in a smoking room, all talking, when suddenly, smack in the middle of a discussion, he disappears. We're lucky if we see him again before lunch or supper. His wife, an odd woman, thirty, a former dancer (just the chorus), seduced by him at 17, pregnant, married, and practically abandoned, has reacted with an extreme hardness for which her wan face and doe-eyed gaze indicate she's not suited. Trapped in resentment, she has, I think, defended herself through contempt: of him and everyone. She's the one who *builds,* he, as Dolorès said, shows up to inspect the finished work. She's a bit crazy, very whimsical, and drinks too much. I'll stop here: this is just a beginning, there are still all the others. I can't say I'm bored. Sometimes I get furious: too much stupidity with the work (even Reinhardt is numb with admiration for Huston). But honestly it's worth living through this once, this solitude in common. Arlette has made no impression: people are here, here they remain, and that's that. They leave her to her own devices with the same equanimity as they do anyone else. *I'm not drinking* (but I miss it): *one* dry martini and *occasionally, one* whisky. I rest, I sleep, I experience the salutary effects of the solitude. I'll be back on *Thursday* at 11:30. Unfortunately they're down to 2 flights a week for Paris, and, in spite of everything, to take the first (on Sunday) would be a pity: for all the reciprocal lack of understanding, something may be brewing (involving the screenplay). I'll drop Arlette at her place and come right over to you. I've told no one else my arrival time; when I get there we'll agree on a suitable hour. If I write to Évelyne[3] before then to make a date, it will be for late afternoon. Tell her you don't know.

Warmest greetings, my sweet. I send you a great big kiss. I've talked only about myself, but that was to entertain you. Till Thursday, little Beaver.

---

[3] Évelyne Rey, an actress of great beauty, sister of Sartre's colleague on *Les Temps Modernes,* Claude Lanzmann. Sartre wrote the lead role in *The Condemned of Altona* for her.

1963

My dear little yourself

I was very pleased (and shamefaced) to get your letter yesterday. I'm sorry about your rain: it's scarcely better in Avignon than here[1] where we're getting the same, but here at least it's appropriate. To tell the truth it doesn't rain that much, but it often does drizzle, there are long showers and then the sky is gray. Sometimes, in the evening, the sun breaks through. That's good enough for Amsterdam: they never see anything better (was the weather perhaps better when we were here? this bad weather seems so pervasive that I feel I've never seen any other in Holland). Oddly, far from complaining, Arlette loves it: she has finally discovered her sense of the exotic, here she's as curious, as much the tourist, as we would be in the Congo. There's talk of pushing on, some other year, as far as the North Cape.

We are *taking pains* to be conscientious: we have seen Haarlem, The Hague, old Amsterdam, new Amsterdam; tomorrow Leyden. We could do better, but we're doing all right. The essential lies less in taking walks than in seeing Museums (we've gone several times to Amsterdam's, and in The Hague I was very pleased to see again both Rembrandt's *Saul* and the Delft landscape by Vermeer. If I remember rightly, you and I preferred—I did, in any case—other

---

[1] She was in Villeneuve-les-Avignon, where he was to meet her once he left Amsterdam.

works of his; I think we were wrong). Actually I've decided to like everything—minor works as well—that's a first. It pays off: you see masses of things, you see them again the moment you're outside. We found an excellent book, *Daily Life in Holland at the Time of Rembrandt*: the book, the paintings, life today, all add up to a dense counterpoint that I find very pleasing. Nonetheless I'd add that there's a shabby side to Amsterdam that I'd never noticed before. Is it Arlette's cult of the miserable? What a shambles, Rembrandt Square! And something else: *There's no whisky anymore.* Anywhere—I mean *anywhere at all*—you ask for a Scotch, mentioning a brand to show you know about such things, you get a smile, they repeat the brand name with a conniving air, and they serve you a dreadful brew that's as much like whisky as hash is like Tournedos. I'm dumfounded.

I've done *no work* for ten days. And since the only available French works are by Simenon, I'm reading two Simenons a day, sometimes three. Here's the daily schedule: I get up at 10:00, I get dressed, I go to wake up Arlette, who successfully resists till 10:45. Breakfast. While she's dressing, first Simenon (begun). We go out. Additional tea or coffee on Rembrandt Square. Then from 11:30 to 5:30, touristic efforts often crowned with success (lunch—generally Indonesian—is included in the schedule). At 17:30, free afternoon, Simenon, tea, Simenon, departure around 9:30 and dinner—anything but Indonesian—disappointed quest for whisky, return around 12:30 a.m., finish Simenons and sleep.

Three scourges:

The most minimal of them: the Permanent Theater Company of Genoa (Drama and Comedy), not so permanent as all that, is wandering around Holland. We had to see them and see their show. As for the show, fine, it was Goldoni, played with gusto, so far so good, but they had to have me photographed in their arms, the traitors. Whence:

Scourge two: the journalists, They swarm, they interview, and who knows what they don't have me saying. I've just phoned to make sure they remove from an article *all* the political declarations that a blond lady put in my mouth. But there are still two others to catch up with. That's the worst of it, for—being humble—I'm hardly counting the devouring sore that's gnawing away at my nose (did Tania take one of my photos and stick pins in my beak?) and turned it into an overripe tomato, it's hideous. Yesterday the appendage was endlessly photographed, as they assured me that my pimple *would not show up on the photo*, which I find absurd: if the photographic art cannot reproduce that vegetal redness—enormous and incandescent—then it's still in diapers. It's getting a bit better. But people peer at my nose; the day before yesterday the bartender didn't take his eyes off it and without my asking gave me some iodine.

Write to me, good little Beaver, it makes me happy. Work, read, take good walks, I'm very eager to see you (the evening of the 31st, your place at 9 o'clock) and I send you a big kiss.

P.S.: Is it because I'd made up my mind to write to you? I reread 19 pages of *Flaubert*.[2]

❧ *to Simone de Beauvoir*

July 25

My dear little yourself

Thank you for your good little letter—though followed by silence, like mine. Listen, you'll still have had better weather than we despite your storms. The strange thing here is that it rains at noon and the sky clears at the end of the day. A nordic custom, I suppose. Which means walking about under the gray sky and reading Simenon in the last rays of a cold and unavailing sun. Aside from that, it's appealing: Utrech, The Hague, Haarlem, particularly Leyden, charming beneath a *blue* sky—there have been 2 days of blue sky. Ultimately, Amsterdam is the pearl. There is everything and that melancholy which suits it alone—which the last minor masters (early 17th century) saw. Did you know that the 17th-century Dutch *did not bathe?* They reeked at ten paces. And that a certain abbé Sartre in a memoir of his trip to Holland said they ate like pigs in those days. That hasn't changed. Since Arlette's cult of misery forbids the 5 Flies, we eat in the normal restaurants which normally serve shit. No one here maintains any illusions; they even exaggerate: to the point that *all* the reporters who interviewed me began by asking suspiciously, "But what could have attracted you to Holland? What do you think of this country?" To tell the truth I like it very much though Cuba is better than Amsterdam for working. Descartes said it: a bad country for the work of understanding. I want you to know that I've maintained my work schedule and that Arlette has adopted it: we have read fifty-seven detective and spy novels of the lowest quality. And baser yet: I've followed with the greatest interest the atrocious tortures that the friendly OSS 117[1] inflicts on men and women to make them talk. But Dutch somnolence muffles my

---

[2] Sartre was working on his multivolume study of Flaubert, *L'Idiot de la famille*, eventually published in the early 1970s and later in English translation as *The Family Idiot*.

[1] Hero of spy stories by Jean Bruce.

indignation; from time to time I ask myself, "But didn't people protest against that a couple of years ago?" and weak-willed drowsiness takes hold of me again, and I suspend judgment. And Simenon, that dirty dog! What a strange portrait of the author arises from 20 Simenons read all in a row: this was not a good young man. He wasn't, he isn't a good man. "He's anti-Semitic," remarks Arlette occasionally, lifting her nose from a Maigret, by way of pure information. Then dives right back in.

Only one event related thus by Puig[2] in his letter of 7/21/63: "I have some very bad news for you: I had an accident with the car, here in l'Ain, I missed a turn and encountered a tree, slightly injuring my arm. As for the car itself, I'm rather afraid it is no more." He wrote from Gex. Said like a gentleman, don't you think? Not one word more: these champions enjoy brevity. At first I lamented: no vacation for Arlette, who feels that *in a pinch*, their relationship allows them to travel together but not to stay together in some country spot. Then a quick line of reasoning convinced me, and later her: since a turn *had* to be missed—and since if it had not been that one, it might have been another with perhaps graver consequences—just as well it occurred at the start and without Arlette: thus the accident portends what Arlette's vacation would have been and at the same time fortunately renders it impossible. "And what on earth was he doing in l'Ain?" she asks me. My ignorance of French *départements* makes me incapable of answering her.

And what about you, little one? I know that you telephoned my mother. As for me, I telegraphed, she seems in seventh heaven that we remembered her and her 81 years. She seems to be adjusting to her room and sent me a *spoken* letter, it's a genre of "epistle" she used to practice but had given up a long time ago. About the muffled noises on the Bd. Raspail, muffled, she says, by the curtains and deafness. "It's loud enough to hear them," she says. "But not to notice."

Little yourself, I'm really, really delighted at the thought of seeing you again. I have the train tickets and will stand before you on the 31st at 9:00 p.m. A big kiss for you.

I sent a telegram to Sourkov: impossible to come the 1st will be in Leningrad the 4th. As for Puig, he's getting senile, I don't know what kind of a mess he's creating over our tickets. We'll get them.

This letter is the last that I received from Sartre. Thereafter, during our brief separations, we used the telephone. (SdB)

---

[2] André Puig, Sartre's secretary.

Select Bibliography

SARTRE'S WORKS

L'Imagination. Paris: Presses Universitaires Françaises, 1936. *Imagination: A Psychological Critique*, trans. Forrest Williams. Ann Arbor: University of Michigan Press, 1979.

La Transcendance de l'égo. Paris: Vrin, 1937. *The Transcendence of the Ego*, trans. Forrest Williams and Robert Kirkpatrick. New York: Noonday Press, 1957.

La Nausée. Paris: Gallimard, 1938. *Nausea*, trans. Lloyd Alexander. New York: New Directions, 1964.

Le Mur. Paris: Gallimard, 1938. *The Wall*, trans. Lloyd Alexander. New York: New Directions, 1948.

Esquisse D'une théorie des émotions. Paris: Hermann, 1939.

L'Imaginaire. Paris: Gallimard, 1940. *The Psychology of Imagination*. New York: Philosophical Library, 1948; New York: Washington Square Press, 1966.

L'Être et le Néant. Paris: Gallimard, 1943. *Being and Nothingness*, trans. Hazel Barnes. New York: Philosophical Library, 1956; New York: Washington Square Press, 1966.

Les Chemins de la liberté, Vol. I, *L'Âge de raison*. Paris: Gallimard, 1945. *The Age of Reason*, trans. Eric Sutton. New York: Vintage Books, 1973.

Les Chemins de la liberté, Vol. 2, *Le Sursis*. Paris: Gallimard, 1945. *The Reprieve*. New York: Knopf, 1947; New York, Vintage Books, 1973.

Les Chemins de la liberté, Vol. 3, *La Mort dans l'âme*. Paris: Gallimard, 1949. *Troubled Sleep*. New York: Knopf, 1950; New York, Vintage Books, 1973.

Les Mouches. Paris: Gallimard, 1943. *The Flies*, trans. Stuart Gilbert, in *No Exit and Other Plays*, New York: Vintage, 1955.

Huis Clos. Paris: Gallimard, 1944. *No Exit* in *No Exit and Other Plays*, New York: Vintage, 1955.

Saint Genet, comédien et martyr. Paris: Gallimard, 1952. *Saint Genet: Actor and Martyr*, trans. Bernard Frechtman, New York: Braziller, 1963; Pantheon, 1983.

Les Séquestrés d'Altona. Paris: Gallimard, 1959. *The Condemned of Altona*, trans. Sylvia and George Leeson. New York: Knopf, 1961.

Les Mots. Paris: Gallimard, 1963. *The Words*, trans. Bernard Frechtman. New York: Braziller, 1964; New York: Vintage Books, 1981.

Bariona, le fils de Tonnère, in *Les Écrits de Sartre*. Paris, Gallimard, 1970.

Bariona: Or the Son of Thunder, in *Selected Prose*, trans. Richard McCleary, Evanston: Northwestern University Press, 1974.

L'Idiot de la famille. Vols 1 and 2. Paris: Gallimard, 1971, vol. 3, 1972. *The Family Idiot: Gustave Flaubert*, vol. 1, trans. Carol Cosman. University of Chicago Press, 1981.

Le Scénario Freud. Paris: Gallimard, 1984. *The Freud Scenario*, trans. Quintin Hoare. University of Chicago Press, 1986.

Oeuvres romanesques, ed. Michel Contat and Michel Rybalka. Bibliothèque de la Pléiade, Paris: Gallimard, 1981.

Les Carnets de la drôle de guerre. Paris: Gallimard, 1983. *The War Diaries*, trans. Quintin Hoare. New York: Pantheon, 1985.

Lettres au Castor et à quelques autres, Vols. 1 and 2. Paris: Gallimard, 1983.

Écrits de jeunesse, ed. Michel Contat and Michel Rybalka. Paris: Gallimard, 1990.

GENERAL BIBLIOGRAPHY

Bair, Deirdre. *Simone de Beauvoir: A Biography*. New York and London: Summit Books, 1990.

Beauvoir, Simone de. *La Cérémonie des adieux*, suivi de *Entretiens avec Jean-Paul Sartre*. Paris: Gallimard, 1981. *Adieux: A Farewell to Sartre*, trans. Patrick O'Brian. New York: Pantheon, 1984.

————. *La Force de l'âge*, Vols. 1 and 2. Paris: Gallimard, 1960. *The Prime of Life*, trans. Peter Green. Cleveland and New York: World, 1954.

————. *L'Invitée*. Paris: Gallimard, 1943. *She Came to Stay*. Cleveland and New York: World, 1954.

————. *Lettres à Sartre*, Vols. 1 and 2. Paris: Gallimard, 1990. *Letters to Sartre*, trans. Quintin Hoare. New York: Arcade Publishing, 1992.

Cohen-Solal, Annie. *Sartre 1905–1980*. Paris: Gallimard, 1985. *Sartre: A Life*, trans. Anna Cancogni, ed. Norman MacAfee. New York: Pantheon, 1987.

Gerassi, John. *Jean-Paul Sartre: Hated Conscience of His Century*. Chicago: University of Chicago Press, 1989.

Hayman, Ronald. *Sartre: A Biography*. New York: Simon & Schuster, 1987.

Index